Pragmatics of Language:

Clinical Practice Issues

Edited by
Tanya M. Gallagher, Ph.D.

Singular Publishing Group, Inc.

Singular Publishing Group, Inc.
4284 41st Street
San Diego, CA 92105

Copyright 1991 by Singular Publishing Group, Inc.

All rights, including that of translation, reserved. No part of this publication may be reproduced, stored in a retrieval system, or transmitted in any form or by any means, electronic, mechanical, recording, or otherwise, without the prior written permission of the publisher.

Library of Congress Cataloging-in-Publication Data

Pragmatics of language : clinical practice issues / edited by Tanya M.
  Gallagher.
        p.   cm.
    Dedicated to the memory of Carol Ann Prutting.
    Includes index.
    ISBN 1-879105-10-1 (hardcover ed.). — ISBN 1-879105-13-6
(softcover ed.)
    1. Language disorders in children.   2. Pragmatics.   3. Prutting,
Carol A.   I. Gallagher, Tanya M., 1945–   .   II. Prutting, Carol A.
    [DNLM: 1. Language—in infancy & childhood.   2. Language
Development Disorders—in infancy & childhood.   3. Language
Disorders—in infancy & childhood.   WL 340 P8987]
RJ496.L35P74   1991
618.92'855—dc20
DNLM/DLC
for Library of Congress   91-4801
                                                                              CIP

This volume is dedicated
to the memory of
Carol Ann Prutting
1941–1989

Contents

List of Contributors

Elizabeth Bates, Ph.D.
University of California, San Diego
La Jolla, California

Elizabeth B. Cole
McGill University
Montreal, Quebec, Canada

Martha B. Crago, Ph.D.
McGill University
Montreal, Quebec, Canada

Holly K. Craig, Ph.D.
University of Michigan
Ann Arbor, Michigan

Judith F. Duchan, Ph.D.
State University of New York
Buffalo, New York

Marc E. Fey, Ph.D.
Kansas University Medical Center
Kansas City, Kansas

Tanya M. Gallagher, Ph.D.
McGill University
Montreal, Quebec, Canada

Diane M. Kirchner, Ph.D.
University of California
Berkeley, California

Laurence B. Leonard, Ph.D.
Purdue University
West Lafayette, Indiana

Brian MacWhinney, Ph.D.
Carnegie-Mellon University
Pittsburgh, Pennsylvania

Michelle Mentis, Ph.D.
Boston University
Boston, Massachusetts

John R. Muma, Ph.D.
Texas Tech University
Lubbock, Texas

Norma S. Rees, Ph.D.
California State University,
  Hayward
Hayward, California

Elizabeth Skarakis–Doyle, Ph.D.
Dalhousie University
Halifax, Nova Scotia, Canada

Donna Thal, Ph.D.
Carnegie-Mellon University
Pittsburgh, Pennsylvania

Sandra M. Thompson, Ph.D.
University of California,
  Santa Barbara
Santa Barbara, California

Amy Wetherby, Ph.D.
Florida State University
Tallahassee, Florida

Foreword

It is a great honor to introduce a volume to recognize Carol Prutting's contributions to the field of human communication and its disorders. Carol was an extraordinary teacher and colleague whose influence went far beyond the classrooms in which she taught and the lecture halls in which she conducted workshops; a mind like Carol's endures through the continuing work of those she taught and those fortunate enough to have talked with her and read her writings.

Carol took a path much different from that of the ordinary scholar. While others were looking at ever smaller bits of knowledge, she was asking the big questions; when others were specializing and dividing, she was looking for connections. Her students were not being trained, they were being educated. They joined her in learning as an adventure, not a chore.

I first met Carol when she attended a lecture I gave. We talked briefly during a break and were friends immediately and permanently. I did not have the good fortune to be one of her students, but could not help but be influenced by her incisive thinking and her infectious enthusiasm. I talked about her work to my own students, who soon came to associate the name of Prutting with imaginative approaches to research and scholarship. I was one of the lucky people who were on Carol's mailing list, which brought me copies of manuscripts in draft form for comment and, from time to time, copies of books. Carol's generous style of communicating with friends and colleagues included sending them copies of books she read and thought they might enjoy.

Early in our acquaintance we talked about the then emerging field of pragmatics of language and its implications for a broader understanding of the nature and handicap of communicative disorders. It is no accident that Carol should have become fascinated by matters pragmatic; her fundamental interest in the human dynamics of communication would predict such a development. Years later, when I asked her how she happened to get interested in pragmatics, she surprised me by saying, "From you." Nothing could have flattered me more, and I hope it is true.

This volume is the enduring record of the deep respect and affection of Carol Prutting's colleagues and students. It is a privilege to be included among that body.

Norma S. Rees
California State University
Hayward, California

Preface

The goals of creating this book were twofold. In the past decade, pragmatic language models have had a major impact on speech-language pathologists' thinking about the nature of language disorders and the goals for
and approach to clinical assessment and intervention. One of the goals of
this book was to bring this literature together to review, clarify, and evaluate the progress that has been made but most importantly to direct our
thinking toward the future. The second goal was to do this so well that it
would be a fitting memorial to Carol Prutting.

The contributors to this book are among the most distinguished scholars
who have written in the area of pragmatics. They also were all Carol's
friends. Diane Kirchner, Elizabeth Skarakis–Doyle, Michelle Mentis, Sandra Thompson, and Amy Wetherby are also her former students. Each con-
tributor to the book deals in depth with a major issue in pragmatics, and the
breadth of the topics addressed across the chapters provides the most comprehensive look at clinical pragmatics to date.

The book is organized in the following sequence: Chapters dealing with
social/cultural issues, chapters dealing with models of language and language disorders and their implications for clinical practice, and chapters
dealing with specific pragmatic assessment or intervention applications. All
of the chapters address these issues in light of their implications for
the future.

Chapter 1, "A Retrospective Look at Clinical Pragmatics," is a review of
the contributions pragmatics has made to the evolution of language assessment and intervention in the last decade. This chapter also discusses what
has not been accomplished, and why all of the field's early expectations for
pragmatics may not have been realized.

Chapter 2, "Language and Social Skills: Implications for Clinical Assessment and Intervention with School-Age Children," examines the social aspects of language use and the role language skills play in the child's interpersonal world. The role of peers in social assessment and intervention
programs is reviewed and the implications of this literature for pragmatic
language assessment and intervention with school-age children is discussed.

In Chapter 3, "Everyday Events: Their Role in Language Assessment and
Intervention," Judith Duchan discusses event representations, action sequences and their temporal and causal relations, normal children's development of event language, and the implications of this literature for
assessing children's event knowledge and event language and for facilitating children's event learning. Particular attention is directed toward classroom events and language intervention in classrooms.

Martha Crago and Elizabeth Cole's chapter, "Using Ethnography to Bring Children's Communicative and Cultural Worlds into Focus," reviews language socialization and ethnography and discusses crosscultural issues relative to communicative competence. Ethnographic methodology is reviewed and the interfaces between clinical and ethnographic procedures are discussed. Particular attention is given to ethnographic perspectives in the assessment of children from minority cultures who are communicatively impaired.

In Chapter 5, "A Functionalist Approach to Language and Its Implications for Assessment and Intervention," Elizabeth Bates, Donna Thal, and Brian MacWhinney present a functionalist approach to language. They contrast "straw man functionalism" with the Competition Model and discuss the model's application to normal adults and children and to individuals with language disorders.

In Chapter 6, "Pragmatic Characteristics of the Child with Specific Language Impairment: An Interactionist Perspective," Holly Craig reviews the pragmatic characteristics of the child with specific language impairment (SLI), discusses the methodological implications of that literature, and presents a revised interactionist model for SLI.

In Chapter 7, "Discourse: A Means for Understanding Normal and Disordered Language," Michelle Mentis and Sandra Thompson consider normal language and language disorders from a discourse perspective and present an integrated approach to language disorders.

John Muma in his chapter, "Experiential Realism: Clinical Implications," presents the principles of experiential realism, contrasts them with objectivism, and discusses the clinical implications of this theory for language assessment and intervention.

In Chapter 9, "Profiling Pragmatic Abilities in the Emerging Language of Young Children," Amy Wetherby discusses the cognitive, social, and communicative bases of symbol use and the importance of profiling these abilities in children with normal language development and children with communicative impairments. She proposes an assessment framework, illustrates its principles using case presentations, and considers the implications of this framework for intervention.

Elizabeth Skarakis–Doyle and Michelle Mentis in their chapter, "A Discourse Approach to Language Disorders: Investigating Complex Sentence Production," review complex sentence development in children and present a case to illustrate that assessment of complex sentence use in children with language disorders is enhanced through discourse analysis.

In Chapter 11, "Reciprocal Book Reading: A Discourse-Based Intervention Strategy for the Child with Atypical Language Development," Diane Kirchner discusses reciprocal reading routines as a discourse context for facilitating language acquisition. She presents procedures for selecting the literature, segmenting the text to be used, and criteria for fitting intervention strategies to children's language profiles.

Laurence Leonard and Marc Fey's chapter, "Facilitating Grammatical Development: The Contribution of Pragmatics," discusses some of the ways grammar and pragmatics interact and how knowledge of pragmatics can be used in intervention programs to facilitate grammatical development of children who have language impairments.

This book was organized in January 1990, shortly after Carol Prutting's death. All of the contributors gave generously of their time and energies and, I think, unquestionably met both of the goals that I had set for the project.

A PERSONAL NOTE

Carol Prutting died of a massive heart attack December 18, 1989 at the age of 48. It was as unexpected to those of us who knew her as it was devastating.

Carol and I were close friends for over twenty years. We were bonded by scholarship, friendship, and a shared history of personal triumphs, defeats, and struggles that naturally comprise twenty years of living. We met as graduate students at the University of Illinois at a time when the intellectual excitement on that campus around the study of language was almost palpable. At the center of this activity was Tom Shriner, our professor and mentor. He was our "academic father" and the three of us spent so much time together we thought of ourselves as a family. Carol used to call us "old friends."

It is difficult to characterize that long history in a truly meaningful way, but what I most want to share is my admiration for her as a teacher. Whether she was teaching a seminar, talking with students and colleagues over coffee, or addressing a huge auditorium full of people, she was the quintessential teacher—personally accessible, inspiring, and empowering. She was what she most admired.

It is, therefore, understandable that what I would like to highlight among Carol's writings is a more personal and perhaps lesser known contribution to the literature than those that are amply referenced throughout this book. It is a short piece that she wrote for the NSSLHA Journal in 1985. She had been asked to write an article for the journal and given its student audience she chose to write a broadly philosophical paper from a very personal perspective. The paper is entitled "The Long Battle for the Light." In it she presents what she refers to as a "few innocent sounding ideas," among them that "dailiness is what one has and therefore matters"; that self-esteem is at the core of what we do "for everything external depends on a trust within"; that "exuberance is a quality to value and embrace"; and that "morality is the 'power to' rather than 'power over.'"

Given the international regard in which Carol was held, her ability to not take herself too seriously was all the more remarkable and endearing. I would like to share just one example of this quality which I remember fondly. Carol had been invited to speak at a workshop, as she frequently was, and when she arrived at the auditorium she saw a large poster board that was propped up on an easel by the door. After she read it she called me and through whole-hearted laughter said, "I just had to call to tell you what this poster says." The poster read, "Carol Prutting, Language Expert, Admission, $1."

When our dear friend and mentor, Tom Shriner, died in December of 1981, Carol and I edited a book in his memory. It means a great deal to me that I was also able to do that in hers.

CHAPTER 1

A Retrospective Look at Clinical Pragmatics

TANYA M. GALLAGHER

Approximately 20 years ago when I was a graduate student in the psycholinguistics and speech-language pathology programs at the University of Illinois, Tom Shriner, Carol Prutting, and I began our endless discussions about pragmatics, although we didn't use that term then. We were trying to integrate three modes of thinking about language that existed in three physically distinct locations on campus. One mode of thinking about language was linguistics. In linguistics classes we discussed Chomsky's theory of generative grammar, a language theory with such profound implications that it was receiving extraordinary attention even in the popular literature. Chomsky's theory rested on three fundamental assumptions. One was that the domain of linguistic theory was the characterization of the abstract rules of language as language competence rather than language performance. The second assumption was that the primary power of language resided in syntax. The third assumption was that knowledge of syntax could be described independently from the other levels of language knowledge, phonology and semantics. In linguistics classes we analyzed sentences as they "might be written on a blackboard" and we conceptualized language as an abstract, symbolic code. In psychology seminars, brilliant scholars, such as Charles Osgood, taught us about the principles of mediational behavioristic psychology and how these principles were evident in language performance. In these classes we discussed behavior and language. In speech-language pathology, we worked with children and adults who were language disordered. These people were having such difficulty communicating that their functional capabilities were reduced significantly from those of their chronological peer groups. Problems with trying to deal with communication difficulties by viewing language as simply a symbolic code, however elegant, or viewing language as simply another form of behavior were haunting. Although we did not have theoretical models that adequately characterized it as such or a vocabulary that provided a means for making clear references to it, we struggled with trying to deal with communication, language as behavior, with language as it was used by people in their daily lives. This meant that we somehow had to conceptualize language as a code that was used by people to do things. As I review the clinical literature over the last 20 years I think that my experience as a graduate student was to some extent a microcosm of the tensions and struggles that have characterized the study of language disorders itself.

In the last 10 years pragmatic language models (Austin, 1962; Bates, 1976; Searle, 1969) have had a major impact on the study of language disorders. The depth and speed of their impact on clinical practice are remarkable features of what has been referred to as the "pragmatics revolution" (Duchan, 1984). Viewed from the broadest perspective, pragmatic language models attempt to characterize communicative competence. This competence reflects the complex interrelationships among three types of knowledge: language structural knowledge, knowledge of the language code; presuppositional knowledge, the ability to make appropriate judgments about the form an utterance must take to adequately communicate the speaker's intent or to adequately understand it; and conversational knowledge, knowledge of the discourse rules governing conversation in the interactants' society. This functionalist perspective focuses on language as it is used for communicative purposes.

Why did this type of model have such a profound impact on the clinical literature? Its acceptance probably was enhanced by three major factors. One was the inadequacies evident in previous types of models, and a growing frustration with their inadequacies. Throughout the 1960s and early 1970s clinicians experienced the limitations of an almost exclusively syntactic/semantic characterization of language behaviors. This constrained their ability to adequately identify the depth and range of communicative problems their clients were experiencing and to facilitate the generalization of newly learned language behaviors to contexts beyond the therapy room. Skarakis–Doyle (1990) recently wrote that

Chomsky may have adopted an ideal methodology for illuminating mechanisms of syntax, but not for how it participates in human endeavors . . . It comes as no surprise then that clinicians who were charged with treating people with language disorders would so readily entertain pragmatic models which 'returned language to its users' (McLean and Snyder–McLean, 1988, p. 255) . . . I believe it was a [humanistic] position that was always held, but in light of behavioral and psychometric influences on our field, it was not always in vogue to articulate it. (pp. 10–11)

A related factor perhaps was an intuitive recognition that there was something fundamentally right about the field's earliest conceptualizations of language disorders as a type of socially defined disability (VanRiper, 1939). Pragmatic models of language had a compelling face validity.

A third factor was the attention that pragmatic models received in the normal language developmental literature. Bates, Bretherton, and Snyder (1988) described the reception of these models in that literature as follows: "In the 1970s this interactive view of language development was so popular that we were preaching among the converted" (p. ix).

The enthusiastic reception that pragmatic models received in speech-language pathology created an atmosphere of high expectation and anticipation for the contributions they would make to the evolution of clinical practice. For example, Norma Rees in 1978 characterized the potential of pragmatic approaches for clinical practice as "limitless" (p. 263). High expectations, however, are sometimes difficult to fulfill. Enough time has passed to permit us to productively review what we have learned from a decade of working within this model.

Clearly, in the last decade pragmatics research has amassed an impressive list of contributions to the clinical literature. These contributions have reflected the influence of three major lines of pragmatic research with language disordered populations: the study of context and the influence of contextual variables on language use; the study of discourse phenomena that had been largely ignored from an exclusively language structural perspective, for example, requests for clarification and turn-taking behaviors; and the study of communicative intentions. To a greater or lesser extent all aspects of language assessment and intervention have been affected in pragmatically based clinical practice.

CONTRIBUTIONS TO LANGUAGE ASSESSMENT PROCEDURES

One of the contributions of pragmatics research to language assessment procedures has been the introduction of the concept of "communicative disability," which has resulted in the expansion of the identification criteria of language disorder. The concept of communicative disability incorporated a broader set of criteria than had been used previously. The result was that adults and children who might not have qualified for inclusion in service delivery programs or who qualified only minimally using exclusively language structural criteria became eligible for service using these expanded criteria.

Spontaneous language sampling protocols also have been modified. As more has been learned about the impact of various types of communicative contexts on the language structures produced by clients, increased understanding of contextual variability led to a realization by speech-language pathologists that it is futile to attempt to strip context effects away from language use. Clinicians learned that it also was not possible to identify a "standardized" context that could be used with all clients as a way of neutralizing idiosyncratic contextual influences on individuals. It could not be assumed that one context was by definition "easier" or at least equally easy for all clients. Two modifications of language sampling procedures that have been recommended are that information be obtained on each client prior to sampling to permit clinicians to individualize the contextual configurations of language sampling, a procedure referred to as "pre-assessment" (Gallagher, 1983; Lund & Duchan, 1988) and that an individual's language use be observed in more than one context.

Language sampling analysis procedures also have been expanded. New behaviors, both verbal and nonverbal, have been added to assessment protocols, and some previously noted behaviors now are analyzed from multiple perspectives. Clarification responses and gaze behaviors are examples of the former and the inclusion of questions within the broader speech act category of requests, which also can include other sentence types such as declaratives, is an example of the latter.

Pragmatic profiles have been introduced (Penn, 1988; Prutting & Kirchner, 1983, 1987; Roth & Spekman, 1984). Prutting and Kirchner's (1983, 1987) and Penn's (1988) protocols are the most elaborate. Prutting and Kirchner's "Pragmatic Protocol" elicits clinician judgments of 30 interactive behaviors which represent three broad categories: verbal behaviors (e.g., the variety of speech acts used), paralinguistic behaviors (e.g., prosody), and nonverbal behaviors (e.g., physical proximity). Penn's "Profile of Communicative Appropriateness" includes 49 client behaviors that are rated on a five-point rating scale. These represent six categories of behavior: responses to interlocutors (e.g., acknowledgment), control of semantic context (e.g., topic adherence), cohesion (e.g., ellipsis), fluency (e.g., false starts), sociolinguistic sensitivity (e.g., indirect speech acts), and nonverbal communication (e.g., facial expression). The use of more real time scoring and checklists has been encouraged.

Some pragmatic tests also have been developed. These include *The Test of Pragmatic Skills* (Shulman, 1986), the *Let's Talk Inventory for Children* (Bray & Wiig, 1987), the *Interpersonal Language Skills Assessment* (Blagden & McConnell, 1985).

CONTRIBUTIONS TO LANGUAGE INTERVENTION PROCEDURES

Many contributions of pragmatics research to language intervention also are evident. One of these contributions relates to goal setting. Intervention goals have been expanded to include communicative functions such as controlling and informing (Wood, 1977a, 1977b), requesting (Olswang, Kriegsmann, & Mastergeorge, 1982), and turn taking (Bedwinck, 1983; Muma, 1975). Clinical tasks and activities also have been modified to highlight natural needs, desires, and consequences of communication. Increased saliency and natural consequences have been emphasized in pragmatically based clinical practice in contrast with other models that emphasize specific clinician evaluations of client behavior or external rewards (see Owens, 1991).

Pragmatically based clinical tasks and activities include routines, scripts, and formulaic utterances. Memorized sequences, once devalued and considered counterproductive, are being incorporated into intervention programs as a means of achieving productive use and/or as compensatory or coping strategies for dealing with interactionally problematic circumstances. As a consequence of these changes the role of the clinician has been expanded from that of facilitator to that of teacher/facilitator as activities that incorporate explicit instructional principles are being included in clinical practice (Craig, 1983).

Finally, the number of intervention agents has been expanded. A number of indirect therapies have been developed, including consultative models that use significant individuals in the client's life as primary intervention agents. The many roles that peers are assuming in child language intervention programs is another example.

WHAT HAS NOT BEEN ACCOMPLISHED

All of the contributions of pragmatics research to language assessment and intervention cited above are significantly expanded by the chapters in this volume. The question that is inevitably raised, however, is what has not been accomplished and why? There is a sense of disappointment that all of the high expectations with which we went into the decade were not fully realized and that the concepts we intuitively grasped easily and readily were not as easily and readily implemented. In peer commentaries of a review of clinical pragmatics by Gallagher (1990), both Brinton (1990) and Craig (1990) emphasized this point. Brinton (1990) wrote: "I must admit that the revolution has not met at least one major expectation; it has not made clinical research and intervention easier. Rather, it has attacked our knowledge base, complicated our methods, and challenged our conclusions" (p. 8). In a similar vein Craig (1990) wrote:

These changes have associated costs. The scope of assessment has increased geometrically. More behaviors must be sampled and analyzed, and their interdependent influences described . . . and across more situational contexts and types of conversational partners . . . Intervention tasks that emphasize natural experiences for the child, conversational symmetry between the child and the intervention agent, and balanced play between interactants . . . may appear imprecise or unfocused, and documentation procedures for intervention may depend upon subjective measures . . . (p. 9)

At least two basic assumptions underlie these types of concerns. One is that pragmatically based clinical practice would be simply another form of language practice as we had come to know it, leaving all of our basic assumptions intact. As a member of a panel discussion at the 1988 American Speech-Language-Hearing Association convention, Norma Rees characterized this assumption as follows:

We assumed . . . that if language has a finite array of phonemes and sentence types, it should behave itself and also have a finite list of speech acts, and our job is to discover it. Once we discovered the correct final comprehensive list of speech acts, it should be pretty short, otherwise it is not too helpful. Then we could discover the order in which children acquire them and so on, building test and therapy protocols. Now of course that hasn't worked terribly well.

Clearly one of the expectations that speech-language pathologists had for pragmatic clinical practice which largely has not been realized was that pragmatic norms, pragmatic skill profiles, and tests of pragmatic skills would be forthcoming and would be similar in form to the language structural norms, profiles, and tests with which they had become familiar and comfortable throughout the generative grammatical period. Thinking in new ways has been difficult, and the degree of change that was needed in order to implement pragmatic models was not fully anticipated. Skarakis–Doyle (1990) wrote, "It is not a flaw of pragmatic models that the elements they seek to organize and explain do not behave as syntactic units; it is our inappropriate assumption that they should, which accounts for our failed expectations" (p. 11).

There are fundamental differences between generative theories and pragmatic theories. Generative theories attempt to characterize universal aspects of grammar. Pragmatic theories, on the other hand, are individualistic and characterize behavior in interactional, culturally sensitive, and highly situational terms. The development of extensive pragmatic paper and pencil tests may be logically inconsistent with features of the theory itself. It is difficult to see how delayed imitation testing formats, for example, could be utilized to answer pragmatic language questions.

The second assumption that has contributed to concerns about successfully implementing pragmatically based language models is that throughout the decade speech-language pathologists were all working from one, cohesive, overarching pragmatic theory. That has certainly not been the case. Within the last decade there have been many interpretations of pragmatics. Craig (1983) referred to two basic types of interpretations, narrow and broad, however, even within these types there has been variability. Unlike generative theory, pragmatic models are not characterized by a single, coherent, explanatory theory that leads to predictable, rigorous, and supportable hypotheses (McTear, 1985). Among the consequences of this lack of theoretical clarity have been terminological confusion, terminological proliferation, and a blurring of the distinctions between the identification of behaviors and their explanation. Even the basic unit of analysis that was finite, clearly identifiable, and, therefore, quantifiable in generative theories varies across pragmatic models. Part of the complication to which Rees (1988) among others refers is the complication that is introduced by the lack of a clearly unifying theory.

Proceeding as though pragmatics is simpler than it is or concluding that it is not useful because it did not meet all of the early expectations for it are not productive options. The more promising course would seem to be to engage in the careful work that is needed to fully realize the potential inherent in this interactional perspective. Brinton (1990) wrote:

Perhaps the pragmatics revolution can be compared to a political revolution. Political revolutions that result in constructive change and growth often begin as violent flurries of activity and upheaval that are followed by years of slow, carefully planned reform measures. The initial pragmatics battle is behind us. Much of the hard work and reforms still lie ahead. (p. 8)

Fundamental questions remain to be explored. For example, will pragmatic analyses clarify long-standing enigmas of language disorder, such as language structural inconsistencies? Are the interactional difficulties exhibited by individuals with language disorders the consequences of limited language structural skills or are they related to broader nonlinguistic impairments that may be cognitive or social in nature? Finally, can the boundaries of pragmatics be made sufficiently clear and delimited enough to support reliable clinical predictions? The chapters in this volume are concrete examples of the promise of pragmatics research for the future.

REFERENCES

Austin, J. (1962). *How to do things with words.* Cambridge, MA: Harvard University Press.

Bates, E. (1976). *Language in context.* New York: Academic Press.

Bates, E., Bretherton, I., & Snyder, L. (1988). *From first words to grammar: Individual differences and dissociable mechanisms.* Cambridge, UK: Cambridge University Press.

Bedwinek, A. (1983). The use of PACE to facilitate gestural and verbal communication in a language-impaired child. *Language, Speech, and Hearing Services in Schools, 14,* 2–6.

Blagden, C., & McConnell, N. (1985). *Interpersonal language skills assessment.* Moline, IL: LinguiSystems.

Bray, C., & Wiig, E. (1987). *Let's talk inventory for children.* San Antonio, TX: Psychological Corp.

Brinton, B. (1990). Peer commentary on "Clinical pragmatics: Expectations and realizations" by Tanya Gallagher. *Journal of Speech Language Pathology and Audiology, 14*(1), 7–8.

Craig, H. K. (1983). Applications of pragmatic language models for intervention. In T. M. Gallagher & C. A. Prutting (Eds.), *Pragmatic assessment and intervention issues in language* (pp. 101–127). San Diego, CA: College-Hill Press.

Craig, H. K. (1990). Peer commentary on "Clinical pragmatics: Expectations and realizations" by Tanya Gallagher. *Journal of Speech Language Pathology and Audiology, 14*(1), 8–9.

Duchan, J. (1984). Language assessment: The pragmatics revolution. In R. Naremore (Ed.), *Language science.* San Diego, CA: College-Hill Press.

Gallagher, T. (1983). Pre-assessment: A procedure for accommodating language use variability. In T. Gallagher & C. Prutting (Eds.), *Pragmatic assessment and intervention issues in language* (pp. 1–28). San Diego, CA: College-Hill Press.

Gallagher, T. (1990). Clinical pragmatics: Expectations and realizations. *Journal of Speech Language Pathology and Audiology, 14*(1), 3–6.

Lund, N., & Duchan, J. (1988). *Assessing children's language in naturalistic contexts.* Englewood Cliffs, NJ: Prentice-Hall.

McLean, J., & Snyder–McLean, L. (1988). Application of pragmatics to severely mentally retarded children and youth. In R. L. Schiefelbusch & L. L. Lloyd (Eds.), *Language perspectives: Acquisition, retardation, and intervention* (2nd ed., pp. 255–288). Austin, TX: Pro-Ed.

McTear, M. (1985). Pragmatic disorders: A question of direction. *British Journal of Disorders of Communication, 20,* 119–127.

Muma, J. (1975). The communication game: Dump and play. *Journal of Speech and Hearing Disorders, 40,* 296–309.

Olswang, L., Kriegsmann, E., & Mastergeorge, A. (1982). Facilitating functional requesting in pragmatically impaired children. *Language, Speech and Hearing Services in Schools, 16,* 202–222.

Owens, R. (1991). *Language disorders: A functional approach to assessment and intervention.* New York: Macmillan.

Penn, C. (1988). The profiling of syntax and pragmatics in aphasia. *Clinical Linguistics & Phonetics, 2,* 179–207.

Prutting, C., & Kirchner, D. (1983). Applied pragmatics. In T. Gallagher & C. Prutting (Eds.), *Pragmatic assessment and intervention issues in language* (pp. 29–64). San Diego, CA: College-Hill Press.

Prutting, C., & Kirchner, D. (1987). A clinical appraisal of the pragmatic aspects of language. *Journal of Speech and Hearing Disorders, 52,* 105–119.

Rees, N. (1978). Pragmatics of language: Applications to normal and disordered language development. In R. Schiefelbusch (Ed.), *Bases of language intervention.* Baltimore, MD: University Park Press.

Rees, N. (Speaker) (1988). *Pragmatics: A retrospective analysis* (Cassette Recording H81118-110). Rockville, MD: American Speech-Language-Hearing Association.

Roth, F., & Spekman, N. (1984). Assessing the pragmatic abilities of children: Part I. Organizational framework and assessment parameters. *Journal of Speech and Hearing Disorders, 49,* 2–11.

Searle, J. (1969). *Speech acts: An essay in the philosophy of language.* Cambridge, UK: Cambridge University Press.

Shulman, B. (1986). *Test of Pragmatic Skills—Revised.* Tuscon, AZ: Communication Skill Builders.

Skarakis–Doyle, E. (1990). Peer commentary on "Clinical pragmatics: Expectations and realizations" by Tanya Gallagher. *Journal of Speech Language Pathology and Audiology, 14*(1), 7–8.

VanRiper, C. (1939). *Speech correction: Principles and methods.* New York: Prentice-Hall.

Wood, B. (1977a). *Development of functional communication competencies pre-K through grade 6.* Urbana, IL: Eric Clearinghouse in Reading Communication Skills.

Wood, B. (1977b). *Development of functional communication competencies grade 7–12.* Urbana, IL: Eric Clearinghouse in Reading Communication Skills.

CHAPTER 2

Language and Social Skills: Implications for Assessment and Intervention with School-Age Children

TANYA M. GALLAGHER

The prominence of pragmatic language theories during the last 15 years has contributed to an increased awareness of the social role of language. Language is a primary means by which we make interpersonal contact, socialize our children, and regulate our interactions. Despite this and the fact that the negative social consequences of communication disorders were among the first problems to be noted in the early speech-language pathology literature (Koepp–Baker, 1937; Travis, 1936), the profession has been slow to develop assessment and intervention programs that deal with language disorders in social-interactional terms.

One of the reasons for this hesitancy may have been a reluctance on the part of speech-language pathologists to expand their sphere of responsibility beyond dealing with the concrete elements of the language structural code, that is, phonology, syntax, and semantics. There is a growing awareness, however, that whether we explicitly acknowledge it or not, when that language code is used to communicate it is an inherently social phenomenon. Pragmatics is the study of language as it is used and when language is used in conversation it is a social behavior. In order to fully understand conversational behavior, it must be studied in its social context. Prutting (1982) wrote:

Some may wonder if there is a danger in clinicians dealing with behavior tied so closely to social development . . . Our intervention goals however have always been toward shaping social growth . . . We have always been in the business of social change . . . The pragmatic shift brings this issue closer to the surface and gently reminds us of our raison d'etre. (p. 132)

For the most part, American psychological theory has not explored the role that language plays in the child's cognitive and social development. Jean Berko Gleason in an address to the Stanford Child Language Conference in 1987 highlighted what she characterized as a "bias" in American psychology that had not been fully recognized. She argued that developmental psychological theories have been essentially nonverbal in their orientation. Consequently, studies of language development, social development, and cognitive development have been, to a large extent, distinct lines of research. Cognitive developmental theory has focused on the child's manipulation and exploration of the physical world (Piaget, 1963) and social psychological theory has focused on the child's acculturation through identification and modeling. Both of these theoretical approaches were primarily nonverbal and did not explore the role that language plays across all of these domains of inquiry.

Recently, there have been appeals to broaden psychological models (Fischer, 1980). Wyer and Srull (1986), for example, have argued that current cognitive theories are not sufficient to account for issues of concern in social cognition. They stated that some of the most important input variables in the social domain, such as prior attitudes, stereotypes, goals, and so forth have been ignored or experimentally controlled in most current cognitive research and that many of the most important output variables also have not been addressed.

In a parallel fashion, language developmental researchers have more often studied the development of language forms than the content of language. The role that language plays in mediating cognitive tasks, establishing social roles, and achieving social goals only recently has begun to be recognized, as has the role of interaction in the development of language itself (Bates & Mac-Whinney, 1982; Bruner, 1978; Golinkoff, 1983; Snow, 1979).

This chapter will review what has been learned about some of the social aspects of language use that speech-language pathologists need to understand in order to frame language assessment and intervention programs within the ecologically valid social contexts that will enable them to address their goals for communicative competence. The specific focus of the chapter will be a review of these social aspects relative to the needs of school-age children with language disorders. The review has been restricted to school-age children not because this is the only age range in which the general principles apply, but because the social world of the child differs in fundamental ways from that of the adult and therefore warrants specific study. In the context of peer relationships the chapter will review the nature of social cognition; the nature of social skills and social competence and how they relate to language skills; the stages of friendship development and the role that language skills play in that development; how social skills and peer status have been assessed; the role of peers in social skill intervention programs; and what implications this literature may have for pragmatic language assessment and intervention with school-age children.

PEER RELATIONSHIPS

In the child development literature it has been proposed that various aspects of the child's functioning are enhanced by peer interaction. Peers are thought to positively contribute to the child's cognitive skills (Piaget, 1963), social-cognitive skills (Selman, 1980), moral development (Damon, 1977; Kohlberg, 1983), maturity (Hartup, 1979; Sullivan, 1953, Youniss, 1980), aggressive impulse control (Hartup, 1978), and sex-role behavioral development (Fine, 1980). Hartup (1983) wrote:

Peer interaction is an essential component of the individual child's development. Experience with peers is not a superficial luxury to be enjoyed by some children and not by others, but is a necessity in childhood socialization. And among the most sensitive indicators of difficulties in development are failure by the child to engage in the activities of the peer culture and failure to occupy a relatively comfortable place within it. (p. 220)

Peers provide opportunities for establishing and practicing language skills and through role modeling and naturally consequent feedback are a major source of information about language use. Social cognition, social skills, and the attainment of age-appropriate friendship skills provide the foundation on which peer relationships are built. Central to each of these is language skill.

SOCIAL COGNITION

In the broadest definition, *social cognition* is the individual's representation of her or his social world. The content of social cognition is social knowledge, constructs that enable the interpretation and ordering of social reality, and social processes, the means by which social information is received, exchanged, and mediated. Social processes include those that are general to other types of cognitive functioning, such as memory and attention, and those that are primarily social in nature, such as communication and social-perspective taking. Through these processes children learn about their social world and construct knowledge structures which contribute to the continual change of social cognition itself (Damon, 1981; Shantz, 1983). Research to date has not resulted in a unified theory of social cognition and most of the work still can be traced to its major intellectual roots (e.g., cognitive-developmental theories [Shantz, 1983] or contextualist or social action theories [Lerner & Lerner, 1986; McGuire, 1983]).

It is beyond the scope of this chapter to discuss whether or not social cognition requires a separate model or can be incorporated into more comprehensive cognitive models, or whether or not developmental social cognition is distinct enough from adult social cognition to also require separate models. For discussions of these issues see Kramer (1986), Wyer and Srull (1986), Edelstein, Keller, and Wahlen (1984), and Selman (1980). As Chandler (1977) has emphasized, however, all models regardless of their differences must address two questions: the general nature of the relationships that are assumed to exist between humans and the world of objects in general and whether humans, in contrast with inanimate or nonsocial objects, have special qualities or characteristics that alter the nature of the processes by which they are understood. In other words, all models must describe the basic features of social cognition and how they differ from those of physical cognition.

Research to date indicates that the basic features of social cognition differ in psychologically important ways from those of physical cognition. Social objects differ from physical objects on a number of dimensions. Social objects are more complex, more variable, and more unpredictable and can be comprehended through self-reflection, a route not available for understanding physical objects (Youniss, 1975). Social objects, with their unique potential for personal interaction, also exist in a special relationship to people that is not shared by physical objects. Only people can intentionally coordinate their interactions, thoughts, and perspectives with each other. Damon (1981) considered intentional coordination, this type of planned and purposeful adaptation to another, to be the hallmark of social cognition and what makes human communication possible. Selman (1980) described the development of social perspective taking as the development of an understanding of how human points of view are coordinated with one another and how they are related. Social perspective taking is not simply the development of a representation of what social or psychological information may be as in the concept of "roles."

The nature of social knowledge also differs from physical knowledge. Physical knowledge can be objectified and scientifically verified. Social knowledge, however, is more arbitrary, less uniform, less predictable, and more dependent on specific social situations and cultural expectations (Muus, 1982). Social knowledge includes relational concepts like friendship, regulational concepts like fairness and politeness, intrapersonal concepts like identity, and extrapersonal concepts like society.

Contrary to earlier assumptions, converging evidence from a number of studies in the last decade suggests that rudiments of these distinct aspects of social cognition are present in children at very young ages (see Miller & Aloise, 1989, for review). Further, although developing social cognitive abilities are related to physical cognitive abilities they are distinctive enough to make adequate predictions of performance from one to the other difficult. For example, there is growing evidence that nonsocial problem solving skills, such as those typically measured with conventional IQ tests, are not transferred easily by some children to social problem-solving tasks (Shantz, 1975; Shure & Spivak, 1980). These children may be able to demonstrate high levels of performance on physical problem-solving tasks but have difficulty performing what may appear to be simpler levels of analysis in social situations.

These data have interesting implications for understanding language-disordered populations, such as children who have specific language impairments. This group of children is defined as having normal intelligence based on nonverbal intelligence measures; however, they are often noted to have social interaction difficulties. When these types of disparities cannot be explained adequately in terms of specific language structure deficits they are often puzzling. Clinicians have shared their surprise that children with IQs of 110 and above can have difficulty understanding the relationship between a socially penalizing conversational behavior they are displaying, for example, frequently insulting their peers, and their peers' negative reactions to them. Children who present this type of profile may be having social cognitive difficulties and would benefit from learning social problem-solving strategies, just as children who evidence other types of cognitive difficulties benefit from learning strategies to facilitate physical problem solving. Alternatively, these children may not have acquired sufficient social knowledge to function effectively in their social world and these knowledge deficits could be contributing to their communicative difficulties. This also could be addressed. Such relationships and their implications for conversational performance should be investigated further.

SOCIAL SKILLS

Among the products of social cognition is social competence. The attainment of age-appropriate social competence facilitates the establishment of successful peer relationships. Various definitions of social competence have been proposed, each entailing specific sets of social skills. The current difficulty in defining social competence and obtaining consensus on an inclusive list of social skills reflects the problems inherent in characterizing behaviors that are value laden, situationally interpreted, variable, and influenced by dominant cultural and subcultural expectations. Given different sets of circumstances, the same behavior by the same individual may be considered in one instance to be appropriate and in another instance to be inappropriate by the same evaluator. In light of these complexities, definitions of social competence that have gained general acceptance have been very broad. An example is the following definition by Ford (1982): "Social competence is the attainment of relevant social goals in specified social contexts, using appropriate means and resulting in positive developmental outcomes" (pp. 323-324). The disadvantage of this breadth, of course, is that it provides only limited guidance regarding the specification of the social skills that comprise this competence.

In January 1973 the Office of Child Development of the U.S. Department of Health, Education, and Welfare convened a panel of experts to define social competence in young children. The panel concluded that 29 social competencies or skills characterized social competence in young children (Anderson & Messick (1974). These competencies are listed in Table 2–1.

Despite the extensiveness, generality, and heterogeneity of the competencies listed, they essentially can be grouped into three major categories. The first deals with the knowledge of specific types of socially relevant behaviors and their roles in social contexts. The second deals with the ability to skillfully perform these behaviors; and the third deals with the ability to select, among candidate behaviors, the most appropriate behaviors to achieve social goals, evaluate their effectiveness in meeting those goals, and substitute behaviors as needed. Examples of children exhibiting problems with each of these types of social skill are numerous in the literature. For example, Asher and Renshaw (1981) noted that some children behave as though they have inappropriately conceived of the social goal of an interaction, such as behaving as though the goal of playing a game with their peers is winning "at all costs" rather than having "fun with other kids." Ladd and Oden (1979) reported that the responses to hypothetical situations of unpopular school-age children compared to those of popular children were more idiosyncratic and ineffectual. Some children may be able to understand the behavior that is needed in a social situation but be unable to perform it (Goetz & Dweck, 1980). Finally, Ladd (1981) reported that children who were social isolates often were unable to describe the reactions of other participants to their behaviors even though they could describe their own behaviors in the same social episodes.

A review of this literature suggests that language skill is a central component of social skill. The 1973 expert panel listed language skills as one of the 29 specific skills comprising social competence in young children (see Table 2–1). Research has further emphasized its significance. Communication skills such as school-age children's ability to adjust their messages in

Table 2–1. Social competencies in young children

1. Differentiated self-concept and consolidation of identity
2. Concept of self as an initiating and controlling agent
3. Habits of personal maintenance and care
4. Realistic appraisal of self, accompanied by feelings of personal worth
5. Differentiation of feelings and appreciation of their manifestations and implications
6. Sensitivity and understanding in social relationships
7. Positive and affectionate personal relationships
8. Role perception and appreciation
9. Appropriate regulation of antisocial behavior
10. Morality and prosocial tendencies
11. Curiosity and exploratory behavior
12. Control of attention
13. Perceptual skills
14. Fine motor dexterity
15. Gross motor skills
16. Perceptual-motor skills
17. Language skills
18. Categorizing skills
19. Memory skills
20. Critical thinking skills
21. Creative thinking skills
22. Problem-solving skills
23. Flexibility in the application of information-processing strategies
24. Quantitative and relational concepts, understandings, and skills
25. General knowledge
26. Competence motivation
27. Facility in the use of resources for learning and problem solving
28. Some positive attitudes toward learning and school experiences
29. Enjoyment of humor, play, and fantasy

Source: Adapted from "Social Competency in Young Children" by S. Anderson & S. Messick, 1974, *Developmental Psychology*, 10(2), 289–292.

light of their listener's needs, to ask appropriate questions, to contribute substantively to ongoing conversations, to initiate communication success-fully, to communicate intentions clearly, to address all participants when joining a group, and to present comments positively more often than nega-tively were among the variables found to be related to measures of peer ac-ceptance and sociometric status (Asher, Oden, & Gottman, 1977; Asher & Renshaw, 1981; Dodge, Pettit, McClaskey, & Brown, 1986; Gottman, Gonso, & Rasmussen, 1975; Ladd & Oden, 1979; Putallaz & Gottman, 1981; Rubin, 1972; Selman, Schorin, Stone, & Phelps, 1983).

A recent study of 44 preschool children, who were approximately 3 to 5 years of age, suggested that the same relationships between peer acceptance and language skills also are evident at these younger ages (Hazen & Black, 1989). The study found that children who were well liked by peers were better able to initiate and maintain coherent discourse by clearly directing their talk to specific others and by responding appropriately to others' initiations than were children who were not well liked.

Numerous studies have reported that social skill problems are prevalent in the social interactions of children with identified deficits in the basic skill areas listed among the 29 competencies in Table 2–1, such as children who are mentally retarded, emotionally disturbed, or learning disabled (see Gresham, 1981, for review). Given the central role that language plays in social competence, children with language disorders are at particular risk for social interactional difficulties, a risk that Wiig and Semel (1976) were among the first to note in the clinical literature. In order to fully understand language problems, their relationships to social interactional problems need to be explored and vice versa.

FRIENDSHIP

Although from the adult perspective there is an impressive list of benefits to be derived from peer interaction, from the child's perspective one of the primary goals of peer interaction is friendship. Ginsberg, Gottman, and Parker (1986) reflected this perspective when they asserted that, ". . . children are not interested in peers in general; they are interested in specific peers, namely, their friends" (p. 5).

Social Needs Met by Friendship

What social benefits does the child derive from friendship? Furman and Robbins (1985) concluded from their research on the development of children's relationships that children meet eight types of social needs in their relationships with peers. These are the need for affection, intimacy, reliable alliance, instrumental aid, nurturance, companionship, enhancement of worth, and a sense of inclusion.

In considering the social needs met by friendship it is helpful to distinguish between two kinds of relationships that are typically subsumed under that term. One type of friendship, being liked or accepted by one's peer group, can be termed "popularity." The other type, having a close, mutual dyadic relationship between co-equals, is "close friendship," originally termed "chumship" by Sullivan (1953). Considering these two types of friendship relative to the social needs each may meet for children, four of them—instrumental aid, nurturance, companionship, and enhancement of worth—can be met in either type of relationship. Three of them—affection, intimacy, and reliable alliance—are met in close friendship or "chumship." And one—a sense of inclusion—is met primarily by general peer group acceptance or "popularity."

As early as preschool age (Hayes, 1978), children seem to be aware of the social expectations they have for friends. Several studies have indicated that most children are capable of stating what they value about friends, what their expectations are of friends, what friends' obligations are to each other, and how friendships differ from other peer relationships (Bigelow, 1977; Furman & Bierman, 1984; Selman, 1980; Wright & Keple, 1981; Youniss & Volpe, 1978).

Developmental Stages of Friendship

Despite the commonalities among the social needs that are met by friends, some needs are more primary than others at some ages. For example, peer group inclusion is a major social need of children in the middle school years.

Friendship relationships throughout the school-age period of childhood can be described in terms of developmental stages. Such age differences are apparent in the following responses, reported by Berndt (1981), of a kindergartner and a sixth grader to the question "How do you know that someone is your best friend?" The kindergartner answered:

I sleep over at his house sometimes. When he's playing ball with his friends he'll let me play. When I slept over, he let me get in front of him in 4-squares. He likes me. (p. 180)

The sixth grader answered:

If you can tell each other things that you don't like about each other. If you get in a fight with someone else, they'd stick up for you. If you can tell them your phone number and they don't give you crank calls. If they don't act mean to you when other kids are around. (p. 180)

The first example highlighted the social needs of companionship, reliable alliance, instrumental aid, and affection. The second example highlighted intimacy, reliable alliance, nurturance, and companionship.

After reviewing the literature, including extensive references to their own work (Gottman, 1983; Gottman & Parker, 1986; Gottman & Parkhurst, 1980), Gottman and colleagues (Gottman & Mettetal, 1986; Parker & Gottman, 1989) divided the course of friendship relationships among children from 3 to 18 years of age into three developmental periods. The first period, termed "Early Childhood," extends from approximately 3 to 7 years of age. The second period, termed "Middle Childhood," extends from 8 to 12 years of age, and the third period, termed "Adolescence," extends from 13 to 18 years of age.

Early Childhood. Parker and Gottman (1989) proposed that the theme of the early childhood period of friendship development was "the maximization of excitement, entertainment, and affect levels of play" (p. 104). They suggested that during this period children meet their peer friendship needs through coordinated play. They categorized coordinated play into various types. Each type had a hierarchial relationship to the others in terms of the degree of coordination it required and the degree of social satisfaction it provided. The lowest level of coordinated play was parallel play, which requires minimal coordination between children and provides the lowest level of satisfaction; the highest level was nonstereotyped fantasy play, which requires the greatest coordination and provides the highest level of satisfaction.

Coordinated play is disrupted by conflict. Parallel play is the least demanding in the degree to which the children need to accommodate to each other and, therefore, has the lowest potential for disagreement and conflict. Conversely, nonstereotyped fantasy play, which places the greatest demands on the children to coordinate and negotiate their play, has the greatest potential for conflict and is easily disrupted. Fantasy play is verbally demanding, because roles, settings, props, and plot are established, negotiated and re-negotiated verbally, and enactment is largely verbal. Successful fantasy play requires clear communication, behavioral inhibition, and perspective-taking on the part of each child in order to be sustained. These features of fantasy play make it fragile. In order to achieve and maintain it, young children must be comfortable with each other, be able to anticipate one another, and be willing to accommodate each other. Gottman and colleagues hypothesized that these features of fantasy play explain its increased frequency as familiarity increases among young children (Matthews, 1978). Doyle, Connolly, and Rivest (1980) also have observed higher levels of social participation in the play of familiar peers compared to that of unfamiliar peers.

Gottman (1986) proposed that one of the benefits of fantasy play for young children is its potential for resolving major fears. Children at these ages have limited self-disclosure and self-analysis capabilities. Gottman observed them working through their fears in the context of peer support by means of fantasy play. Friends would take turns acting out fantasies dealing with their fears. They would set up a drama pertaining to a fear, ensuring that there was a satisfactory solution regardless of how improbable it might be, and then repeat the drama over and over again with some variations. Fantasy play provided a safe means for expressing their fears and resolving them since the children did not have to attribute the fears to themselves. The fears belonged to the "pretend" characters. Gottman concluded that repetition was an important part of the process. It increased the children's comfort levels by giving them a sense of order and mastery. The following is an example of this aspect of fantasy play from Gottman (1986). The children are two preschool-age friends, Eric and Naomi. Gottman wrote:

During the period of time that Eric and Naomi's conversations were recorded, Naomi was afraid of the dark and slept with a night light. The theme of their pretence play often involved dolls being afraid of the dark. They would turn the lights off and Naomi, pretending to be the doll, would scream and then, as the mommy, comfort the doll. Eric would also comfort the doll. After a few months, Naomi announced to her parents that she no longer needed the night light. Also, the theme of being afraid of the dark disappeared from their fantasy play. Both Naomi and the doll were cured. (p. 160)

Although the particular circumstances, experiences, and temperaments of individual children contribute to the themes they enact in their fantasy play, Gottman noted that generally in the play of young children there were several recurrent themes. These were parental abandonment, growing up, power and powerlessness, life and death, and transformations of the self. Similar themes were noted in the fantasy play of preschool-age children by Corsaro (1985). He identified three recurrent themes in the fantasy play of the children he observed. These were "lost-found," "danger-rescue," and "death-rebirth."

Within this period, children's regard for each other relates to their potential as play partners (Berndt & Perry, 1986; Furman & Buhrmester, 1985), most particularly their potential to engage in fantasy play (Connolly & Doyle, 1984). In a sample of 91 preschool children, Connolly and Doyle (1984) found that the complexity levels of fantasy play and the frequency with which fantasy play occurred among the children predicted four measures of their social competence: teacher ratings, popularity, affective role taking, and "a behavioral summary score reflecting positive social activity" (p. 794).

The major role that language plays in supporting play activities was explicitly noted by George and Krantz (1981). Their observational study of 11 pairs of preschool-age children indicated that compared to nonpreferred partners, preferred play partners talked significantly more, were more successful in sharing information, produced more related utterance sequences, produced more relevant responses, and were better able to use language to support their interaction. They concluded that conversational ability may serve as a "developmental constraint" with regard to social competence and may have a causal relationship to both the development of social competence and the attainment of social status. Similar relationships between social success and conversational skills were reported by Putallaz and Heflin (1986).

Middle Childhood. The theme of the next period of friendship development, middle childhood, which extends from 8 to 12 years of age, is inclusion by peers. Predictable corollaries are a concern about self-presentation and a desire to avoid rejection. The effects of the social complexity of schools are evident in this stage of friendship development. In schools, children encounter a complex social world. Typically, the number and diversity of children with whom they interact is much greater than they have experienced at younger ages. One of the consequences of this increased social complexity is that children form peer groups that differ in status and power (Hartup, 1984). Children's insecurities about peer acceptance are heightened by the formation of these peer groups, whose membership is seen as "volatile" and to some extent "capricious."

According to Gottman and colleagues (Gottman & Mettetal, 1986; Parker & Gottman, 1989), the most salient social process in middle childhood is successful negative-evaluation gossip. Negative-evaluation gossip is talking negatively about an aspect of some person, or stereotype. Success is reflected in the gossip's ability to elicit interest among peers and in its ability to elicit more negative gossip. Success is highest if the gossip helps to establish the child's solidarity with a group. Negative-evaluation gossip is the primary means by which children establish solidarity, reaffirm group membership, and determine peer attitudes about behaviors for which probable group reactions are unknown. Teasing also is used to serve these functions. Parker and Gottman (1989) regard negative-evaluation gossip and teasing, both verbal behaviors, as low risk strategies for sampling peer group attitudes. Children can use these strategies to obtain the information they need to avoid peer exclusion and rejection without risking personal exposure by actually displaying the behaviors themselves.

Language also plays a major role in this stage of friendship development. Furman and Childs (1981), for example, observed 40 dyads of third graders and found that the first time unacquainted children met they usually began their interactions by asking one another questions in an attempt to discover their common attitudes and orientations. Gottman (1983) also emphasized the role of language in the early interactions of unacquainted children. He observed 18 dyads of unacquainted children during three consecutive play sessions. He concluded that the emergence of friendship among these children could be accurately predicted by examining their conversations within their first meeting. Six specific conversational processes were identified: the extent to which the children communicated clearly and effectively, exchanged information successfully, explored their similarities and differences, successfully established common-ground activities, resolved conflicts amicably when they arose, and, to a lesser degree, engaged in self-disclosure.

Adolescence. The theme of the third period of friendship development, adolescence (13 to 18 years), is self-exploration and self-definition. Social processes include self-disclosure, positive and negative evaluation gossip, and problem solving. The most salient of these social processes is intimate self-disclosure. The means for addressing the theme of the adolescent period is highly verbal. Adolescents spend several hours a day talking with their friends. In the context of discussions with friends, adolescents explore who they are, what they believe, what they want to become, and so forth, and they help each other solve problems. Gottman and colleagues (Gottman & Mettetal, 1986; Parker & Gottman, 1989) observed that in adolescence self-disclosures lead to lengthy discussions focusing on the problems the friend is experiencing and possible ways that the problems may be resolved. Gottman and Mettetal (1986) concluded that these conversations require honesty, vulnerability, reciprocity of risk, and the willingness to persevere regardless of how difficult the solutions may be to find. Although peer group inclusion is still important, meeting the needs of this stage requires that children develop close friends. Adolescents need some friends who can be counted on to provide unquestioned loyalty and intimacy. Several studies of children's friendship expectations have indicated that between middle childhood and adolescence the frequency with which expectations of friendship include sharing personal thoughts and feelings increases dramatically (Furman & Bierman, 1984; Youniss, 1980).

Children with language disorders are at risk in each of these stages of friendship development. Whether the goal is to have a trusted play partner with whom a child can, among other things, explore and resolve his or her fears through highly coordinated fantasy play, as in early childhood; or whether the primary goal is peer group inclusion through the use of negative-evaluation gossip and teasing, as in middle childhood; or whether the goal is to learn about him- or herself through discussions with close friends, as in adolescence, language skills are paramount to achieving it. Children with language disorders, therefore, are at an extreme disadvantage throughout these stages because their facility with the major means for establishing friendships in each of the developmental stages is limited. Limited access to friends reduce their opportunities to gain social and conversational knowledge from peers and to use and strengthen their language skills.

Recently, Mabel Rice shared the following example in a lecture she gave at McGill University (Rice, 1990). She observed two four-year-old boys with normal language skills playing together in a preschool classroom. A third boy, a child with limited language skills, approached them and tried to join their play. One of the boys turned to the other and said, "Don't talk to him. He's weird." The boy then turned without saying anything and walked away. Social problems may be an inherent aspect of language disorders, and the pervasive role they may play in children's lives needs to be more carefully assessed and addressed in clinical programs. Social research further suggests that adult intuitions about highly regarded social competencies may differ from those of peers. Peer perspectives, therefore, require explicit study. For example, Cartledge, Frew, and Zaharias (1985) investigated classmates' and teachers' perceptions of the social skills that students with learning disabilities would need in mainstreamed classrooms. Teachers tended to rate most highly social competencies that directly contributed to academic performance, such as being able to pay attention to tasks, and so forth. They rated communication and peer interactional skills as least important. Peer classmates, however, rated these skills as the most important.

SOCIAL ASSESSMENT METHODOLOGIES

Children's social competence and friendship status across the age range of approximately 3 to 18 years of age have been assessed using various methodologies. These methodologies obtain information from three perspectives: the peers' perspective, the adults' perspective, and the child's own perspective. Each of these perspectives is an important source of information about the child's social world, and the ecological validity of a social assessment is increased by using them in combination. Major methodologies representing each of these perspectives are summarized below.

PEER ASSESSMENT METHODOLOGIES

Three major types of peer assessment methodologies have been used: peer nominations, rating scales, and interviews. Each type of assessment can be adapted to accommodate age range differences and to derive estimates of popularity as well as close friendship.

Peer Nominations

Using the nomination method children are asked to respond to a set of questions about their peer preferences. Any number of questions can be posed and any limit can be set to the number of answers the children are asked to provide or this can be left open-ended. For example, Gottman, Gonso, and Rasmussen (1975) asked children to provide answers to the following questions: who were their best friends (any number could be listed); what three children would they like to work with; what three children would they go to for help; what three children "really listen" to them; what three children "really like" them; and what three people they liked to play with "best." Since these children were third graders they were asked to write their answers. In an individual interview format children can verbalize their answers. With very young children, pictures can be used and the children can point to indicate their answers to the questions.

   Among the advantages of the nomination method are its adaptability and versatility. For example, possible memory and verbal problems can be accommodated by using the picture format. Recently, Krantz and Burton

(1986) modified this method to obtain more information about perceived friendship reciprocity by asking kindergarten, first, second, and third graders to identify their own best friends and the friendship choices that their peers would make. This is an example of method's versatility. Using this method popularity is determined by counting the number of positive nominations received by each child in the peer group (e.g., classroom). Rejection is determined by counting the number of negative nominations received, visibility is determined by counting the total number of nominations received, and close friendship is determined by counting the number and reciprocity of best or close friend nominations received.

There are concerns about using the nomination method, however. Children must actively select among their peers, making explicit what they previously may not have fully realized. Making preferences explicit may reinforce the inclusion of some children and the exclusion of others in the children's minds and inadvertently imply that their preferences are expected and acceptable. Children also may share their nominations with each other, and unpopular children may feel badly about not being included positively or being mentioned negatively. Further, if negative questions are asked (e.g., "Who would you not like to play with?"), some children may be viewed even more negatively as a result of the probing. Although little research has addressed the possible consequences of using negative nomination procedures on peer group perceptions, and the limited research that is available (e.g., Hayvren & Hymel, 1984) does not support these concerns, nomination is still used with care. Rating scale techniques provide a reasonable and widely used alternative to negative nomination questions.

Rating Scales

Rating scales provide many of the same features as nomination procedures. The same flexibility is available in determining the precise wording and number of questions the children address. With reference to each question posed, however, each child is asked to make a judgment about all members of the group. Memory problems are minimized because all children are listed and the procedure is more comprehensive than the nomination method because every child receives a rating relative to the question asked, (e.g., "How much do you play together?"). With paper and pencil administration, a 5-point scale typically is used. Pictures can be substituted for the children's names and smiling faces can be substituted for the rating points for preschool children. Asher, Singleton, Tinsley, and Hymel (1979) developed this modification for preschool children. They asked four-year-old children to sort pictures of their classmates into three boxes. One box had a happy face on it, another had a neutral face on it, and a third had a sad face on it. They found that the children were not only able to successfully complete the task but that the test-retest reliability for this procedure was higher than that for the nomination method.

The distribution and numerical average of the ratings each child receives are computed. Rating distributions are important to note because the same mean value can be obtained from very different sets of ratings. Reciprocally high ratings between children would indicate close friendship. Popularity would be indicated by numerous high scores, and rejection by numerous low scores. It is also typical in the lower grades for scales to be grouped and averaged by gender, with boys' scores being treated as one set and girls' scores treated as another set (e.g., Bierman & Furman, 1984).

Interview

A third method is the interview. Children are interviewed individually and asked a series of questions that are usually broad and open-ended. This method also can be used as a follow-up to clarify data from peer nominations and rating scales.

The nomination, rating scale, and interview methods can be used together to characterize children's peer group status as (a) *popular,* highly visible and well liked; (b) *rejected,* highly visible and not well liked; (c) *controversial,* highly visible, and disliked by some children and liked by others; (d) *neglected,* low visibility and neither liked nor disliked; and (e) *average,* at or about the mean on both visibility and likeability (Asher & Dodge, 1986), distinctions that have important intervention and predictive significance (Table 2–2). For example, rejected children are more aversive in their interactional style, have a social status that is more stable over time, are more lonely, and are at greater risk for adjustment problems in later life than are neglected children (see Asher, 1985, for a review).

ADULT ASSESSMENT METHODOLOGIES

School personnel are the adults typically sampled in assessments of school-age children's social competence. The nomination, rating scale, and interview procedures described above also can be used to sample the children's peer group status from the adult's perspective. For example, the teacher can be asked to list the names of each child's best friends, to characterize each

Table 2–2. Characteristics of peer group membership (Asher, 1985)

Popular	Highly visible and well liked
Rejected	Highly visible and not well liked
Controversial	Highly visible and liked by some children and disliked by others
Neglected	Low visibility and neither liked nor disliked
Average	At or near the group mean on both visibility and likeability

child in terms of how well they are liked by the other children on a rating scale of 1 to 5, to identify children who are having social difficulty, and so on. These procedures offer the same advantages of versatility and flexibility as discussed above.

Formal Test Instruments

Formal instruments also have been developed to sample teacher perspectives. These are available for children across the age range of preschool through Grade 12. The most comprehensive teacher rating scale is the *Social Behavior Assessment* (SBA) (Stephens, 1978, 1981). The scale contains 136 items, each sampling a social skill from one of four broad categories: environmental behaviors, task-related behaviors, self-related behaviors, and interpersonal behaviors. The teacher rates each child on a 4-point scale with 0 indicating *not applicable* and 3 indicating *behavior never exhibited*. Despite the fact that the test has good psychometric characteristics, it is time consuming to administer.

The *Teacher Rating of Social Skills—Children* (TROSS-C) (Clark, Gresham, & Elliott, 1985) is a 52-item scale that was developed to be more time efficient than the SBA. The TROSS-C samples social skills related to academic performance, social initiation, cooperation, and peer reinforcement. Teachers rate each item on a 5-point scale with 1 indicating that the behavior is *never exhibited* and 5 indicating that the behavior is *frequently exhibited*. Preliminary psychometric data on the TROSS-C suggests that it is a promising screening measure of children's social skills (Clark, Gresham, & Elliott, 1985).

The *Waksman Social Skills Rating Scale* (Waksman, 1985) is a 21-item screening instrument designed for teachers' use with children from kindergarten through Grade 12. The items, like those of the other rating scales, are heavily weighted toward the assessment of communication skills. Items on the Waksman include, for example, "interrupts often," "speaks rudely," "avoids looking others in the eye," "fails to acknowledge compliments," and "fails to initiate conversations" (p. 113). Teachers rate each student on a 4-point scale with 0 indicating *never* and 3 indicating *usually*. Normative data on a random sample of teachers of 331 kindergarten through high school students is provided.

One of the major disadvantages of using teacher rating scales is that they are subject to bias if administered repeatedly. This limits their usefulness in single-subject intervention designs, for example, or time-series designs. Although this is also a concern with the repeated use of peer rating scales, children tend to have more difficulty remembering their previous ratings.

Behavioral Observation

Observation of natural, spontaneous peer interactions is another adult assessment methodology. Corsaro (1981) suggested that adult observers be alert to three potential indices of social interactional problems: social isolation and/or an overdependence on adults for interaction; difficulty initiating peer interactions and entering peer groups; and whether once having gained entry the child participates in a limited manner or is disruptive. Quantitative guidelines are rare since appropriateness is a social-cultural judgment. Roopnarine and Field (1984), however, have suggested that nursery school children who interact with peers less than one third of the time they are observed should be considered to have social difficulties.

Priority should be given to observing situations and types of behaviors that have been identified by signficant others, such as parents, teachers, or other children, as being particularly socially penalizing for the target child. Observations also can be organized around major social tasks. Are there particular social tasks that are problematic for the target child? Dodge (1985) has suggested that there are six types of social tasks that are frequently problematic for young children. These can serve as a taxonomy to guide adult observation. The six tasks were (a) peer group entry, (b) responses to ambiguous peer provocations, (c) responses to their own failures, (d) responses to their own successes, (e) responses to peer group norms and expectations, and (f) responses to teacher expectations.

The face validity of naturalistic observation is its major advantage. If concerns about intrusiveness and the possible distortions adult observation might introduce can be reduced, this is a comprehensive and versatile technique. Disadvantages include its inefficiency, particularly regarding observations of low frequency behaviors or situations, and concerns about reliability and generalizability. These can be addressed to some extent through the use of multiple observations and checklists that are coded on-line. Rice, Sell, and Hadley (1990) recently developed an on-line coding system that allows the observer to index conversational assertiveness/responsiveness as a function of play level, addressee, and type of play.

Analogue Situations

Analogue situations, for example, role play, are another type of adult assessment methodology. In analogue assessment the situation is manipulated in some way to provide opportunities to observe target behaviors. Settings, props, puppets, and so forth may be used. This methodology permits the assessment of relationships among variables that may be difficult to discern in natural observation situations and, therefore, can be used as a follow-up procedure. Analogues also can be used as a primary means for sampling behaviors that occur with such low frequency in the natural environment that natural observation is not feasible. The major disadvantage of using analogue situations as an assessment methodology concern the generalizability of the information obtained. Analogue situations themselves may introduce an element of complexity, for example, that reduces their potential for generalizing observed behaviors to natural settings. The more contrived the analogue situation is the more susceptible the observation is to this interpretive limitation.

SELF-ASSESSMENT METHODOLOGIES

It is important to try to obtain children's perceptions of their own social competence. This is particularly helpful in identifying discrepancies between self-perceptions and the perceptions of others, and other possible distortions or misperceptions, and in designing intervention goals related to what children perceive as most problematical.

Interview

Individual oral interviews or written interviews can be used to obtain children's assessments of their own social strengths and weaknesses. This method is versatile and flexible. If children's oral skills are limited or if they are uncomfortable talking about themselves, puppets and other objects can be used to elicit this type of information.

Self-Assessment Scales

Self-assessment scales also have been developed for use with children. One of these is the social subscale of Harter's (1982) *Perceived Competence Scale for Children*. This subscale contains seven items that can be presented in written form or read aloud. The items consist of a pair of social competence statements that are oppositional to each other. An example is, "Some kids find it hard to make friends BUT for other kids it's pretty easy." The children are asked to select the statement that best describes them and to rate how well it describes them on a 4-point scale. A broader scale which includes cognitive skills, physical skills, popularity, acceptance by parents, morality, personality traits, physical characteristics, and affect assessments is the *Piers-Harris Self Concept Scale* (Piers, 1969).

As a component of self-assessment it is important to determine children's perceptions of locus of control. If children indicate that they are having difficulty, to what do they ascribe that difficulty? Dweck and her colleagues have found that rejected and neglected children tend to associate their social difficulties with invariant factors, factors over which they have no control. (See Dweck and Goetz, 1983, for review.) They noted two attributional patterns. Either these children view their difficulties as the result of unchangeable, personal characteristics, or they believe them to be the result of an arbitrary, hostile environment. In either case the relationships among the social behaviors exhibited by the children and the impact those behaviors have on other children would need to be clarified for new behav-

ior patterns to be adopted. This is an important component of most social
skills intervention programs.

SOCIAL SKILL INTERVENTION: THE ROLE OF PEERS

Many studies in the last 10 years have examined the effectiveness of social
skill intervention programs on the social behaviors and social status of children who have been identified as withdrawn from or rejected by peers. Although there are differences among the intervention goals and techniques
that have comprised these programs, they have tended to focus on interactionally relevant conversational behavior patterns and to employ methods
of instruction that include direct instruction or coaching, modeling, role
play and practice, and feedback designed to build self-evaluative and self-
monitoring skills. (See Conger and Keane, 1981; Ladd, 1975; and Hansen,
Watson–Perczel, and Christopher, 1989, for reviews.)

The prominent role that peers play in both the establishment and maintenance of positive social behaviors has become increasingly apparent. Price
and Dodge's (1989) reciprocal influence model of peer transactions provides an interesting framework for interpreting the results of a number of
these studies. In this model both the withdrawn or rejected target child's behaviors and peers' behaviors contribute to the target child's social problems.

According to the model the target children's behaviors contribute to their
negative social status because they exhibit more anti-social and/or inept social behaviors than their peers exhibit. For example, Coie and Kupersmidt
(1983) and Dodge (1983) reported observing a higher frequency of aggressive and inappropriate behaviors among rejected boys than among
their peers.

Peers, who cannot attend to all stimuli within interpersonal contexts, utilize processing strategies such as selective attention and perceptual readiness to focus on interactionally relevant information. Over time, they
develop schemas for interacting with other children. Stereotypes, reputations, and so forth are established. Although the development of schemas is
a natural strategy that aids perceptual processing efficiency, negative
schemas work to the disadvantage of socially unpopular children because
once they are established they contribute to the stability of reputations.
Dodge (1980) and Hymel (1986), for example, both reported that ambiguous behaviors were more likely to be interpreted by peers as negative if
they were attributed to a disliked child than if they were attributed to a
liked child, indicating that children's reputations biased peers' perceptions
of their behaviors.

As a consequence of their negative perceptions, the behaviors that peers
direct toward disliked children are more frequently negative than the behaviors they direct toward other children. This can set up a self-fulfilling

prophecy that reinforces the peers' negative biases. Therefore, both peers' perceptions of disliked children and the behaviors they direct toward them can serve as precipitating and maintaining factors for social interactional problems. Dodge and Frame (1982), for example, found that peers directed a higher frequency of aggressive behavior toward children that they perceived as being aggressive than they directed toward other children.

The final component of the model relates to the target children's perceptions of the behaviors that peers direct toward them. Dodge and Tomblin (1987), among others, have found that children with social problems tend to misinterpret peer intentions and are more inaccurate than their peers in predicting probable outcomes of social situations. The fact that a disproportionate frequency of negative behavior may actually be directed toward them only exacerbates these problems.

The reciprocal influence model has important implications for the role of peers in social skill intervention programs. These implications include:

1. The prediction that intervention programs that focus exclusively on the target child's behaviors are insufficient and would result in limited changes because they do not address the precipitating and maintaining behaviors of peers.
2. Target children and their peers need to be involved in the change process.
3. The goals of intervention should address the behavioral and perceptual changes needed by both the target children and their peers.

Most intervention studies have focused on changing target children's behaviors. Price and Dodge's (1989) model would predict that intervention programs would be more efficient and effective over time if peers were taken into account as well. Bierman and Furman's (1984) data support these predictions.

Bierman and Furman (1984) studied the effects of social skills training and cooperative peer involvement on the peer acceptance of fifth and sixth grade children who were identified as deficient in conversational skills and not accepted by their peers. Fifty-six children were randomly assigned to one of four experimental conditions. Children in one group, Condition 1, received conversational skills training that focused on sharing information about themselves, asking others about themselves, and giving help, suggestions, invitations, and advice to other children. Each child in this group received individual coaching that included instruction, rehearsal, and performance feedback. In Condition 2, children were involved in cooperative group experiences that were directed toward making videotapes together. In this condition the children met in groups of three, composed of one target child and two peer classmates. Children assigned to Condition 3 were involved in both the individual coaching program and the cooperative group experiences described in the previous two conditions. Condition 4 was a no-treatment control group. Treatment effects were observed at the conclusion of the intervention program and at a six-week follow-up assessment. The results indicated that only the children in the combined condition, who had received both coaching and cooperative group experiences, evidenced sustained improvements in peer acceptance, social skill performance, and peer interaction rates.

Peers can play many roles in social skills intervention programs. They can become directly involved in the intervention program by serving as peer partners or be involved more indirectly through their participation in cooperative group experiences.

PEER PARTNERS

Peers can particpate in social skill intervention programs in various ways. They can serve as models either through direct observation or indirectly through the use of videotape. Peer behavior can be used to teach new behaviors that can be substituted for the target child's socially penalizing behaviors while still meeting the functional needs those behaviors served. For example, if a child is using a socially penalizing verbal behavior to gain peer group entry, highly valued peers can be used to illustrate more successful substitute behaviors. The inclusion of popular peers in intervention programs serves the dual purpose of providing examples of skilled behavior and also changing the negative perceptions of highly valued children in the target children's social world (see Furman and Gavin, 1989, for review).

After the target child has learned the new behaviors, peers can be trained to elicit and reinforce the use of these behaviors in the target child's natural, interpersonal contexts (e.g., Solomon & Wahler, 1973; Wahler, 1967). Again, this serves the additional purpose of changing peer perceptions of the target child by directing their attention to the target child's positive social behaviors, and increasing the target child's attention to self-monitoring skills.

PEER GROUP EXPERIENCES

Peer group experiences can, but need not, be used in combination with the use of peers in partner roles. Since a major goal of peer group experiences in social skill intervention programs is altering peers' perceptions of target children and the behaviors they direct toward them, cooperative group interactions are emphasized. Increased interaction with peers can exacerbate target children's social problems by reinforcing negative biases unless the interactions are carefully structured. If the interactions confirm peers' negative biases about target children, increasing the frequency with which children interact would only strengthen those biases.

The major characteristics of cooperative group experiences are that (a) the goal of the experience is a group goal; (b) the reward for achieving the goal is a group reward; (c) each child has a specialized task such that the group's reward depends on the successful contribution of each member; (d) the target child can competently perform the task assigned to her/him; and (e) the activity elicits positive interactions among children (see Table 2–3). Furman and Gavin (1989) provide a recent review of this literature.

Recently a clinician shared an example of a cooperative group experience that she had organized in a first grade classroom. She divided the children into small groups and provided one piece of drawing paper for each group. Each group was asked to draw a picture of a sunny day. Each child in the group was given a different color crayon and was told that she or he could only use that crayon. In one group she gave a boy who was language disordered the yellow crayon. This insured that, regardless of what the group decided to draw, it could not successfully complete the task without his participation. He had to be included as a productive member of the group in order for their picture to have a sun and be hung on the wall with the others. This is an example of a group activity that has all of the major characteristics listed in Table 2–3.

Bierman's (1986) further analysis of the Bierman and Furman (1984) data confirmed the importance of cooperative group experiences in social skill intervention programs. She concluded that participating in cooperative activities that provided opportunities for target children to display newly learned positive social behaviors improved both the attitudes of peers, as evidenced by rating scale and interaction rate data, and the frequency of their positive behaviors toward target children.

IMPLICATIONS FOR PRAGMATIC LANGUAGE ASSESSMENT AND INTERVENTION

Experiencing appropriate peer relations throughout childhood is important for the development of successful social communication skills, for

Table 2–3. Characteristics of cooperative peer group experiences

Goal	The goal of the experience is a group goal.
Reward	The reward for achieving the goal is a group reward.
Task	Each child is assigned a specialized task.
Contribution	The group's reward depends on the successful contribution of each member.
Competence	Each child can competently perform the task assigned to her or him.
Positive affect	The activity elicits positive interactions among children.

the development of a sense of social support and security, and for the development of self-concept and self-esteem. Language is the primary means by which school-age children establish and maintain peer relationships.

The central role that language plays in social cognition, social competence, and social access to peer acquaintances and friends places children with impaired language skills at social-communicative risk. Hartup (1977) has argued that "without an opportunity to encounter individuals who are co-equals children do not learn effective communication skills" (p. 1). Despite the historical reluctance of speech-language pathologists to deal with the social aspects of communicative problems, there are numerous indications that children with language disorders are socially disadvantaged. An example of this literature is the work of Bryan and colleagues (Bryan, 1974; Bryan & Bryan, 1981; Bryan & Wheeler, 1972). They found that children who were learning disabled were less popular than their peers, less socially skilled, and more frequently inadvertently negative toward their peers.

A major implication of the literature reviewed in this chapter is that speech-language pathologists need to become more concerned about the social aspects of language disorders because they may be inherent to language disorder and/or may contribute as precipitating and maintaining factors. Peers play a primary role in the child's social world. Another implication, therefore, is that peers are not simply a context for language assessment and intervention but may be central to accomplishing assessment and intervention goals.

Social assessment methodologies can be used to gain a fuller understanding of children's conversational skills. These methods can include questions about children's social goals. What are the child's social goals compared to the child's peer group? What behavioral and conversational strategies does the child use to accomplish social goals? What are their frequencies, types, and diversity? What roles do language structural limitations play in the social interactional patterns observed? How effective and socially acceptable are the behavioral and conversational strategies the child uses?

Particular emphasis could be placed on identifying communicative behaviors for which there are social penalties. The relationships between highly socially penalizing behaviors and children's social acceptance could be explored. Gallagher and Craig (1984) and Loucks and Gallagher (1988, 1989) have reported examples of interactional behaviors of children with language disorders that did not achieve their communicative goals and resulted in social penalties. The behaviors noted in these studies were aversive to peers. Identifying aversive behaviors and noting the communicative purposes they were intended to serve is an important first step in designing intervention programs to substitute more acceptable alternatives for meeting children's communicative needs.

Finally, how responsive is the child to interactive feedback? How persistent or flexible is the child? Is there evidence of social self-monitoring skills?

The answers to these questions provide a fuller context for the interpretation of a child's communicative profile and could aid speech-language pathologists in identifying and prioritizing intervention goals. For example, behaviors that have high social penalties could be given high priority in intervention programs. Contexts that sample behaviors that facilitate friendship formation at the child's developmental stage also could be included. For example, during a developmental period in which peer group inclusion is a high priority, analyzing the dyadic conversations of close friends may not provide an adequate sample of all relevant communicative behaviors. Similar assessment data also could be used periodically throughout the course of intervention as documentation of the child's improvement.

An important caution is that sociometric data, such as that described above, should be used by speech-language pathologists to aid interpretation of children's communicative disorders. Children may not be socially acceptable to peers for a variety of reasons other than language problems. An abused child who is hostile to peers and frequently insulting, for example, would not be an appropriate candidate for pragmatic language intervention. The problems that this child has would need the primary attention of a specialist trained to address the underlying emotional issues involved. A child, however, who has limited language skills and inadvertently insults peers may appear to be hostile, but that perception is a social consequence of behavior that reflects the child's basic language problems. This type of child could benefit from pragmatic language intervention. McDermott (1985) has suggested that these types of social consequences of communicative problems should be considered in caseload decisions in school settings.

There also are implications regarding the role of peers in intervention programs. The social-interactional literature suggests that peers can serve in a variety of capacities as an integral part of the intervention program. They may serve as role models, as direct intervention agents, as monitors and reinforcers, or more indirectly by changing their perceptions of and behaviors toward the child with language disorders. Consultative intervention models and classroom-based interventions are both examples of peer-oriented intervention programs. Again, the major implication is that peers are not simply a context for intervention but may be essential to accomplish the goals of intervention. In-depth study of the social interactional literature suggests that there are aspects of social competence that must be developed through interactions with peers and social needs that can only be addressed through those interactions. As a result, clinicians' roles may be expanded to include the role of coach and indirect intervention agent. In a recent text, which refers to this type of intervention as the "functional language approach," Owens (1991) summarized it as a "communication-first approach." He wrote, "In short, in a functional language approach, conversation between children and their commuunicative partners becomes the vehicle for change" (pp. 3–4).

A final caution regards the cultural specificity of the literature reviewed in this chapter. The research reflects Western middle-class culture. The multi- and cross-cultural concerns reviewed in Chapter 4 should be noted relative to the details presented. The assumptions and philosophy of the social interactional perspective discussed, however, is a highly contextualized one and therefore is generalizable in principle across cultures. One of the strengths of this approach is that it uses children's peer culture as the standard against which they are compared. This is preferable to establishing norms that may not be specific enough to reflect the variety of social contexts within which children with language disorders live.

Aram and Nation (1982) shared a poignant description of a client with language disorders named Gary. Despite having normal nonverbal intellectual performance, Gary was described throughout his school years as a "loner" and was considered "strange" by his peers, teachers, and other adults. Aram and Nation wrote:

Twenty-four years after his mother raised questions, Gary continues to present a host of language, learning, social, and vocational problems. Although he is gainfully employed, talks in sentences, has completed high school, and occasionally dates, he has not grown out of or been remediated out of the language and learning problems he presented as a young child. Although he has made immeasurable progress, using all aspects of development as a floating referent, he has never been able to close the gap between himself and his peers." (p. 68)

Developing pragmatic language assessment and intervention programs from a social-interactional perspective will not be easy and we still have much to learn. The promise that this approach holds for cases like Gary, however, is an exciting one.

REFERENCES

Anderson, S., & Messick, S. (1974). Social competency in young children. *Developmental Psychology, 10*(2), 282–293.

Aram, D., & Nation, J. (1982). *Child language disorders.* St. Louis, MO: C. V. Mosby.

Asher, S. (1985). An evolving paradigm in social skill training research with children. In B. Schneider, K. Rubin, & J. Ledingham (Eds.), *Children's peer relations: Issues in assessment and intervention.* New York: Springer-Verlag.

Asher, S., & Dodge, K. (1986). Identifying children who are rejected by their peers. *Developmental Psychology, 22,* 444–449.

Asher, S., Oden, S., & Gottman, J. (1977). Children's friendships in school settings. In L. Katz (Ed.), *Current topics in early childhood education.* Norwood, NJ: Ablex Publishing.

Asher, S., & Renshaw, P. (1981). Children without friends: Social knowledge and social skills training. In S. Asher & J. Gottman (Eds.), *The development of children's friendships.* Cambridge, UK: Cambridge University Press.

Asher, S., Singleton, L., Tinsley, B., & Hymel, S. (1979). A reliable sociometric measure for preschool children. *Developmental Psychology, 15*(4), 443–444.

Bates, E., & MacWhinney, B. (1982). Functionalist approaches to grammar. In E. Wanner & L. Gleitman (Eds.), *Language acquisition: The state of the art.* Cambridge, UK: Cambridge University Press.

Berndt, T. (1981). Relations between social cognition, non-social cognition, and social behavior: The case of friendship. In J. Flavell & L. Ross (Eds.), *Social cognitive development: Frontiers and possible futures.* Cambridge, UK: Cambridge University Press.

Berndt, T., & Perry, T. (1986). Children's perceptions of friendships as supportive relationships. *Developmental Psychology, 22,* 640–648.

Bierman, K. (1986). Process of change during social skills training with preadolescents and its relation to treatment outcome. *Child Development, 57,* 230–240.

Bierman, K., & Furman, W. (1984). The effects of social skills training and peer involvement on the social adjustment of preadolescents. *Child Development, 55,* 151–162.

Bigelow, B. (1977). Children's friendship expectations: A cognitive developmental study. *Child Development, 48,* 246–253.

Bruner, J. (1978). The role of dialogue in language acquisition. In A. Sinclair, R. Jarvella, & W. Levelt (Eds.), *The child's conception of language.* New York: Springer-Verlag

Bryan, T. (1974). Peer popularity of learning disabled children. *Journal of Learning Disabilities, 7,* 621–625.

Bryan, T., & Bryan, J. (1981). Some personal and social experiences of learning disabled children. In B. Keogh (Ed.), *Advances in special education.* Greenwich, CT: JAI Press.

Bryan, T., & Wheeler, R. (1972). Perception of children with learning disabilities: The eye of the observer. *Journal of Learning Disabilities, 5,* 484–488.

Cartledge, G., Frew, T., & Zaharias, J. (1985). Social skill needs of mainstreamed students: Peer and teacher perceptions. *Learning Disability Quarterly, 8,* 132–139.

Chandler, M. (1977). Social cognition: A selective review of current research. In W. F. Overton (Ed.), *Knowledge and development.* New York: Plenum Press.

Clark, L., Gresham, S., & Elliott, S. (1985). Development and validation of a social skills assessment measure: The TROSS C. *Journal of Psychoeducational Assessment, 4,* 347–356.

Coie, J., & Kupersmidt, J. (1983). A behavioral analysis of emerging social status in boys' groups. *Child Development, 54,* 1400–1416.

Conger, J., & Keane, S. (1981). Social skills intervention in the treatment of isolated or withdrawn children. *Psychological Bulletin, 90,* 478–495.

Connolly, J., & Doyle, A. (1984). Relation of social fantasy play to social competence in preschoolers. *Developmental Psychology, 20*(5), 797–806.

Corsaro, W. (1981). The development of social cognition in preschool children: Implications for language learning. *Topics in Language Disorders, 2*(3), 77–95.

Corsaro, W. (1985). *Friendship and peer culture in the early years.* Norwood, NJ: Ablex Publishing.

Damon, W. (1977). *The social world of the child.* San Francisco: Jossey-Bass.

Damon, W. (1981). Exploring children's social cognition on two fronts. In J. Flavell & L. Ross (Eds.), *Social cognitive development: Frontiers and possible futures.* Cambridge, UK: Cambridge University Press.

Dodge, K. (1980). Social cognition and children's aggressive behavior. *Child Development, 51,* 162–170.

Dodge, K. (1983). Behavioral antecedents of peer social status. *Child Development, 54,* 1386–1399.

Dodge, K. (1985). Facets of social interaction and the assessment of social competence in children. In B. Schneider, K. Rubin, & J. Ledingham (Eds.), *Children's peer relations: Issues in assessment and intervention.* New York: Springer-Verlag.

Dodge, K., & Frame, C. (1982). Social cognitive biases and deficits in aggressive boys. *Child Development, 53,* 620–635.

Dodge, K., Pettit, G., McClaskey, C., & Brown, M. (1986). Social competence in children. *Monographs of the Society for Research in Child Development, 51*(Serial No. 213).

Dodge, K., & Tomblin, A. (1987). Utilization of self schemas as a mechanism of interpretational bias in aggressive children. *Social Cognition, 5,* 280–300.

Doyle, A., Connolly, J., & Rivest, L. (1980). The effect of playmate familiarity on the social interactions of young children. *Child Development, 51,* 217–223.

Dweck, C., & Goetz, T. (1983). Attributions and learned helplessness. In W. Damon (Ed.), *Social and personality development: Essays on the growth of the child.* New York: W. W. Norton.

Edelstein, W., Keller, M., & Wahlen, K. (1984). Structure and content in social cognition: Conceptual and empirical analyses. *Child Development, 55,* 1514–1526.

Fine, G. (1980). The natural history of preadolescent male friendship groups. In H. Foot, J. Chapman, & J. Smith (Eds.), *Friendship and social relations in children.* New York: John Wiley and Sons.

Fischer, K. (1980). A theory of cognitive development: The control and construction of hierarchies of skills. *Psychological Review, 87,* 477–531.

Ford, M. (1982). Social cognition and social competence in adolescence. *Developmental Psychology, 18*(3), 323–340.

Furman, W., & Bierman, K. (1984). Children's conceptions of friendships: A multimethod study of developmental changes. *Developmental Psychology, 20,* 925–931.

Furman, W., & Buhrmester, D. (1985). Children's perceptions of the personal relationships in their social networks. *Developmental Psychology, 21,* 1016–1024.

Furman, W., & Childs, M. (1981). *A temporal perspective on children's friendships.* Paper presented at the biennial meeting of the Society for Research in Child Development, Boston.

Furman, W., & Gavin, L. (1989). Peers' influence on adjustment and development. In T. Berndt & G. Ladd (Eds.), *Peer relationships in child development.* New York: John Wiley and Sons.

Furman, W., & Robbins, P. (1985). What's the point? Selection of treatment objectives. In B. Schneider, K. Rubin, & J. Ledingham (Eds.), *Children's peer relations: Issues in assessment and intervention.* New York: Springer-Verlag.

Gallagher, T., & Craig, H. (1984). Pragmatic assessment: The analysis of a highly frequent repeated utterance. *Journal of Speech and Hearing Research, 29,* 375–377.

George, S., & Krantz, M. (1981). The effects of preferred play partnership on communication adequacy. *The Journal of Psychology, 109,* 245–253.

Ginsberg, D., Gottman, J., & Parker, J. (1986). The importance of friendship. In J. Gottman & J. Parker (Eds.), *Conversations of friends: Speculations on affective development.* Cambridge, UK: Cambridge University Press.

Goetz, T., & Dweck, C. (1980). Learned helplessness in social situations. *Journal of Personality and Social Psychology, 39,* 246–255.

Golinkoff, R. (1983). The preverbal negotiation of failed messages: Insights into the transition period. In R. Golinkoff (Ed.), *The transition from preverbal to verbal communication.* Hillsdale, NJ: Lawrence Erlbaum.

Gottman, J. (1983). How children become friends. *Monographs of the Society for Research in Child Development, 48*(Serial No. 201).

Gottman, J. (1986). The observation of social process. In J. Gottman & J. Parker (Eds.), *Conversations of friends: Speculations on affective development.* Cambridge, UK: Cambridge University Press.

Gottman, J., Gonso, J., & Rasmussen, B. (1975). Social interaction, social competence, and friendship in children. *Child Development, 46,* 709–718.

Gottman, J., & Mettetal, G. (1986). Speculations about social and affective development: Friendship and acquaintanceship through adolescence. In J. Gottman & J. Parker (Eds.), *Conversations of friends: Speculations on affective development.* Cambridge, UK: Cambridge University Press.

Gottman, J., & Parker, J. (1986). *Conversations of friends: Speculations on affective development.* Cambridge, UK: Cambridge University Press.

Gottman, J., & Parkhurst, J. (1980). A developmental theory of friendship and acquaintanceship processes. In W. Collins (Ed.), *Minnesota Symposia on Child Development: Development of cognition, affect, and social relations.* Hillsdale, NJ: Lawrence Erlbaum.

Gresham, F. (1981). Social skills training with handicapped children: A review. *Review of Educational Research, 51*(1), 139–176.

Hansen, D., Watson–Perczel, M., & Christopher, J. (1989). Clinical issues in social-skills training with adolescents. *Clinical Psychology Review, 9,* 365–391.

Harter, S. (1982). The Perceived Competence Scale for Children. *Child Development, 53,* 87–97.

Hartup, W. (1977, Fall). Peers, play, and pathology: A new look at the social behavior of children. *Newsletter of the Society for Research in Child Development,* pp. 1–3.

Hartup, W. (1978). Children and their friends. In H. McGurk (Ed.), *Issues in childhood social development.* London: Methuen.

Hartup, W. (1979). The social worlds of childhood. *American Psychologist, 34,* 944–950.

Hartup, W. (1983). Peer interaction and the behavioral development of the individual child. In W. Damon (Ed.), *Social personality development: Essays on the growth of the child.* New York: W. W. Norton.

Hartup, W. (1984). The peer context in middle childhood. In W. Collins (Ed.), *Development during middle childhood: The years from six to twelve.* Washington, DC: National Academy Press.

Hayvren, M., & Hymel, S. (1984). Ethical issues in sociometric testing: The impact of sociometric measures on interactive behavior. *Developmental Psychology, 20,* 844–849.

Hazen, N., & Black, B. (1989). Preschool peer communication skills: The role of social status and interaction context. *Child Development, 60,* 867–876.

Hymel, S. (1986). Interpretation of peer behavior: Affective bias in childhood and adolescence. *Child Development, 57,* 431–445.

Koepp–Baker, H. (1937). *Handbook of clinical speech.* Ann Arbor, MI: Edwards Brothers.

Kohlberg, L. (1983). The development of children's orientations toward a moral order. In W. Damon (Ed.), *Social and personality development: Essays on the growth of the child.* New York: W. W. Norton.

Kramer, D. (1986). A life-span view of social cognition. *Educational Gerontology, 12,* 277–289.

Krantz, M., & Burton, C. (1986). The development of the social cognition of social status. *The Journal of Genetic Psychology, 147*(1), 89–95.

Ladd, G. (1981). Effectiveness of a social learning method for enhancing children's social interaction and peer acceptance. *Child Development, 52,* 171–178.

Ladd, G. (1985). Documenting the effects of social skill training with children: Process and outcome assessment. In B. Schneider, K. Rubin, & J. Ledingham (Eds.), *Children's peer relations: Issues in assessment and intervention.* New York: Springer-Verlag.

Ladd, G., & Oden, S. (1979). The relationship between peer acceptance and children's ideas about helpfulness. *Child Development, 50,* 402–408.

Lerner, R., & Lerner, J. (1986). Contextualism and the study of child effects in development. In R. Rosnow & M. Georgoudi (Eds.), *Contextualism and understanding in the behavioral sciences: Implications for research and theory.* New York: Praeger.

Loucks, Y., & Gallagher, T. (1988, November). *Dispute initiations among SLI and normal language preschoolers.* Paper presented at the American-Speech-Language-Hearing Association Convention, Boston, MA.

Loucks, Y., & Gallagher, T. (1989, November). *Disputes among SLI and NL preschoolers: Responses to violations.* Paper presented at the American Speech-Language-Hearing Association Convention, St. Louis, MO.

Matthews, W. (1978). Sex and familiarity effects upon the proportion of time young children spend in spontaneous fantasy play. *Journal of Genetic Psychology, 133,* 9–12.

McDermott, L. (1985). Service alternatives. In American Speech-Language-Hearing Association (Ed.), *Caseload issues in schools: How to make better decisions.* Rockville, MD: Editor.

McGuire, W. (1983). A contextualist theory of knowledge: Its implications for innovation and reform in psychological research. In L. Berkowitz (Ed.), *Advances in experimental social psychology.* New York: Academic Press.

Miller, P., & Aloise, P. (1989). Young children's understanding of the psychological causes of behavior: A review. *Child Development, 60*(2), 257–285.

Muus, R. (1982). Social cognition: Robert Selman's theory of role taking. *Adolescence, 17*(67), 499–525.

Owens, R. (1991). *Language disorders: A functional approach to assessment and intervention.* New York: Macmillan.

Parker, J., & Gottman, J. (1989). Social and emotional development in a relational context. In T. Berndt & G. Ladd (Eds.), *Peer relationships in child development.* New York: John Wiley and Sons.

Piaget, J. (1963). *Psychology of intelligence.* Paterson, NJ: Littlefield, Adams.

Piers, E. (1969). *Manual for the Piers-Harris Children's Self-Concept Scale.* Nashville, TN: Counselor Recordings and Tests.

Price, J., & Dodge, K. (1989). Peers' contributions to children's social maladjustment. In T. Berndt & G. Ladd (Eds.), *Peer relationships in child development.* New York: John Wiley and Sons.

Prutting, C. (1982). Pragmatics as social competence. *Journal of Speech and Hearing Disorders, 47*(2), 123–134.

Putallaz, M., & Gottman, J. (1981). An interactional model of children's entry into peer groups. *Child Development, 52,* 989–994.

Putallaz, M., & Heflin, A. (1986). Toward a model of peer acceptance. In J. Gottman & J. Parker (Eds.), *Conversations of friends: Speculations on affective development.* Cambridge, UK: Cambridge University Press.

Rice, M. L. (1990, October). *Specific language impaired preschoolers' verbal interactions with their peers.* Paper presented at McGill University, Montreal, Canada.

Rice, M., Sell, M., & Hadley, P. (1990). The Social Interactive Coding System (SICS): An on-line, clinically relevant descriptive tool. *Language, Speech, and Hearing Services in Schools, 12,* 2–14.

Roopnarine, J., & Field, T. (1984). Play interactions of friends and acquaintances in nursery school. In T. Field, J. Roopnarine, & M. Segal (Eds.), *Friendships in normal and handicapped children.* Norwood, NJ: Ablex Publishing.

Rubin, K. (1972). Relationship between egocentric communication and popularity among peers. *Developmental Psychology, 7,* 364.

Selman, R. (1980). *The growth of interpersonal understanding: Developmental and clinical analyses.* New York: Academic Press.

Selman, R., Schorin, M., Stone, C., & Phelps, E. (1983). A naturalistic study of children's social understanding. *Developmental Psychology, 19*(1), 82–102.

Shantz, C. (1975). The development of social cognition. In E. Hetherinton (Ed.), *Review of child development research.* Chicago: University of Chicago Press.

Shantz, C. (1983). Social cognition. In P. Mussen, J. Flavell, & E. Markman (Eds.), *Handbook of child psychology: Cognitive development.* New York: John Wiley and Sons.

Shure, M., & Spivak, G. (1980). Interpersonal problem solving as a mediator of behavioral adjustment in preschool and kindergarten children. *Journal of Applied Developmental Psychology, 1,* 29–44.

Solomon, R., & Wahler, R. (1973). Peer reinforcement of classroom problem behavior. *Journal of Applied Behavior Analysis, 6,* 49–55.

Snow, C. (1979). The role of language acquisition. In W. A. Collins (Ed.), *Minnesota Symposia on Child Psychology* (Vol. 12). Hillsdale, NJ: Lawrence Erlbaum.

Stephens, T. (1978). *Social skills in the classroom.* Columbus, OH: Cedars Press.

Stephens, T. (1981). *Technical information: Social behavior assessment.* Columbus, OH: Cedars Press.

Sullivan, H. (1953). *The interpersonal theory of psychiatry.* New York: W. W. Norton.

Travis, L. (1936). A point of view in speech correction. *Quarterly Journal of Speech, 22,* 57–61.

Wahler, R. (1967). Child-child interactions in five field settings: Some experimental analyses. *Journal of Experimental Child Psychology, 5,* 278–293.

Waksman, S. (1985). The development and psychometric properties of a rating scale for children's social skills. *Journal of Psychoeducational Assessment, 3,* 111–121.

Wiig, E., & Semel, E. (1976). *Language disabilities in children and adolescents.* Columbus, OH: Charles E. Merrill.

Wright, P., & Keple, T. (1981, August). Friends and parents of a sample of high school juniors: An exploratory study of relationship intensity and interpersonal rewards. *Journal of Marriage and the Family,* 559–570.

Wyer, R., & Srull, T. (1986). Human cognition in its social context. *Psychological Review, 93*(3), 322–359.

Youniss, J. (1975). Another perspective on social cognition. In A. Pick (Ed.), *Minnesota Symposia on Child Psychology.* Minneapolis: University of Minnesota Press.

Youniss, J. (1980). *Parents and peers in social development: A Sullivan-Piaget perspective.* Chicago, IL: University of Chicago Press.

Youniss, J., & Volpe, J. (1978). A relational analysis of friendship. In W. Damon (Ed.), *Social cognition.* San Francisco: Jossey-Bass.

CHAPTER 3

Everyday Events: Their Role in Language Assessment and Intervention

JUDITH FELSON DUCHAN

If you were to ask a fish about how he likes his water, he would probably be unable to answer. Water for a fish is such an everyday aspect of life that it is taken for granted. So it is for people in their everyday life contexts. They take for granted the events they regularly participate in. If you were to ask a normal adult how he liked getting dressed, he would construe the question as one which asks something unusual about getting dressed, not as one about putting on his clothes. Thinking about the mundane part of everyday events is for people like being a fish out of water. They must step out of the context which they ordinarily take for granted in order to see it. Perhaps that is why the practice of speech-language pathology, until the pragmatics revolution in the 1970s, did not regard language as being part of everyday life events. Knowledge of events was neither assessed nor taught to children with language impairments.

The 1970s represented a consciousness raising era with regard to events and language learning. Research such as that done by Bruner and his colleagues (Bruner, 1975; Bruner & Sherwood, 1976; Ninio & Bruner, 1978; Ratner & Bruner, 1978) on routine events in the lives of infants, cast events in a central role in the language learning process. Bruner saw these routinized events such as peek-a-boo, give and take games, and naming pictures in a book as providing children with knowledge which led them to understand conversational rules and the process of mutual referencing.

A second wave of consciousness-raising about everyday events came from the work of researchers in artificial intelligence who were attempting to provide computers with sufficient knowledge to understand sentences such as: The woman is hungry; she went to get a phone book. In order to understand the relationship between hunger and phone books, a computer would need to understand that phone books list numbers of take-out restaurants, and that the woman must be looking up such a number in order to achieve her goal of getting food. In their effort to provide computers with background information for responding intelligently to such input, Schank and Abelson (1977) suggested that computers be provided with information about everyday events and that that information be organized as a script, including information about the people, their goals, and their activities. The script, then, provides a means for framing or structuring information needed to understand why a hungry woman would go to get a telephone book. Information contained in such scripts can offer both human and artificial systems a knowledge base to respond intelligently to such everyday-like situations.

Although Schank and Abelson later abandoned their original formulation of fully elaborated scripts (e.g., what ordinarily happens in restaurants), replacing it with a more circumscribed unit of event knowledge (e.g., how to pay for something), their insight about the need for background knowledge to understand what is going on remained. Knowledge about people's goals, about how their actions relate, and about how everyday events are ordinarily carried out is needed to understand and participate in everyday life experiences.

Following the insight provided in Schank and Abelson, researchers in child development began to examine the role of scriptal knowledge in children's early learning. At the forefront of this development were Katherine Nelson and her colleagues who began examining children's acquisition of event knowledge and the role that knowledge played in children's conversations, descriptions, and recall of everyday events. For example, Nelson and Gruendel (1981) asked children as young as three years of age to describe familiar events and found that they were better able to do that than to describe particular instances of events. That is, they were better able to describe birthday parties in general than yesterday's birthday party. Nelson and Gruendel hypothesized that children had learned a generalized event representation (GER) of familiar events, what Schank and Abelson had been calling scripts, and that their young subjects used this script-like representation in carrying out conversations and in describing and recalling the past events.

Influenced by Bruner and Nelson's research in the late 1970s and early 1980s, speech-language pathologists have begun to think about events when they assess children's language (Lund & Duchan, 1988; Ross & Berg, 1990) and when they design intervention approaches for helping children learn language (Constable, 1986; Snyder–McLean, Solomonson, McLean, & Sack, 1984). This chapter is an attempt to elaborate on that effort, and to develop a systematic approach to making events — especially familiar, everyday events — more central to language assessment and intervention. A theoretical framework will be presented that argues for the importance of events in communication, and a review of how normal children conceive of and describe events will then be offered. Ways in which speech-language pathologists might incorporate events into clinical approaches will be discussed. The chapter will conclude with a consideration of how greater attention to events in clinical interventions might dramatically alter what speech-language pathologists are currently doing clinically.

FRAMEWORKS FOR STRUCTURING AND INTERPRETING EVENTS

A century ago William James described the world construed by infants as a "booming buzzing confusion" (James, 1890, p. 488). People and objects make noise and move, activities happen, and young children have little idea about what is going on. As they put together the various relations, the various aspects of the happenings around them, they come to understand their world in terms of events. These new understandings are seen as conceptual, structured units which have been called "event representations." Normal children, even within their first year of development, come to form event representations of everyday happenings, and use those representations to guide their participation in them and to anticipate and remember what happens.

Event representations can be structured in a variety of ways. Different interpreters will experience and interpret the same event differently. One possible way to form a mental representation of an event is to focus on what has been called the "role structure" of the event (Wolf & Gardner, 1981). Children at a very young age notice the activities of a person in the event, assign an agency role to that person, and interpret the actions as intended by the agent and as being directed toward a goal or goals. For recurring events, the role structure can include responsibilities assigned to the various participants. For example, Bruner and Sherwood (1976) found that peek-a-boo events are interpreted by children at first as having a fixed role structure with the mother responsible for hiding the child, trying to find him, and saying peek-a-boo. Later the child sometimes assumes the role of the "hider" and sometimes the one who is hidden. Bruner and Sherwood take this shift to reflect a new understanding, one of role reciprocity. The child comes to realize that different participants have assigned activities and that both activities and participants relate to one another.

Knowledge of roles can also include cultural definitions of status and gender. So in pretend play children enact adult roles, with those playing the father, doctor, mother, or nurse doing different things (Bretherton, 1984). They also assign one another role status, with certain children playing the dominant roles such as doctor, father, or mother, and others playing the submissive roles of patient or baby (Miller & Garvey, 1984; Sachs, 1987).

Children's knowledge representation of daily events, then, can include their sense of people's roles as defined by their culture, their ideas of pre-negotiated roles, and their ideas about the different roles and goals carried out by the participants in a particular event. These ideas about roles can serve as a frame for creating and understanding event meaning.

A second way to interpret an event is to focus on the activities being carried out and to note their temporal relationships. Temporality is more important for some events than for others. Mental representations of getting dressed contain segments which require that clothes be put on in an ordered sequence. First things are put on first, second things second, and not vice versa. Dressing usually involves finishing one segment before beginning a second. Other events can involve temporally overlapping sequences, where another activity starts before the first is finished—the teen-aged brother joins a breakfast in progress, a duck is put into the bath water during the course of taking a bath. Some events are related temporally, but in a nonimmediate way—breakfast and dinner, greeting and departing rituals in a school day. Some events involve negotiations for the temporal sequence of its constituents, such as taking turns in a play activity, where who goes next may vary with the results of the negotiation; other events are temporally ordered but the order is arbitrary and varies from one event to the next (e.g., for some people, eating different foods during the main course of the meal).

The ordering of activities within an event is often dictated by the logic of the event. Socks must be put on before shoes, the cap of the toothpaste tube must be removed before putting the paste on the toothbrush. These logical relationships are part of a third type of structuring which frames mental representations of events—causality. In the case of socks and tops of containers, the putting on and taking off enables one to proceed to the second activity in the event. The causal relation is one of enablement. Causal relations also can be interpreted in an instrumental sense, where one activity such as a ball hitting a window causes it to break. In this case, no agent is identified; the cause is a physical one. When agents are identified as causing something to happen, the type of causality being expressed is motivational or intentional—the boy threw the ball at the window—he caused the window to break. One can go beyond the relations between a few adjacent activities, and create a mental representation of an entire activity sequence by having an agent devise an elaborate plan and carry out a number of actions to achieve a distant goal. Thus the boy may have spent the morning carrying out several activities to achieve his goal of breaking the window (finding his bat, talking his mother into allowing him to play outside, missing, and trying again).

A fourth way for happenings to be construed is through their deictic organization. Events are both experienced and imagined from a particular center in space and time and often from a particular person's point of view. The event involving the boy throwing the ball through the window can be interpreted from the point of view of the boy, and thought of with him as the spatial center and with the event occurring in the temporal "now." The same event can be thought of from the point of view of an observer, say the owner of the window watching the boy from the garage in the temporal "now." Or the event can be cast in the temporal past relative to the time of remembering, in the temporal "then," or in another place, the spatial "there," or both. The deictic point of view might also shift within an interpretation of a single event. The interpreter might first assume the point of view of one of the participants, then another; might think of the event as having occurred in the past and then begin reliving it as if it were in the present; or might imagine moving around a scene as the event takes place, changing the spatial perspective accordingly. The following description of a picture by a child reported in Westby (1984) indicates how the child established a deictic point of view by imagining himself with the gorilla at the top of the mountain, looking at the snow coming up, and the people down below. The child's viewpoint is indicated through the deictic spatial terms "come" and "up" and "down" and "there."

The gorilla is climbing up the mountain.
snow's *comin' up* [italics added].
and the people are *down there* [italics added]
and all the houses
and all the trees
It's all black
and its all brown. (Westby, 1984, p. 115)

These four interpretive frameworks (see Table 3–1) have been found to be used by young children to structure event representations. They are not a complete list of the possibilities available for children to interpret events. Nor are all four interpretive frameworks likely to be equally important in the interpretation of a particular event. What is being suggested here is that event representations require one or more interpretive frames for the event to be understood as coherent and sensible. Understanding how a child's event representation is organized includes finding out how the child is framing the event. Knowledge about how the child frames events will provide insight into how the child makes sense of his everyday life experiences.

Table 3-1. Frameworks for structuring and interpreting events

1. Role relations
2. Temporal relations between actions
3. Causal relations between actions and between agents and actions
4. Deictically centered relations

The same event will be interpreted within different frameworks, even by the same child. The special circumstances surrounding an event will influence which frames the child will use in its interpretation. For example, two children in a power struggle are more likely to focus on the role structuring of an event in which they both participate. An event that takes place in several spatial locations such as a birthday party that moves from an eating area to a play area to an area where presents are opened is likely to have those locations highlighted in its representation.

The notion of focus in event representation is parallel to the notion of topic in conversation; that is, the structural elements are not just accumulated over the different frames, but rather are interpreted in terms of an overall thematic understanding. The child mentioned before who described the gorilla as on the mountain and the people below was focused more on the spatial deictic aspects of the events in the picture than on the characters' roles, the causal structure, or the temporal relations between the action components.

NORMAL CHILDREN'S EARLY
EVENT REPRESENTATIONS

Katherine Nelson has developed a theory of children's cognitive development that casts event understanding in a central role (Nelson, 1986). She has argued that children first understand the world in terms of unrelated event episodes, that they later combined similar episodes to form generalized scripts, and that they learn to differentiate categories of objects, actors, and actions by observing which things fit into the same slots in the scripts (Nelson, 1983; Nelson & Gruendel, 1981). Thus, Nelson considers the generalized event representation to be a basic building block of cognitive development.

Research on infants has shown that by age one normal babies have developed a variety of primitive event representations, which they use to understand, anticipate, and engage in repeating events. Stern (1985) has argued that these event representations are at play when the infant comes to recognize a breast feeding situation as an event that she has experienced before. Bruner and associates studied social exchanges between children as young as nine months and found that children participate knowingly in games involving give and take and hiding (Ratner & Bruner, 1978). Nelson's research has focused on children's first verbal descriptions of events, which she finds fairly well developed for familiar routines by age three. Nelson illustrated by providing examples of children's answers to questions such as "What happens when you make cookies?" A child age 3 years 1 month answered "Well, you bake them and eat them" (Nelson & Gruendel, 1981).

What, according to these researchers, is the composition of these early event representations? Nelson (1983) answered the question as follows: "The event representation as we view it includes action schemata and much more, in particular, representation of objects, persons and person roles, and sequences of actions appropriate to a specific scene. In other words, it includes specific social and cultural components essential for carrying through a particular activity" (Nelson, 1983, pp. 134–135). Bretherton (1984) and Stern (1985) added to Nelson's list a strong affective component. The various frames that children may use to build into their event representations will be presented next by reviewing the research literature on when and how knowledge in those domains is acquired by normally developing children.

ROLE STRUCTURING OF EVENT REPRESENTATIONS

During the first three years of their lives normal children display a developing knowledge that they and others behave in characteristic ways, can cause things to happen, and can alter roles depending on the social and physical circumstances. Notions of role relations such as these are built up over time. Infants younger than one month prefer social to nonsocial stimuli (Fantz, 1963; Fitzgerald, 1979; Stechler & Latz, 1966). Between 9 and 15 months children show fear of separation from caregivers (Ainsworth & Wittig, 1969; Bowlby, 1969), they engage in sharing games (Bruner & Sherwood, 1976; Ratner & Bruner, 1978), and they communicate requests to others for objects, actions, and attention (Dore, 1975). At two years (but not at 16 months) of age children show surprise when they see inanimate objects act in animate ways (Golinkoff & Harding, 1980); and by three years of age they are able to pretend to be different characters in a play scenario (Wolf, 1982; Wolf & Gardner, 1981).

Knowledge used to achieve understandings of role relations allows children to understand that participants can serve as primary actors in an event, initiating, intending, and carrying out actions to achieve their goals. The knowledge that they as well as others can act as independent agents is developed, according to Wolf (1982), by age two. Children also come to understand that participants can serve a passive role in an event, in that things can happen to them. This recipient or "patient" role is understood by 14 months, as indicated by their surprise response when a participant in a film serving as an agent shifts to being the patient (Golinkoff, 1975).

A type of role understanding that develops later is children's understanding that participants in event descriptions or stories can have subjective states, that different characters can ponder and have feelings about events which are different from how the child feels about them. Their notions about subjective states, or what some have called their "theory of mind" (e.g., Leslie, 1987), also pass through a series of developmental stages. Wolf, Rygh, and Altshuler (1984) in their longitudinal study of the pretend play of nine normally developing children found that the children passed through five stages in their understanding of agents, the last three having to do with their acquisition of knowledge about subjectivity. The stages are based on Wolf and colleagues' observation of children's play with objects, what they call replica play. Examples of behaviors exhibited in each of the five stages are provided in Table 3–2.

ACTION SEQUENCES AND THEIR TEMPORAL AND CAUSAL RELATIONS

When children perform actions in a sequence, they often are given credit for understanding the temporality of the event. There is, however, some evidence that children first learn an event by associating actions without

Table 3–2. Wolf's levels of acquisition of subjectivity in pretend play

Stage	Description of behavior	Examples
Level 1 1 year	Child treats a doll as a passive recipient of the child's actions	Wraps doll in blanket and lays it in a box.
Level 2 1½ to 2 years	Child treats doll as an independent agent, but without internal states	Walks doll over blocks saying, "She climbed up here."
Level 3 2½ years	Child ascribes sensations, perceptions, and physiological states to doll	Puts doll in bath making it say, "Ouch, too hot."
Level 4 3 years	Child ascribes emotions, obligations, simple moral judgments, and elective social relations to doll	Makes two figures fight and then face each other saying, "No, now let's be friends."
Level 5 4 years	Child ascribes cognitions like thinking, planning, wondering, and knowing to doll	Makes doll look for others saying, "He wonders where they went. He can't see them."

Source: Adapted from "Agency and Experience: Actions and States in Play Narratives" by D. Wolf, J. Rygh, & J. Altshuler, 1984. In I. Bretherton (Ed.), *Symbolic Play: The Development of Social Understanding* (pp. 195–217). New York: Academic Press.

focusing on their temporal relations. For example, O'Connell and Gerard (1985) found that, when asked to imitate a three-sequence activity using toys as props, children at 20 months were able to imitate actions performed in an order reverse of that of daily life (e.g., drying a baby then putting him in the tub) just as easily as they were able to imitate actions performed in their correct order. O'Connell and Gerard argued that these 20-month-old children had knowledge of the event, which they used to carry out their reproductions, but they did not yet understand the temporal or causal relations between items. The authors based their conclusions on the fact that the children did better on the regular and reverse order conditions in which the actions formed a coherent event, than they did on the scrambled condition in which actions from one event (e.g., bathing) were mixed with actions from a second sequence (e.g., eating). By 24 months of age the children did better on the forward condition than the reversed condition, suggesting that they had developed an understanding of the temporal relations (which things happen first, which next, and which last).

Fivush and Mandler (1985), like O'Connell and Gerard (1985), created a forward and backward sequencing task, which in their study involved picture sequencing rather than enactments with toys. They asked children ages 3, 4, and 5 years old to sequence groups of six pictures in forward or backward order and compared their performance on the two conditions. They also compared the children's performance for sequencing familiar (going to McDonalds) and unfamiliar (going on a train ride) events. Children at all ages had more difficulty sequencing the familiar than the nonfamiliar events in backward order than sequencing them in a forward order, indicating that they were using knowledge of temporal aspects of familiar events to guide their sequencing.

Piaget's extensive studies of causality (Piaget, 1963, 1972) have shown that by age two, at the end of the sensorimotor period of development, normally developing children have acquired notions that they can cause things to happen (means-ends) and that causality can be interpreted from happenings in the physical world (physical causality).

Children's acquisition of understanding of how several actions can work together in causal relations was studied by DasGupta and Bryant (1989). They found that 4-year-old, but not 3-year-old children, were able to understand that an object could be caused to change to a new state through an instrument. For example, 3- and 4-year-old children who were shown pictured objects (e.g., a broken cup and a broken, wet cup) and pictured instruments (water, hammer) could select which instrument went with which change of state. Three-year-old children chose the hammer, indicating that they did not focus on the change between earlier and later states (nonwet changing to wet) but instead associated the instrument with the picture in a general, noncausal way (hammers break things).

DEICTIC ORGANIZATION OF EVENTS

Like the understanding of temporality and causality children's development of deictic understandings begins before the age of two. Mutual referencing between children and adults, in which the children follow the
trajectory of an adult's finger or eye gaze develops within the first year of
life (Scaife & Bruner, 1975). Children in their first year also check the
adult's direction of attention during showing, giving, and hiding activities
(Bates, Benigni, Bretherton, Camaioni, & Volterra, 1979; Murphy & Messer,
1977). It is not until much later, at about age three, that children can take the
deictic perspective of another person (Astington, Harris, & Olson, 1988).

NORMAL CHILDREN'S DEVELOPMENT
OF EVENT LANGUAGE

BEGINNING STAGES OF LANGUAGE
AND EVENT REPRESENTATION

During the stage just before normal children begin to produce their first
words, they produce phonetically consistent noises that are situated in familiar events (Carter, 1975; Dore, Franklin, Miller, & Ramer, 1976). For example, they may say "uh oh" when something falls or spills, "bye-bye"
when someone leaves, and "peek-a-boo" when someone uncovers his or
her face. Often these vocalizations, sometimes called "vocables," are characterized by their close ties to activity, and thus qualify as components of
events. These vocables have served some children as an entree into the language system. For example, a child studied by Menn (1976) first used a vocable "oioioi" as he was spun around in a swivel chair and later used it to
ask for a spin in that chair. The vocable when used in the context of the
event (e.g., the child's noise as he is spun) is part of the child's event representation. It is what he says during or at a particular time in an event. Later,
when he uses it as a word to request the event, it serves as a label or title for
that event. In both instances, when the vocalization is part of the event or
when it is a request for the event, the child is revealing his knowledge of
that event. In this sense, a look at the language children use as they are engaged in activities allows us a peek at their ideas about such activities, as
well as a way to understand how their language relates to these ideas.

Many of the semantic notions expressed by children in their one- and
two-word utterances can be interpreted as their comments on what they
are noticing about what is happening around them. Gopnik (1982) studied
children's early use of an interesting set of words that seem to be used
when they are getting ready to carry out an event. Children just over 1 year
old, who were still in the one-word stage of language development, were

found to use "gone" and "down" just before they made objects disappear or fall, "there" and "oh dear" when their actions were completed or failed, "no" when something interfered with the execution of their plan, and "more" when they were repeating an action they had just finished. Greenfield and Smith (1976) also studied children in the one-word stage and noted that they tend to indicate the components of events that are most uncertain, or most informative. For example, when a child is holding an object and something happens to that object, the child will comment on what happened: "gone" when he puts it in a cup, "drop" when he drops it. On the other hand, when the object is first obtained, the child refers to the object rather than what changes (e.g., picks up nut and says "nut"). Greenfield and Smith (1976) depicted this version of the uncertainty principle in two steps:

When the object is securely in the child's possession while it is undergoing its process or state change, it becomes relatively certain and the child will first encode Action-State. When the object is not in the child's possession, it becomes more uncertain and his first utterance will express the Object. (p. 188)

Thus, the child, even at this early stage of language development, comments differently depending on what is being noted about what is going on.

Children's first verbs also can serve as indicators of how they construe events. Gleitman (1989), in her recent reflections on how children learn verb meanings, observed that for children to understand the difference in meaning between verb pairs such as "chase" and "flee" in a context where hounds and foxes are running they must understand not only the events but also the perspective assumed by the speaker who uses one of the verbs. According to Gleitman (1989), "since verbs represent not only events but the intents, beliefs, and perspectives of the speakers on those events, the meanings of the verbs can't be extracted solely by observing the events" (p. 13).

The two-word semantic relations that make up typical lists of first-word combinations also contain a healthy representation of candidates for event descriptions (e.g., Brown, 1973). The lists invariably contain an agent-action relation, action-patient or object relations, and an action-locative relation. These expressions qualify as event descriptions because they indicate how animate agents act, how objects are affected, and deictic changes in object location. The prevalence of the use of these forms as event descriptions in children's early language attests to the importance of events in their thinking and in their language development.

The same knowledge frames that influence the conceptual organization of events are in play when a child describes and verbally participates in events. Children talk about role relations, they mark temporal and causal relations, and they indicate their deictic centering linguistically.

THE LANGUAGE OF ROLES

Once children have progressed beyond their first event descriptions, expressed in one- and two-word utterances, they begin to describe multiple events. Sutton–Smith (1981) provided examples from a 2-year-old child, Alice, whose early stories involved playing with elements by casting them in different role relations, first passive and then active:

The dog went on the puppet
The puppet went on the house
The house went on the pigeon. (Sutton–Smith, 1981, p. 48)

Similarly, Farrah a 4-year-old story-teller substituted various elements in the patient role in her stories as can be seen in the following:

A monster
the monster ate the house
the monster ate the kids
the monster ate the dad
the monster ate the cat and also the dog
he ate the furniture
and then he went home to the zoo
the end. (Sutton–Smith, 1981, p. 101)

Children's first expressions of role relations can be found in the semantic role relations within their uttterances, such as agent and patient relations shown in the example above. By assigning roles to participants in events, the child conveys how they relate to one another and assumes a perspective on the event about the relative importance of participants. These role expressions are tied to observed activities, which are depicted by action verbs (e.g., eating, going, running). By age three children are able to describe events using mental state verbs that depict how participants think, feel, or perceive a real or imagined event. Three-year-olds can describe the desires, intents, or beliefs of participants. For example, the 3-year-old, Abe, who was studied by Shatz, Wellman, and Silber (1983) commented on mental states in a number of ways, exemplified by the following two excerpts (reported in Wellman, 1988).

    Mom: Don't touch this cloth when your hands are dirty.
     Abe: Do my hands *look like* [italics added] they're dirty?
    Mom: Yes, they look very dirty.
     Abe: Why I painted on them?
   Other: Why did you?
     Abe: Because I *thought* [italics added] my hands are paper! (p. 82)

Abe: This don't have a hole in it yet.
     You're *going to* [italics added] cut it, OK?
Dad: OK, Lets find some scissors.
Abe: Scissors won't work.
Dad: What do you need?
Abe: You get a little saw.
Dad: Oh, I'm not sure that'll work.
Abe: I *think* [italics added] with Mommy's scissors will be a good idea.
Dad: You think I need to use Mommy's scissors?
Abe: Yeah, they will work pretty easy. (p. 83)

With the evolution of the ability to understand that participants in events are motivated to do things through their intents, desires, and goals, children's conception of events and participants' roles in them expands considerably. By five years of age some children can describe events and produce narratives in which participants have a fully evolved role, including psychological states that motivate their actions. We found, for example, that Ellie, a precocious 5-year-old child know among her friends and family as a "good story-teller" included in her self-generated stories descriptions of her character's thoughts ("So the little bear thought about all the things that could happen scary") and feelings ("One little bear was afraid"). She also used expressions that showed the internal monologue of her characters (" 'I wonder how long I can keep this up' ") as well as quoted them directly (" 'I'm scared, I'm scared' said the little boy"). Finally, she was able to represent her characters' thoughts, not as they would say them to themselves or others, but as they might think them ("It was night and night and night" where she used repetition to depict endlessness felt by her character) (Hewitt & Duchan, 1989).

THE LANGUAGE OF TEMPORALITY AND CAUSALITY

When children first describe event sequences, they most often mention the events in the order of their occurrence. Ferreiro and Sinclair (1971) found that French speaking children between ages four and six described observed events in the order of their occurrence 80% of the time. For example, after just witnessing an enactment of two dolls in which a girl doll washed a boy doll and the boy doll then left and went up some stairs, they said something like: "she cleaned him and then he went up" (age 4 years, 2 months). However, some of the least mature children (still in the preoperational stages of cognitive development) responded in inverse order, such as: "he went upstairs and she washed him" (age 4 years, 5 months). When the least mature children described the event in chronological order, they were then asked to describe the same event again, but this time to talk first about the boy.

Just as in their inverse descriptions, these children failed to linguistically indicate that the boy's going upstairs followed the girl's washing him. A more
advanced group of children also were unable to use temporal indicators to
show that the boy's going upstairs followed the girl's washing him, but their
responses reflected that they felt confusion and conflict about having to describe the second event prior to the first. One child, for example, said, "he
goes downstairs again and the girl washes his arms" (age 5 years, 10 months).
The most advanced group used adverbs to indicate that the reverse in order
of mention did not mean that the events actually occurred in reverse order
(e.g., "The boy will go upstairs when the girl finishes washing him").

Ferriero and Sinclair (1971) interpreted their findings to mean that when
children first form event descriptions, they "regard the two events as separate entities, neither of which constitutes a reference point for the other" (p.
45). Later, as indicated by the children's apparent struggle in expressions of
inverse order, they make note of the temporal link between events but have
difficulty in expressing the relationship to indicate that the order of mention is a reverse of the order of occurrence of the two events. In a third stage
of development, the children are able to use adverbs and conjunctions to
express events that need to be described in the reverse of their order of occurrence, and "it is only at a much more advanced level that the different
tenses of the verbs themselves are apprehended as an indication of the temporal relationships" (p. 46).

There has been an effort to study children's development of the term
"then" in an attempt to trace the acquisition of temporality in their verbal
descriptions of sequential events (Bloom, Lahey, Hood, Lifter, & Fiess,
1980). Such studies often take "then" to be a marker of time; however, recent studies of adult language have shown that "then" more typically serves
as a marker of a change in discourse continuity (Schiffrin, 1987; Segal, Duchan, & Scott, in press). The marked discontinuities may be in the spatial location of the described events (and then they went home); the temporal
progression of events (then it was morning); or the appearance of a new
character (then a monster came). Studies of children's language also have
shown that children use "then" as an indicator of discourse discontinuity
(Cassell, 1986; Duchan, 1990). For example, Duchan (1990) found that children's use of "then" coincided with the first appearance or reappearance of
characters into a story scene as can be seen from the following story told by
3-year-old Clarence and reported by Sutton–Smith (1981):

Cowboys fight
cowboys shoot the robbers
then the bad guys
and *then* horsey came
then the cowboy came and fight
then big horsey (p. 68)

Like "then," the term "after" seems to be used by children as a marker of completion, more often than as a marker of time. For example, in a study by French and Nelson (1985) all 33 examples of "after" used by children between ages 3 and 6 in their event descriptions occurred in contexts where children were indicating that one entire episode was completed and another was about to begin as in:

After the birthday, they go home (3:1 years)
After I get dressed, I just go to school (4:1 years)
Go out and play. Um, *after* that ice cream and cake and *after* that, go home (5:0 years) [italics added] (p. 111)

Beginning at about age three, normal language learners, use connectives of "so" and "because" to express causal relations between subevents when they tell stories or describe events (Bloom et al., 1980; Hood & Bloom, 1979; McCabe & Peterson, 1985). They sometimes use the terms to indicate relations of physical causality, as when forces in the world are interpreted as causing things to happen (e.g., the tree fell over 'cause the wind was so strong); but most often they use the terms to express psychological causality where events are interpreted as being caused by people (e.g., she told him to do it, so he did). McCabe and Peterson (1985) found that children between the ages of four and nine expressed five types of psychological causality when they related their personal experiences: *explicit intentions* in which the cognitive state is described (she wanted to hurt him so she hit him); *implicit intentions* in which the cognitive state must be inferred (I scratched her so she scratched me); *emotions* in which an emotional state is related to an occurrence (she was mad so she hit him); *directives* in which one person desires an action from another person (Daddy said: "get that girl out of here and get her to the hospital!" So we went to the hospital); and *reasoning* in which a conclusion is made from a piece of data (she adopted us and everything so she was really our real mother).

THE LANGUAGE OF DEIXIS

Normal children begin using deictic terms of space, time, and character early in their language development. A child's first spoken word often is something like "da" said in combination with a finger point. It is interpreted as "That one there" (Gopnik & Meltzoff, 1985; Werner & Kaplan, 1963). Deictic verbs such as "come" and "gone" also are among the words children develop early, and they have been found to be used by children to indicate the appearance (for "come") and disappearance (for "gone") of objects in the situational present (Clark & Garnica, 1974; Macrae, 1976). Later to emerge are deictic indicators of person, such as personal pronouns

("I" and "you"), and of time, including past tense markers and temporal markers such as "now" and "then" (Wales, 1986; Weist, 1986). The deictic terms used by normal language learners in these early stages of their development are centered in the child's own perspective, with the "I" or "me" and "here" referring to entities near the child and "you" and "there" indicating observable objects or actions away from the child.

Later, children begin to converse about past events which took place somewhere and sometime other than the present (Gerhardt, 1988; Miller & Sperry, 1988; Nelson & Gruendel, 1981). This stage of understanding an event can be thought of as a projection of the here-and-now deixis onto a second conceptual field. The second deictic field is still perceived from the current point of view of the child, since the notion of a past or distant event is in relation to where the child is centered. The verbs take a past tense marker in this context because the event occurred before the current time. Further, the personal pronouns are referenced with the child as deictic center so that "I" or "we" refers to the child. However, deictic verbs such as "come" and "go" are referenced to the projected spatial center of the event being described, a center that may be different from the spatial center of the current situation in which the event is being described. An example of this projected deixis can be seen in the following transcript of an event description made by a child, Emmy, as she was talking to herself which was reported by Gerhardt (1988). (Parentheses were used when transcriber was uncertain about what Emmy said, and ellipses indicate that a few lines are omitted.)

1. Yesterday my slept
2. (   ) um, in Tanta house
3. (And) Mommy woke my up
4. (   ) 'Go/Time go home'
   . . . . .
5. When Mormor came in
6. And Mommy shouted 'make my bed'
7. When when Mommy came in
8. When my (bed)
9. (Wh-wh) I sleeping Tanta house
10. Mommy came wake my up
11. Because time t'go home
12. Drink P-water [Perrier water] (p. 389)

Emmy indicated that the event being described occurred in the past by using the adverb "yesterday" and past tense. She also referred to herself as "my" and "I" and her relatives as "mommy," her mother; "Tanta," her aunt; and "Mormor," her grandmother. These also are deictically referenced in that they are interpretable only when one knows who the speaker is. Her use of "came" and "go" is referenced as centered at her aunt's house rather than her own home, where she was when she said them. She uses "came" to depict others approaching her at her aunt's house and "go" to depict her leaving for home from her aunt's house.

A third type of deictic organization that can occur in an event description is one in which the center is shifted to a character who is imagined as being located in a place and at a time other than that of the child's present. In this case no reference is made to the deictic circumstances of the current situation. It is this sort of shifted deictic center that is found in narratives where characters are described as "coming" into the story scene, where the "I" refers to the character rather than the narrator, and where the past tense is that of the narrative genre. Thus one finds sentences such as the following in the language of young children as well as novelists:

Now the daddy went away. (Beatrice, age 2, reported in Sutton–Smith, 1981, p. 52)

The house was truly sad now. (Flaubert in *Madame Bovary*, cited in Banfield, 1982)

The events described by the children in the previous examples were specific events that actually occurred. Nelson and Gruendel (1981) distinguished a different type of event description, which they termed "generalized event description." They asked preschool children to describe familiar events such as birthday parties, making cookies, going to McDonald's, and having lunch at the day-care center. The researchers found that children as young as age three were able to produce a one- or two-sentence description of activities. The language of the descriptions was in some ways general. Children often used the general pronoun "you" instead of the first person pronoun "I"; and they used unmarked verbs such as "eat" rather than verbs marked with tense or aspect such as "ate" or "eating." Nelson and Gruendel viewed the language of children's descriptions as evidence that the children were representing familiar events in a general, abstract way, rather than as specific recollected episodes, hence, the researchers' use of the term "generalized event representations."

Although general in reference to characters and time, the descriptions made by Nelson and Gruendel's children were specific in reference to a deictic perspective. The two following extracts from Nelson and Gruendel (1981) demonstrate two different deictic centers in the description of a birthday party, the first from the perspective of the child hosting the birthday party, and the second from the perspective of the guest.

The host as deictic center:

1a. . . . and then all the people come you've asked
2a. . . . and then they give you some presents
3a. and then you play with them
4a. and then that's the end
5a. and then they go home
6a. and they do what they wanta. [told by child age 4 years 9 months old]
(Nelson & Gruendel, 1981, p. 135)

The guest as deictic center:

1b. ... Then you go to the birthday party
2b. ... Then usually they always want to open one of the presents
3b. ... then they have the birthday cake
4b. then sometimes they open up the other presents
5b. or they could open them all at once
6b. after that they like to play some more games
7b. and then maybe your parents come to pick you up
8b. and then you go home. [told by child age 8 years 10 months old]
(Nelson & Gruendel, 1981, p. 135)

The "you" in the above examples is the deictically centered character; in the first example it is the host (3a) and in the second it is the guest (8b). Both children use "they" to refer to the noncentered characters, with the child giving the party using "they" to refer to the guests (5a) and the one attending the party using "they" to refer to the host (2b). Further, the use of "come" and "go" is deictically referenced, with the host having guests "come" to the party (1a) and the guest "going" to the party (1b).

ASSESSING CHILDREN'S EVENT KNOWLEDGE AND EVENT LANGUAGE

The above reviews indicate that by age three normal children have many specific and generalized event representations which they use to guide their participation in everyday events and to structure their event descriptions. Children with communication problems are likely to have difficulty in creating event descriptions. Because event description requires not only sophistication in language and discourse, but also knowledge of the event itself, it behooves the clinician to consider what children know about events when evaluating how well they describe them. Children's knowledge of events will be considered in the next section, beginning with an outline of problems children have been found to have with event knowledge. Then a procedure for assessing children's event knowledge and their event descriptions will be outlined.

CHILDREN'S PROBLEMS WITH EVENT KNOWLEDGE

Children have been found to have a variety of problems when participating in events. They may lack knowledge of the event, may be over committed to a particular way the event is carried out, or may have unconventional ideas of events. Each type of problem can be assessed by finding out how others perceive the child (ethnographic assessment) and by analyzing the child's behavior as it naturally occurs (event analysis). This section will begin with examples from the literature of the problems children have with event knowledge and then discuss ethnographic and event analysis as assessment approaches.

Lack of Knowledge of the Event Sequence

Sometimes children participate in events through improvisation. In an example from Verba, Stambak, and Sinclair (1982), which is described further in the section on event transcriptions, four children watched one another, as they explored and imitated one another, without following a pre-established script. Other times, successful participation requires that children know the event sequence and organizational structure in advance. Shultz (1979) described the problems experiences by a kindergarten child, Angie, on her fourth day of class because she lacked the knowledge needed to participate in a school activity. The activity was a game of tic-tac-toe, which Angie had not played before. The teacher assigned Angie to play the game, along with two of her classmates who had experience with the game. The teacher also participated. Angie asked a number of questions throughout the activity that indicate her ignorance about the event. Shultz's (1979) conclusions from her questions were:

a. She doesn't know what tic-tac-toe is:
   Child 1: Angie, you wanna play tic-tac-toe?
   Angie: What's tic-tac-toe mean?
b. She doesn't know what tic-tac-toe looks like:
   Teacher: (sets up three dimensional version of the game)
   Angie: What's it called?
c. She doesn't know the aim of the game:
   Teacher: You want to get four in a row. If you put one here it won't be a row.
   Angie: Where, where's four?
d. She doesn't know how someone wins:
   Teacher (to Angie): If she puts one and makes four in a row, then she wins.
   Angie: And me too? (p. 276)

Shultz's (1979) analysis of postures, verbal accompaniments, and interruption patterns during the game revealed that it was divided into three segments: set up, serious play, and wind up. The teacher and children changed their postures during the different segments, with the most consistent finding being that during the serious play phase they leaned into the game. During the first segment, the less serious portion of the game, children outside the game readily interrupted the teacher, and game participants talked about topics other than those related to the game. Once the game entered its serious phase children seldom interrupted, and when they did the teacher did not respond. Nor were extraneous topics talked about during the serious phase. Angie not only had difficulty with the rules of the particular game, but she also violated the participation rules. She did not shift her posture when others did, and she asked an off-topic question during the serious play phase.

Shultz argued that these types of mistakes, due to a lack of event knowledge, led Angie's teacher to characterize Angie as being "dependent and not a leader" (Schultz, 1979, p. 273).

Problems with Event Flexibility

Children's lack of experience with events is not the only type of difficulty they have with event knowledge. Some children have been found to have event knowledge but to lack flexibility in thinking about and using their knowledge. This problem has been described as obsessiveness, fixation, and broadly as preservation of sameness. An often cited example is from Kanner's (1943) early descriptions of autistic children. Donald T., one of his subjects, was committed to a naptime ritual described by Kanner (1943) as follows:

> A great part of the day was spent in demanding not only the sameness of the wording of a request but also the sameness of the sequence of events. Donald would not leave his bed after his nap until after he had said, "Boo, say 'Don, do you want to get down?' " and the mother had complied. But this was not all. The act was still not considered completed. Donald would continue, "Now say 'All right.' " Again the mother had to comply, or there was screaming until the performance was completed. All of this ritual was an indispensable part of the act of getting up after a nap. (p. 245)

Unconventional Views of Events

A third difficulty children have with events is that they think of them in an idiosyncratic way or in ways that are different from the mainstream culture. Michaels and Cazden (1986) gave as an example the difficulty experienced by Deena, a normal learner from a black community, who was interrupted by her teacher as she was contributing in sharing time and given a negative evaluation. Evidence that Deena thought of the event differently from her teacher came from her own insights given in an interview in which the researchers asked her a year later about her earlier experiences in the sharing time event. When asked how she liked sharing time she said, "sharing time got on my nerves. She was always interruptin' me, sayin' 'that's not important enough' and I hadn't hardly started talkin'!" Deena apparently had a concept of what the teacher wanted from her as evidenced by her response to Michaels' question about what her teacher meant by "tell about one thing." Deena said: "She meant tell about one thing, not 35,000 other things. Like, don't say 'Yesterday, I had a fight. I saw some roses.' " Michaels went on to ask what Deena thought her teacher wanted the children to do at sharing time. Deena answered:

She just wanted us to, say like, well
well yesterday
blah blah blah
blah blah blah
blah blah blah blah
blah blah blah blah
blah blah blah blah

Michaels (1986) commented on her reply:

Deena begins with the sharing time formula, "yesterday," using pronounced sharing intonation. She then provides an account without words which is segmented prosodically into what sounds like a beginning, middle, and end. Interesting enough, this captures precisely the intonational pattern of topic centered discourse. This indicates that Deena had a sense of what topic-centered discourse sounded like, and knew this was what Mrs. Jones wanted, but did not impose this prosodic framework on her own narrative style and presentations. (p. 111)

Undue Focus on Events

A fourth type of problem children have with event knowledge occurs when they focus too much on the event, at the expense of other aspects of the context. I have come to call these children "event kids" because they care more about what should be going on than about what it might mean or how it might vary. Evidence that they are fixed on the event structure comes from their language, which has to do with what is about to happen, or what should have happened during regularly occurring events, and from their lack of participation in unfamiliar or newly created events. Below is an excerpt from a diagnostic report of such a child whom my student, David Hill, and I evaluated. The evaluation was based on observations of him in his classroom, and interviews with his classroom teacher and speech-language pathologist:

Clark's talk revolves around his ideas about routine events. He often requests routines by asking for the first action in the routine. For example, he asks "I go to the rug?" for the event which begins when all children are seated on the rug, and "I want to see the green line?" for the event which begins with them lining up behind the green line. The action requests are made during activities that occur just prior to the one being requested.

Once a routine has begun, Clark's talk has to do with the prescribed utterances involved in the routine. For example, he asks the teacher's questions before she does during calendar routine (e.g., What was yesterday?). He can substitute elements appropriately such as the name of the day or the weather, indicating that he is not simply rotely reciting the routine, but is understanding what is being asked for.

When routines do not go according to plan, Clark comments on the departures or assures himself that it is okay. For example he indicates what should have been done by using the word "later" as when he said "I do 'g' later" when the teacher failed to call on him.

Clark's dependency on routines for his communications is apparent from his behavior in nonroutinized events. During snack preparation in his classroom, Clark remains uninvolved. Instead, he comments on what is going on, such as indicating where the children are sitting. Often, after the non-predictable event has continued for a while, Charles becomes agitated and eventually asks to be removed from the activity by requesting the "time-out" chair ("Karen will put me on the chair?"). If he cannot remove himself from the context, he works into a full blown temper tantrum.

In summary, Clark's language can be characterized as primarily consisting of "stage manager talk" which is about what is going on or about to happen. His goal seems to be to stage the sequence of scenes and to recite his lines, with little other interest in the goings-on, and with little facility for contributing to what goes on in a spontaneous, unprescribed way. His behavior problems occur during the time that he is not in a comfortable event, and seems to be his reaction to not being able to understand what is going on.

ETHNOGRAPHIC INTERVIEWS

In two of the above analyses, the participants in the event were asked about their views of what was going on in the event and their answers were considered as valid renditions of their event representations. Interviewing people about how they think about events has been a consistent aspect of a newly evolving approach to language assessment, the ethnographic approach. (Evidence for its newness is the emergence in October 1989 of a newsletter, *Ethnotes*, for those in communication disorders interested in ethnographic approaches to assessment.) Imported from anthropology, the ethnographic approach includes interviews (the ethnographic interview); direct participation with the child in the events being studied (participant observation); noting and transcribing observations of events and their possible meanings (field notes); analyzing different perspectives held on the same event by participants or observers (triangulation); and imputing thoughts and attitudes to the participants (thick description). (See Damico, Maxwell, and Kovarsky, 1990; Kovarsky and Crago, 1991; and Chapter 4 for a sampling of these techniques.)

The ethnographic approach differs from traditional approaches to assessment in the assumption that there are differences between the clinician's world view and those of the persons or group being assessed; the aim of the approach is to discover, respect, and work within those differences. Westby (1990) described the difference between traditional and ethnographic approaches when she compared the ethnographic interview with the traditional parent interview:

In traditional interviews, interviewers predetermine the questions that are to be asked, and in some cases they predetermine the range of responses that can be given. In ethnographic interviewing both questions and answers must be discovered from the people being interviewed. Different information is collected from different families because the values, beliefs, strengths, and needs of each family are different. (p. 105)

Westby (1990) also provided specific examples of how the ethnographic interview requires a different attitude from the clinician:

Ethnographic interviewing differs from other types of interviewing by the absence of "why" and "what do you mean" questions. For example, if a parent says "Sara is really hyper," [the ethnographic interviewer says] "Tell me what she does when she's acting hyper" not "What do you mean by hyper?" (p. 106)

Ethnographic interviews with children, family members, and teachers can reveal how they think about one another and about various events that take place. Hints as to the usefulness of such information already exist in the literature on autism. For example, Temple Grandin, a woman who reported on her autistic experiences in her autobiography (Grandin & Scariano, 1986), described her own "fixations" from the point of view of others who respond to her:

Constantly asking questions was another of my annoying fixations, and I'd ask the same question and wait with pleasure for the same answer—over and over again. If a particular topic intrigued me, I zeroed in on that subject and talked it into the ground. It was no wonder I was nicknamed "Chatterbox." (p. 35)

Grandin regards fixations as "bad habits" but ones that should not be merely eliminated. She recalled that her early fixations "reduced arousal and calmed" her (Grandin & Scariano, 1986, p. 36), and recommended that fixations be "guided into something constructive" rather than trying to eliminate them. She commented that, "a compulsive talking fixation in a child can release some of the pent-up frustration and isolation that an autistic child so often feels" (p. 37).

Reactions of family members to Grandin's fixations were provided in a letter from her aunt to Grandin's mother, which was written while Grandin was spending a summer on her aunt's farm.

On the debit side she did, as advertised, get on one subject and ride it to death. Temple deals in symbols and when she finds one which would, so to speak, bear the weight of some of her fears and frustrations, she never lets go of it. The "door" which stood for venturing forth into new realms and endeavors, I heard about until I could tell the story verbatim. Several times I interrupted in the middle of her subject. She allowed me to finish my interjection and then resumed her story exactly where she's left off. Yes, it was a little aggravating, but Temple is so basically sensible, so obviously intelligent and so willing to help with any problem we had, that listening to her was a small price to pay. (Grandin & Scariano, 1986, p. 93)

Thus, Temple Grandin as well as her family saw her fixations as problematic, but as necessary, and a minor irritation. They saw them as being caused by Temple's frustration emanating from her condition of autism.

Simons (1974) provided an example of how different construals of autistic children's compulsive behavior can lead to different interactions with the child. Simons sees the source of compulsive behavior in autism as related to the child's anxiety which accompanies a new awareness of others. She comments: "Thus, the autistic child who begins to emerge from his aloneness tends to become more compulsive in an effort to cope with anxiety" (Simons, 1974, p. 6). For the children she described as using compulsions to consciously manipulate the environment, she recommended "cutting through" the compulsion by dealing with it directly and restricting it; for children whose compulsions she described as potentially constructive she recommended "broadening compulsive behavior into constructive pursuits" (Simons, 1974, p. 8).

The comments of Grandin, her aunt, and Simons demonstrate how attitudes of others toward the autistic person, and toward the particular behavior, affect their responses to the person and the behavior. The same behavior seen as a handicap and a serious problem in one event context is seen as a minor irritation in another.

ELICITING DISPLAYS OF EVENT KNOWLEDGE

Children need to know about events in order to participate in them and to talk about them. Research by Nelson (1986) and others has shown that some events are easier than others to learn and use. Events which are easiest for the child to display event knowledge are highly familiar, shared between the child and the partner, situated in contexts of support (e.g., when there are pictures or props available), and short, rhythmic, and simple. Events that are more difficult to carry out or talk about are less familiar to the child, not shared between the elicitor and the child, not context bound, and long, complex, and nonrepetitive. When evaluating children's event knowledge, as in evaluating other knowledge, one might want to elicit events by progressing from those that are easy to those that are more difficult for the child.

Naturally Occurring Events

The most direct way to elicit children's knowledge of events is to watch what they do and say as they are engaged in familiar events. That is what Bruner and Sherwood (1976) did when they studied children enacting peek-a-boo. Bruner and Sherwood videotaped multiple episodes of a child and his mother playing peek-a-boo. They then transcribed the verbal-action sequences and examined the commonality across sequences and the changes in format as the child learned the event. They found four phases in the event, which they called the basic rules, and found that each of the phases or rules varied in well defined ways. Their rules were: (a) initial contact, (b) disappearance, (c) reappearance, and (d) re-establishment of contact. Bruner and Sherwood (1976) described the variations:

Within this rule context, there can be variations in degree and kind of vocalization for initial contact, in kind of mask, in who controls the mask, in whose face is masked, in who uncovers, in the form of vocalization upon uncovering, in the relation between uncovering and vocalization, and in the timing of the constituent elements. (p. 61)

The authors concluded that the children were learning not only the rules, but also how they could vary.

Replica Play

A second way to elicit knowledge from children about events, and one that requires more abstract thinking from the children than their straightforward enactment, is to use replica objects and to invite them to enact events. This method has been used by Bretherton (1984) and Wolf (1982). These authors focused on particular aspects of the children's event depiction: the use of agent, action, and props. Rather than present his results as a schematic representation in the style of Bruner and Sherwood, Wolf (1982) summarized them in a narrated form. The following example is an illustration of how the child J. created equivalences, as he worked out how others were similar to himself:

O. presents a bag of toy implements to J. at 1:4. Each one that he tries out he tries first on himself and then on a big doll. He takes out a comb and combs the back and then the front of his hair, then the doll's. He takes the toy scissors, clipping at the hair around his and then the doll's ears. (Wolf, 1982, p. 314)

Sequence Cards

A third way to elicit event knowledge, and one that is commonly used in the field of communication disorders, is to ask children to arrange a series of picture cards in a sequence depicting a temporal or causal ordering for the pictured event. If they fail to perform the task successfully they are considered to have a "sequencing problem" which implies to some that the children are unable to sequence all sorts of elements, such as sounds, digits, and words, along with action sequences. This representation of the child's failure takes the problem as one of memory, and of the child's inability to remember multiple items. The memory explanation for the child's problems with picture sequencing does not entertain the possibility that the child's failure may be much more specific, and related to his knowledge of events. Because the picture sequencing task is highly complex, requiring both knowledge of the event and memory of how the elements are ordered, one cannot tell which of the two interpretations is valid. Indeed, other interpretations are also plausible. The problem may be in knowing picture sequencing conventions involving left-to-right temporal progression, or even in understanding that people and objects depicted in one picture are the same as those depicted in the next picture.

To find out whether a child's poor performance on a picture sequencing task stems from a problem with event knowledge, one can turn to more direct approaches to assessing event knowledge, such as observing the child as he or she enacts the events in everyday life. If the pictures show someone brushing his teeth, and a child being assessed places the picture of the boy brushing his teeth to the left of the one with the boy putting the toothpaste on the toothbrush, one cannot assume that the child makes this mistake every morning. In conclusion, if children perform poorly on picture sequencing tasks, it tells us very little about their knowledge of events, but if they are successful on such tasks, we can assume that they know about the events being depicted. It is only when children are successful, then, that sequence pictures offer information about their event knowledge.

Event Descriptions

A fourth method for eliciting children's event knowledge, and the most difficult for children with language problems, is to ask the children to verbally describe events that are familiar to them. The typical format is to ask questions such as "what happened in school yesterday?" This elicitation format has been found to be particularly difficult for children, even those who have been found, through other elicitation techniques, to have considerable event knowledge (Fivush, 1984). Fivush hypothesized that the difficulty arises from the fact that children with event knowledge may not know what yesterday means, and that there is nothing in the question that focuses the child on a possible answer. Many events occur in school, none of which are suggested by the question. Children do better if asked about deictically centered particulars—"what happened when Mary got hurt on the playground?"

Peterson and McCabe (1983) devised an elicitation procedure for event descriptions that is embedded in conversational discourse. They interacted with a child as the child was putting together a picture out of construction paper and paint. The adult, in the course of the interaction, began talking about an interesting experience such as a car wreck, a trip to the doctor, and so on. Once the experience had been described the adult asked the child if she or he had ever had a similar experience. For example, the experimenter might say: "One time I was on a trip and our tire blew up and we crashed into the guard rail. Have you ever been in a car wreck?"

TRANSCRIBING EVENT SAMPLES

Analyzing children's action and verbal behavior as they engage in everyday happenings offers a new challenge to transcription procedures, as well as to analytic techniques. In the traditional approach to language sample analysis, transcriptions have involved writing down what the participants say, with an additional column for context notes (Bloom & Lahey, 1978; Brown, 1973). If the focus is on discovering event knowledge, the transcription is of the activity, rather than the verbal performance during the activity. Verba and colleagues (1982) offered an approach, in which they transcribed what two children were doing and who they were looking at during the course of a collaborative activity with blocks (see Table 3–3).

Verba and colleagues (1982) discovered by analyzing their transcript that the two children began a tapping activity, and in the course of successive variations transformed it into a building towers activity. From their analysis one can see how event structuring can evolve collaboratively.

For action-based activities that have verbal components, transcriptions should include depictions of both action and verbal components. In some events, such as "Ring Around the Rosey," the action and verbal components are combined; in others, such as the card game, "Fish," the action and the verbal components are interwoven (the requests for cards are between the playing of the cards). Because the aim of doing the transcription is to discover the child's knowledge of a particular event, the goal should be to transcribe the actions and verbal components that are essential to the event interpretation. Thus, if a fight erupts between the children during a particular activity but it seems unrelated to the activity, it might be noted but need not be transcribed in detail unless it always erupts at that point during that activity.

ANALYSIS OF EVENTS

Once the child's activity structuring is captured in a transcription one can proceed to analyzing how the event is framed. The four types of structuring outlined in the beginning of this chapter each require that the activity be analyzed in a variety of ways.

Analyzing for Role Structure

For activities that have multiple roles, an analysis for role structuring might provide insight into how they are organized conceptually by the child. For

Table 3–3. A transcription of a play sequence between two children

Karine	Bertrand
Looks at Bertrand	Taps block
Taps block	
Tries to take Bertrand's block	Refuses
Taps block	
	Gives Karine block
Offers block to Bertrand	
	Taps block
Builds structure with blocks	
Taps block	
	Offers block to Karine
Builds second structure	Watches Karine
Taps block	
Builds third structure	
	Builds structure similar to Karine's second one

* Vertical lines indicate continuation of the activity.
Source: Adapted from "Physical Knowledge and Social Action in Children 18 to 24 Months of Age" by M. Verba, M. Stamback, & H. Sinclair, 1982. In G. Forman (Ed.), *Action and Thought*. New York: Academic Press.

example, changing voices, who the participants or play-acted characters are, and their role relations can be noted. A basic role relation to examine is that of actor and recipient within a particular activity. Indicators of the child's awareness of these role relations would be their nonverbal enactments in which dolls interact with one another and their verbal use of semantic relations including actor, agent, and patient. Other, more permanent role relations to note are those between mother, child, teacher, and student.

More cognitively and linguistically advanced children can depict roles through subjective language. The easiest indicators of subjectivity to find are mental state verbs (e.g., verbs of perception such as "see"; verbs and adjectives describing emotion such as "felt sad"; kinship terms showing relationships such as "daddy"; verbs describing cognitive acts such as "thought," "wanted," "guessed"). Also easy to discern are examples of quoted speech and use of different voices to depict different characters. Finally, first person pronouns, especially when used to refer to someone other than the person speaking provide an indicator of subjectivity.

To analyze the transcribed action and verbal behavior of a child for its subjective indicators, one can progress through the verbal and action transcript, line by line. If the event being analyzed is pretend play, Wolf's stages can be used to assign the child's performance to a developmental level.

A sample analysis of subjectivity expressed by a child is presented below. The data was from a partial transcript of a story told by a 5-year-old child, Ann. The story was among those reported in Sutton–Smith (1981):

1. When Red Riding Hood opened the door.
2. There was grandma.
3. Why do you have such big ears?
4. They're good to hear with.
5. Why do you have such big eyes?
6. They're good to see with.
7. Why do you have such big teeth?
8. They're good to eat with.
9. She ran away from her grandmother.
10. She wouldn't do that again. (p. 129)

Sutton–Smith's transcription does not indicate whether the child used different voices for the different characters. Nonetheless, the question-answer format and the pronoun "you" indicate that the characters are depicted as talking, indicating that Ann has entered the subjective world of each. Her use of the perception verbs "see" and "hear" hint at her understanding that the characters can experience their own sensations, although some analysts might suggest that since the story is a frequently heard one, it is not possible to tell whether Ann is repeating what she has heard or whether she understands that characters can have subjective experiences. There is considerable evidence, however, that Ann's features are creative, and not simply copied from an original version. In line 2, for example, she depicts Red Riding Hood's subjective feelings upon seeing who she thought to be her grandmother. The "there" is an indicator of original notice as in "there it is!" (Duchan, 1990). Since the narrator and the listener already know that it was the wolf in the bed dressed as the grandmother, it should come as no surprise to them. Rather, it is Red Riding Hood who is experiencing the surprise. Further, the character in the bed is referred to as "grandma," a name referring to her relationship with Red Riding Hood. It might have been called "the wolf" or, as later in the story in line 9, "her grandmother" in which case it would have been outside the subjective perspective of the child.

Analyzing for Temporal and Causal Structure

If a child picks up a ball and throws it, is she thinking of the two acts as temporally related? Probably not. But what if the child describes a school day in order of the activities, indicating that first there is reading and then recess? Is the child relating these activities temporally? Probably so. Why are we willing to say the child understands the temporality of the second case but not the first? This problem also relates to causality. When the child talks about going to the doctor and getting a shot, does he think that getting there enables him to get the shot? Probably not. But when he describes killing the lion to save the boy we feel certain that the two events are understood by the child as causally related.

The problem with assessing children's ability to understand temporal and causal relations is that clinicians operate from adult intuitions about which event descriptions are focusing on time and causality, rather than from what they know about the child's understanding of events. Usually there is no basis for determining whether the child is just carrying out the event or thinking of the components as being temporally or causally related. For example, in the following story related by Sutton–Smith (1981), does Alice think that a dog is going on a puppet prior to a puppet going on a house?

The dog went on the puppet
The puppet went on the house
The house went on the pigeon. (p. 48)

Lahey (1988, p. 269) regarded Alice's description as organized around repeated actions, and lacking in temporality. Her intuitions were based on her assumption that the child was focused on the similarity in activities across events rather than in their temporal relations.

The same dilemma holds when trying to assign causal relations to event descriptions. In the following example from 3½-year-old Watson, reported by Pitcher and Prelinger (1963), does he see his dog's going to the doctor as causally related to him getting a shot?

1. About Noodle.
2. He went to the doctor.
3. He give a shot.
4. He go home.
5. He drink milk.
6. He didn't drink his milk. (p. 27)

Lahey (1988) argued that in this case items 2 and 3 in the event description are temporally but not causally related. She commented, "while it is possible that the dog went to the doctor in order to get a shot, such a causal relation is not coded nor is it implied. Thus, this was called a temporal chain" (Lahey, 1988, p. 269). By "coded" Lahey seems to be referring to something in the child's language that would indicate that the event is causal, such as a connective "because" or "so."

Lahey assigned children logical knowledge based on whether or not they coded it in their language. From her examination of children's stories she argued that some children specialize in certain types of logical relations. Thus certain children emphasized temporal relations in their descriptions, whereas others emphasized causal ones. Even more strongly, Lahey suggested that children go through three stages in the development of narrative competence. In the first stage components have no temporal links, but one component is added to the next as an additive relation. According to Lahey, the child then proceeds to a second stage of temporally chained descriptions, in which the elements are connected by virtue of one occurring later than another. The last stage is a causal one in which the child focuses on forming descriptions that have causal relations. As part of the causal stage children begin to create descriptions which include thwarted plans and in so doing develop the ability to tell stories with plots based on blocked goals.

Lahey's ideas are not yet verified because she did not follow children as they developed. If found to be valid, her idea is appealing because it allows for the possibility of studying children's event descriptions to determine whether they include linguistic indicators of additive, temporal, or causal relations. If they do, it would provide stronger evidence for children assigning temporal and causal relations to their narratives or event descriptions. That is to say, if most of a child's descriptions were focused on temporal relations, and few on causal, as was the story from Watson above, we would have more evidence for his descriptions being expressions of temporal relatedness and less evidence for them being causally related. Lahey's (1988) insight would be even more strongly validated if children were found to shift from temporal to causal descriptions within an identifiable and circumscribed period of time.

Analyzing for Deictic Organization

Analyses of preverbal children's knowledge of deixis can be done by examining how the children go about getting the attention of others and whether they engage in showing, pointing, and giving activities, and if so how. Efforts to get the attention of others would indicate that they have a beginning notion that others have a point of view, and pointing, or following others' points, would suggest that they are attending to spatial deictics. Analyses of their performance in games of hiding or peek-a-boo, in the manner of Ratner and Bruner (1978) and Bruner and Sherwood (1976), would indicate that the children know and care about the perspective in events, both their own and their partners'.

Problems with deixis in the formative stages of children's development can create problems in their beginning understanding of events. For example, Roberts (1989), in her study of interactions between autistic children and their mothers, found that the autistic children initiated requests, and the mothers responded, but that the autistic children did not look at the mothers as the mothers responded to them. This failure to attend to what others do in response to a request may be foundational for later learning about others' points of view, a problem that gives autistic children special difficulties (Baron–Cohen, 1989).

Analyses of deictic organization of event knowledge in verbal children can be done by examining the deictic terms they use as they carry out their events, or as they describe events. Systematic analysis of their use of personal pronouns, spatial prepositions, temporal adverbs, deictic verbs, verbs expressing states of mind, and discourse markers such as "then" can lead to an understanding of the children's ideas about how events are organized deictically. Descriptions that are confusing because one cannot tell who was doing the acting or when or where the actions took place can be analyzed to determine the source of confusion. For example, the 5-year-old child (designated "M" below) who created the following event description caused deictic confusion in her listener because she did not indicate the spatial shifts in scene clearly enough:

    E: Did your dog ever run away?
    M: Noo. 'Cept when we moved over to *the old house* cause he missed it.
    E: When you were over to the old house?
         Cause you moved and he ran away?
    M: Yeah, but we didn't move that day,
         we're at, we lived at out own, *our new house.*
    E: Oh, I see.
    M: Then when we went to our old house, Fritz ran away.
         We have a *cousin by the old house.*
    E: Oh, you do?
    M: Yep.
    E: What happened?
    M: I don't re...
         We had to call him, Fritz, back.
         He wouldn't come when we were calling him.
         Cause he saw a real rabbit,
         he couldn't find it,
         and all of a sudden Jim went out in the back and Fritz came in.
(Peterson & McCabe, 1983, p. 227)

The passage includes at least two houses, an old house and a new one (and maybe a third, the cousin's). The child at first seems to be saying that the dog ran from the new to the old house, but later says that the dog ran away from the old house which is located near where their cousin lived. The problem may be that the child is not clear about the deictic arrangement of the houses or that she fails to convey her knowledge through language that offers a clear deictic picture to the listener (note E's confusion in the passage).

As summarized in Table 3–4, the procedures recommended to assess children's event knowledge and the language they use to describe events combine ethnographic approaches of interviewing and participant observation with traditional informal analysis techniques involving transcription and structural analysis (Lund & Duchan, 1988).

FACILITATING CHILDREN'S EVENT LEARNING

Organizing language intervention around events is nothing new to speech-language pathologists. For years, therapies have been conducted within event structures such as games, lesson-like activities, simulations of activities of daily living; and for years, sequence cards, stories, and event descriptions have been used as a method for helping children learn about language. What is different about the approach recommended here is that events are focused on directly, and are the target of the child's learning, rather than treated as a tool for teaching other things.

FACILITATING BEGINNING EVENT KNOWLEDGE

There are a few clinical methods now available that focus on helping children learn about events which occur in their world, and help them learn the language of these events. The VanDijk method for teaching deaf-blind children is a good example of how children might be taught events, although the author and his supporters do not talk about the method in this way

---

Table 3–4. Steps to assessing children's event knowledge and event descriptions

1. Conduct ethnographic interviews of the child, teacher, family members, or peers to determine their event interpretations.
2. Elicit different displays of child's event knowledge.
3. Make field notes during observations and transcribe recorded samples elicited.
4. Analyze interviews, field notes, and transcriptions.
5. Make recommendations and write reports based on findings.

(Sternberg, Battle, & Hill, 1980; Stillman & Battle, 1984). The method is designed for children who have very little knowledge of their world. VanDijk begins his training by interacting physically with the child to create a pleasurable, repetitive, and rhythmic action sequence, such as rocking back and forth. The clinician and child rock together, then the clinician stops rocking and waits for the child to initiate a continuation. This activity has the potential of helping the child develop a primitive event structure. The clinician first assumes the role of agent, stopping the event. The child's attempts to resume the event can be seen as an initiation and an act of agency. The rhythmic, repetitive nature of the event provides a simple and ongoing activity structure which can be requested and mentally represented by the child even when he or she has very little other conceptualization of world knowledge. VanDijk has called these activities "resonance activities."

Once the child is able to engage in the resonance activities, VanDijk recommends moving to "co-active activities" in which the separation between clinician and child increases and the child develops a clearer idea of "other." These activities are also rhythmic, pleasurable, and conceptually simple and progress naturally from the resonance activities.

When the child has acquired a group of interactive sequences, or events that he requests and is able to engage in, VanDijk suggests that the child be given a tangible means for requesting the activities, such as an object that has been associated with the activity or a person who engages in the activity. These objects then are placed in a box, with a separate box for each event. These sequence boxes allow the child to request events and remind the child of the ordering of events in his day (e.g., the leftmost box might have a ball in it, to be used in a ball-rolling activity; the next box to the right might have a spoon to indicate a snack event, etc.).

SCAFFOLDING EVENT KNOWLEDGE
THROUGH REPEATED DEMONSTRATIONS

Scaffolding is a term coined by Bruner (1983; Bruner & Sherwood, 1976) when he described how parents of normal children teach them social actions routines such as peek-a-boo. The parent first provides a full rendition for the child, taking all of the turns. Later, the parent remains silent during some parts, waiting for the child's response. This provision of parts of the model to allow the child to participate is seen as providing the child with a frame or scaffold upon which to build his response. Snyder–McLean, Solomonson, McLean, and Sack (1984), borrowing from Bruner's approach, have developed intervention programs related to joint action routines. The programs were designed for older children, who are severely retarded. The method calls for designing joint action routines that involve (a) the creation of a product (e.g., preparing a snack), (b) a story (e.g., a circus event or putting out a fire), or (c) a cooperative turn-taking game (e.g., a circle time event). Snyder–McLean and her colleagues recommend presenting the routine to the children several times each day, and inviting their participation, following the scaffolding methods used by parents in Bruner's studies. The routines should have a unifying theme, involve interaction of two or more people, and have clearly defined and exchangeable roles. The sequence of elements in the routine should be logical, with clearly delineated beginnings and endings, and the routine should have clear turn-taking rules. Students who were initially nonverbal and preintentional were found by Snyder–McLean and colleagues to have improved significantly after a two-year program emphasizing routines of food preparation, vocational skills, and leisure skills. Students made improvements not only in performance of the routines, but also in their overall communication and peer interaction.

ELABORATING ON ROUTINES ALREADY PERFORMED BY THE CHILD

The Snyder–McLean and associates program scaffolds routines for the child that are preplanned and not tailored to what the child already knows. Sugarman (1984) outlined a second approach to getting children to participate in events. Sugarman's approach is for the clinician to engage in routines that are already being performed by the children. In the case she reported, Sugarman entered the activities already being engaged in by an autistic 2-year-old named Lee, and in so doing altered the child's conceptualization of the event. For example, she handed the child crayons as he engaged in an activity of lining up crayons. The child came to expect Sugarman's offerings. Prior to Sugarman's inclusion in the routine, the activity lacked role structure (the child performed it alone) and action structure (there was one activity, lining up). Sugarman's entry provided a dual role and variation in activity (taking the crayon, lining it up) and she also added to the child's activity (she scribbled with a crayon before giving it to the child). The notion of joining what the child is doing has been elaborated in what has come to be called the "Sonrise" method of therapy which involves working with the child's rituals to make them more elaborate and conventional (Kauffman, 1976).

SCAFFOLDING EVENT DESCRIPTIONS THROUGH QUESTIONS AND FORMATS

Judging from research on first words of normal children (e.g., Gopnik, 1982), many of the first words of children with language impairments will be related to their observations about what is happening (e.g., "done" or "there" when an event is completed, "uhoh" when something goes wrong, etc.). Thus, rather than select frequently occurring nouns as items for vocabulary training with children in the one-word-stage, it is recommended that things be made to happen and children be given words to talk about what is exciting about what happens. Interventions that facilitate their evolution to the two-word stage can also be event related.

Some procedures that lend themselves to teaching children at the one-word stage to combine words in making event descriptions have already been developed. For example, Schwartz, Chapman, Terrell, Prelock, and Rowan (1985) have proposed that children well into the one-word stage be asked guiding questions which provide a structure for creating two-word utterances. Children with language impairments were presented with a situational happening, through a picture or the experimenter's manipulation of toys, and asked: "What's this?" or "Who's that?" Once the child responded by naming the object, the experimenter then asked a question to elicit a second noun from the child (e.g., "What's the boy throwing?" or "What's the block in?") as he pointed to the answer. The experimenter then produced a complete response containing the noun-noun relation (e.g., "The boy is throwing the ball" or "The block is in the truck"). Schwartz and colleagues (1985) found notable improvement in most of their eight experimental subjects, not only in production of two-word noun-noun utterances but also in other semantic relations and in use of new words.

There are a few problems with the method developed by Schwartz and his colleagues. First, the questions posed by the adults are not real questions for them. Rather, they are test questions which the adults already know the answers to. This creates a teaching rather than a conversational atmosphere. Second, the items are not related to each other, so that moving from one question pattern to another fails to follow coherent discourse principles. Third, the adult controls the event, and does not build on the child's meaning formation. The method can, however, be adjusted and carried out in more naturalistic ways. Indeed, the method was derived from naturally occurring incidents noted by Scollon (1976). In his study of a child in the single word stage, Scollon found that she often said one word first and then waited to be asked about it at which time she said a second, related word (e.g., Child to adult: "Hiding." Adult: "Hiding? Who's hiding?" Child: "Balloon"). Scollon dubbed this sequence one of *vertical structuring,* and Schwartz and his colleagues based their intervention program on it.

Lucariello (1990), from the results of a study of how mothers of normal language learners format event descriptions, recommended intervention programs that contain wh-questions presented in lingusiticaly formatted or repetitive frames for children with language impairments. The wh-questions should relate to who, what, when, where, and how events occurred. The formatted language consists of repeated comments such as the following (M = mother; C = child):

M: Then we'll go to the club and go see Diane
C: Yeah
M: You wanna go to the club, don't you?
M: Wanna get dressed to go to the club?
M: We're gonna go see Kevin at the club, Jimmy
M: Where we going today, Jimmy?
C: Club
M: We're going to the club?
C: Yeah (Lucariello, 1990, p. 24)

Lucariello also recommended, based on the performance of normal children, that the scaffolding questions and formats be about scripted events—ones quite familiar to the child. It was in these contexts that children were first able to talk about past and future, rather than present, events.

An extension of the scaffolding-through-questioning and formatted exchanges approach has been proposed by Lund and Duchan (1987) to help children with language impairments form event descriptions in response to questions such as "What happened in school today?" The authors recommended keeping a notebook that the child takes to and from home and school which has in it questions for scaffolding children's event descriptions. For example, the teacher might include in the notebook questions for the parents to ask about something significant that happened during the school day such as: "Ask Jose about why Elise cried on the playground? Ask him what he did when Elise cried and whether Elise is better now." The teacher can then rehearse the answers to the questions with the child, so that the child can convey the information to his or her mother using familiar language forms.

The relevance of questions as a means of scaffolding children's event descriptions and story-telling is evidenced from the following excerpt of Vivian Paley's student, Rose, whom Paley (1981) described as having difficulty participating in story-telling. Paley commented about Rose's strategy: "She began to question herself. She modeled her own Thanksgiving story after Wally's but asked herself a question following each line. Her answer then became part of the story" (p. 85). Paley (1981) transcribed the results of the self-questioning scaffolding:

A girl said, "Can I go for a walk?" Who'd she say it to? Her mother. "Okay, you can go." We went to the forest and saw Squanto. Who's Squanto? An Indian. "Do you want to live with me?" Yes, she did. She asked could her mother come too? "Yes." (p. 85)

LEARNING TO BE FLEXIBLE

Children with communication disorders not only have problems learning events and talking about them, but also may have problems in being flexible in carrying out events they already know. This difficulty is particularly pronounced among autistic children and has been identified as part of the syndrome. Rather than thinking of this problem of "rigidity" or "preservation of sameness" as a symptom of a disorder, one can analyze the difficulty in terms of how it seems to function for the autistic child, and respond to it accordingly. Simons (1974) followed this philosophy and proposed four approaches for working with autistic children who have what she calls "compulsive behaviors."

Limiting the Area of Compulsive Activity

This procedure is used when the compulsive behavior becomes too disruptive. She described a 3-year-old, Timmy, who sat in the middle of the playroom and "proceeded to accumulate visible and invisible wires or strings which he then attached to every possible object in sight (Simons, 1974, p. 6). She established limits by designating a special corner in the room for Timmy to create his "wire mechanisms." His behavior diminished to using only one string in the rest of the room within a few hours following the creation of his corner, and he abandoned the activity within a few weeks.

Ignoring Compulsive Manifestations

Simons (1974) used this method if the compulsion did not create undue problems. She argued for its use because she found that attempts to stop or suppress compulsive behaviors were often unproductive and, indeed, sometimes led to an increase in such behaviors.

Cutting Through a Compulsion

Simons (1974) used this method when she found that the child was aware of the compulsion and used it as a "conscious weapon" to "manipulate the environment." She described, as an example, an autistic 6-year-old child, Jack, who "had to march up and down the stairs in a straight line like a soldier, turn back, and proceed to the bathroom, and start screaming on this way" (p. 7). Simons noted that Jack only did this when someone else was on the stairs and that the behavior increased when the stairs were in greatest use. Simons' therapy was to tell Jack "that we understood that he did not want his straight line to be crossed, and that this could be henceforth accomplished if he were to either confine himself to a path adjacent to the wall or alternatively restrict his trips to a time schedule which I would have to establish" (p. 8). The child abandoned the entire routine immediately.

Broadening Compulsive Behavior into Constructive Pursuits

Under this intervention approach Simons (1974) described a 6½-year-old child, Pierre, who "could not resist a powerful urge to appropriate every possible key or key chain" (p. 8). Simons allowed him to play with her personal keys in her presence twice a day. She then created activities around his interest in keys, such as learning the shapes and colors of the different keys on the chain. Within eight weeks his attachment to keys diminished; "he was ready to move on to unrelated constructive activities involving shapes, numbers, and letters" (p. 9).

Approaches to intervention that build different kinds of event understandings are in keeping with approaches to assessment that analyze how children interpret events. Both approaches suggest that clinicians need to understand the children they serve in light of the world they live in; in so doing they may be better able to help them live in that world.

CLASSROOM EVENTS

Assessment procedures for analyzing children's understanding of events include ethnographic approaches as well as direct analysis of children's participation in particular events. These procedures can be applied to events that occur at home, at school, and in the community. To illustrate, the literature on ethnographies of classrooms, analyses of classroom events will be reviewed, and its applicability to assessing the classroom performance of children with language impairments will be discussed.

DOING CLASSROOM ETHNOGRAPHIES

Ripich and Spinelli (1985) conducted ethnographic interviews with a child and his teacher. Although both agreed that the child was having problems in school, each had a different version of it. The results of the interviews along with an analysis of the classroom event revealed that the child's problems may have been confined to situations in which he did not understand the teacher's instructions. Shultz (1979), using a similar methodology (see page 61), found that the child he studied who did not know how to play the tic-tac-toe game created an impression in the teacher that she was "dependent."

Ethnographic approaches to the study of school events have been carried out for a number of years following the leads of Dell Hymes (1972) and Courtney Cazden (1979). Both researchers found from their ethnographies that school events can be divided into two general types: events based on action and events based on discourse. Cazden illustrated: "Among classroom contexts, a tic-tac-toe game is a speech situation, and teacher-led lessons are speech events" (p. 2). Cazden depicted the distinction between action and discourse events as a continuum, with some activities having features of both. A math lesson involving an abacus could contain an action sequence as well as the Initiation-Response-Evaluation (IRE) discourse exchange structure. Cazden argued that children may be using their preschool experiences with action events, such as peek-a-boo or labeling pictures in a book, as a basis for participation in the lessons, because the infant games are organized around the IRE three-part exchange sequence (Cazden, 1979).

Action-Based Classroom Events

Group projects involving collaborative activities occur often in American classrooms. Examples of such events are the tic-tac-toe sequence described by Shultz (1979) and the block play described by Verba and her colleagues (Verba et al., 1982). Each event takes on its own life, and neither is predetermined ahead of time. For example, Verba elaborated on the block play of four children between the ages of 19 and 24 months old, who were playing together in a day-care center in Paris, France. The children were given manipulable objects such as beads, sticks, clay, string, and cardboard tubes and were videotaped as they played together with the objects. The play was interactive, and event sequences emerged as children gave each other ideas for how to act on the objects. The following are excerpts taken from the description given by Verba and colleagues (1982):

Karine then offers one of her cubes to Bertrand and, with the one still in her possession, taps with him on the parallelogram. Karine next uses the two objects she has in her hands to construct two towers by putting each of them on one of the two large cubes on the table. She then offers one little cube to Bertrand, who refuses her offer. Karine then taps with this cube on the base of the dismantled tower. Bertrand, who has been observing Karine, gives her his parallelogram. She then constructs two identical towers. Each has a large cube at the base and a parallelogram at the top. . . . Next she inserts a small cube between the base and the top of one of the towers and calls Bertrand to look. He looks and also begins to construct a tower with three cubes. (p. 288)

The authors concluded that "the common activity develops not only through imitation of a neighbor's actions but equally through exhortations addressed to the other to join one's own activity." (Verba et al., 1982, p. 288). This study illustrates how manipulative play takes its shape on the spot and how children influence one another's formation of action events. The "tower" event emerges as a social and action collaboration between children.

Action events that occur during the school day may either be formed on the spot, such as the ones described above by Verba and her colleagues

(1982), or they can be already formed, such as the scripted events described by Nelson and Gruendel (1981). School action scripts may be planned, controlled, and enacted by children as a repeating scripted event which occurs in the doll corner or a game which takes place on the playground; or they may be teacher controlled such as the script followed as children carry out their jobs or have their snack. In either circumstance, an already established action sequence is followed, and children must know that sequence to be able to perform in and understand the event.

An assessment of how well particular children engage in events therefore should include an analysis of what type of event they are engaging in, whether it is an action or discourse event (or contains both action and discourse), and if it is an action event, whether it has an established structure or is extemporaneous.

Discourse-Based Classroom Events

Many events in classrooms, especially those in the upper grades, revolve around discourse structure rather than action. Lessons, for example, are typically structured verbally, with physical activity being derived from the verbal organization. The lessons have beginnings, middles, and ends and are built from a sequentially organized turn-taking exchange structure (Cazden, 1988; Mehan, 1979). Lesson beginnings involve getting set up, teacher's instructions, and the teacher's discourse signal to begin (e.g., Okay, now . . .). Middles, the heart of the lesson, are often organized in the three-part sequence where the teacher initiates (I), the child responds (R), and the teacher evaluates (E), forming the IRE structure. Ends involve such things as planning for next time and cleaning up. So, lessons, like birthday parties, are made up of temporally related components that become part of children's generalized event representations for that event.

Lessons are only one type of classroom discourse event. Another commonly occurring discourse event, especially in preschool and kindergarten classrooms, involves an activity variously described as "show and tell" or "sharing time." Children stand before the entire class and report on something "interesting." Many of their contributions involve describing a past event or past events, and thereby require not only knowledge of the event, but also how to organize and select language to describe it.

Sharing time events differ considerably with different teachers, and for different children, yet there are some commonalities across classrooms. For example, Michaels and her colleagues (Michaels, 1981, 1986; Michaels & Collins, 1984; Michaels & Cazden, 1986) have observed that white teachers from middle-class backgrounds value event descriptions that have a single topic and are organized around a single deictic center. Michaels and Cazden (1986) described this as discourse which "tended to be tightly organized around a single topic with a high degree of cohesion, and lexically explicit referential, temporal, and spatial relationships. There was a marked beginning, middle and end, with no shifts in time or place" (p. 136). For example, the following event description by a first grader, about one topic and with the time and participants specified, was enthusiastically received by the teacher:

> *Jerry:* Ummmmm. (pause)
> Two days ago, ummm
> my father and my father's friend were doin'
> somethin' over the other side
> and my sister wanted uhh, my father's friend
> to make her a little boat outta paper
> 'n' the paper was too little.
> He used his dollar
> and, umm, my sister undoed it
> and we, ah, bought my father and my mother
> Christmas presents.
>
> *Teacher:* A man made a boat out of a dollar bill for you?
> Wow!
> That's pretty expensive paper to use! (Cazden, 1988, p. 7)

Michael and Cazden (1986) contrasted the single topic event description given by Jerry above with the multiple episodes description given by Deena below. Deena's style is described by Michaels and Cazden as consisting of "a series of implicitly associated anecdotal segments or episodes. Temporal orientation, location, and focus often shifted across episodes, but the episodes themselves were linked thematically to a particular topical event or theme" (p. 143). As reported by Michaels and Cazden (1986), Deena's event description went as follows:

> *Deena:* I went to the beach Sunday
> and to McDonalds
> and to the park
> and I got this for my birthday (holds up purse)
> my mother bought it for me
> and I had two dollars for my birthday
> and I put it in here
> and I went to where my friend named Gigi
> I went over to my grandmother's house with her
> and she was on my back
> and I and we was walking around by my house
> and she was HEAVY
> she was in the sixth or seventh grade

Teacher: OK I'm going to stop you
I want you to talk about things that are
really really very important
that's important to you
but can you tell us things that are sort of
different
can you do that? (p. 137)

Cazden (1988) found that adults from different ethnic backgrounds responded differently to the episodically organized description:

In responding to the mimicked version of this story (by Deena), white adults were uniformly negative, with comments such as "terrible story, incoherent." . . . When asked to make a judgment about this child's probable academic standing, they without exception rated her below children who told topic-centered accounts . . . The black adults reacted very differently, finding this story well formed, easy to understand, and interesting, "with lots of detail and description." . . . All but one of the black adults rated the child as highly verbal, very bright and/or successful in school. (p. 18)

ASSESSING CLASSROOMS FOR CHILD PLACEMENT DECISIONS

Ethnographic analyses of events in classrooms and children's participation in them also can yield information about what types of classrooms offer children who are communicatively handicapped the most opportunities for success and growth in language. That is to say, rather than analyzing the children's knowledge, the classroom itself might be assessed. This approach is in accord with the ethnographic approach of McDermott (1987), who argued that handicaps should not be seen as merely problems of individual children, but rather as problems in how the performance of particular children becomes part of the classroom culture. From his study of the interactions between his subject, Adam, and his peers and teacher, McDermott found that Adam was being systematically excluded from participating as a full-fledged member of the class. Further, he found that Adam was competent in some contexts, especially those in which he worked with his friend, Peter, and incompetent in other contexts, such as test situations. McDermott argued from his findings that the event and social interactions within it create experiences of success or failure in children. The problem is with the context, not with the so-called "disabled" child.

A vivid example of how children with problems can be successful is the following spontaneous exchange between children in a kindergarten class, which was transcribed by Vivian Paley (1981), the classroom teacher:

Lisa: (pouring tea.) My daddy says black people come from
Africa.

Wally: I come from Chicago.

Lisa: White people are born in America.

Wally: I'm black and I was born in Chicago.

Rose: Because more people come dressed up like they want to.

Wally: How do they dress up?

Rose: You know, like going to church or someplace.

Wally: You mean if they're black?

Rose: They can dress up like they want to.

Wally: I see what she means.
Like getting dressed up to go to church?

Rose: Like they want to.

Wally: Not in a black dress, right?
You can wear a white dress?

Rose: Yes. (p. 47)

Following McDermott's approach (McDermott, 1987), the degree of support offered by classmates and teachers during different classroom events can be assessed to determine whether a particular child is likely to be successful in them. Through such an analysis McDermott found that certain events allowed full participation of children with learning difficulties, whereas others, such as test taking or reading groups, promoted failure.

Besides interviewing and analyzing particular interactions between children and teachers, a classroom ethnography can include an analysis of how daily activities are structured. Ethnographic interviews can be done with participants in classroom events to obtain their depictions of the types and structure of events that take place regularly. Information of this kind can be used when designing interventions to help children participate better in their classrooms, and can help clinicians develop collaborative relationships with classroom teachers to design congenial learning events for children with language-learning problems.

This focus on particualr events in classrooms can supplant current approaches that classify educational approaches as "structured" or "nonstructured" and assign children to classrooms on the basis of what is seen as their "need for structure." The approach presented here suggests that the ways in which events promote success or failure may be a more relevant dimension than degree of structure, and that children's knowledge of events may be more crucial to their performance than the degree to which the events are structured.

LANGUAGE INTERVENTION IN THE CLASSROOM

Ethnographic analyses can lead naturally to classroom interventions in which activities are designed to create more congenial learning environments for children with problems. An example of a classroom that carries no penalty for problem performances of children with learning difficulties is Vivian Paley's kindergarten. Paley (1990) discussed her approach to such children, laying out her philosophy that children are not "learning disabled" or "slow" or even "misbehaving." She provided the following example in her recount of a conversation with her student teachers:

> I could view misbehavior as "bad" and therefore punishable, or consider these unwanted acts to be misreading of a script-in-progress, awkward stage business that needed reworking. We don't fire the actors just because the early rehearsals are unwieldy. We analyze the script to bring out its inherent logic and to improve the acting.
>
> This notion of viewing misbehavior as poor stage acting appealed to me. Why not create my own stories in which to suggest alterations in behavior. Certainly William needed another perspective in the doll corner.
>
> "William, could you pretend to be a wolf that doesn't knock things over? 'Once upon a time there was an angry wolf and his wolf mother was far away in the den but a different mother let him in and he didn't growl...'" (pp. 90–91)

Paley aims to create classroom events in which children can learn and feel successful. So, rather than focus solely on helping the child fit the classroom context, one might take Paley's approach and change the contexts to be in keeping with the child's understandings and abilities. One way Paley developed facilitatory contexts in classrooms was to encourage children to work cooperatively, as exemplified by the support that Wally gave to Rose when she was attempting to convey her thoughts (see p. 86).

A second way Paley created contextual support for children with learning problems was to understand the child's apparently inappropriate performance and figure out how to respond positively to it. Examples of this are given throughout her book, *The Boy Who Would Be a Helicopter* (Paley, 1990; see Paley's comments above). Another example of the potential of this competency-based approach is provided by Michaels (1990) in a description of how a classroom teacher with a bias toward topic-centered discourse began to appreciate and respond positively to the episode structure of her black student. Rather than devalue the student's event description, which seemed to her to be disorganized, the teacher asked the student how the parts of the description were related. The student replied easily and matter of factly. The teacher reported to Michaels: "You know, its a whole lot easier to get them to make the connections clear, if you assume that the connections are there in the first place" (p. 115).

A third approach, also exemplified by Paley, is to create classroom contexts that focus directly on students' understanding of events. In Paley's case, she couched her event learning in the form of stories which the children told and enacted. This "event-based curricular approach" already exists in many classrooms for children who are severely handicapped. The

goal of "functionally based classrooms" is to teach students how to participate in everyday events. The emphasis may be on "activities of daily living,"
which has been part of the specialty of occupational therapy, or on vocational training, the specialty of teachers of retarded children. Both types of
training are ready-made contexts for the speech-language pathologist who
is interested in using events to help children think about the world and
communicate appropriately in different, commonly occurring contexts. The
addition of speech-language pathology to the event-based training programs already in place could help children create event representations
that allow them to make sense of the event and to communicate creatively
within it.

The following example illustates how an event representation focus can
be added to already developed programs. The training procedure is taken
from a vocational program developed by Black (1984) for preparing students who are severely handicapped for community jobs:

Activity: Waiting for, boarding, and riding bus

Skill:
1. Identifies bus stop.
2. Estimates time of arrival.
3. Waits with socially appropriate behavior.
4. Watches for bus.
5. When bus comes into view, reads signs and readies token.
6. Lets passengers disembark from bus.
7. Waits turn and boards bus.
8. Deposits token.
9. Sits with peer.
10. Watches for exit landmarks.
11. Pulls cord.
12. Exits bus. (p. 3)

As the program is presented, the goal is to get the student to carry out the
12 steps of the program. Taking the event representation focus, we could
add to the behavioral goals of performing the steps a second goal: understanding the events presupposed by the steps. This focus would lead to a
different presentation of the sequences of behaviors to promote a structuring of the elements into a coherent event representation. For example, the
behaviors might be conceptually organized into segments that involve
waiting for the bus, getting on it, keeping track of when to get off, and getting off, relating socially to a peer, to the bus driver, and/or to a stranger.
Each segment has its own logic, deictic organization, action, and role structure. Understanding that buses cost money would create a meaningful context for figuring out what to do with the token. Understanding that the cord
rings a bell which signals the driver to stop the bus would take care of what
to do to get off the bus.

WHERE MIGHT WE GO FROM HERE?

What is likely to be the effort of speech-language pathologists considering event representations as they carry out assessments and intervention with children who have language impairments? There are two possible scenarios for how event analysis and event therapy will affect current clinical approaches. Attention to events might simply be added to what clinicians currently do and be embraced by them as communicative intent or as conversational turn-taking was in the 1970s. *The additive scenario* would mean that clinicians do everything they are already doing, and add analysis and therapy approaches for dealing with children's event representations. A second possibility is that a full consideration of events will lead to substantive changes in clinical approaches, as did the pragmatics revolution of the late 1970s and 1980s (Duchan, 1984). My hope is that the *substantive change scenario* will be played out in the next 10 years. If this were to take place, speech-language pathologists will change how they think about children with communication disorders, how and where they do assessments and therapy, and what they assess and teach; and those changes will lead to different types of diagnostic reports.

CHANGING CLINICIANS' VIEWS OF CHILDREN WITH COMMUNICATION DISORDERS

The incorporation of event evaluations into clinical procedures, if done with care and insight, could allow clinicians to better understand why children behave in unconventional ways. Children who are now considered to be inappropriate, incoherent, disorganized, or inattentive, once evaluated within their own ways of understanding might be seen as appropriate, given the way they frame the world. Several examples have been given in the literature reviewed here for how this change could take place: The child whose teacher saw her as dependent was found to be unfamiliar with the event (tic-tac-toe) (Schultz, 1979). The child who seemed to have difficulty creating organized event descriptions was able to provide a coherent rendition of her ideas when asked (Michaels, 1986). The child whose teacher rejected her contributions during sharing time understood what the teacher wanted, but preferred her own cultural form of topical organization (Michaels & Cazden, 1986).

Notions of diagnostic categories, such as "preservation of sameness" in autism or "behavioral disorder," can be more richly understood within an event-based approach which includes ethnographic methods such as interviews and participant observation and field notes. For example, Temple Grandin's fixations on events were seen as functional and minor irritations by her and her relatives; Clark's temper tantrums in the classroom occurred during unstructured time so they were interpreted as reflections of his insecurities about not being able to predict what was going to happen.

Clinicians' current inadvertent biases toward children from cultural backgrounds different from their own may become apparent and minimized when they begin to understand how a child's cultural group carries out and interprets events. For example, Westby (1990) has pointed out how role relations differ in different cultures and can account for a child's or family member's apparent reticence to participate in a school event or an interview (see Westby, 1990, for specific examples).

CHANGING ASSESSMENT APPROACHES

Determining what children know about everyday events can best be done by observing children as they engage in them. This would require that clinicians conduct assessments in arenas familiar and significant to the child. Given this goal, the place in which assessments are done will need to change so that events can be studied as they happen, where they happen.

Current views of language are also likely to change when children's event participation and knowledge of events are evaluated, resulting in a change in the target areas of assessment. Rather than seeing morphology and syntax as a system of isolatable rules, from an event perspective, certain forms can be seen to serve particular functions in event descriptions: past tense serving as expressions of past events and being used most efficiently in contexts in which familiar or emotional events are described (Lucariello, 1990; Miller & Sperry, 1988); embedded clauses as first appearing in contexts of consciousness verbs (think, wish, afraid) which express characters' subjective impressions of the event being described (Bloom et al., 1980); and interclausal connectives serving as discourse markers which express discontinuity, temporal and causal relations in children's early event descriptions (Segal, Duchan, & Scott, in press).

Further, early communicative acts and first words can be seen as event related (requests for routines; indicators that events are completed) and as contextually tied to the children's event representations rather than as isolatable intents and unrelated vocabulary items. Techniques for coding intents and assessing vocabulary will need to include their contextual embeddedness.

Also, rather than seeing children as having fixed knowledge of language, a single competence, it would be predicted from the performance of normal children that children who are communicatively handicapped will perform more competently when they are engaged in familiar events. So clinicians will need to talk about different capabilities of children in different event contexts.

Evaulations not only of children's knowledge of language structure (phonology, morphology, and syntax) but also their participation in and knowledge of events will need to be added. Attention to event knowledge is likely to lead to an improvement in clinicians' ability to evaluate events for whether they provide positive learning contexts. Thus event analysis can be used to assess contexts such as classroom events for whether they would offer congenial experiences for children who are communicatively handicapped.

Finally, ways to collect naturally occurring events and to analyze them as structured entities will need to be added to assessment approaches. Besides analyzing for roles, time, cause, and deictic structuring, clinicians will need to be open to other areas which hold the events together such as affect relations or different types of topical coherences.

CHANGING APPROACHES TO LANGUAGE INTERVENTION

The focus on event representation will give new importance to events in language intervention. Moving from traditional language intervention methods which have, until recently, been formatted in lesson-like discourse (see Panagos, Bobkoff, & Scott, 1986; Prutting, Bagshaw, Goldstein, Juskowitz, & Umen, 1978), interventions of the future will focus on teaching language structures in contexts in which they will be actually used—grocery stores, restaurants, classroom reading groups, work settings. This shift will require new skills in creating nonintrusive elicitation approaches when particular language structures are targeted and will require that therapy be conducted outside the "speech room" and in the world in which the everyday events take place.

A second possibility for carrying out intervention in the contexts in which the events ordinarily occur is to have the parents and teachers do it. (For well-developed examples of such an approach see Bromwich, 1981; Girolametto, Greenberg, and Manolson, 1986.) Under this concept, the clinician assumes the role of consultant and advisor rather than working directly with the child. Parents and teachers are in a better position than clinicians to carry out scaffolding and formatting procedures because they have a more developed understanding of the children's event knowledge for events that regularly occur at home and at school.

Besides the where and who of intervention, the what or content of intervention is likely to change with a shift in emphasis from language form to event knowledge. Once assessment approaches can identify particular aspects of event knowledge that are absent or underdeveloped in the child's representation, clinicians will be able to set goals and design methods to help the child acquire that knowledge. For example, it has been hypothesized that autistic children lack knowledge of how others think or feel, which would lead them to have representations lacking in the area of role structuring. Therapy techniques could be devised to help children understand role reciprocity and the subjectivity of different participants.

CHANGING APPROACHES TO REPORT WRITING

I have been arguing that a focus on children's event knowledge can lead to notable changes in how clinicians think about children, and how they carry out clinical approaches to them. These changes will be directly reflected in report writing, since reports are closely tied to what clinicians' think and do. I would propose several directions for changes in reports which would be consistent with the new concepts emanating from considerations of events.

First, the sections of current reports that describe the child and the child's medical and developmental history will need to be broadened to include ethnographic interview information. This section of diagnostic reports ordinarily is written as factual and objective and includes information about developmental milestones and significant health problems. Information that has not been witnessed directly or reported in professional documents is treated as nonfactual and marked with evidentials such as "reported by the mother," "according to Mr. Gonzales," or "the teacher indicated."

Evidentials, which credit someone else with the information, can be interpreted to mean that the clinician does not necessarily agree that the information provided is true. Reports by parents of the child's birthdate or address are not couched in evidentials, whereas information about high fevers or age of first words are. This separates information marked with evidentials as less believable than information asserted directly.

The idea of the ethnographic interview, on the other hand, is to regard information provided by an informant as legitimate and to include it as part of the record. When a teacher reports that a child is distractible, the interviewer presupposes the category and asks when he is distractible (Westby, 1990). The idea tied to ethnographic approaches is that there may be a number of interpretations of particular people, behaviors, and events, and each is important and worthy of consideration. The goal is not to find the facts, but to uncover how people interpret the facts and to compare their interpretations with one another.

Thus the background history section of reports written with ethnographic sensitivity is likely to indicate who the informant is at the beginning of a section and to indicate within the section (free from evidential language) the information presented by that person.

The section that describes the assessment procedures would need to indicate what events the child engages in, with whom, and in what situations. Also relevant would be how familiar the child is with the events and the interactants. Samples of the child's behaviors need to be collected in different events that are selected to answer particular assessment questions. Given the understanding that events can affect the degree of competence shown by the child, details of the events used to collect information about the child would be needed no matter what is being assessed, whether it be phonology, syntax, or event knowledge.

Results of an assessment done with a sensitivity to the role of events might report the child's performance in different types of events. This would be especially significant if the child's performance differs depending on his or her event familiarity. Thus, rather than having sections on the child's test results and language sample analyses, one might find sections on the child's performance in events that provide contextual support, such as everyday, enjoyable events in which the child experiences success versus events that are context stripped, such as tests or lessons. Taking this tack, McDermott found that his subject, Adam, appeared learning disabled in some contexts, but not in others.

A clinician is in a much better position to draw ecologically valid conclusions if the assessment includes an analysis of the child's performance in everyday contexts and a report of how the child and others interpret the events. One might conclude, for example, that the child's difficulty is due to a cultural difference. The ethnographic approach to analyzing children's event knowledge should result in more reports that conclude that the problem is in the meeting of different cultures, not in the child.

If the child is found to have a problem, the event assessment can lead to better motivated recommendations. Events that were found in the assessment to provide conditions for facilitating the occurrence of the targeted structures should be incorporated in early therapy, moving from those types of supportive events to ones within which the child produced more "errors." Or events can be constructed which would provide contexts for using targeted forms. For example, having a child talk about immediately preceding, emotionally laden, highly familiar events would be a logical context for teaching past tense forms. Or, if the aspects of event knowledge itself are targeted as an area of intervention, then scaffolding and formatting techniques for teaching event structure would be warranted.

These changes will require a spirit of adventure and a willingness and know how to create social change. One person who assumed such a leadership role in creating changes in the field was Carol Prutting. She was always walking along our frontier, pointing to where we should go and leading us in that direction. I trust she would be in sympathy with the event-based approach taken in this chapter. It is consistent with her ideas about cohesion in text (Mentis & Prutting, 1987), her ideas about synergy in systems of knowledge (Prutting, 1979; Prutting & Elliott, 1976), and her focus on pragmatics and ecological validity in assessment (Prutting, 1982). I wonder what Carol would project over the next few years. She would have loved to have been asked. All we can do now is build upon Carol's past contributions and take up her spirit of adventure. In so doing, we can show our appreciation to her for having brought us so far.

REFERENCES

Ainsworth, M., & Wittig, B. (1969). Attachment and exploratory behavior in one year olds in a stranger situation. In B. Foss (Ed.), *Determinants of infant behavior.* New York: John Wiley and Sons.

Astington, J., Harris, P., & Olson, D. (Eds). (1988). *Developing theories of mind.* New York: Cambridge University Press.

Banfield, A. (1982). *Unspeakable sentences: Narration and representation in the language of fiction.* Boston, MA: Routledge & Kegan Paul.

Baron–Cohen, S. (1989). The autistic child's theory of mind: A case of specific developmental delay. *Journal of Child Psychology and Psychiatry, 30,* 285–297.

Bates, E., Benigni, L., Bretherton, I., Camaioni, L., & Volterra, V. (1979). Cognition and communication from 9–13 months. In E. Bates (Ed.), *The emergence of symbols.* New York: Academic Press.

Black, J. (1984). A step-by-step-process for developing a vocational job site in the community. Unpublished handout. Syracuse, NY.

Bloom, L., & Lahey, M. (1978). *Language development and language disorders.* New York: John Wiley and Sons.

Bloom, L., Lahey, M., Hood, L., Lifter, K., & Fiess, K. (1980). Complex sentences: Acquisition of syntactic connectives and the semantic relations they encode. *Journal of Child Language, 7,* 235–261.

Bowlby, J. (1969). *Attachment and loss* (Vol. 1). London: Hogarth Press.

Bretherton, I. (1984). Representing the social world in symbolic play: Reality and fantasy. In I. Bretherton (Ed.), *Symbolic play: The development of social understanding.* New York: Academic Press.

Bromwich, R. (1981). *Working with parents and infants.* Baltimore, MD: University Park Press.

Brown, R. (1973). *A first language: The early stages.* Cambridge, MA: Harvard University Press.

Bruner, J. (1975). The ontogenesis of speech acts. *Journal of Child Language, 2,* 1–19.

Bruner, J. (1983). The acquisition of pragmatic commitments. In R. Golinkoff (Ed.), *The transition from prelinguistic to linguistic communication.* Hillsdale, NJ: Lawrence Erlbaum.

Bruner, J., & Sherwood, V. (1976). Early rule structure: The case of peekaboo. In J. Bruner, A. Jolly, & K. Sylva (Eds.), *Play: Its role in evolution and development.* New York: Penguin.

Carter, A. (1975). The transformation of sensorimotor morphemes into words: A case study of the development of "more" and "mine." *Journal of Child Language, 2,* 233–250.

Cassell, J. (1986). Then . . . and then . . . and then: The acquisition of temporal reference in children's narrative. Unpublished thesis, University of Edinburgh, UK.

Cazden, C. (1979). Peekaboo as an instructional model: Discourse development at home and at school. *Papers and Reports on Child Language Development, 17,* 1–29. (Available from Department of Linguistics: Stanford University.)

Cazden, C. (1988). *Classroom discourse,* Portsmouth, NH: Heinemann.

Clark, E., & Garnica, O. (1974). Is he coming or going? On the acquisition of deictic verbs. *Journal of Verbal Learning and Verbal Behavior, 13,* 559–572.

Constable, C. (1986). The application of scripts in the organization of language intervention. In K. Nelson (Ed.), *Event knowledge* (pp. 205–230). Hillsdale, NJ: Lawrence Erlbaum.

Damico, J., Maxwell, M., & Kovarsky, D. (Eds.). (1990). Ethnographic inquiries into communication sciences and disorders. *Journal of Childhood Communication Disorders, 13*(1).

DasGupta, P., & Bryant, P. (1989). Young children's causal inferences. *Child Development, 60,* 1138–1146.

Dore, J. (1975). Holophrases, speech acts, and language universals. *Journal of Child Language, 2,* 21–40.

Dore, J., Franklin, M., Miller, R., & Ramer, A. (1976). Transitional phenomena in early language acquisition. *Journal of Child Language, 3,* 13–28.

Duchan, J. (1984). Language assessment: The pragmatics revolution. In R. Naremore (Ed.), *Language sciences.* San Diego, CA: College-Hill Press.

Duchan, J. (1990). Deictic centers in children's oral narratives. Unpublished manuscript.

Fantz, R. (1963). Pattern vision in new born infants. *Science, 140,* 296–297.

Ferreiro, E., & Sinclair, H. (1971). Temporal relationships in language. *International Journal of Psychology, 6,* 39–47.

Fitzgerald, H. (1979). Autonomic pupillary reflex activity during early infancy and its relation to social and nonsocial visual stimuli. *Journal of Experimental Child Psychology, 6,* 470–482.

Fivush, R. (1984). Learning about school. *Child Development, 55,* 1679–1709.

Fivush, R., & Mandler, J. (1985). Developmental changes in the understanding of temporal sequence. *Child Development, 56,* 1439–1446.

French, L., & Nelson, K. (1985). *Children's acquisition of relational terms: Some ifs, ors, and buts.* New York: Springer-Verlag.

Gerhardt, J. (1988). From discourse to semantics: The development of verb morphology and forms of self reference in the speech of a two-year-old. *Journal of Child Language, 15,* 337–393.

Girolametto, L., Greenberg, J., & Manolson, A. (1986). Developing dialogue skills: The Hanen early language parent program. *Seminars in Speech and Language, 7,* 367–381.

Gleitman, L. (1989). The structural sources of verb meaning. *Papers and Reports on Child Language Development, 28.* (Available from Department of Linguistics, Stanford University.)

Golinkoff, R. (1975). Semantic development in infants: The concepts of agent and recipient. *Merrill-Palmer Quarterly, 21,* 181–193.

Golinkoff, R., & Harding, C. (1980, March). *Infants' expectations of the movement potential of inanimate objects.* Paper presented at the International Conference on Infant Studies, New Haven, CT.

Gopnik, A. (1982). Words and plans: Early language and the development of intelligent action. *Journal of Child Language, 9,* 303–318.

Gopnik, A., & Meltzoff, A. (1985). From people, to plans, to objects: Changes in the meaning of early words and their relation to cognitive development. *Journal of Pragmatics, 9,* 495–512.

Grandin, T., & Scariano, M. (1986). *Evergence: Labeled autistic.* Novato, CA: Arena Press.

Greenfield, P., & Smith, J. (1976). *The structure of communication in early language development.* New York: Academic Press.

Hewitt, L., & Duchan, J. (1989). *Subjectivity in child narrative: Beyond story grammars.* Paper presented at the New York State Speech, Language, and Hearing Association, Kiamesha, NY.

Hood, L., & Bloom, L. (1979). What, when, and how about why: A longitudinal study of early expressions of causality. *Monographs of the Society for Research in Child Development, 44*(6).

Hymes, D. (1972). Models of the interaction of language and social life. In J. Gumperz & D. Hymes (Eds.), *Directions in sociolinguistics: The ethnography of communication* (pp. 35–71). New York: Holt, Rinehart & Winston.

James, W. (1890). *Principles of psychology* (Vol. 1). New York: W. W. Norton.

Kanner, L. (1943). Autistic disturbances of affective contact. *Nervous Child, 2,* 217–250.

Kauffman, B. (1976). *Sonrise.* New York: Warner Books.

Kovarsky, D., Crago, M. (1991). Toward the ethnography of communication disorders. *National Student Speech Language Hearing Association Journal, 18.*

Lahey, M. (1988). *Language disorders and language development.* New York: Macmillan.

Leslie, A. (1987). Pretense and representation: The origins of "theory of mind." *Psychological Review, 94,* 412–426.

Lucariello, J. (1990). Freeing talk from the here-and-how: The role of event knowledge and maternal scaffolds. *Topics in Language Disorders, 10,* 14–29.

Lund, N., & Duchan, J. (1987, April). What happened in school today? Mini-seminar presented to New York State Speech, Language, and Hearing Association Convention, Monticello, NY.

Lund, N., & Duchan, J. (1988). *Assessing children's language in naturalistic contexts,* (2nd ed.). Engelwood Cliffs, NJ: Prentice-Hall.

Macrae, A. (1976). Movement and location in the acquisition of deictic verbs. *Journal of Child Language, 3,* 191–204.

McCabe, A., & Peterson, C. (1985). A naturalistic study of the production of causal connectives by children. *Journal of Child Language, 12,* 145–149.

McDermott, R. (1987, July). *The acquisition of a child by a learning disability.* Paper presented at a conference on Context, Cognition, and Activity, New York.

Mehan, H. (1979). *Learning lessons.* Cambridge, MA: Harvard University Press.

Menn, L. (1976). *Pattern, control, and contrast in beginning speech: A case study in the acquisition of word form and function.* Unpublished doctoral dissertation, University of Illinois, Champaign-Urbana.

Mentis, M., & Prutting, C. (1987). Cohesion in the discourse of normal and head-injured adults. *Journal of Speech and Hearing Research, 30,* 88–98.

Michaels, S. (1981). "Sharing time": Children's narrative style and differential access to literacy. *Language in Society, 10,* 423–442.

Michaels, S. (1986). Narrative presentations: An oral preparation for literacy with first graders. In J. Cook–Gumperz (Ed.), *The social construction of literacy* (pp. 94–116). New York: Cambridge University Press.

Michaels, S., & Cazden, C. (1986). Teacher/child collaboration as oral preparation for literacy. In B. Schieffelin & P. Gilmore (Eds.), *The acquisition of literacy: Ethnographic perspectives.* Norwood, NJ: Ablex Publishing.

Michaels, S., & Collins, J. (1984). Oral discourse styles: Classroom interaction and the acquisition of literacy. In D. Tannen (Ed.), *Coherence in spoken and written discourse.* Norwood, NJ: Ablex Publishing.

Miller, P., & Garvey, C. (1984). Mother-baby role play: Its origins in social support. In I. Bretherton (Ed.), *Symbolic play: The representation of social understanding.* New York: Academic Press.

Miller, P., & Sperry, L. (1988). Early talk about the past: The origins of conversational stories of personal experience. *Journal of Child Language, 15,* 293–315.

Murphy, C., & Messer, J. (1977). Mothers, infants, and pointing: A study of a gesture. In H. Schaffer (Ed.), *Studies in mother-infant interaction.* New York: Academic Press.

Nelson, K. (1983). The derivation of concepts and categories from event representations. In E. Scholnick (Ed.), *New trends in conceptual representation: Challenges to Piaget's theory?* Hillsdale, NJ: Lawrence Erlbaum.

Nelson, K. (1986). *Event knowledge, structure, and function in development.* Hillsdale, NJ: Lawrence Erlbaum.

Nelson, K., & Gruendel, J. (1981). Generalized event representations: Basic building blocks of cognitive development. In M. Lamb & A. Brown (Eds.), *Advances in developmental psychology,* (pp. 131–158). Hillsdale, NJ: Lawrence Erlbaum.

Ninio, A., & Bruner, J. (1978). The achievement and antecedents of labeling. *Journal of Child Language, 5,* 1–15.

O'Connell, B., & Gerard, A. (1985). Scripts and scraps: The development of sequential understanding. *Child Development, 56,* 671–681.

Paley, V. (1981). *Wally's stories.* Cambridge, MA: Harvard University Press.

Paley, V. (1990). *The boy who would be a helicopter.* Cambridge, MA: Harvard University Press.

Panagos, J., Bobkoff, K., & Scott, C. (1986). Discourse analysis of language intervention. *Child Language Teaching and Therapy, 2,* 211–229.

Peterson, C., & McCabe, A. (1983). *Developmental psycholinguistics.* New York: Plenum.

Piaget, J. (1963). *The origins of intelligence in children.* New York: W. W. Norton.

Piaget, J. (1972). *The child's conception of physical causality.* Totowa, NJ: Littlefield Adams & Co.

Pitcher, E., & Prelinger, E. (1963). *Children tell stories: An analysis of fantasy.* New York: International Universities Press.

Prutting, C. (1979). Process\processin\: The action of moving forward progressively from one point to another on the way to completion. *Journal of Speech and Hearing Disorders, 44,* 3–30.

Prutting, C. (1982). Pragmatics as social competence. *Journal of Speech and Hearing Disorders, 47,* 123–134.

Prutting, C., Bagshaw, N., Goldstein, N., Juskowitz, S., & Umen, I. (1978). Clinician-child discourse: Some preliminary questions. *Journal of Speech and Hearing Disorders, 47,* 123–133.

Prutting, C., & Elliott, J. (1976). *Synergy: Toward a model of language.* Paper presented at the Annual Convention of the American Speech and Hearing Association, Houston, TX.

Ratner, N., & Bruner, J. (1978). Games, social exchange and the acquisition of language. *Journal of Child Language, 5,* 391–401.

Roberts, E. (1989). *Communication during the transition to first words: A look at the autistic and normal dyadic process.* Unpublished doctoral dissertation. The Graduate School and University Center of the City University of New York.

Ripich, D., & Spinelli, F. (1985). An ethnographic approach to assessment and intervention. In D. Ripich & F. Spinelli (Eds.), *School discourse problems* (pp. 199–217). San Diego, CA: College-Hill Press.

Ross, B., & Berg, C. (1990). Individual differences in script reports: Implications for language assessment. *Topics in Language Disorders, 10,* 30–44.

Sachs, J. (1987). Preschool boys' and girls' language use in pretend play. In S. Philips, S. Steele, & C. Tanz (Eds.), *Language, gender, and sex in comparative perspective* (pp. 178–188). New York: Cambridge University Press.

Scaife, M., & Bruner, J. (1975). The capacity for joint visual attention in the infant. *Nature, 253,* 265–266.

Schank, R., & Abelson, R. (1977). *Scripts, plans, goals, and understanding.* Hillsdale, NJ: Lawrence Erlbaum.

Schiffrin, D. (1987). *Discourse markers.* New York: Cambridge University Press.

Schwartz, R., Chapman, K., Terrell, B., Prelock, P., & Rowan, L. (1985). *Journal of Speech and Hearing Disorders, 50,* 31–39.

Scollon, R. (1976). *Conversations with a one-year-old.* Honolulu: University Press of Hawaii.

Segal, E., Duchan, J., & Scott, P. (in press). The role of interclausal connectives in narrative structuring: Evidence from adults' interpretation of simple stories. *Discourse Processes.*

Shatz, M., Wellman, H., & Silber, S. (1983). The acquisition of mental verbs: A systematic investigation of the first reference to mental state. *Cognition, 14,* 301–321.

Shultz, J. (1979). Its not whether you win or lose, it's how you play the game. In O. Garnica & M. King (Eds.), *Language, children, and society.* New York: Pergamon Press.

Simons, J. (1974). Observations of compulsive behavior in autism. *Journal of Autism and Childhood Schizophrenia, 4,* 1–10.

Snyder–McLean, L., Solomonson, B., McLean, J., & Sack, S. (1984). Structuring joint action routines: A strategy for facilitating communication and language development in the classroom. *Seminars in Speech and Language, 5,* 213–228.

Stechler, G., & Latz, E. (1966). Some observations on attention and arousal in the human infant. *Journal of the American Academy of Child Psychiatry, 5,* 517–525.

Stern, D. (1985). *The interpersonal world of the infant.* New York: Basic Books.

Sternberg, L., Battle, C., & Hill, J. (1980). Prelanguage communication programming for the severely and profoundly handicapped. *JASH, 5,* 224–233.

Stillman, R., & Battle, C. (1984). Developing prelanguage communication in the severely handicapped: An interpretation of the VanDijk method. *Seminars in Speech and Language, 5,* 159–168.

Sugarman, S. (1984). The development of preverbal communication: Its contribution and limits in promoting the development of language. In R. Schiefelbusch & J. Pickar (Eds.), *The acquisition of communicative competence* (pp. 23–67). Baltimore, MD: University Park Press.

Sutton–Smith, B. (1981). *The folkstories of children.* Philadelphia: University of Pennsylvania Press.

Verba, M., Stambak, M., & Sinclair, H. (1982). Physical knowledge and social interaction in children from 18 to 24 months of age. In G. Forman (Ed.), *Action and thought.* New York: Academic Press.

Wales, R. (1986). Deixis. In P. Fletcher & M. Garman (Eds.), *Language acquisition.* New York: Cambridge University Press.

Weist, R. (1986). Tense and aspect. In P. Fletcher & M. Garman (Eds.), *Language acquisition.* New York: Cambridge University Press.

Wellman, H. (1988). First steps in the child's theorizing about the mind. In J. Astington, P. Harris, & D. Olson (Eds.), *Developing theories of mind* (pp. 64–92). New York: Cambridge University Press.

Werner, H., & Kaplan, B. (1963). *Symbol formation.* New York: John Wiley & Sons.

Westby, C. (1984). Development of narrative language abilities. In G. Wallach & K. Butler (Eds.), *Language learning disabilities in school-age children.* Baltimore, MD: Williams & Wilkins.

Westby, C. (1990). Ethnographic interviewing: Asking the right questions to the right people in the right ways. *Journal of Childhood Communication Disorders, 13,* 101–111.

Wolf, D. (1982). Understanding others: A longitudinal case study of the concept of independent agency. In G. Forman (Ed.), *Action and thought: From sensorimotor schemes to symbol use.* New York: Academic Press.

Wolf, D., & Gardner, H. (1981). On the structure of early symbolization. In R. Schiefelbusch & D. Bricker (Eds.), *Early language acquisition and intervention* (pp. 287–327). Baltimore, MD: University Park Press.

Wolf, D., Rygh, J., & Altshuler, J. (1984). Agency and experience: Actions and states in play narratives. In I. Bretherton (Ed.), *Symbolic play: The development of social understanding* (pp. 195–217). New York: Academic Press.

CHAPTER 4

Using Ethnography to Bring Children's Communicative and Cultural Worlds into Focus

MARTHA B. CRAGO AND ELIZABETH COLE

This is a decade in which we shall once again connect up individuals and their place in society with an appraisal of the disordered.

(Carol Prutting, 1983, p. 251)

In one way or another, all of the chapters in this book are attempts to capture an accurate and intervention-useful picture of the child who is communicatively disordered. The present chapter is about using a special kind of camera lens in striving to achieve a very wide angle as well as a deep dimensional focus. This "lens" provides a view of communicative competence that is well grounded in a language socialization perspective. Taken seriously, this perspective has the potential to create major changes in thinking about language acquisition, usage, assessment, intervention, and research. These changes may prove to be crucial for meaningful intervention with children, in general, but they have particular importance for the rapidly increasing number of children from minority cultures who are being treated by speech-language pathologists from mainstream cultures. Population forecasts for both Canada and the United States show that as much as one third of the speech-language pathology and audiology case-load in the schools will be children from black, Hispanic, Asian, and Native North American cultures within the next decade (ASHA, 1988; Cole, 1989; Crago, 1990a; Shewan, 1988). Speech-language pathologists from these cultures comprise a very small minority of the profession and the vast majority of speech-language pathologists already in practice feel they are unprepared to provide adequate service to children of other cultures (ASHA, 1988; Cole, 1989; Des Bois, 1989; Shewan & Malm, 1989). The stark reality of such demographics is only enhanced by research findings on language socialization that attest to the intertwined nature of culture and language. A culturally sensitive refocusing of our assessment and intervention practices is long overdue.

In the field of communication disorders, a prevailing view of language is that of clinical pragmatics which is thoroughly discussed in other chapters of this volume and elsewhere (Gallagher, 1990; Gallagher & Prutting, 1983; Rees, 1988). The perspectives of clinical pragmatics and language socialization have a number of commonalities. For example, both were derived from a variety of disciplines including linguistics, anthropology, philosophy, and psychology; both can claim early formulations in the late 1960s and early 1970s; both are concerned with how language is used; and both derive meaning regarding communication events from context. However, there are some key conceptual differences between the two which are highlighted in the next section. Inclusion of these key concepts in theoretical, research, and clinical endeavors in the field of communication disorders may help to unlock the full, rich, culturally grounded, and informative context of communicative competence and incompetence.

THE OTHER LENS: ROOTS AND RUDIMENTS OF A LANGUAGE SOCIALIZATION PERSPECTIVE

In the 1970s, Hymes (1974) stated that there was a need for and "an opportunity to develop new bonds, through contributions to the study of verbal behavior that collaboration between anthropology and linguistics can alone provide" (p. 190). He called this new area of study "the ethnography of speaking" and specified the importance of looking at the role of speaking in the socialization of children.

Gumperz and Hymes (1964) formulated the term "communicative competence" (later adopted by the field of communication disorders) to reflect the enlarged scope of communicative abilities that an anthropological ethnography of communication was intended to address. This concept of communicative competence suggested the need for both a new and interdisciplinary approach to language acquisition research. It is evident from the term "ethnography of speaking" that Hymes (1972) felt the ethnographic methodology used in anthropological research would be appropriate to the study of language as a socially and culturally situated phenomenon.

Throughout the 1980s, a number of ethnographic studies of language use have followed Hymes' early lead. Some researchers looked at speech events across cultures (Baugh & Sherzer, 1984; Bauman & Sherzer, 1975, 1989). Others looked at the acquisition of language as it intersects with becoming a competent cultural member (Heath, 1989; Ochs, 1979; Ochs & Schieffelin, 1984; Schieffelin & Eisenberg, 1984). Still others have used the ethnographic approach to study language use in educational contexts (Cook–Gumperz, 1986b; Duranti & Ochs, 1988; Gumperz, 1986; Heath, 1983; Schieffelin & Gilmore, 1986). Although certain ethnographic concepts have been reflected in the clinical practice literature of communication disorders (Cheng, 1987; Iglesias, 1985; Omark, 1981; Rice, 1986; Taylor, 1986a, 1986c; Westby, 1985a, 1985b; Westby & Rouse, 1985), only very recently has the ethnography of speaking approach to research been developed within the field (Damico, Maxwell, & Kovarsky, 1990).

How does this fit with clinical pragmatics in communication disorders? Duranti (1988) provided a cogent explanation of the differences and similarities. He wrote: "What usually distinguishes the ethnographic approach from pragmatic analysis is [ethnography's] stronger concern for the sociocultural context of the use of language, with the specific relationship between language and the local systems of knowledge and social order . . . (p. 213).

The ethnography of speaking approach does not attempt to establish universals and its goal is to preserve the complexity of language use in the descriptions that it produces. This means that:

ethnographers . . . like the people they study . . . struggle both to capture and maintain the whole of the interaction at hand. The elements of one level (e.g., phonological register, lexical choice, discourse strategies) must be related to elements at another level (e.g., social identities, values). . . . In this process, ethnographers act as linking elements between different levels and systems of communication. (p. 220)

For effective intervention with minority culture children, this linking of information among the levels and systems of communication and culture is essential.

RUDIMENTS OF THE LANGUAGE SOCIALIZATION PERSPECTIVE

Following Hymes' lead, a number of anthropological and linguistic researchers have applied ethnographic methodology to the crosscultural study of the development of communicative competence in children

(Boggs, 1985; Clancy, 1986; Crago, 1988; Demuth, 1986; Eisenberg, 1982; Heath, 1986a, 1989, 1990; Ochs, 1988; Philips, 1983; Schieffelin, 1990; Scollon & Scollon, 1981; Smith–Hefner, 1988). In 1986, Ochs and Schieffelin described this approach to the study of language as language socialization (Ochs, 1986; Schieffelin & Ochs, 1986b). Language socialization research, they wrote, differs from other language research, including observational studies and developmental research into pragmatics, because it aims to link "the microanalytic analyses of children's discourse to more general interpretive ethnographic accounts of cultural beliefs and practices of the families, social groups, or communities into which the children are socialized" (Schieffelin & Ochs, 1986a, p. 168). In the same year, Cook–Gumperz (1986a) also articulated the importance of considering language as a "web of words" that helps the child to become a full-fledged member of its society. Language acquisition, according to her, is part of a more general theory of socialization.

The problem for study is how children draw on their knowledge of the world to do things with words and how their perception of the social setting or context shapes the outcomes of the verbal exchanges. . . . To create an adequate theory of language socialization both linguistic and social knowledge must be seen to focus on the social transmission process and the linguistic means through which social knowledge is reproduced. (pp. 47–48)

The result of such a formulation has been an emphasis in the study of language and socialization on the process by which children become competent members of their societies and/or cultures (Cook–Gumperz, 1986a; Cook–Gumperz & Cosaro, 1986; Duranti, 1988; Gumperz, 1986; Heath, 1989, 1990; Ochs, 1988, 1990; Schieffelin, 1990).

Language socialization research has demonstrated that several features of adult-child interaction, discourse patterns, and conversational systems are not universal in nature. Many of the findings reported in the clinical pragmatics studies now appear to be influenced by the fact that the children and parents studied have come predominantly from the North American white middle class. The culturally veiled and socially arranged nature of much of this research (the fact that it is carried out on first-born children interacting primarily with mothers as caregivers in laboratories or in mainstream middle-class homes) has led to a number of misleading conclusions regarding its universality (Ochs & Schieffelin, 1984).

Despite the rich clinical ramifications of this research approach for the communicatively disordered, only a very limited amount of research with a stated language socialization perspective has been undertaken in the field of communication disorders (Crago, 1990b; Rice, 1990). Rice's work with preschoolers with specific language impairments has revealed the social risks and consequences suffered by children whose language disorders make them vulnerable to a breakdown in socialization. Crago's ethnographic language socialization study of Inuit children in northern Quebec has shown that many of our clinical assumptions about communicative interactions between children and their families as well as about language disorders are culturally relative.

CENTRAL CONCEPTS FROM CROSSCULTURAL STUDIES OF COMMUNICATIVE COMPETENCE

Several central concepts have emerged in the literature on language socialization. Schieffelin and Ochs (1986a, 1986b), Ochs (1988) and Schieffelin (1990) have discussed a number of them. Table 4–1 gives an idea of the diversity of cultures that have been studied and the types of issues dealt with in crosscultural language socialization studies. Such studies have shown that by changing the focus and the method of investigation, researchers have begun to unlock notions of language acquisition and language usage as they relate to the social lives of children from numerous and varied cultures.

The features of language socialization shown in Table 4–1 and the cultural roots that underlie them vary from one cultural group to another. It can, therefore, be expected that speech-language pathologists from the majority culture will not share values, assumptions, and patterns of communication with the children from minority cultures that they serve. Frequently such differences or "discontinuities," as they have been called in educational literature, are interpreted by professionals as deficiencies in the children or in their parents. The power differential between the professional and the client can transform interactional differences to which both the professional and the client contribute into an official diagnosis of client deficiency (Cummins, 1989; Erickson, 1987; Gal, 1989). Such deficiency interpretations persist despite the fact that children from minority cultures have been shown to be competent and appropriate learners and communicators in their natal cultures (Tharp, Jordan, Speidel, Hu-Pei Au, Klein, Calkins, Sloat, & Gallimore, 1984) and in school settings where the instructional process has been made culturally congruent (Kawakami & Hu-Pei Au, 1986; Vogt, Jordan, & Tharp, 1987). The penalization of Native and minority culture children that results from the "discontinuities" between home and school have been poignantly documented (Boggs, 1985; Duranti & Ochs, 1988; Erickson, 1987; Heath, 1983; Philips, 1983; Tharp et al., 1984; Trueba, 1988). The practice of speech-language pathology is also affected by cultural differences in the patterns of white middle-class communicative interactions and those of children from minority cultures. After all, speech-language pathologists are, by necessity, in the role of communicative partners with the children who need their services. Taylor and Payne (1983) and Taylor, Payne, and Anderson (1988) have described the sources of cul-

Table 4–1. Language socialization studies: Cultures and concepts

	Routines	Expression of Affect	Clarification
Africa			
Luo (Blount, 1969)			
Kipsigis (Harkness, 1977)			
Basotho (Demuth, 1986)	•		
Canada			
Athabaskans (Scollon & Scollon, 1981)			
Japan			
Japanese			
(Clancy, 1986;		•	
Fischer, 1970)			
Melanesia			
Kawara'ae			
(Watson–Gegeo & Gegeo, 1986)	•		
Polynesia			
Kaluli (Schieffelin, 1979, 1990)	•	•	
Samoans (Ochs, 1982, 1988)		•	•
Tamil Malaysians (Williamson, 1979)			
U.S.A.			
Apache (Basso, 1972)			
Warm Spring Indians (Philips, 1983)			
Navajo (Saville–Troike, 1982)			
Poor Rural Blacks (Ward, 1971)	•		
Working Class Whites (Miller, 1986)	•		
Working Class Blacks (Heath, 1983)	•		
Working Class Whites (Heath, 1983)			
Middle Class Whites			
(Heath, 1983;			
Psycholinguistic Literature)	•		•
Mexicano / Chicano			
(Eisenberg, 1986;	•	•	
Coles, 1977)			
Hawaiians (Boggs, 1985)	•		

Acknowledgment of Others	Questioning	Accomodation	Silence	Genres of Narrative	Literacy
			•		
			•		
			•		•
			•		
		•			
•		•	•		•
			•		
			•		
	•		•		
			•		
	•			•	•
	•			•	•
	•			•	•
		•			
			•		
				•	•

tural bias that exist in most of the evaluative measures presently in use with children from minority cultures. Furthermore, Taylor (1986a) claimed that:

All clinical encounters are cultural events and, as such, the clinician should develop an ethnological approach to all clinical practice. . . . Clinicians should

1. View each clinical encounter as a socially situated communicative event that is subject to the cultural rules governing such events by both the clinician and the client.
2. Recognize possible sources of conflicts in cultural assumptions and communicative norms in clients prior to clinical encounters, and take steps to prevent them from occurring during service delivery.
3. Recognize that learning and culture are ongoing processes that should result in constant reassessment and revision of ideas and greater sensitivity to cultural diversity. (p. 17)

The socialization of children to their culture is, indeed, an important and delicate process in which language and communication patterns have an integral and crucial role. The violation of minority cultures' cultural and socialization practices by a lack of awareness of the importance of this relationship prevents the formulation of appropriate assessment and intervention strategies for these populations.

The ethnographic, language socialization perspective, therefore, can infuse pragmatic study with an increased amount of context and, in doing so, change the nature of it. The interpersonal context usually associated with pragmatic and conversational analysis is broadened to include a wider context (Lavandera, 1988). In this approach to language study, then, socialization and the study of communicative competence can be seen as phenomena that sustain and are sustained by social and cultural context. The goal of such study is "not to strive for simplicity measures or one-dimensional patterns, but rather to capture, through ethnography and linguistic analysis, the complexity of the human experience as defined and revealed in everyday discourse" (Duranti, 1988, p. 225). In communication disorders, the goal is to inform and transform our clinical practice in such a way that the variability and complexity of human discourse and human experience can become an asset, not a deficit, in our intervention efforts.

THE UNLOCKING OF SOCIOCULTURAL CONTEXT: ETHNOGRAPHIC METHODOLOGY

Preserving and investigating the complexity of human experience is not a simple matter in research or in clinical endeavors. It requires going beyond "multi-level, multi-variate, interactive behavioral descriptions" (Gallagher, 1990, p. 5) to evolve a highly contextualized and flexible approach to the

study of communication and its disorders. Along with a socially construc-
tionistic view of the study of language has come a movement away from experimental and hypothesis-testing methods to naturalistic and interpretive
ones (Corsaro & Streeck, 1986). Linking now occurs between the microanalysis of interactional fragments provided by clinical pragmatics studies
with society's macro-structures, that is, the cultural values and patterns as
well as the historical, political, and economic situations that surround a
child (Gal, 1989; Heath, 1990; Mehan, 1987).

Schieffelin (1979) has described the importance of this flexibility and
sensitivity in the crosscultural study of child language by recounting the
difficulties that researchers encountered when using Slobin's (1967) *A Field
Manual for the Cross-Cultural Study of the Acquisition of Communicative Competence*. This manual consisted of, among other things, certain specified experimental procedures. Many of these procedures required the people being
studied to carry out tasks that were inappropriate to their particular cultures. The lack of utility of such tasks led researchers to the realization that a
much more flexible approach was needed. The ethnographic methodology employed in language socialization studies provides researchers with
this kind of flexible and sensitive tool for studying language in a variety of
settings. A priori decisions need not be made about the kind of tasks participants will be asked to do; they are simply studied in the context of their
everyday lives. Moreover, ethnographic descriptions provide additional information by seeking the participants' point of view and their interpreta
tions of events.

The remainder of this chapter, then, clarifies and expands on the assumptions and processes of ethnographically based knowledge. The aim is to
provide a way for clinicians to carry out their clinical investigations of communicative competence and incompetence in a more culturally flexible
manner. The socially and culturally situated nature of language means that
a methodology that is sensitive to context is of particular utility to professionals in communication disorders.

ASSUMPTIONS OF ETHNOGRAPHY

This section describes nine basic assumptions that characterize the ethnographic approach and its methodology.

1. *The everyday details of life can be made comprehensible.* Ethnography studies the details of people's everyday lived experiences. In doing so, it attempts to build knowledge in which the social action of one group of people
can be made coherent and comprehensible to another group of people
(Agar, 1986). The knowledge base of ethnography is constructed from the
daily life details of what people do, what people say, and what people say
they ought to do or say.

Clinically, in the field of communication disorders, an attempt is made to make sense out of the lived experience of the client being treated. What they are able to say, what they do with what they say, and what they or their significant others feel they ought to be saying or doing is all investigated. Ideally, assessment will lead not only to a description of the speech and language abilities but also to a sensitive understanding of the communicative world and world view of the children and families that we serve.

2. *Accurate description requires extensive contact.* Ethnography is empirical study based on extensive contact with the people being studied. Theories and hypotheses are based or "grounded" in data rather than proposed beforehand and proven by testing (Glaser & Strauss, 1967; Rennie, Phillips, & Quartaro, 1988).

In clinical practice, the concept of diagnostic therapy implies long-term empirical study and the development of a diagnosis that is grounded in rich experimental findings. In addition, appropriate service to a cultural minority group implies speech-language pathologists need to learn about and, if possible, steep themselves in the ways of the cultural groups that they treat.

3. *Interpretation is an inherent part of observation.* The job of the ethnographer and of the clinician is not just to describe what is going on, but rather to make sense of it. Heath (1982) likened ethnography to a "background tapestry . . . busily detailed, seemingly chaotic; [which] however, upon closer look, reveals patterns, and with repeated scrutiny reveals other patterns" (p. 44). Ethnography is an interpretative enterprise (Erickson, 1986; Geertz, 1973; Wolcott, 1987) which seeks to understand the meaning of what is observed. Meaning or interpretation is derived partly through inference and partly by representing the world views and stated concepts of the people being investigated.

Crago (1988) in her work with the Inuit discovered that talking during mealtime had a completely different meaning in that culture than it does in the white middle-class culture. When Crago suggested to Inuit teachers that morning soup time in school would be a good time for facilitating children's oral language, they laughed and one explained, "It's a joke. We say white people talk while they eat because their food is so bad" (p. 4). Ethnography helps to unlock the meaning that various forms of communicative interaction have for the people involved in them. Seeking for and capturing accurate interpretations of people's beliefs and actions helps steer clinicians to appropriate times, forms, places, and people for intervention.

4. *Analysis is an iterative spiral and not predetermined.* Ethnography does not proceed in a predetermined manner. Instead, the process is rather like a bloodhound sniffing out a trail, making decisions as it goes. The Spindlers (1987b) refer to the tenacity of enterprise and curiosity that characterizes ethnography as "being pesky" (p. 20).

Ethnographic analysis is ongoing and determines successive rounds of data collection. Gladwin (1989) has diagrammed a research cycle in which the ethnographer asks an initial set of questions, collects data, analyzes it, and then formulates a better set of questions, collects more data, and so on in an interative spiral that leads to a set of assertions. Successive data are then collected to prove and disprove the validity of the assertions "until the patterns of behavior and the native explanations of them coalesce into repetitive sequences and configurations" (Spindler & Spindler, 1987a, p. 3).

In clinical practice, when a child enters our caseload, we start with a referral and some basic information that leads to an initial set of questions. We collect an initial set of data, which leads to more questions, and in response we structure successive rounds of data collection.

5. *All descriptions are partial and subjective.* Polkinghorne (1983) described the open-ended nature of ethnographic investigations. They are assumed to be subject to self-correction and to improvement by successive study. Two other features of ethnography give it partiality. Reliance on informants and the fact that these informants may not adequately represent all sectors of a population or all opinions means that there may be implicit limits on the nature of ethnographic findings. The ethnographic approach also assumes subjectivity. The investigator is understood to influence the findings. Accounting for the sources and forms of partiality then becomes a part of the ethnographic process. Ethnographic reporting normally includes a natural history of the study in which the investigators describe and account for their own life situations, predispositions, and a priori concepts. In this way, an attempt is made to reveal the subjective and partial nature of the study and to understand the effects of this on the results.

Clinicians are often constrained by partiality. They rely on parents or teachers to tell them what happens at home or in the classroom. Representations by others may be partial. The clinicians' own understanding and interpretation of their meanings may, in turn, also be partial. Cultural and social biases and blinders may lead to biased conclusions (Damico, 1988). Following the ethnographic lead, open, honest reckoning and accounting for this partiality might lead to more productive clinical outcomes.

6. *Descriptions have emic and etic dimensions.* Agar (1986) has described the "emic" and "etic" dimensions of ethnography as an issue of control. It is assumed that ethnographies will be constructed on a rich base of information coming from and, in that sense, controlled by the people being investigated (the emic dimension). It is also assumed that ethnographies will represent the point of view of the people being investigated as thoroughly and accurately as possible. On the other hand, no matter how steeped researchers are in the people they study, they still represent an outsider (etic) perspective. It is the interplay between the etic and the emic that makes the two conceptual frameworks mutually comprehensible. The ethnographer begins with a certain etic framework and then hones and adapts that framework by constantly holding emic actions and points of view up to it. Furthermore, some ethnographers dare to step over and have the people

they are studying analyze and comment on their ways. In doing so, the ethnographer becomes the object of study and the emic and etic dimensions are reversed. The outsider becomes the insider and the insider becomes the outsider.

Clinicians enter the clinical situation with etic frameworks based on their own life of experiences, the present state of clinical training, their experience with other clients, and a series of standardized measures. Through their information gathering, they need to shape these outsider frameworks to suit the client at hand, who may or may not fit into such a mold. Clinicians also need to step over and understand how their perspectives, actions, and interpretations are seen by their clients.

7. *More than one perspective is needed.* Coming at something from different angles is an implicit part of ethnography. The details of the use of multiple perspectives for ethnographic data collection and analysis are described in more detail later in this chapter. The essential concept that reality is more tangibly understood when viewed from more than one perspective was introduced by Bateson (1979). In ethnography, this concept has been called "triangulation."

The idea of multiple sources of information is not new to clinical practice. For instance, observation of the classroom or peer-group play can be combined with language sampling, standardized testing, interviews with significant others, and with other professionals' reports. These multiple sources allow a fuller, more complete assessment of the child than any single source allows. Furthermore, in the treatment of minority culture children, multiple perspectives on the child's functioning have special significance. Other culturally informed points of view can help clinicians avoid misinterpretations, particularly deficiency interpretations, of cultural difference.

8. *Both macro and micro levels of analysis are needed.* Ethnographic studies that involve an in-depth analysis of an isolated event, a particular situation, or a small group of people are referred to as micro studies. Sometimes this approach has led to analyzing specific behavior patterns with little attention to the culture or society as a whole (Gilmore & Smith, 1982). Language socialization studies, as pointed out before, link the microanalysis of children's discourse with more encompassing cultural and societal factors. This attention to wider social context is one of the important assumptions of ethnography that renders it particularly informative (Collins, 1987; Mehan, 1987).

Micro clinical findings, such as language samples that are structurally analyzed, may pinpoint certain important grammatical gaps in a child's language, but they do not inform us about how the child uses language, with whom, for what purposes, and why. Furthermore, ignoring how language is integrated into the more macro levels of the cultural patterning of interaction and the socioeconomic and historical dimensions of communication can lead to limited models of intervention and erroneous assessment and placement decisions (Harris, 1985; Heath, 1986a; Mehan, 1987; Taylor & Payne, 1983).

9. *Themes are generalizable from the careful study of a small number of people.*
Ethnographic language studies often involve small numbers of people. The
depth and accuracy of the study, however, can lead to information that is authentic enough to be generalizable. A high point of Crago's study of the communicative interaction of four Inuit children in northern Quebec came when
she presented her findings at an international conference of Inuit studies
(Crago, Ningiuruvik, & Annahatak, 1988). A native woman from Greenland
stood up and beamed. "They are just like us. It was like being in my mother's
house to hear you talk," she said. Then, an Inupiaq lady from Alaska stood up
with tears in her eyes and said quietly, "For me, it was recognizable but I only
know some of it from my grandmother's house." Despite the fact that cultural
change has happened at a different rate, people thousands of miles apart recognized and identified with findings based on only four children.

On the other hand, a number of authors (Cheng, 1989; Lee, 1989; Lewis,
Vang, & Cheng, 1989; Matsuda, 1989) caution that what may appear to the
outsider as one cultural group (e.g., Asians) with one set of practices may,
in fact, have numerous subgroups with substantially different belief systems, political and economic histories, and cultural patterns of communication. It is important not to overgeneralize from one group to the next.
Cultural boundaries need to be understood and respected.

Every child who is seen clinically is, in a sense, a study of one. However,
careful comparisons and multimodal documentation often can allow common patterns and threads to come into view. For example, parents of children who have language impairments share some of the same experiences
and frustrations. Accounts of their lived experiences can contain themes
that are identifiable to others and from which others can benefit. Similarly,
information gathered on the communicative interactions of a few families
of a particular cultural group can provide information that can be pertinent
to several children in a caseload.

THE INTERFACE BETWEEN CLINICAL
AND ETHNOGRAPHIC PROCEDURES

The Research-Clinical Continuum

People involved in the ethnographic enterprise can be seen as spanning a
continuum (Hymes, 1982; Schein, 1987). At one end are researchers such
as the ethnographers of speaking and of language socialization who were
mentioned in the first part of this chapter. At the other end of the continuum is the general population whose knowledge of the intricacies of life
(including language) has been acquired in a less conscious type of process
(Hymes, 1982; Wolcott, 1987).

The two ends of the continuum do have some elements in common.
Ochs (1979) and Saville–Troike (1982) have pointed out that children

learning language attend to context in much the same way that clinicians and researchers should. "Children are essentially participant observers of communication, like small ethnographers, learning inductively, developing the rules of their speech community through the process of observation and interaction" (Saville–Troike, 1982, p. 205). The discourse practices of children's worlds are important resources for children's socialization in much the same way as these practices inform researchers about the acquisition of culture and language (Schieffelin, 1990).

The middle group on the continuum are practitioners. As Hymes (1982) wrote, "in between . . . would be those able to combine some disciplined understanding of ethnographic inquiry with the pursuit of their vocation, whatever that might be" (p. 30). An increased awareness of the ethnographic approach and the conscious use of ethnographic techniques may have the potential to enhance professional speech-language pathology practice in general (Gleason, 1990; Rice, 1986). Moreover, such awareness on the part of speech-language pathologists should have particular utility in helping them unlock a much needed perspective on language as a culturally and socially embedded phenomenon. By doing so, an ethnographic approach should provide useful procedures for the clinical study and development of treatment alternatives aimed at maximizing the effectiveness of the intervention and assessment of children from minority cultures (Taylor, 1986b). The remainder of this section will, therefore, describe the adaptation of certain ethnographic procedures and decision-making processes to the clinical treatment of children from minority cultures.

Who Studies Whom?

In ethnographic research, the selection of participants is often a process of "informed" rather than random selection. People are included in a study, for instance, because they represent a prototype within a population or some particular source of information. Selection is also linked to analysis. In the successive process of analyzing data and asking new questions, additional or different types of people may become included in the study in order to test a hypothesis.

In the school or the clinic, on the other hand, speech-language pathology clients come for services either by self- or family-referral, by the referral of another professional, or as a result of the diagnostic screening procedure. However, in ethnographic terms, speech-language pathology clients can be considered as "tracer units" (Green, 1983). Through them, the professional traces a path to other people in their lives who can provide relevant information concerning these clients' communicative abilities and environment. In inter-ethnic clinical service delivery, it is of utmost importance that the clinician seek information from cultural informants or resource collaborators. This means reaching outside the walls of the clinic into the child's family and community to access information on social and cultural expectations of communicative interaction and impairment as well as on the cultural and socioeconomic factors that may constrain or affect the way the family or child might become involved in the process of speech-language pathology intervention (Cheng, 1987; Gallimore, Weisner, Kaufman, & Bernheimer, 1989). The role of such community and family resource collaborators can vary a great deal, but the idea is to rely on some representative member(s) of the child's world for information. This could include having the resource collaborator(s) react to any tentative hypotheses the clinician develops or formulate their own hypotheses about the nature of the child's problem. The idea is also to "cast the net" as widely and systematically as possible in order to get as rich a picture of the client as possible.

In clinical investigations, family members (parents, siblings, grandparents, aunts, or uncles), teachers, peers (classmates or friends), medical personnel, or social workers can become resource collaborators (Kelly & Rice, 1986; Rice, 1986). It is important to remember that in different cultural groups there are different caregiver roles and personnel as well as different caregiving practices (Rogoff, 1990; Thayer, 1988; Westby, 1985b). This means that what might be done by a mother in the white middle class may be done by a grandparent or an older sibling in another cultural group. In inter-ethnic clinical settings, clinicians need to be sure to obtain information on culturally expected caregiving practices so that they can access appropriate resources for information and communicative interaction in children's worlds.

In ethnographic research, researchers have to decide whether they are well suited to the population being studied. Clinicians, too, as they set about gathering clinical information relevant to minority culture populations need to ask themselves how well suited they are to deliver service to certain populations. They need to inspect their own culturally grounded assumptions and values about communicative interaction, caregiving, and handicap. Clinicians need to become aware of and record observations of their own behavior, reactions, and thoughts as they deal with clients from other cultural groups. Ethnographic researchers frequently do this by keeping a personal journal as they undertake their studies. The contents of such a journal help make researchers or clinicians aware of their subjectivity. Clinicians may also want to consider whether there are more culturally appropriate personnel who could be trained to deliver services in conjunction with professionals (Adler, 1990; Cheng, 1987; Crago, Annahatak, Doehring, & Allen, in press; Crago, Ayukawa, & Hurteau, 1990).

Gathering Information

Data collection in an ethnographic study continues throughout the study and is intricately and systematically interwoven with data analysis. Despite the constraints on time and type of information imposed by Individualized Educational Plans (IEPs) and Individualized Family Service Plans (IFSPs) (Adler, 1990; Damico, 1988), clinical information gathering needs to be a continuous process. Findings from an interview or from a language sample should lead to questions that have to be answered in successive testing, referral, or discussions. This process is very similar to what has been referred to in speech-language pathology as diagnostic therapy. Spradley (1980) has described ethnographic information gathering as a kind of funnelling process in which the ethnographer begins with a wide sweep of data collection. When the central issues are identified, ongoing data collection becomes more precise and specific.

In both clinical practice and ethnographic research, three crucial issues need to be reckoned with in data collection (Erickson, 1986). First, one must be sure to identify and collect information on a full range of events. Second, recurrent instances of an event must be sought and recorded to insure that the event is not a chance occurrence. Finally, events at different levels in the system must be looked at. For instance, children's communication needs to be observed at home and in a classroom as well as in a clinical setting. Furthermore, for children from minority cultures, communication needs to be linked to cultural values and socioeconomic issues. A set of questions that can be used to guide clinicians in their information gathering on the communicative patterns and values of various cultural groups is presented in Table 4–2. These questions are inspired by the work of Ochs and Schieffelin (1984), Taylor and Payne (1983), and Taylor, Payne, and Anderson (1989).

Ethnographic data collection is multimodal. The process known as triangulation that was mentioned earlier occurs, in part, by insuring that data is collected in a number of different ways. The most commonly used modes of collecting data are participant observation, machine recordings, open-ended interviews, and gathering archival information. Each of these modes produces different kinds of information and has different advantages and disadvantages. Agar (1986) has referred to these pieces of ethnographic data as "strips." Each mode will be described in turn and then related to its utility in assessment and intervention with minority culture populations.

Participant observation can be superficially described as hanging around and taking notes. The important thing is that the researcher is present and, to one degree or another, participates in and/or manipulates the scene. The effect of the presence of the researcher on the situation has often been questioned. However, as Agar (1986) pointed out, normally the researcher's presence is only minimally disruptive. Traditions and behavior patterns are usually so strong that the presence of a stranger does not significantly alter them. Furthermore, there is a continuum of participation. Researchers can take a very unassuming role, positioning themselves inconspicuously and not interfering with the flow of events. Ethnographic re-

Table 4–2. Some cultural dimensions to consider in interacting, assessing, and/or intervening in children's communicative worlds

Dimensions	Characteristics
Conversational partners	What proportion of the child's interacting is with adults, peers, older or younger siblings, others?
	How many people are usually involved in an interaction? (two, three, more?)
	in adult-child interactions
	in child-child interactions
	in adult-sibling interactions
	in other interactions
Mode of communication	What proportion of the interacting is verbal versus nonverbal?
	What is the meaning and use of silence in interactions? Are children expected to be seen and not heard? Can people sit together comfortably without talking?
	What is the meaning and use of gaze direction? Where do people look when they are speaking, listening, directing, questioning, scolding, being reprimanded, joking, threatening, deceiving?
Duration of conversation	How long does a typical interaction last?
	in adult-child interactions
	in child-child interactions
	in adult-sibling interactions
	in other interactions
Amount of talk	Do children talk less or more in conversations with particular other participants?
	Do children talk less or more in interactions with particular purposes or settings?
Conversational structure	Who initiates, maintains, and/or ends interactions?
	How is the other person's attention secured?
	How are turns passed back and forth?
Topics	What are typical topics? (e.g., here-and-now play activities, getting things done, imaginative play, dreams and aspirations, daily events, behavior, verbal nonsense [play], rhymes and songs, jokes, family or community news, world news, literature, politics, religion)

continued

Table 4-2. *(continued)*

Dimensions	Characteristics
Topics *(continued)*	What topics or uses of language are considered to be offensive or rude?
Adult talk to children	How complex is it? Does it have "motherese" features? Do adults do minimal or expanded responses to child utterances?
	Is adult talk contingently related to the child's talk?
Speech acts	Are certain types of speech acts performed only by certain interactants?
	What is the use and meaning of questions? (frequency, by whom to whom, real questions or test questions, how often answered)
	What is the role of directives? (frequency, by whom to whom, nature of response)
	What is the role of labeling objects or pictures in storybooks? (frequency, who does it with whom)
	Who can joke, tease, threaten? (frequency, appropriate response)
	When do children use direct versus indirect request forms?
Some relevant social norms	What are the culture's beliefs about how language is learned by small children?
	What activities or uses of language are considered to be play, fun, and/or humorous?
	What are the conventions for male-female communication?
	How does the culture define and view "handicapped?"

searchers sometimes deliberately manipulate a situation in order to confirm their analysis by ascertaining what people's reactions to the change are. The outcome of participant observation is a series of field notes. These are usually taken in a hasty, brief format and later expanded to include fuller detail. The advantage of participant observation is that it allows the unencumbered observation of a fuller range of events than is usually possible with machine recordings. A visit to a classroom, for instance, is often easier to arrange than a videotaping of the classroom. On the other hand, participant observation implies a considerable amount of decision making. The observer has to decide when, where, and what to observe. In addition, field note recording is less inclusive than transcripts of machine recordings.

Clinically, it can be highly informative for the clinician to gather information by participant observation (Nelson, 1989). Many clinical and intervention procedures already automatically place the therapist in the role of a participant observer who often manipulates the situation to determine what the outcome will be. Clinicians could profit from extending their domains of observation into classrooms and homes. Participant observation in homes and communities of children from minority cultures is particularly important for clinicians from the majority culture. In these situations, it is necessary to enter such observations free of already existing taxonomies of behavior because they may have been derived from and be limited to certain cultural patterns of communicative interaction. Making more open-ended observations and writing them up in the form of field notes should allow clinicians fuller insights into the details of communicative patterns of other cultures.

The advantages of machine recordings (audiotapes, videotapes, and photographs) are that they can be played back for multiple viewings. People can be asked to watch or listen to recordings and then comment on them. Furthermore, in the analysis stage, the ability to check out one's impressions by microanalysis of a transcript of a tape recording helps to eliminate errors. On the other hand, the disadvantages of machine recordings, as many clinicians well know, are the time and expense of transcription, the limits they place on access, and possible distortions of the subject's behavior that might result from the presence of the equipment. Nevertheless, videotapes made in home settings and viewed by parents themselves have been shown to be clinically useful (Cole & St. Clair-Stokes, 1984). Furthermore, such family, community, and classroom taping and reactions to tapes are particularly important in inter-ethnic service delivery. They can serve as a means of letting different personnel (families, teachers, and health care professionals) see, comment on, and eventually learn from each other's realities.

Ethnographic interviews are open-ended discussions with the people being studied. The aim is to obtain their stated concepts related to the topic under investigation. Briggs (1986), Mishler (1986), and Crago, Ningiuruvik, and Annahatak (1989) have documented how the interview process itself is a speech event and is therefore culturally determined. Briggs warned that inter-ethnic interviews can become a locus for communicative misunderstandings and misinterpretation, most often to the detriment of the people being interviewed. Furthermore, people can say things about what they do that are not necessarily borne out by observation or recordings (Crago et al., 1989). It is the ethnographer's (and clinician's) job to make sense out of such differences. Spradley (1979) and McCracken (1988) have described in detail how ethnographic interviews can be conducted. Westby (1990) has explained and adapted Spradley's model of ethnographic interviewing and shown how it can be used to advantage by speech-language pathologists in their work with minority culture populations. Once again, the importance of the ethnographic process, in interviewing as in observing, is that the clinician proceed in an open-ended fashion without predetermining categories or questions. McCracken pointed out that interviewers must avoid specifying the substance of interviewees' responses by the way they frame their questions. She suggested that interviewers use only a skeletal set of predetermined questions and then proceed by a series of indirect prompts to elicit information from their interviewees, all the while listening carefully for topics that are avoided and for evidence of misunderstandings.

Archival information is essentially site documentation. In ethnographic research studies, it can include the collection of any document or article that might be related to the phenomena or group being studied. Archival information is usually limited in scope but provides important supplementary information. On site visits to classrooms, homes, and communities of children from minority cultures, clinicians need to draw sketches of space utilization as well as look at and note the kinds of materials used by the children being observed. Such materials can include but not be limited to their books, notebooks, and toys. Without making judgments about the nature and availability of such materials and spatial arrangements, clinicians can, nevertheless, use archival information to become more aware of the world children live and function in.

There is a final method of collecting data that is often used in ethnographic research. This process has been called lamination (Goffman, 1974) or indefinite triangulation (Agar, 1986). It is a layering of different levels of data. First level data is collected by any of the methods described above. This data is then shown to people for their reactions or interpretations. As we noted, machine recordings are particularly useful in this regard. The outcome is a reflective level of data that has particular significance in understanding people of other cultures.

Ethnographic Analysis

Ethnographic analysis has been described by Agar (1986) as "a movement from breakdown through resolution to coherence" (p. 26). How, then, does such a process take place?

One means of obtaining resolution of ethnographic data is by comparing data derived from different sources. When data from different sources are not congruent, the ethnographer must determine why. Usually this means collecting more data, collecting data from additional subjects, or seeking opinions from collaborators or subjects about why discrepancies exist. The latter process is an example of the kind of inquiry that was described as "lamination."

One assumption about ethnography has been that researchers should attempt to wipe out any preconceptions they might have before beginning their study. Both Erickson (1986) and Agar (1986) claim that this, in fact, is impossible to do. Instead, they maintain that researchers enter with schema or frameworks in their heads. These schema may derive from concepts in the literature, from the initial visit to the site, or from the researchers' own world views. In any case, the process of ethnographic analysis is one of holding "strips" of collected data up to the researchers' schema to determine if they fit or are coherent. When the fit is not good, Agar says a breakdown occurs. The schema is then changed and the data strips are held up against this new hypothesis. Or, alternatively, the new hypotheses or schema force a new round of data collection. This process of resolving strips of multimodal data with the researchers' hypotheses continues until all strips of data fit one or another of the researchers' schema. If researchers do not work through their schema in such a way, they are likely to end up with incomplete and unjustified conclusions.

Clinically, a very similar process can take place. Clinicians have expectations and preconceptions of the children that they work with. These may be based on a referral letter or on the parents' cultural or socioeconomic status. Damico (1988) described the unconscious sources of bias that surfaced in his assessment of a child. He pointed out that certain oversights in his assessment decision making might have been avoided by collecting more data and checking his schema against them until there was a better fit.

Similarly, assessments of minority culture children have the potential to lead to inaccurate results if a clinician's schema has not been appropriately supported by data. For instance, the taciturn nature of Native children and Asian children (Cheng, 1987; Crago, 1990b; Harris, 1985) might be inaccurately interpreted by professionals from the white middle-class culture as language impairment. If, however, the same professionals had shown examples of the children's communicative behavior to members of the children's community or family, it is possible that they would have discovered that, in many situations, Native and Asian children's silent behavior is considered not only normal but desirable.

Finally, ethnographic data often contain very complex and entangled phenomena, which make them hard to analyze unless they are categorized. In ethnographic research, categories sometimes derive from literature, but categories that emerge from the data or are found in the stated concepts of the people being studied must also be included (Crago, 1988; Rennie et al., 1988; Strauss & Corbin, 1990). Furthermore, categories derived for one culture may be quite inadequate or misleading for another.

Ethnographic Reporting

Ethnographic writing has been described as "writing close to the ground" (Spindler & Spindler, 1987b, p. 28). This means that it is richly descriptive and is intended to capture the sights and sounds of a person's everyday life. It includes a large quantity of examples of data which are reported as narrative vignettes, direct quotes, or segments of transcripts. However, these strips are embedded in interpretive commentary and theoretical discussion. Furthermore, the natural history of the study must be reported. This is a discussion of the evolution of the key concepts and encounters with the unexpected. It is a kind of map of the data analysis process. The essence of ethnographic writing is conveying credibility and authenticity.

Clinical report writing, particularly as it pertains to minority culture populations, might convey a more accurate picture if it contained several exemplars of multimodal data from which the conclusions were drawn. These anecdotes help to create what Lahey (1988) has referred to as a communication-referenced description of the child. Test scores and reports of grammatical analyses need to be supplemented by reports on families' reactions to children's use of language as well as information on cultural structures of caregiving that would be informative in the development of appropriate and effective intervention strategies.

Establishing Credibility

Agar (1986) describes what he calls "comprehension displays" as a way of accounting for the authenticity of ethnographic research. The basic concept is that ethnographic researchers must make sure that their schema are comprehensible to their informants. To do this, schema have to be described in language that their informants can understand and discuss. Schema can also be checked by predicting a situation based on the formulation of a hypothesis and then seeing if the prediction is borne out.

Another way to determine the authenticity of an ethnographic study is to verify that the evidence gathered is adequate to the conclusions derived (Erickson, 1986; Maxwell, 1990). Inadequacy can result from inadequate amounts of evidence, an inadequate variety of evidence, premature interpretations of evidence, and inadequate discrepant analyses.

ETHNOGRAPHIC PERSPECTIVES ON THE ASSESSMENT OF CHILDREN FROM MINORITY CULTURES WHO HAVE COMMUNICATION IMPAIRMENTS

In the last 10 years, a number of works that have taken an ethnographic perspective on the assessment of children from minority cultures have appeared in the field of communication disorders. The majority of these report extrapolations derived from research done in other fields. Only a small number are based on ethnographic research studies done in the field of communication disorders. The final section of the chapter will describe some of these existing perspectives as well as a future for the field in which ethnographic sensibilities can help clinicians meet the challenges of the multicultural world in which they increasingly will work.

EXISTING PERSPECTIVES

Information that helps clinicians develop a general sensitivity to culturally different modes of communication has been produced by the Office of Minority Concerns of the American Speech-Language-Hearing Association (ASHA). A chart reported in Cole (1989) describes possible verbal and nonverbal sources of miscommunication for blacks, Hispanics, Asians, and Native Americans. The information on this chart is the kind of ethnographically based knowledge that helps practitioners understand the contrast between their own and others' ways of communicating. Cheng (1987) has also charted two different interpretations of Asian children's communicative behavior. Again, this chart helps practitioners compare their own schema with information on another cultural group. The act of contrasting two different culturally based interpretations of the same behavior is at the heart of the ethnographic process.

Several authors in the field have described the ethnographic nature of the overall clinical assessment process (Cheng, 1987; Kovarsky, Crago, Damico, & Maxwell, 1990; Taylor, 1986a; Taylor, Payne, & Anderson, 1989). Cheng constructed a format to be used in the naturalistic and holistic assessment of Asian children which she claimed produced an ethnographically based picture of their communicative functioning. Damico in Kovarsky and colleagues (1990) stated that assessments could never be assumed to be true ethnographies, but should instead be considered as "ethnographic-like" events. Taylor (1986a) has written that the clinical encounter is a culturally and socially situated phenomenon that is best understood from an ethnographic perspective. A flow chart of the assessment process for minority culture children was designed by Taylor and colleagues (1989). It includes stages of the assessment process that involve the collection or review of information on the norms and idiosyncratic sociocultural features of communication in the client's speech community. It also includes the process of corroborating the test and naturalistic data with the client's community before arriving at a diagnosis. These stages of information gathering and verification are similar to stages described in this chapter for ethnographic research.

Other authors have extrapolated information from ethnographic cross-cultural research on parenting and caregiver-child communicative interaction and used it to describe several sensitizing concepts for clinicians working with parents and children of other cultures (Cheng, 1989; Crago, 1990b; Harris, 1985; Matsuda, 1989; Rice, 1986; Thayer, 1988; Westby, 1985b). This information is particularly helpful to consider in the assessment of parent-child interaction and in the development of intervention goals as mandated by Public Law 99-457 in the United States. Matsuda (1989), in particular, has shown how this kind of information interfaces with parental interviews.

Ethnographically based information that is useful in the assessment and management of school-age children from minority cultures has also been reported. Westby and Rouse (1985) and Iglesias (1985) have described models and procedures for understanding and promoting better matches of home and school communicative patterns. Westby (1989) and Heath (1986b) have documented the cultural variety in narratives that is necessary for clinicians to understand before they can successfully assess this form of communication.

Of additional utility in the assessment of children from minority cultures is Taylor and Payne's (1983) description of the cultural biases of certain standardized measures. Their explanation of situational, format, and value bias shares several concepts that are articulated in language socialization studies. Formulations about the utility of nonstandardized assessment approaches with minority culture populations are also congruent with ethnographic perspectives (Holland & Forbes, 1986; Leonard & Weiss, 1983; Naremore, 1985).

Although language socialization and ethnographic research are quite new and undeveloped in the field of communication disorders, there is, nevertheless, an increasing awareness of ethnographic perspectives and their utility in the assessment of children from minority cultures. The need for cultural sensitivity on the part of clinicians has been stated and re-stated. The understanding that such sensitivity is constructed from the findings of ethnographic research and by engaging in an ethnographic approach to the assessment of children from minority cultures is coming of age.

FUTURE PERSPECTIVES

Despite these developments, numerous concerns about the ability of speech-language pathologists to meet the challenge of treating multicultural populations remain. It has been pointed out that only a very small minority of the practicing speech-language pathologists in the United States are from cultural minorities and that universities need to recruit students from these groups. However, it will be a number of years before this group of recruits swells the ranks of the professionals to the extent that they will be able to handle the large number of children from minority cultures that will appear in caseloads across North America. Furthermore, the education of these students requires that university training programs meet another challenge. Cheng (1987) has described the differences in the learning styles of Asian students and how training programs in communication disorders need to become cognizant of the consequences of these differences in the formulation of their programs and in the support systems that they provide to such students. If universities are to train professionals from minority cultures who will remain aware and in touch with their cultural backgrounds, several changes will need to be made in both the content and form of courses taught to students in communication disorders who are from minority cultures. Otherwise, the same cultural discontinuities between the educational setting and home culture that have been documented for school-age children will lead to unsuccessful outcomes for these university students.

Another intertwined concern in the field is the large number of practicing clinicians who report that they have had no education in the area of multicultural and multilingual service issues (Shewan & Malm, 1989). This fact clearly indicates that the university programs have another challenge in addition to the education of students from minority cultures. They must educate mainstream students to be crosscultural communicators who are culturally literate. This education, at both the university level and through continuing educational programs, needs to be fed by ongoing research that documents the linkages between culture and communication. Ethnographic language socialization research in the field needs to be expanded so that the information base for effective education and clinical practice in multicultural service issues can be developed.

In the meantime, the service delivery challenge is a pressing one. While the educational systems adjust and research is underway, mainstream clinicians will need to deal with the current situation. Past experience has shown that many speech-language pathologists can rise to meet multicultural challenges when they are provided with appropriate information. Findings on nonstandard dialect and information on how it influences clinical assessments (Seymour, 1986a, 1986b; Taylor, 1986b) have led to the formulation of more positive clinical strategies, many of which have been put into effect by mainstream clinicians. Ethnographically based information has the potential to help mainstream clinicians understand and treat clients from varied cultural backgrounds. Cummins (1989) and Damico and Hamayan (1990) have described the importance of an advocacy orientation in the assessment and education of children from minority cultures. The profession of speech-language pathology needs to adopt the same advocacy orientation toward the development of skills in handling children from minority cultures. Rather than blame individual clinicians for a lack of knowledge, we need, at many levels, to address our ignorance and build our knowledge base. Moreover, even though a clinician does not have a thorough knowledge of a cultural group, attitudes of respect, sensitivity, and interest are usually appreciated by clients from other cultures. Crago (1988) discovered that even though she spoke only rudimentary Inuktitut and had very limited understanding of Inuit ways at the outset of her research, her efforts to gain understanding were appreciated by the people she studied. Attitudes of respect, sensitivity, and interest for people of other cultures are fostered by the findings from ethnographic research and can be developed by using ethnographic methodology for clinical information gathering with children from minority cultures.

CONCLUDING ISSUES

The more systematized, authentic, contextualized, and culturally informed our clinical investigations are, the closer they will bring us to unlocking not only the linguistic but also the lived experiences of children of all cultures who are communicatively impaired. Ethnography provides us with an investigatory approach that grapples with context and culture by rendering it comprehensible.

Ethnographic methodology need not stand alone. Methodological pluralism is what modern postpositivistic thinking is all about (Kovarsky & Crago, in press; Polkinghorne, 1983). Ethnographic approaches can be usefully linked to other ways of gathering and analyzing information (Fielding & Fielding, 1986; Weller & Romney, 1988). Different approaches to knowledge can support and augment each other (Corsaro & Streeck, 1986). In our clinical and research endeavors, the critical act is to piece together a picture of communicative competence and incompetence that maximizes our understanding. This understanding, however, will not be complete if it remains circumscribed to include only the listener and the speaker to the exclusion of their social and cultural worlds.

In the final analysis, this chapter is meant to be about the children whom we study and serve. These children inhabit a variety of worlds: clinical ones, family ones, school and daycare ones. They are interlocutors carving out a life experience and a cultural identity. Yet, "besides our own memories of childhood we have little first-hand ethnographic information on the worlds children live in" (Corsaro & Streeck, 1986, p. 15) or of the language they use to construct these worlds and interact within them. In an effort to understand and to do something about how children who have communicative impairments socialize and are socialized through language, clinicians and researchers need to investigate communication within an enlarged sphere of sociocultural context. In short, clinical pragmatics can no longer stay off the streets. Time and support must be given to clinicians so that they can venture forth to investigate the lived experiences and culturally based patterns of communication of their clients.

REFERENCES

Adler, S. (1990). Multicultural clients: Implications for the SLP. *Language, Speech, and Hearing Services in Schools, 21*(3), 135–139.

Agar, M. H. (1986). *Speaking of ethnography*. Newbury Park, CA: Sage Publications.

ASHA. (1988). Inside the national office: Office of minority concerns. *Asha, 30*(8), 23–25.

Basso, K. H. (1970). "To give up on words": Silence in Apache culture. In P. P. Giglio (Ed.), *Language and social context* (pp. 67–86). Harmondsworth, UK: Penguin.

Bateson, G. (1979). *Mind and nature: A necessary unity*. New York: E. P. Dutton.

Baugh, J., & Sherzer, J. (Eds.). (1984). *Language in use: Readings in sociolinguistics*. Englewood-Cliffs, NJ: Prentice-Hall.

Bauman, R., & Sherzer, J. (1975). The ethnography of speaking. *Annual Review of Anthropology, 4*, 95–119.

Bauman, R., & Sherzer, J. (Eds.). (1989). *Explorations in the ethnography of speaking* (2nd ed.). Cambridge, UK: Cambridge University Press.

Boggs, S. T. (1985). *Speaking, relating, and learning: A study of Hawaiian children at home and at school*. Norwood, NJ: Ablex Publishing.

Blount, B. (1972). Aspects of Luo socialization. *Language in Society, 1*, 235–248.

Briggs, C. L. (1986). *Learning how to ask: A sociolinguistic appraisal of the role of the interview in social science research*. Cambridge, UK: Cambridge University Press.

Cheng, L. (1987). *Assessing Asian language performance*. Rockville, MD: Aspen Publications.

Cheng, L. (1989). Service delivery to Asian/Pacific LEP children: A cross-cultural framework. *Topics in Language Disorders, 9*(3), 1–11.

Clancy, P. M. (1986). The acquisition of communicative style in Japanese. In B. B. Schieffelin & E. Ochs (Eds.), *Language socialization across cultures* (pp. 213–250). Cambridge, UK: Cambridge University Press.

Cole, L. (1989). E pluribus pluribus: Multicultural imperatives for the 1990s and beyond. *Asha, 31*(8), 65–70.

Cole, E. B., & St. Clair-Stokes, J. (1984). Caregiver-child interactive behaviors: Videotape analysis procedure. *The Volta Review, 86*(4), 200–216.

Coles, R. (1977). Growing up Chicano. In R. Coles (Ed.), *Eskimos, Chicanos, Indians* (pp. 100–151). Boston, MA: Little-Brown.

Collins, J. (1987). Conversation and knowledge in bureaucratic settings. *Discourse Processes, 10*, 303–319.

Cook-Gumperz, J. (1986a). Caught in a web of words: Some considerations on language socialization and language acquisition. In J. Cook-Gumperz, W. Corsaro, & J. Streeck (Eds.), *Children's worlds and children's language* (pp. 37–64). New York: Mouton de Gruyter.

Cook-Gumperz, J. (1986b). Introduction: The social construction of literacy. In J. Cook-Gumperz (Ed.), *The social construction of literacy* (pp. 1–15). Cambridge, UK: Cambridge University Press.

Cook-Gumperz, J., & Corsaro, W. (1986). Introduction. In J. Cook-Gumperz, W. Corsaro, & J. Streeck (Eds.), *Children's worlds and children's language* (pp. 1–10). New York: Mouton de Gruyter.

Corsaro, W., & Streeck, J. (1986). Studying children's world: Methodological issues. In J. Cook-Gumperz, W. Corsaro, & J. Streeck (Eds.), *Children's worlds and children's language* (pp. 13–35). New York: Mouton de Gruyter.

Crago, M. B. (1988). *Cultural context in communicative interaction of young Inuit children*. Unpublished doctoral thesis, McGill University, Montreal.

Crago, M. B. (1990a, April). Professional gatekeeping: The multicultural, multilingual challenge. *Communiqué*, pp. 10–13.

Crago, M. B. (1990b). Development of communicative competence in Inuit children: Implications for speech-language pathology. *Journal of Childhood Communication Disorders, 13*(1), 73–84.

Crago, M. B., Annahatak, B., Doehring, D., & Allen, S. (in press). Evaluation of Inuit children's first language by a Native speaker. *Journal of Speech-Language Pathology and Audiology.*

Crago, M. B., Ayukawa, H., & Hurteau, A. M. (1990). Culturally based audiological services for hearing-impaired Inuit of northern Quebec. *Journal of Speech-Language Pathology and Audiology, 14*(2), 33–46.

Crago, M. B., Ningiuruvik, L., & Annahatak, B. (1988, October). *Cultural change in the communicative interaction of young Inuit children and their caregivers.* Paper presented at the Sixth International Conference of Inuit Studies, Copenhagen, Denmark.

Crago, M. B., Ningiuruvik, L., & Annahatak, B. (1989, February). *Cultural context in the communicative interaction of young Inuit children: Educational and methodological highlights.* Paper presented at the Tenth Annual Ethnography in Education Research Forum, Philadelphia, PA.

Cummins, J. (1989). *Empowering minority students.* Sacramento, CA: California Association for Bilingual Education.

Damico, J. S. (1988). The lack of efficacy in language therapy: A case study. *Language, Speech, and Hearing Services in Schools, 19,* 51–66.

Damico, J., & Hamayan, E. (1990). Implementing assessment in the real world. In E. Hamayan & J. Damico (Eds.), *Limiting bias in the assessment of bilingual students* (pp. 303–318). Austin, TX: Pro-Ed.

Damico, J., Maxwell, M., & Kovarsky, D. (Eds.). (1990). Ethnographic inquiries into communication sciences and disorders. *Journal of Childhood Communication Disorders, 13*(1).

Demuth, K. (1986). Prompting routines in the language socialization of Basotho children. In B. B. Schieffelin & E. Ochs (Eds.), *Language socialization across cultures* (pp. 51–79). Cambridge, UK: Cambridge University Press.

Des Bois, V. (1989). *Multilingual and multicultural issues: A survey of practicing speech-language pathologists in the Montreal area.* Unpublished manuscript, McGill University, Montreal.

Duranti, A. (1988). Ethnography of speaking: Toward a linguistics of praxis. In F. J. Newmeyer (Ed.), *Linguistics: The Cambridge survey: Vol. 4. Language: The socio-cultural context* (pp. 210–228). Cambridge, UK: Cambridge University Press.

Duranti, A., & Ochs, E. (1988). Literacy instruction in a Samoan village. In E. Ochs (Ed.), *Culture and language development: Language acquisition and language socialization in a Samoan village* (pp. 189–209). Cambridge, UK: Cambridge University Press.

Eisenberg, A. (1982). *Language acquisition in cultural perspective: Talk in three Mexicano homes.* Unpublished doctoral dissertation, University of California, Berkeley.

Eisenberg, A. (1986). Teasing: Verbal play in two Mexican homes. In B. B. Schieffelin & E. Ochs (Eds.), *Language socialization across cultures* (pp. 182–198). Cambridge, UK: Cambridge University Press.

Erickson, F. (1986). Qualitative methods in research on teaching. In M. C. Wittrock (Ed.), *Handbook of research on teaching* (Vol. 3, pp. 119–161). New York: Macmillan.

Erickson, F. (1987). Transformation and school success: The politics and culture of educational achievement. *Anthropology and Educational Quarterly, 18,* 335–357.

Fielding, N. G., & Fielding, J. L. (1986). *Linking data: The articulation of qualitative and quantitative methods in social research.* Newbury Park, CA: Sage Publications.

Fischer, J. S. (1970). Linguistic socialization: Japan and the United States. In R. Hill & R. Konig (Eds.), *Families in east and west* (pp. 107–119). The Hague, The Netherlands: Mouton.

Gal, S. (1989). Language and political economy. *Annual Review of Anthropology, 18,* 345–367.

Gallagher, T. M. (1990). Clinical pragmatics: Expectations and realizations. *Journal of Speech-Language Pathology and Audiology, 14*(1), 3–6.

Gallagher, T. M., & Prutting, C. A. (Eds.). (1983). *Pragmatic assessment and intervention issues in language.* San Diego, CA: College-Hill Press.

Gallimore, R., Weisner, T., Kaufman, S., & Bernheimer, L. (1989). The social construction of ecocultural niches: Family accommodation of developmentally delayed children. *American Journal on Mental Retardation, 94*(3), 216–230.

Geertz, C. (1973). *The interpretation of cultures.* New York: Basic Books.

Gilmore, P., & Smith, D. M. (1982). A retrospective discussion of the state of the art in ethnography and education. In P. Gilmore & A. A. Glatthorn (Eds.), *Children in and out of school: Ethnography and education* (pp. 3–18). Washington, DC: Center for Applied Linguistics.

Gladwin, C. H. (1989). *Ethnographic decision tree modeling.* Newbury Park, CA: Sage Publications.

Glaser, B. G., & Strauss, A. L. (1967). *The discovery of grounded theory: Strategies for qualitative research.* New York: Aldine.

Gleason, J. J. (1990). Meaning of play: Interpreting patterns in behavior of persons with severe developmental disabilities. *Anthropology & Education Quarterly, 21,* 59–77.

Goffman, I. (1974). *Frame analysis.* New York: Harper & Row.

Green, J. (1983). Research on teaching as a linguistic process: A state of the art. In E. Gordon (Ed.), *Review of research in education* (Vol. 10, pp. 151–252). Washington, DC: American Educational Research Association.

Gumperz, J. (1986). Interactional sociolinguistics in the study of schooling. In J. Cook–Gumperz (Ed.), *The social construction of literacy* (pp. 45–68). Cambridge, UK: Cambridge University Press.

Gumperz, J., & Hymes, D. (1964). The ethnography of communication. *American Anthropologist, 66*(b, Pt. 2) [Special Publication].

Harkness, S. (1977). Aspects of social environment and first language acquisition in rural Africa. In C. E. Snow & C. A. Ferguson (Eds.), *Talking to children* (pp. 309–318). New York: Cambridge University Press.

Harris, G. (1985). Considerations in assessing English language performance of Native American children. *Topics in Language Disorders, 5*(4), 42–52.

Heath, S. B. (1982). Ethnography in education: Defining the essentials. In P. Gilmore & A. A. Glatthorn (Eds.), *Children in and out of school: Ethnography and education* (pp. 33–55). Washington, DC: Center for Applied Linguistics.

Heath, S. B. (1983). Ways with words: Language, life and work in communities and classrooms. Cambridge, UK: Cambridge University Press.

Heath, S. B. (1986a). Sociocultural contexts of language development. In *Beyond language: Social and cultural factors in schooling language minority children* (pp. 143–186). Developed by the Bilingual Education Office, California State Department, Sacramento. Los Angeles: Evaluation, Dissemination and Assessment Center.

Heath, S. B. (1986b). Taking a cross-cultural look at narratives. *Topics in Language Disorders, 7*(1), 84–94.

Heath, S. B. (1989). The learner as cultural member. In M. L. Rice & R. L. Schiefelbusch (Eds.), *The teachability of language* (pp. 333–350). Baltimore, MD: Paul H. Brookes.

Heath, S. B. (1990). The children of Trackton's children: Spoken and written language in social change. In J. W. Stigler, R. A. Shweder, & G. Herdt (Eds.), *Cultural psychology* (pp. 496–519). Cambridge, UK: Cambridge University Press.

Holland, A., & Forbes, M. (1986). Nonstandardized approaches to speech and language assessment. In O. L. Taylor (Ed.), *Treatment of communication disorders in culturally and linguistically diverse populations* (pp. 49–66). San Diego, CA: College-Hill Press.

Hymes, D. H. (1972). Toward ethnographies of communication: The analysis of communicative events. In P. P. Giglio (Ed.), *Language and social context* (pp. 21–44). Harmondsworth, UK: Penguin.

Hymes, D. H. (1974). The ethnography of speaking. In B. G. Blount (Ed.), *Language, culture, and society: A book of readings* (pp. 189–223). Cambridge, MA: Winthrop.

Hymes, D. H. (1982). What is ethnography? In P. Gilmore & A. A. Glatthorn (Eds.), *Children in and out of school: Ethnography and education* (pp. 21–32). Washington, DC: Center for Applied Linguistics.

Iglesias, A. (1985). Communication in the home and classroom: Match or mismatch? *Topics in Language Disorders, 5*(4), 29–42.

Kawakami, A., & Hu-Pei Au, K. (1986). Encouraging reading and language development in cultural minority children. *Topics in Language Disorders, 6*(2), 71–80.

Kelly, D. J., & Rice, M. (1986). A strategy for language assessment of young children: A combination of two approaches. *Language, Speech, and Hearing Services in Schools, 17*, 83–94.

Kovarsky, D., & Crago, M. (in press). Toward an ethnography of communication disorders. *Journal of the National Students of Speech-Language & Hearing Association.*

Kovarsky, D., Crago, M., Damico, J., & Maxwell, M. (1990, November). *What is ethnography: Implications for assessment.* Miniseminar presented at the American Speech-Language-Hearing Association Conference, Seattle, WA.

Lahey, M. (1988). *Language disorders and language development.* New York: Macmillan.

Lavandera, B. R. (1988). The study of language in its socio-cultural context. In F. J. Newmeyer (Ed.), *Linguistics: The Cambridge survey: Vol. 4. Language: The socio-cultural context* (pp. 1–13). Cambridge, UK: Cambridge University Press.

Lee, A. (1989). A socio-cultural framework for the assessment of Chinese children with special needs. *Topics in Language Disorders, 9*(3), 38–44.

Leonard, L., & Weiss, A. L. (1983). Application of nonstandardized assessment procedures to diverse linguistic populations. *Topics in Language Disorders, 3*(3), 35–45.

Lewis, J., Vang, L., & Cheng, L. (1989). Identifying the language-learning difficulties of Hmong students: Implications of context and culture. *Topics in Language Disorders, 9*(3), 21–37.

Matsuda, M. (1989). Working with Asian parents: Some communication strategies. *Topics in Language Disorders, 9*(3), 45–53.

Maxwell, M. M. (1990). The authenticity of ethnographic research. *Journal of Childhood Communication Disorders, 13*(1), 1–12.

McCracken, G. (1988). *The long interview.* Newbury Park, CA: Sage Publications.

Mehan, H. (1987). Language and power in organizational process. *Discourse Processes, 10*, 291–301.

Miller, P. (1986). Teasing as language socialization and verbal play in a white working class community. In B. B. Schieffelin & E. Ochs (Eds.), *Language socialization across cultures* (pp. 199–212). Cambridge, UK: Cambridge University Press.

Mishler, E. (1986). *Research interviewing: Context and narrative.* Cambridge, MA: Harvard University Press.

Naremore, R. (1985). Explorations in language use: Pragmatic mapping in L1 and L2. *Topics in Language Disorders, 5*(4), 66–79.

Nelson, N. (1989). Curriculum-based language assessment and intervention. *Language, Speech, and Hearing Services in Schools, 20*, 170–184.

Ochs, E. (1979). Introduction: What child language can contribute to pragmatics. In E. Ochs & B. B. Schieffelin (Eds.), *Developmental pragmatics* (pp. 1–17). New York: Academic Press.

Ochs, E. (1982). Talking to children in Western Samoa. *Language in Society, 11*, 77–104.

Ochs, E. (1986). Introduction. In B. B. Schieffelin & E. Ochs (Eds.), *Language socialization across cultures* (pp. 1–16). Cambridge, UK: Cambridge University Press.

Ochs, E. (1988). *Culture and language development; Language acquisition and language socialization in a Samoan village.* Cambridge, UK: Cambridge University Press.

Ochs, E. (1990). Indexicality and socialization. In J. W. Stigler, R. A. Shweder, & G. Herdt (Eds.), *Cultural psychology* (pp. 287–308). Cambridge, UK: Cambridge University Press.

Ochs, E., & Schieffelin, B. B. (1984). Language acquisition and socialization: Three developmental stories and their implications. In R. A. Shweder & R. A. LeVine (Eds.), *Culture theory: Essays on mind, self, and emotion* (pp. 276–322). New York: Cambridge University Press.

Omark, D. (1981). Pragmatics and ethnological techniques for the observational assessment of children's communicative abilities. In J. Erickson & D. Omark (Eds.), *Communication assessment of the bilingual bicultural child: Issues and guidelines* (pp. 249–284) Baltimore, MA: University Park Press.

Polkinghorne, D. (1983). *Methodology for the human sciences: Systems of inquiry.* Albany, NY: State University of New York Press.

Philips, S. U. (1983). *The invisible culture.* New York: Longman.

Prutting, C. A. (1983). Scientific inquiry and communicative disorders: An emerging paradigm across six decades. In T. Gallagher & C. A. Prutting (Eds.), *Pragmatic assessment and intervention issues in language* (pp. 247–266). San Diego, CA: College-Hill Press.

Rees, N. (Speaker). (1988). *Pragmatics: A retrospective analysis* (Cassette Recording H81118-110). Rockville, MD: American Speech-Language-Hearing Association.

Rennie, D. L., Phillips, J. R., & Quartaro, G. K. (1988). Grounded theory: A promising approach to conceptualizing in psychology? *Canadian Psychology, 29*(2), 139–150.

Rice, M. L. (1986). Mismatched premises of the communicative competence model and language intervention. In R. L. Schiefelbusch (Ed.), *Language competence: Assessment and intervention* (pp. 261–280). San Diego, CA: College-Hill Press.

Rice, M. L. (1990, June). "Don't talk to him, he's weird": The role of language in early social interactions. Paper presented at the Social Use of Language: Pathways to Success Conference, Nashville, TN.

Rogoff, B. (1990). *Apprenticeship in thinking: Cognitive development in social context.* Oxford, UK: Oxford University Press.

Saville–Troike, M. (1982). *The ethnography of communication.* Baltimore, MD: University Park Press.

Schein, E. H. (1987). *The clinical perspective in fieldwork.* Newbury Park, CA: Sage Publications.

Schieffelin, B. B. (1979). Getting it together: An ethnographic approach to the study of the development of communicative competence. In E. Ochs & B. B. Schieffelin (Eds.), *Developmental pragmatics* (pp. 93–108). New York: Academic Press.

Schieffelin, B. B. (1990). *The give and take of everyday life.* Cambridge, UK: Cambridge University Press.

Schieffelin, B. B., & Eisenberg, A. (1984). Cultural variation in children's conversations. In R. L. Schiefelbusch & J. Pickar (Eds.), *Communicative competence: Acquisition and intervention* (pp. 377–422). Baltimore, MD: University Park Press.

Schieffelin, B. B., & Gilmore, P. (Eds.). (1986). *Acquisition of literacy: Ethnographic perspectives.* Norwood, NJ: Ablex Publishing.

Schieffelin, B. B., & Ochs, E. (1986a). Language socialization. *Annual Review of Anthropology, 15*, 163–246.

Schieffelin, B. B., & Ochs, E. (Eds.). (1986b). *Language socialization across cultures.* Cambridge, UK: Cambridge University Press.

Scollon, R., & Scollon, S. (1981). *Narrative, literacy and face in interethnic communication.* Norwood, NJ: Ablex Publishing.

Seymour, H. (1986a). Clinical principles for language intervention for language disorders among nonstandard speakers of English. In O. L. Taylor (Ed.), *Treatment of communication disorders in culturally and linguistically diverse populations* (pp. 115–134). San Diego, CA: College-Hill Press.

Seymour, H. (1986b). Clinical intervention for language disorders and nonstandard speakers of English. In O. L. Taylor (Ed.), *Treatment of communication disorders in culturally and linguistically diverse populations* (pp. 135–152). San Diego, CA: College-Hill Press.

Shewan, C. (1988). 1988 omnibus survey: Adaptation and progress in times of change, *Asha, 30*(8), 27–30.

Shewan, C., & Malm, K. E. (1989). The status of multilingual/multicultural service issues among ASHA members. *Asha, 31*(9), 78.

Slobin, D. I. (Ed.). (1967). *A field manual for cross-cultural study of the acquisition of communicative competence.* Berkeley: University of California, Language Behavior Research Laboratory.

Smith–Hefner, N. J. (1988). The linguistic socialization of Javanese children in two communities. *Anthropological Linguistics, 30*(2), 166–198.

Spindler, G., & Spindler, L. (1987a). Issues and applications in ethnographic methods (Editorial introduction). In G. Spindler & L. Spindler (Eds.), *Interpretive ethnography of education: At home and abroad* (pp. 1–7). Hillsdale, NJ: Lawrence Erlbaum.

Spindler, G., & Spindler, L. (1987b). Teaching and learning how to do the ethnography of education. In G. Spindler & L. Spindler (Eds.), *Interpretive ethnography of education: At home and abroad* (pp. 17–33). Hillsdale, NJ: Lawrence Erlbaum.

Spradley, J. P. (1979). *The ethnographic interview.* New York: Holt, Rinehart, & Winston.

Spradley, J. P. (1980). *Participant observation.* New York: Holt, Rinehart, & Winston.

Strauss, A., & Corbin, J. (1990). *Basics of qualitative research: Grounded theory, procedures, and techniques.* Newbury Park, CA: Sage Publications.

Taylor, O. L. (1986a). Historical perspectives and conceptual framework. In O. L. Taylor (Ed.), *Treatment of communication disorders in culturally and linguistically diverse populations* (pp. 1–19). San Diego, CA: College-Hill Press.

Taylor, O. L. (1986b). Teaching Standard English as a second dialect. In O. L. Taylor (Ed.), *Treatment of communication disorders in culturally and linguistically diverse populations* (pp. 153–178). San Diego, CA: College-Hill Press.

Taylor, O. L. (1986c). *Nature of communication disorders in culturally and linguistically diverse populations.* San Diego, CA: College-Hill Press.

Taylor, O. L., & Payne, K. (1983). Culturally valid testing: A proactive approach. *Topics in Language Disorders, 3*(3), 8–20.

Taylor, O. L., Payne, K., & Anderson, N. (1989, November). *Distinguishing between communication disorders and communication differences: Methods and procedures.* Miniseminar presented at the American Speech-Language-Hearing Association Conference, St. Louis, MI.

Thayer, J. T. (1988). Assessing the communicatively handicapped minority preschooler. *Seminars in Speech and Language 9*(1), 55–62.

Tharp, R. G., Jordan, C., Speidel, G. E., Hu-Pei Au, K., Klein, T. W., Calkins, R. P., Sloat, K. C. M., & Gallimore, R. (1984). Product and process in applied developmental research: Education and the children of a minority. In M. E. Lamb, A. L. Brown, & B. Rogoff (Eds.), *Advances in developmental psychology* (Vol. 3, pp. 91–144). Hillsdale, NJ: Lawrence Erlbaum.

Trueba, H. T. (1988). *Raising silent voices: Educating the linguistic minorities for the 21st century.* New York: Harper & Row.

Vogt, L., Jordan, C., & Tharp, R. G. (1987). Explaining school failure, producing school success: Two cases. *Anthropology and Education Quarterly, 18,* 276–286.

Ward, M. (1971). *Them children: A study in language learning.* New York: Holt, Rinehart, & Winston.

Watson–Gegeo, K. A., & Gegeo, D. W. (1986). Calling-out and repeating routines in Kwara'ae children's language socialization. In B. B. Schieffelin & E. Ochs (Eds.), *Language socialization across cultures* (pp. 17–50). Cambridge, UK: Cambridge University Press.

Weller, S. C., & Romney, A. K. (1988). *Systematic data collection.* Newbury Park, CA: Sage Publications.

Westby, C. (1985a). Learning to talk—talking to learn: Oral-literate language differences. In C. Simon (Ed.), *Communication skills and classroom success* (pp. 181–218). San Diego, CA: College-Hill Press.

Westby, C. (1985b, November). *Cultural differences in caregiver-child interaction: Implications for assessment and intervention.* Paper presented at American Speech-Language-Hearing Association Conference, San Francisco, CA.

Westby, C. (1989, November). *Cultural variations in story telling.* Miniseminar presented at the American Speech-Language-Hearing Association Conference, St. Louis, MI.

Westby, C. (1990). Ethnographic interviewing: Asking the right questions to the right people in the right way. *Journal of Childhood Communication Disorders, 13*(1), 101–111.

Westby, C., & Rouse, G. (1985). Culture in education and the instruction of language learning-disabled students. *Topics in Language Disorders, 5*(4), 15–28.

Williamson, S. G. (1979). *Tamil baby talk: A cross-cultural study.* Unpublished doctoral dissertation, University of Pennsylvania, Philadelphia.

Wolcott, H. F. (1987). On ethnographic intent. In G. Spindler & L. Spindler (Eds.), *Interpretive ethnography of education: At home and abroad* (pp. 37–57). Hillsdale, NJ: Lawrence Erlbaum.

CHAPTER 5

A Functionalist Approach to Language and Its Implications for Assessment and Intervention

ELIZABETH BATES, DONNA THAL
AND BRIAN MacWHINNEY

There is a constant tension in the field of speech-language pathology between researchers who are wedded to the use of carefully controlled and designed conditions for the study of language and clinicians who need to know how to remediate language disorders in the much more messy real world. The problems created by this tension have been the topic of many discussions, including a recent ASHA Report (Shewan, 1990). Yet, over the past 20 years, a number of approaches to the study of language and language disorders have been developed that provide a better framework for clinician-researcher communication. One of these is Functionalism, an approach to the study of language which Carol Prutting pioneered. Her appli-

Portions of this chapter previously appeared in "Functionalism and the Competition Model" by E. Bates & B. MacWhinney, 1989, in B. MacWhinney & E. Bates (Eds.), *The Crosslinguistic Study of Sentence Processing* (Chapter 1). New York: Cambridge University Press. A preliminary version was also printed as "What Is Functionalism?" by E. Bates & B. MacWhinney, 1988, in *Papers and Reports in Child Language*. Palo Alto, CA: Stanford University Press.

cation of pragmatics to the study of language assessment and intervention was an important step toward bridging the gap between theoretical approaches and clinical applications. This chapter represents our attempt to continue the bridge building that Carol exemplified in her productive career by describing a recent functionalist model and suggesting how insights derived from the model may be applied to real-world clinical situations.

Functionalism can be defined as the belief that, the forms of natural languages are created, governed, constrained, acquired and used in the service of communicative functions. So defined, functionalism is the natural alternative to theories of language that postulate a strict separation between structure and function, and/or theories that attempt to describe and explain structural facts *sui generis,* without reference to the constraints on form that are imposed by the goals of communication and the capabilities and limitations of human information processing.

Although this definition seems sensible enough as stated, it has become sadly clear over the years that the term "functionalism" alone does not communicate very well. It means different things to different people, and worst of all there seems to be a "Straw Man" Functionalism that causes trouble wherever we go. In this chapter, the principles of the Straw Man Functionalism are compared and contrasted with an approach that is much more reasonable and much more likely to succeed. Some possible applications of this approach to language assessment and intervention are then suggested.

The straw man form of functionalism can be summarized with the following six beliefs:

1. Grammer is a direct reflection of meaning.
2. Grammer is iconic.
3. Mappings from meaning to grammar are one to one.
4. Mappings from meaning to grammar are deterministic.
5. Functionalism is anti-nativist.
6. Functionalism is anti-linguistic.

In the next few pages, these six straw man beliefs will be reviewed one at a time, and each will be replaced with a more viable functionalist account. The particular functionalist theory used in this chapter is called the *Competition Model.* It is based on two decades of research on more than a dozen languages, including studies of language acquisition in children, language processing in adults, and language breakdown in aphasia (Bates, 1976; Bates & MacWhinney, 1979, 1982, 1987, 1989; Bates, Thal, & Marchman, in press; MacWhinney, 1978, 1987; MacWhinney & Bates, 1989).

FROM STRAW MAN FUNCTIONALISM
TO THE COMPETITION MODEL

1. GRAMMAR IS NOT A DIRECT REFLECTION OF MEANING

Instead, grammars reflect the interaction between cognitive content and cognitive process. Grammars carry out important communicative work. Like individual lexical items, specific grammatical devices (word order principles, bound and free morphemes, suprasegmental cues) are associated with meanings and/or communicative goals. But the association is rarely direct. It may be more useful to think of language as a complex traffic control problem, with many different meanings competing for expression in a linear (i.e., time-delimited) channel. The limits imposed by human information processing (limits of perception, articulation, learning, and memory) may ultimately prove more important than meaning itself in elucidating why grammars come to look the way they do.

Figure 5–1 illustrates a two-pronged approach to the explanation of linguistic form, representing an attempt to explain why languages look the way they do. On the one hand, we agree with the proponents of functionalist linguistics and/or cognitive grammar (Chafe, 1971; Dezso, 1972; Dik, 1980; Driven, & Fried, 1987; Fillmore, 1987; Firbas, 1964; Firth, 1951; Foley & Van Valin, 1984; Givón, 1979; Halliday, 1966; Lakoff, 1987; Langacker, 1987) that linguistic forms are associated with and motivated by specific kinds of semantic and/or pragmatic content. In other words, linguistic forms exist to convey messages between human beings. But we disagree with many functionalist linguists who believe that they can explain a given language solely through detailed descriptions of its message constraints (i.e., the restrictions on form-function mappings). That kind of explanation is, we think, only one half of the functionalist story. The other half includes a complex, interacting set of human information processing constraints that operate whenever we use language in real time. These include the opportunities and limitations imposed by memory, perception, planning and articulation of speech movements, and the learning process itself. These message constraints and information processing constraints pose a number of problems that have to be solved together. Hence every natural language can be viewed as a "constraint satisfaction network" (Rumelhart, McClelland, & the PDP Research Group, 1986), a system of converging and (often) competing forms and functions that must be understood to explain how languages evolved in the first place, how they are used by speakers and listeners today, how they are acquired by children, and how they go awry under a range of pathological conditions. We have called out theory the "Competition Model" to capture the highly interactive nature of the form-function mappings that comprise any natural language.

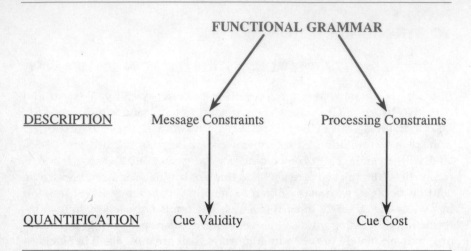

Figure 5–1. Two-pronged view of linguistic form.

In the Competition Model two fundamental principles are used to conceptualize and quantify this traffic control problem: cue validity and cue cost.

The term *cue validity* refers to the information value of a given lexical or grammatical device for any particular meaning or function. The term comes from Gestalt psychology (Brunswik, 1956), where it was broadly used to refer to the information structure of some aspect of the environment for any goal or condition that is of interest to the organism; it is related to (perhaps equivalent to) the better-known term ecological validity, which is widely used in the study of animal behavior (Eibl–Eibesfeldt, 1975) and in the Gibsonian approach to perception (Gibson, 1966, 1969). Later on we will talk about how to calculate cue validity from samples of real language use. For present purposes, it is important to emphasize that validity refers to the environment *from the language user's point of view*. Unlike frequency (which really is an objective property of the environment, whether anyone cares about it or not), validity refers to the signal value of some piece of the environment for a goal or event that is important for the organism that we are trying to study. For example, instead of measuring the absolute frequency of a grammatical device like subject-verb agreement, the value of subject-verb agreement can be measured as a cue to the agent role (i.e., who did what to whom?).

The term *cue cost,* also derived from the study of perception, is used to explain why cue validity does not predict behavior perfectly. In an ideal world, an ideal animal would behave in perfect accordance with cue validity. But people do not live in an ideal world, and they are not ideal animals.

The relationship between meaning and form in language cannot be perfect, because of all the constraints imposed by human information processing systems. Our experiments to date have shown that cue validity strongly determines the order of acquisition of cues by children and the extent to which adult speakers rely on those cues during sentence interpretation. Cue validity also plays a major role in the sentence comprehension and production profiles displayed by adults suffering from severe forms of aphasia. However, there are still many systematic exceptions to this principle. Most of these exceptions can be accounted for by invoking principles of cue cost, that is, the information processing costs associated with the real-time use of any given lexical or grammatical cue. For example, cues that are equally informative can vary in their perceivability (e.g., because two syllables are easier to hear than one, the form of the plural morpheme that follows a voiceless fricative, as in "glasses," is easier to perceive than that in the word "cats"). Cue cost will influence the degree to which adults "trust" this particular cue to meaning, the age at which children come to rely on the cue, and the degree of resistance to impairment associated with this particular cue in sentence processing by adults with brain damage. Similarly, cues can vary in the demands they place on memory. "Local cues" (e.g., a case suffix marked directly on the noun) can be used as soon as they are encountered (providing immediate information about the semantic role that noun is going to play in the sentence). These linguistic forms appear to have an advantage over "long-distance cues" which distribute the same semantic information across a set of discontinuous elements (e.g., subject-verb agreement in a sentence like "The *boys* I told you about *are* coming over tonight"). A full account of how grammars come to look the way they do, and how and when they are acquired by children will require an analysis of the complex interplay between meaning (quantified as cue validity) and information processing (quantified as cue cost). Grammars represent a compromise among these forces, and for this reason, the communicative function of a given grammatical form may be quite opaque.

2. GRAMMAR IS NOT ICONIC

Instead, the relations between form and function are symbolic and indexical. Linguistic forms rarely, if ever, resemble their meanings. There are of course a few examples of words that "sound like" the things they stand for (e.g., Bang!), but these are few and far between. It is even more difficult to think of grammatical devices that bear a literal physical resemblance to their meanings. There is of course the apocryphal claim that natural languages prefer basic word orders in which the subject precedes the verb because human beings "naturally" tend to perceive actors before they perceive their actions. This claim is silly enough that it is not worth pursuing. But if grammars do not "look like" their meaning, what kind of natural cause-and-effect relationship could be said to hold between form and function?

C. S. Peirce (1932) provided an analysis of sign-referent relations that may be as useful in the study of grammar as it is in the study of single signs. *Icons* are signs that come to stand for their referents because of a literal physical resemblance (e.g., a stylized picture of a cigarette to indicate a smoking zone). *Indices* are another class of "natural" signs that come to stand for their referents, not because of a physical resemblance but because of their participation in the same event (e.g., contiguity rather than similarity). For example, smoke can serve as an index to fire because the two are commonly associated in real life. *Symbols* are signs that bear no natural relation to their referents (neither iconic nor indexical); instead, they carry meaning only because of an arbitrary convention, an agreement that was reached by a particular community of users. As Langacker (1987) pointed out, most lexical and grammatical signs bear a symbolic relationship to their meanings. Grammatical devices exist to carry out communicative work, but the work they do does not determine their form. However, in the domain of grammar there may well be many cases of indexical causality if we keep in mind that grammars are jointly caused by cognitive content *and* cognitive processing.

To offer just one example, consider the relative clause. This device typically is used to identify referents in discourse, for example, "The man that sold me the car," a clause that picks one particular man out of a range of other possibilities. In principle, the reference specification function could be served by a purely arbitrary (i.e., symbolic) device. However, the reference specification function itself tends to call indexical factors into play that help to determine its shape and position of the relative clause. Bindings between a referent and its modifier are easier to make if the two are in close proximity. Hence the function of referent identification is best served if the relative clause is placed near its governing noun phrase, where other modifiers are located. However, this solution poses another problem: the relative clause must interrupt a main clause. Such interruption is costly for two reasons. First, because relative clauses are longer than most modifiers, the main clause has to be held open for a rather long time. Second, because relative clauses resemble main clauses in many respects, there is a potential for confusion (e.g., which verb goes with which noun). In principle, this problem could be solved by placing a warning signal at the beginning of a sentence to indicate that "a relative clause will be placed within the following sentence at some point; you guess which point." Although this is a logical possibility, it should be obvious why it would not work very well. It makes much more sense to place the marker *at the point of interruption,* to keep the listener from chasing down some garden path and to help him or her construct and attach the clause right where it belongs (i.e., near the element that it modifies). Finally, insofar as an interruption places quite a burden on the processor, the interruption-marking device had best be kept short and sweet. Hence the functions of the relative clause have an effect not only on the existence of certain devices (symbolic determinism), but also on their position and overall shape (indexical determinism). In neither case is it reasonable to say that the resulting grammatical device "looks like" its meaning!

3. MAPPINGS BETWEEN FORM AND FUNCTION ARE NOT ONE TO ONE

Instead, they are many to many. Grammars can be viewed as a class of solutions to the problem of mapping nonlinear meanings onto a highly constrained linear medium. The universal and culture-specific contents of cognition interact with universal constraints on information processing, creating a complex multivectorial problem space with a finite number of solutions. Natural languages exhaust the set of possible solutions to this mapping problem, and because these solutions represent many competing forces, they invariably involve many-to-many mappings between form and function (cf. Karmiloff–Smith, 1979), with correlated meanings riding piggyback on correlated bits of grammar. No single meaning (however abstract) can be allowed a grammatical monopoly.

Figure 5–2 illustrates a network of such form-function mappings, a fragment of the large network that constitutes our knowledge of "subjecthood" in English. The network includes three communicative roles that are usually, but not always, assigned to the same referent in an English sentence:

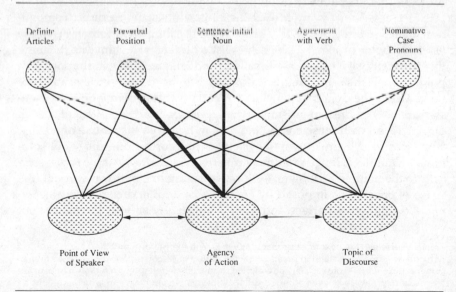

Figure 5–2. Fragment of the sentence role(s) network.

agency (e.g., the actor role for a transitive action verb), topic-hood (the element that we have been talking about so far), and point of view (usually the point of view of the speaker). Because these three important communicative functions go together much of the time, most languages have evolved ways to map them together as a block. The English subject role is a typical example of such a "block assignment." The subject role is referred to as a block or coalition because subjecthood refers to a range of different and potentially separate linguistic devices. In English, the subject tends to be the first noun in the sentence, the noun that comes directly before the verb, and the noun that agrees with the verb in person and number. If the subject is expressed in a pronominal form, it is usually expressed in nominative case (e.g., "I" rather than "me"; "she" rather than "her"). Interestingly, although it is not usually thought of as a cue to the subject role, across most natural languages statistically the subject is particularly likely to be a first person pronoun ("I"). Presumably this is because people like to talk about themselves, that is, their point of view and the topic of the sentence tend to be the same.[1] Finally, because the subject coalition is usually mapping topichood as well as agency, the subject tends to be "old information," which is in turn likely to be expressed with definite reference (e.g., using the definite article "the" when an article is used at all). All of these correlated surface devices can be used in comprehension as cues to sentence role to help the listener figure out who did what to whom.

The many-to-many nature of grammatical mapping is both a cause and a result of the instability inherent in linguistic systems. In fact, there may be no stable, perfect pathway through the linguistic problem space. As Slobin (1982) pointed out, many processing constraints stand in direct competition; hence stability in one area may create instability in another. From the listener's point of view, a given linguistic marker will signal its meaning most efficiently if it is consistent, salient, and unique. But from the speaker's point of view, the same linguistic device has to be easy to retrieve and produce. Hence the clear and perceivable markers that evolve for comprehension are often subject to erosion in the service of rapid and efficient speech output. Faced with these competing demands, across the course of history, languages have been known to cycle back and forth from one set of solutions to another. Hence grammars must be viewed as a set of *partial solutions* to the mapping problem, each representing one pathway through the space of constraints imposed by cognitive content and cognitive processing. No solution is perfect, and each is constantly subject to change; but

---

[1] Not surprisingly, the next most probable subjects tend to be "you" and "he/she/it," a reflection of how human goals and interests shape the nature of discourse. Indeed, in some human languages the subject role can only be assigned to an animate referent, preferably a human animate referent; there are even some so-called split-ergative languages in which one kind of "special" subject role is reserved for first and second person only; a different treatment is given for third person topics (Silverstein, 1976).

every grammar used by a community of human adults and acquired by their children has to meet certain implicit but implacable limits of tolerance.

4. MAPPINGS FROM MEANING TO GRAMMAR ARE NOT DETERMINISTIC

Grammatical mappings are inherently probabilistic. Languages differ qualitatively in the presence or absence of certain linguistic devices (e.g., word order constraints, case-marking), but they also differ quantitatively in the extent to which the same linguistic device is used at all and in the range of functional roles it has come to serve. One of the ways in which the Competition Model differs from other functionalist approaches to language lies in its heavy emphasis on the probabilistic nature of linguistic knowledge as well as language use. In a sense, in constructing the Competition Model, we have followed the same path that physicists followed in embracing quantum mechanics: the probabilistic nature of our data is not just a reflection of our imperfect measures; rather, we have been forced to conclude that nature itself is probabilistic at its core. (For a lucid discussion, see Stephen Hawking's *A Brief History of Time*, 1988.) In everyday terms, this means that the relationship between form and meaning is inherently imperfect; when we learn a language, we learn not only *that* a given form and meaning go together, we also learn *how strongly* they go together in our native language. This also means that the "same" mapping from form to meaning (e.g., the relationship the actor role and preverbal position) can vary systematically in strength from one language to another.

We have given a number of examples of such quantitative differences between languages throughout our work (see especially papers in MacWhinney and Bates, 1989). One particularly important example has to do with the relative strength of word order versus subject-verb agreement as cues to sentence meaning. In English, word order is rigidly preserved; in almost all structures, the order that is preserved is Subject-Verb-Object or SVO. In Italian, word order can be varied extensively for pragmatic purposes—a fact that comes as something of a surprise to those who believe that such pragmatic word order variation occurs only in case-inflected languages (i.e., languages with markers on the noun to indicate who did what to whom). The following list (from Bates & MacWhinney, 1989) illustrates some possible variations in the order of major constituents in Italian in a hypothetical restaurant conversation. This short conversation (hypothetical but quite plausible according to our Italian informants) contains all possible orders of Subject, Verb, and Object.

1. SVO: *Io mangerei un primo.*   I would eat a first course.
2. OSV: *La pastasciutta Franco la*   Pasta Franco it orders always
   prende sempre qui.   here.

3. VSO: *Allora, mangio anche io la pastasciutta.*   Well then, am eating also I pasta.

4. VOS: *Ha consigliato la lasagna qui Franco, no?*   Has recommended the lasagna here Franco, no?

5. OVS: *No. la lasagna l'ha consigliata Elizabeth.*   No, the lasagna (it) has recommended Elizabeth.

6. SOV: *Allora, io gli spaghetti prendo.*   In that case, I the spaghetti am having.

Some of these require particular intonation patterns to sound exactly right, and some are definitely better with particular grammatical markers like the object clitic. But all of these orders can be found in a large enough sample of free speech, and all of them occur at some point in the input received by Italian children (Bates, 1976).

At one level, this discourse serves merely to illustrate a well-known qualitative difference between languages: Italian has word order options that do not exist in English at all. However, this quanitative variation also has quantitative implications. In several different experiments it has been demonstrated that Italian listeners "trust" word order—even good old-fashioned Subject-Verb-Object order—less than their English counterparts. Given a sentence like "The pencil hits the cow," English listeners from ages 2 to 80 have a strong tendency to pick the pencil as the agent/subject. Given the Italian equivalent (*"La matita colpisce la vacca"*), Italians of all ages are much more likely to choose the cow as the agent/subject. Hence a qualitative difference in the availability of word order types has a quantitative effect even on a subset of grammatical structures that both languages share (e.g., SVO order).

Most of our joint research to date has concentrated on sentence comprehension. But we have also discovered some interesting quantitative differences in the domain of sentence production. For example, Bates and Devescovi (1989) described some robust differences between Italian and English in the use of relative clauses. The structural options available in the two languages are the same, at least for the set of structures studied by these investigators. In both languages, it is perfectly grammatical to describe a picture of a monkey eating a banana by saying either "A monkey is eating a banana" or "There is a monkey that is eating a banana." However, English speakers typically use the first option; Italian speakers describing exactly the same picture, under the same conditions, are three to five times more likely to produce a relative clause. This cross-linguistic difference in relative clause use is already well established in children by the age of three, and it tends to persist even in elderly patients who have suffered left-hemisphere damage. How can we capture a quantitative difference between two structures that are equally grammatical from a traditional grammatical perspective? To be sure, there are some differences between the two languages in the range of functions that control these particular forms. In particular, Italians appear to use the relative clause as a kind of topic marker. But in addition to (and perhaps because of) these differences in function, there are also clear processing differences between English and Italian in the "accessibility" of the relative clause. Similar statistical differences between Italian and English children have been found in rates of article omission (greater in English children well before the age of three) and in rates of subject omission (with much higher rates of subject omission in Italian children even in the stage of first word combinations [Bates, 1976]). Some of these differences (e.g., subject omission) are treated in current linguistic theory in terms of a discrete set of rules or parameters; others (e.g., article omission) receive no treatment at all in current linguistic theory. It may be that these early differences in performance can only be captured by assuming that very small children are sensitive to statistical as well as structural facts about the language they are trying to acquire. Function and frequency codetermine the selection of grammatical forms in sentence production, in language use by adults, and in language acquisition by children.

As noted earlier, physicists have made their peace with the counterintuitive predictions of quantum mechanics, and they now accept the premise that the position of a subatomic particle may be unknowable *in the absolute.* Uncertainty lies at the core of the universe; it is not just a byproduct of man's imperfect measures. We argue that the human language processor is also probabilistic at its core. In the Competition Model, the adult speaker's knowledge of his native language is represented in a probabilistic form, and probabilities play a fundamental role in the process of language acquisition. The difference between obligatory rules and statistical tendencies is simply a matter of degree. This does not mean that we ignore the powerful laws that separate one language from another. After all, the values "0" and "1" do exist even in a probabilistic system, and an adult native speaker thus may come to know with some certainty that a particular structure is impossible in his or her language. The difference between this characterization of adult knowledge (i.e., "competence to perform") and the characterizations offered in most competence models lies in its ability to capture the many values that fall between 0 and 1. Linguistic representations are described in terms of a complex set of *weighted form-function mappings,* a dynamic knowledge base that is constantly subject to change. Returning to the network described in Figure 5–2, a fragment of the English subject system, in principle the weight or strength of the relationship between each form (e.g., preverbal position, subject-verb agreement) and each of the three related functions (agency, topic-hood, point of view) can be calculated. In the Competition Model, these weights would be used to predict the degree to which listeners "trust" each of the subject cues when they are trying to decide who did what to whom. In English, positional cues (e.g., sentence-initial position, preverbal position) are strongly associated with the actor role (i.e., their weights are strong), and they are used quickly and reliably to assign sentence roles during comprehension; in Italian, the same cues are much less reliable (i.e., their weights are small), and as a result, Italian listeners tend to rely more on other, stronger sources of information to assign the actor role (e.g., subject-verb agreement, lexical contrasts, definiteness).

Within this framework, language acquisition can be viewed as a process of *meaning-driven distributional analysis,* similar in spirit to the approach outlined some time ago by Maratsos (1982). However, the Competition Model also furnishes some nonlinear principles that permit the capture of sudden phase transitions, U-shaped functions, and the effect of rare events—all of the phenomena that forced psychologists to abandon the simple linear associative models of American Behaviorism. Many of these discoveries within our model have fallen out of two approaches to the quantification and formalization of language learning: (a) mathematical modeling of the effects of cues on choice behavior in sentence comprehension (McDonald, 1986; McDonald & MacWhinney, 1989) and (b) computer simulations of the learning process (Taraban, McDonald, & MacWhinney, in press). For example, we have discovered that cue validity can be operationalized in two ways: *overall cue validity* (the proportion of all the cases in which an interpretation must be made in which a given cue is available and leads to a correct interpretation) and *conflict validity* (the proportion of cases in which one cue competes with another in which the cue in question "wins"). Both of these metrics can be calculated objectively from texts of real speech, and used to predict the choice behavior of children and adults in sentence comprehension experiments. Interestingly, we have discovered that overall cue validity drives the early stages of language acquisition; conflict validity (affected primarily by rare cases, particularly those that are encountered in complex discourse) drives the late stages of learning in older children and adults. With these two statistical principles, abrupt changes in sentence processing strategies that occur as late as 7 to 10 years of age can be captured.

Although the Competition Model was developed independently (to deal with facts of acquisition and processing across different natural languages), in its current form the model has a great deal in common with a recent movement that is alternatively referred to as *connectionism, neural modeling* and/or *parallel distributed processing* (e.g., Elman, 1990; Rumelhart, et al., 1986). It remains to be seen how strong that relationship will be, but we are at least convinced that the tools we share will prove to be exceptionally important in the next era of language acquisition research. Cognitive psychology has proceeded for more than 30 years without an adequate model of learning. Unfortunately, research in language acquisition has done the same. The new focus on learning in "brain-like systems" is a healthy one, whatever its limits may prove to be. And the new tools (i.e., mathematical modeling, multivariate statistics, computer simulation) are bound to lead to progress. Natural languages are so complex that "eyeball analysis" alone can only take us so far—probably no farther than we have come to date.

5. FUNCTIONALISM IS NOT ANTI-NATIVIST

It is, in fact, based on the unique biological heritage of humans. The innateness issue is one of the major sources of anger and misunderstanding in the field of psycholinguistics. Much of this misunderstanding comes from a failure to distinguish between *innateness* and *domain-specificity*. The innateness issue has to do with the extent to which human language is determined by the unique biological heritage of our species. But this biological heritage may include many capacities that are not unique to language itself: the large and facile brain, particular social organization, and protracted infancy of the human species, and a variety of unknown factors that may contribute in indirect but very important ways to the problem of mapping universal meanings onto a limited channel, and to the particular solutions that we have found to that problem. Hence the human capacity for language could be both innate and species-specific, and yet involve no mechanisms that evolved specifically and uniquely for language itself. Language could be a new machine constructed entirely out of old parts (Bates, 1979). The universal properties of grammar may be *indirectly innate,* based on interactions among innate categories and processes that are not specific to language. In other words, we believe in the innateness of language, but we are skeptical about the degree of domain specificity that is required to account for the structure and acquisition of natural languages.

6. FUNCTIONALISM IS NOT ANTI-LINGUISTIC

Instead, functionalist claims are made at different levels of evidence. Functionalist theories of performance are not in direct competition with any linguistic theory. Different kinds of functionalist claims require different kinds of evidence. This is a point that has been made before in several places (notably Bates & MacWhinney, 1982, 1987, 1989), but it is sufficiently important that it deserves reiterating here. Four different levels of functionalist claims, ordered from weakest to strongest (in the sense that claims at the higher levels presuppose that claims at the lower levels are true) can be distinguished.

Level 1 focuses on the role of cognitive and communicative functions in the evolution of language proper, and the history of individual languages. Claims at Level 1 constitute a kind of linguistic Darwinism, that is, arguments that functional constraints have played a role in determining the forms that grammars take today. Where did the tiger get his stripes? Why do grammars have relative clause markers? A great deal of work in functionalist linguistics is of this historical sort, in particular studies of "grammaticization" (e.g., Bybee, 1985; Givón, 1979). Although this work is extremely interesting in its own right, claims at the historical level do not necessarily have implications for current language use by adults, language acquisition by children, or the proper characterization of grammatical knowledge. Like the large-scale forces that operate to create mountains and rivers across geological time, the forces that operate across many individuals to bring about historical language change may not be detectable (or even operative) in every individual case.

Level 2 is a synchronic variant of Level 1, focusing on the causal relationship between form and function in real-time language use by adult speakers of the language. Much of our own work with adults is of this sort: We manipulate competing and converging sets of grammatical forms as "causes" to see what interpretations our subjects derive; conversely, we manipulate competing and converging meanings in picture and film description, to see what expressive devices our subjects produce to meet these demands. However, even if we could show a perfect cause-and-effect relation in adults, we could not immediately conclude that children are able to perceive or exploit these relations.

Level 3 presupposes but goes beyond Level 2, focusing on the causal role of cognitive and communicative functions in language acquisition by children. The cause-and-effect work of Level 2 must be repeated at every stage of language acquisition to determine empirically if and when children are sensitive to the form-function correlations available in the adult model. Furthermore (as noted earlier), we need a well-articulated theory of the learning process, one that can adequately describe, predict, and explain the stages that children go through on their way to adult performance.

Finally, *Level 4* is reserved for the claim that facts from Levels 1 through 3 play a direct role in the characterization of adult linguistic competence. A variety of competence models of this sort have been proposed within the functionalist tradition, ranging from *Eastern European functionalism* (i.e., the so-called Prague School—Dezso, 1972; Driven & Fried, 1987; Firbas, 1964; Firth, 1951), *British functionalism* (e.g., Halliday, 1966), the American school of *generative semantics* (e.g., Chafe, 1971; Fillmore, 1968) to more recent proposals that include *cognitive grammar* (Lakoff, 1987; Langacker, 1987), *construction grammar* (Fillmore, 1987), *role and reference grammar* (Foley & Van Valin, 1984), and several other approaches that either retain the simple term "functionalism" or elect to avoid labels altogether (e.g., Dik, 1980; Givón, 1979; Kuno, 1986). For the sake of simplicity, these otherwise rather disparate linguistic theories will be referred to with the single term *functional grammar*. Although functional grammars are not designed to account for real-time processing, they are most compatible with highly interactive models of performance, that is, like the Competition Model. For obvious reasons, "modular" theories of performance are instead more compatible with "modular" theories of competence, that is, with linguistic theories that emphasize the autonomy of various components and subcomponents of the grammar (cf. Berwick & Weinberg, 1984; Bresnan, 1982; Pinker, 1984). It is quite possible that ultimately there will be a convergence between some Level 4 versions of functional grammar and the performance model that we have developed to account for data at Levels 1 to 3. But it is also possible, at least in principle, that there may be a rapprochement between a functionalist model of performance and the various rules and representations that have been proposed within the many-times-revised-and-extended school of generative grammar.

In short, we are not anti-linguistic, nor is our work directly relevant to any particular class of competence models. We are consumers of linguistic theory, and we have our own bets about which linguistic theory or class of theories ultimately will prevail. But we are much too preoccupied with problems of a different sort to enter into the linguistic fray. This is an exciting new era in language acquisition research, and time is too precious to be wasted on battles that are best waged elsewhere.

APPLICATIONS OF THE COMPETITION MODEL TO NORMAL ADULTS AND CHILDREN

As summarized in MacWhinney and Bates (1989), the Competition Model has provided a framework for the study of sentence comprehension, sentence production and grammaticality judgments, in child and/or adult speakers of more than a dozen different languages (English, Italian, German, French, Dutch, Spanish, Serbo-Croatian, Hungarian, Turkish, Hebrew, Japanese, Chinese, and Warlpiri). In all of these studies, dramatic cross-linguistic differences in the relative "strength" and timing of grammatical cues have been explained using the twin principles of cue validity and cue cost.

A particularly clear example comes from a recent "on-line" study of grammaticality judgments by Wulfeck, Bates, and Capasso (1991). This study compared American and Italian college students listening to errors of agreement (e.g., "She are selling books down by the river") and to errors of word order involving the same sentence elements (e.g., "She selling is books down by the river"). In both languages, college students were able to detect these errors almost 100% of the time. However, Americans were significantly faster at detecting word order errors; conversely, Italians were significantly faster at detecting errors of agreement. These results follow directly from differences between English and Italian in the cue validity or information value of agreement (high in Italian, low in English) and word order (high in English, lower in Italian). Of course both languages have word order, and both languages have agreement. However, the relative importance of these two sources of information influences the way that native speakers distribute their attention as a sentence comes in.

The Competition Model has also been applied to the acquisition of a second language by normal adults (Kilborn & Ito, 1989; McDonald, 1989). In these studies, cross-linguistic differences in cue validity can be used to predict patterns of transfer from the adult's first language (L1) to the adult's second language (L2). For example, native speakers of German and/or Italian tend to rely primarily on subject-verb agreement when they are asked to interpret English sentences (e.g., given an "odd" sentence like "The dog are kicking the cows," German-English and Italian-English bilinguals tend to choose "the cows" as the subject; monolingual English speakers are much more likely to choose "the dog," rigidly following SVO word order). Conversely, native speakers of English tend to pay more attention to word order than any other cue when they are trying to process a second language. A particularly compelling example of this kind of transfer comes from a study of English-Japanese bilinguals by Harrington (1987), which was described by Kilborn and Ito (1989). In Harrington's study, bilingual subjects were presented with Japanese sentences in which the basic word order of that language (SOV) was placed in competition with semantics (e.g., The pencil the cow is kicking) and/or with morphological cues. Surprisingly, the English subjects actually relied more on SOV word order than their Japanese counterparts (e.g., choosing the pencil as the agent in a sentence like "The pencil the cow is kicking"). Since SOV is not a realistic option in English, Kilborn and Ito interpreted this result as evidence for a kind of "meta-transfer": faced with a new and unfamiliar language like Japanese, these English adults looked for the relevant word order cues in that language and used them as their main source of information. As Kilborn (1987) has shown in other studies, this kind of transfer can be very costly: bilingual listeners may "get the right answer" most of the time with their L1 strategies, but they pay a high price in processing efficiency (i.e., slower reaction times, particularly in situations that require rapid and immediate integration of semantic and grammatical cues). Put somewhat differently, use of the wrong cue validity structure results in high cue cost.

In studies of first language acquisition, the general rule appears to be that children start out by learning the most valid cues in their language (e.g., Turkish children rely on case morphology more than word order from the very beginning; English children rely on word order from the very beginning and make little use of other grammatical cues for several years). However, there are some important exceptions to this general rule which underscore the interaction between cue validity and cue cost. For example, we now know that of all forms of agreement (subject-verb, object-pronoun) as primary cues to sentence meaning in comprehension tend to be "postponed" by children until 6 or 7 years of age, even though the same children often know how to produce those forms in their own speech by the age of 2! French, Italian, Spanish, Serbo-Croatian, and Hebrew are all languages in which adults rely heavily on agreement cues in our sentence comprehension task (e.g., given a sentence that is equivalent to "The dog is kicking the cow," they tend to choose "the cow" as the actor); however, in all four languages this adult profile of sentence processing does not show up until 7 years of age (Devescovi, D'Amico, Smith, Mimica, & Bates, 1990; Kail, 1989; Sokolov, 1989). The reason appears to be that use of agreement cues in comprehension (but not production) requires the listener to keep a lot of elements in mind (first listen to and remember the first noun, check it against the verb, but then wait until you hear the next noun because you could be fooled, check it against the verb, and so on). Children appear to operate under memory limits of some kind that are "lifted" around 6 to 7 years of age, when they finally "calibrate" to interpret sentences in an adult mode.

Other cue cost factors that have been studied to date include *perceivability*, that is, differences in phonological salience between cues that are equally high in information value. For example, MacWhinney, Pléh, and Bates (1985) have studied the acquisition and use of the Hungarian accusative case inflection "–t" under two different conditions: after a strong vowel (e.g., "bear-nominative" or *maci*—> "bear-accusative" or *macit*) and after a final consonant (e.g., "squirrel-nominative" or *mokus*—> "squirrel-accusative" or *mokust*). The same inflection is easier to hear in the first condition, and it is in this condition that Hungarian children first demonstrate an ability to use accusative case markings as a cue to sentence meaning.

Another cue cost factor is one that Bates and MacWhinney (1989) have called *functional readiness*, that is, the conceptual difficulty or cognitive cost of the communicative function that underlies a given grammatical cue. For example, some grammatical devices (e.g., the relative clause) bear a very strong and consistent relationship to their primary functions (e.g., specifying the identity of the intended referent for one's listener). However, it may be relatively difficult for young children to understand this reference-specification function (i.e., how much information the listener needs for successful communication to take place) because their cognitive skills are not yet sufficiently developed. In a case like this, a grammatical device may be acquired relatively late despite its high cue validity.

APPLICATIONS OF THE COMPETITION MODEL TO LANGUAGE DISORDERS

During the 1970s and 1980s, many English-speaking aphasiologists were drawn to the notion that grammatical impairment is somehow uniquely associated with nonfluent Broca's aphasia (see especially Caramazza & Berndt, 1985; Heilman & Scholes, 1976; Zurif & Caramazza, 1976). By definition, individuals with Broca's aphasia display reduced syntactic complexity and omission of bound inflections and free-standing grammatical function words in their expressive language—a form of "expressive agrammatism." The further conclusion that this syndrome reflects a kind of "central agrammatism" was based (at least in part) on the finding that individuals with Broca's aphasia display a form of *receptive agrammatism*, that is, deficits in receptive processing of the same morphosyntactic elements that are missing or impaired in their expressive language. For example, patients who appear to comprehend reasonably well at a conversational level (i.e., in a bedside clinical examination) fail to comprehend the difference between sentences like "He showed her the baby pictures" and "He showed her baby the pictures." From this point of view, the deficits displayed by adults with Wernicke's aphasia could be reinterpreted to reflect a form of "central semantic deficit." If adults with Broca's aphasia are impaired in receptive and expressive processing of grammatical elements, those with Wernicke's aphasia may suffer from a complementary impairment in the receptive and expressive processing of content words. This claim appears to unify several of the behavioral symptoms that define Wernicke's aphasia: moderate to severe problems in language comprehension in patients with fluent but empty speech, marked by moderate to severe word-finding deficits and a tendency toward word substitutions, word blends, and/or neologisms.

Taken together, these complementary forms of aphasia appear to constitute strong evidence for the modularity and dissociability of grammar and semantics—in direct contrast to the most central tenets of the Competition Model. How can a functionalist theory that insists on an intimate relationship between grammar and meaning deal with findings of this kind? As it turns out, our model fits the cross-linguistic evidence on aphasia surprisingly well.

In our cross-linguistic research program, the Competition Model was recently extended to the study of language breakdown in patients with non-fluent Broca's aphasia and fluent Wernicke's aphasia. These two forms of aphasia were chosen because they permit the broadest possible survey of grammatical symptoms across natural languages. This may seem surprising, in view of the above claim that adults with Wernicke's aphasia have "preserved" grammar but "impaired" semantics. However, a more careful examination of speech by fluent aphasics suggests that these patients also suffer from *paragrammatism*, that is, a tendency to substitute one grammatical form for another (a grammatical analogue to the word substitutions and blends that characterize the speech of adults with Wernicke's aphasia at a lexical level). These symptoms are often difficult to see in English. If a patient says "I went the train to London," has he committed a lexical error (substituting "went" for "took") or a grammatical error (omitting the function word "on")? In richly inflected languages like German or Hungarian, the grammatical problems associated with Wernicke's aphasia are much more obvious, because these patients frequently produce the wrong inflected form for nouns, articles, and other content words. Indeed, the pioneering German aphasiologist Arnold Pick (who invented the term "agrammatism") (Pick, 1913/1973) insisted that there are two forms of agrammatism, frontal and posterior. In fact, Pick argued that the agrammatism associated with fluent (posterior) aphasia may be much more interesting, reflecting deficits at a deeper stage of speech production when grammatical forms are selected for use.

Our cross-linguistic results support Pick's view of agrammatism; in a sense we have merely rediscovered cross-linguistic facts that were known a hundred years ago, but temporarily lost in the 1970s and 1980s when English-language studies dominated the field of aphasiology (see Bates & Wulfeck, 1989a, 1989b, for a detailed discussion). However, the Competition Model has permitted us to take a number of steps beyond Pick's original insights to develop a theory of grammatical processing in aphasia that is compatible with the basic principles of the Competition Model. Briefly summarized, our research to date leads to the following five conclusions (for reviews, see Bates & Wulfeck, 1988a, 1989b; Bates, Wulfeck, & MacWhinney, in press)

Cross-Linguistic Variation

First, cross-linguistic studies by our research team and by other research groups (see Menn & Obler, 1990) have clearly demonstrated that the "same" aphasic syndromes look very different from one language to another. Indeed, in many of our cross-linguistic experiments to date language differences account for more variance than patient group differences (e.g., Bates, Friederici, & Wulfeck, 1987a, 1987b, 1988; Bates, Friederici, Wulfeck, & Juarez, 1988; Vaid & Pandit, in press; Wulfeck, Bates, Juarez, Opie, Friederici, MacWhinney, & Zurif, 1989). English, Italian, and German patients tend to preserve SVO word order—often to a greater extent than normal speakers of the same language. But Turkish aphasics tend to preserve SOV word order—again, to an extent that often exceeds word order usage by normal adults, as though the aphasic patients were sticking with canonical word order as a kind of "safe harbor" for their disturbed sentence planning. Additionally, in all of the languages that have been studied, patients are generally "right more often than they are wrong" at the level of grammatical morphology, producing correct case endings, forms of the article, forms of modifier agreement, and conjugations of the verb at a level that would be impossible to explain if we still believed that grammar had somehow been "disconnected" from the rest of language processing. We conclude that the "shape" of grammatical impairment in aphasia reflects the basic principles of cue validity: strong mappings between form and function tend to "protect" areas of grammar from omission or substitution; weak mappings tend to be "at risk."

Performance Deficits

The existence, strength, and nature of the cross-linguistic differences uncovered in these studies lead to the conclusion that language-specific knowledge (i.e., competence) is largely preserved in Broca's and Wernicke's aphasia, requiring an account of language breakdown based on deficits in the processes by which this preserved knowledge base is accessed and deployed (i.e., performance). In the Competition Model, this means that grammatical deficits in aphasia must be explained by some form of cue cost. This conclusion had led, in turn, to an expanded use of "on-line" or "real-time" experimental procedures that yield information about how patients from different language groups arrive at a correct or incorrect response in receptive and expressive language use (see especially Friederici & Kilborn, 1989; Wulfeck, Bates, & Capasso, in press).

Selective Vulnerability of Morphology

Overlaid on these language differences, there is some evidence for a modified version of the closed-class theory of agrammatism, the idea that grammatical inflections and function words can be selectively impaired in aphasia. In these and other papers by the same research team, evidence has been found for closed-class impairments in production, comprehension, and error detection, although the degree and nature of those impairments vary greatly from one language to another. We have to conclude that closed-class elements are particularly "expensive" to process, that is, they are particularly vulnerable to general or specific deficits in processing capacity (see below). At the same time, these cross-linguistic studies have also helped to distinguish between aspects of morphology that are "at risk" (e.g., case contrasts that are irregular and/or relatively difficult to perceive) and those that appear to be "protected" (e.g., case contrasts that are regular and/or relatively easy to perceive) within and across language types (see especially Friederici, Weissenborn, & Kail, in press; MacWhinney, Osmán-Sági, & Slobin, in press).

Patient Group Similarities

The selective vulnerability of morphology described above is apparently not restricted to individuals with agrammatic Broca's aphasia. We have observed equivalent morphological deficits in the expressive language of individuals with fluent Wernicke's aphasia; receptive deficits appear in an even wider range of patient groups, including some patients who are neurologically intact (see especially Bates et al., 1987a; MacWhinney, Osmán–Sági, & Slobin, in press). This suggests that closed-class items might be vulnerable to global forms of cue cost that are only indirectly related to the effects of focal brain injury (e.g., perceptual degradation, cognitive overload). Such findings point to the need for experiments that control for the contribution of a global reduction in perceptual and/or cognitive resources to isolate forms of grammatical impairment that are specific to particular types of aphasia from those that can be induced in normals under stressed or nonoptimal processing conditions (e.g., Kilborn, in press).

Patient Group Differences

Finally, although there are indeed more similarities than differences in the patterns of sparing and impairment observed in patients with Broca's and Wernicke's aphasia, a set of contrasts that holds up across very different language types has been found: differential success in the production of nouns (higher in Broca's) and verbs (higher in Wernicke's) (Bates, Tzeng, & Chen, in press), differences in the ability to exploit both grammatical and lexical redundancy (higher in Broca's) (Bates et al., 1987a, 1987b), and differences in the nature of morpheme substitution errors (patients with Broca's aphasia tend to substitute neutral or high-frequency forms, where as those with Wernicke's aphasia tend toward a more random pattern of substitutions) (Bates, Friederici, & Wulfeck, 1988). Although the reason for these "neurolinguistic universals" is still not understood, the cross-linguistic approach has brought us one step closer to a model of intrahemispheric organization that can handle universal and language-specific differences between syndromes. Specifically, we have begun to explore processing factors that could produce contrasting forms of grammatical impairment within a single interlocking network of form-function mappings. For example, Dell (1990) showed that variations in the timing and activation of speech forms can produce qualitatively different error patterns: high speed and/or underinhibited patterns of activation result in substitution errors (including low-probability substitutions); low speed and/or underexcited patterns of activation result in omission errors (i.e., failure to reach threshold) or in conservative patterns of substitution (a high-frequency form is substituted for a lower frequency target). Schwartz and Dell (1990) demonstrated that the complementary error patterns displayed by patients with Broca's and Wernick's aphasia could reflect just such a "speed/accuracy tradeoff" or "fluency/precision tradeoff" (see also Bates, Appelbaum, & Allard, in press). Although a complete model of the complementarities between fluent and nonfluent aphasia is not yet available, it appears that an interactive, functionalist model can be extended to account for qualitative variations in language impairment.

In short, the Competitive Model is not "defeated" by patterns of language breakdown in aphasia. It contains principles that can account for cross-linguistic variations in the symptoms displayed by patients from the same patient group, and within-language variations in the elements of grammar that are "protected" or "at risk" across patient groups. This kind of variability is difficult to explain in traditional modular or "disconnection" approaches to aphasia. And it appears that by manipulating dimensions of activation and cue cost, the model can also be extended to account for qualitatively different forms of aphasia.

To date, the Competition Model has not been extended to the study of language disorders in children. However, Leonard and his colleagues have begun to carry out cross-linguistic studies of specific language impairment (SLI) in English and Italian (Leonard, 1989; Leonard, Sabbadini, Leonard, & Volterra, 1987; Leonard, Sabbadini, & Volterra, 1988). His results to date are quite compatible with our studies of language breakdown in aphasic adults. For example, he has found that (a) grammatical morphology is generally richer and better preserved in Italian children with SLI, compared with their English counterparts (in line with predictions based on cue validity), but that (b) grammatical morphology is still the most vulnerable area of development *within* each language group (in line with predictions based on cue cost). Furthermore, Leonard, Bartolini, Caselli, McGregor, and Sabbadini (1991) have been able to predict specific patterns of grammatical strength and vulnerability within each language, based on a specific set of cue cost principles that he terms "the surface hypothesis."

What do these findings mean for clinical practice? The Competition Model provides a coherent theoretical framework within which to analyze language disorders and devise intervention strategies in an ecologically sound manner. Since the "pragmatics revolution" of the 1970s and 1980s, clinicians have come to trust their intuitions about "real talk," about evaluating and treating language in valid communication contexts (Gallagher & Prutting, 1983; Lund & Duchan, 1988; Prutting, 1982; Prutting & Kirchner, 1987; Roth & Speckman, 1984). However, it isn't always clear how to proceed to implement this belief. If plain everyday talk were enough, children with communication disorders would have already learned language in its ecological niche. Clearly something else is wrong. For children with mental retardation or autism, one probable factor is lack of "functional readiness." According to Bates and MacWhinney (1987) "Functional readiness means that children will not acquire a complex form until they can assimilate it, directly or indirectly, to an underlying function" (p. 176). Clearly children with mental retardation have cognitive limitations that may prevent development of functional readiness at some levels. Similarly, many children with autism have broad cognitive limitations as well. On the other hand, Wetherby and Prutting (1984) noted heterochronous development of communicative skills in autistic children. They described superior development of skills that can be learned through trial-and-error type problem solving and deficient development of skills that require observational learning. This suggests a potential processing problem which creates higher than normal cue costs for the development of symbolic and social communicative devices such as symbolic play and conventional communicative gestures. Analysis of cue cost factors may also be most appropriate for children with specific language impairment who, by definition, are acquiring linguistic forms at levels below those expected by their development in other areas of cognition. For example, the kinds of auditory processing deficits described by Tallal and her colleagues (Tallal, 1988) would affect the perceivability of critical (and highly valid) cues. Limitations on memory and attention would also affect what is learned. Specific examples from two classes of communication disorders are briefly described below.

One obvious example is the oral language problems associated with hearing loss. In such children cues are reduced or distorted, thus interfering with their usefulness. In the case of severe or profound hearing loss the validity of the auditory cues in the language of the community in which the children are being raised is irrelevant because the cues are not heard and thus are not available for use. This is a major cue cost factor based on a biologically based sensory deficit.

Another interesting example is the language impairment seen in children with autism. A widely recognized characteristic of children who are autistic but not mute is the use of immediate and delayed echolalia. The functional uses of this speech form have been described (Prizant & Duchan, 1981) and attributed to extreme reliance on a "Gestalt" language learning style (Prizant, 1983; Prizant & Wetherby, 1988; Wetherby, 1984). This may create a cue cost by preventing or bypassing perception of the sequential ordering of auditory information and the fact that the speech stream is composed of important individual parts. Thus, the appropriate form to function mapping is missed despite the presence of valid cues. As noted above, another communicative problem of children with autism is the heterochronous development of communicative functions. Wetherby (1986) proposed that children with autism acquire the functions of language one at a time rather than in the parallel manner observed in infants who are developing normally. Functions for regulating behaviors to achieve environmental ends are acquired first, those for achieving social ends considerably later. Wetherby hypothesized that this may be due to delayed or impaired cortical inhibition of the limbic system which would allow continued dominance of limbic-controlled vocal signals which are of low information value and are thought to be emotional or self-stimulatory vocalizations. If form-function mappings occur on a cortical level and if inhibition of the limbic system is necessary for the development of the higher cortical function of communication for social purposes, this could account for the later development of social form-function connections. This then would be another cue cost factor, but at the level of brain development.

The immediately preceding discussion describes how the Competition Model could be used to account for certain observable phenomena in language disorders. Another question remains, however. Can it be a useful guide to assessment and intervention? Again we are just beginning to consider these issues, and again our answer is a tentative yes. Analysis of cue validity for the communication system being learned by individuals who are communicatively impaired will allow us to identify which factors usually work for normal individuals. Assessment of the individual who is com-

municatively impaired will focus on functional readiness and on perceptual, memory or other information processing difficulties that create cue
costs for the individual. Further assessment would include the environments in which the individual must communicate to identify environmental cue cost factors. Most of this is what speech-language pathologists
already do. What is new is a coherent theoretical framework that can be
used to structure and guide clinical practice from a functionalist point of
view. Here are just a few suggestions.

Identify Cue Costs and Manipulate Them Directly

The easiest and most straightforward example of a manageable cue cost factor is oral language delay due to hearing impairment. Amplification will decrease the cue costs associated with hearing impairment, costs that might
otherwise have a particularly severe effect on the acquisition of closed-class
morphemes, because those morphemes are more difficult to detect and
identify in a fluent speech stream. (See Volterra and Bates [1989] for a discussion of the relationship between hearing impairment and selective deficits in grammatical morphology.) It could also be speculated that amplification of closed-class morphemes might assist children with specific language impairment to overcome the selective vulnerability of morphology
(Withee & Tallal, 1989). This is clearly speculative because the cue cost factors that are responsible for the selective vulnerability of morphology are not
known. However, it is not far-fetched if one considers the successful use of
mild amplification for remediating disorders of phonology (Hodson & Padden, 1991). Hopefully, this will be a productive area of clinical research.

Provide Strong Examples of Form-Function Mapping

In some cases it will not be possible to eliminate or decrease cue costs directly. In such cases therapists need to find a way to get around the cue cost
limits by finding and exaggerating "natural" cue validity to make the necessary relationship between form and meaning particularly clear for the child.
Cue validity estimation can be used by the clinician to figure out (a) what
the ecological niche of a given linguistic device ought to be, (b) which of the
network of meanings served by a given device is the most reliable guide to
its use (i.e., the best candidate for a therapeutic "caricature" or exaggera-
tion), and (c) the specific items to present in context, providing repeated
opportunities to observe "natural" instances of form-function mapping. To
some extent, this is exactly what most good clinicians already do. An example comes from a strategy for intervention proposed by Prizant and
Wetherby (1988) for children with autism, in which they recommend moving gradually from the existing form-function mappings to the use of more
sophisticated forms to map the same functions. The same may be said for

the commonly used ecologically and pragmatically sound practices of modeling, expansion, and extension (Duchan & Weitzner–Lin, 1987) and the long known practices of self-talk and parallel talk (Norris & Hoffman, 1990). The key point is that "real talk" alone is probably not sufficient for effective intervention; if it were, children with normal language input would already have the problem solved. Cue validity analysis is a technique that can help clinicians identify specific targets for intervention-in-context, a kind of "amplified pragmatics" that goes beyond normal input but preserves its most essential characteristics.

This "cartoon" approach is not without problems. According to the Competition Model (and to all serious functionalist theories of grammar), the mappings between form and meaning are many to many (see also Karmiloff–Smith, 1979, on "plurifunctionality" in language use). Because cues and functions form a whole network of interlocking relations, an intervention that exaggerates one piece of the mapping could skew the whole system (at least temporarily), presenting the child with an unrealistic picture of the competitions, cooperations, and conspiracies among pieces of the language that characterize real-time language use. The solution to this problem is old-fashioned bootstrapping: if we can help the child to "break into" the most reliable mappings between grammar and meaning, we may start a benign cycle of incidental learning in the child's home and school environment that ultimately will lead to the acquisition of the complete form-function network that underlies a speakers knowledge of what to do and when to do it in his native language.

In short, the Competition Model provides a rigorous and potentially quantifiable framework for doing what speech-language pathologists already know they should be doing: finding out what communicative work language really does and what processing limits prevent the "natural" environment from working in specific cases. This is the approach that characterized Carol Prutting's work on pragmatics and language processing; these were the key insights that she taught to her students, and conveyed to her friends and colleagues, in a career that illustrated why research and clinical practice belong together.

REFERENCES

Bates, E. (1976). *Language and context*. New York: Academic Press.
Bates, E., with Benigni, L., Bretherton, L., Camaioni, L., & Volterra, V. (1979). *The emergence of symbols*. New York: Academic Press.
Bates, E., Appelbaum, M., & Allard, L. (in press). Statistical constraints on the use of single cases in neuropsychological research. *Brain and Language*.
Bates, E., Chen, S., & Tzeng, O. (1991). The noun-verb problem in Chinese aphasia [Special issue on crosslinguistic aphasia]. *Brain and Language*.
Bates, E., & Devescovi, A. (1989). A functionalist approach to sentence production. In B. MacWhinney & E. Bates (Eds.), *The crosslinguistic study of sentence processing*. New York: Cambridge University Press.

Bates, E., Friederici, A., & Wulfeck, B. (1987a). Grammatical morphology in aphasia: Evidence from three languages. *Cortex, 23,* 545–574.

Bates, E. Friederici, A., & Wulfeck, B. (1987b). Comprehension in aphasia: A cross-linguistic study. *Brain and Language, 32,* 19–67.

Bates, E., Friederici, A., & Wulfeck, B. (1988). Grammatical morphology in aphasia: A reply to Niemi et al. *Cortex, 24,* 583–588.

Bates, E., Friederici, A., Wulfeck, B., & Juarez, L. (1988). On the preservation of word order in aphasia: Cross-linguistic evidence. *Brain and Language, 33,* 323–364.

Bates, E., & MacWhinney, B. (1979). A functionalist approach to the acquisition of grammar. In E. Ochs & B. Schieffelin (Eds.), *Developmental pragmatics.* New York: Academic Press.

Bates, E., & MacWhinney, B. (1982). A functionalist approach to grammar. In E. Wanner & L. Gleitman (Eds.), *Language acquisition: The state of the art.* New York: Cambridge University Press.

Bates, E., & MacWhinney, B. (1987). Competition, variation and language learning. In B. MacWhinney (Ed.). *Mechanisms of language acquisition.* Hillsdale, NJ: Lawrence Erlbaum.

Bates, E., & MacWhinney, B. (1989). Functionalism and the competition model. In B. MacWhinney & E. Bates (Eds.), *The crosslinguistic study of sentence processing.* New York: Cambridge University Press.

Bates, E., Thal, D., & Marchman, V. (in press). Symbols and syntax: A Darwinian approach to language development. In N. Krasnegor, D. Rumbaugh, R. Schiefelbusch, & M. Studdert–Kennedy (Eds.), *Behavioral foundations of language.* Hillsdale, NJ: Lawrence Erlbaum.

Bates, E., & Wulfeck, B. (1989a). Crosslinguistic studies in aphasia. In B. MacWhinney & E. Bates (Eds.), *The crosslinguistic study of sentence processing.* New York: Cambridge University Press.

Bates, E., & Wulfeck, B. (1989b). Comparative aphasiology: A cross-linguistic approach to language breakdown. *Aphasiology, 3,* 111–142, 161–168.

Bates, E., Wulfeck, B., & MacWhinney, B. (1991). Cross-linguistic research in aphasia: An overview [Special issue on crosslinguistic aphasia]. *Brain and Language.*

Berwick, R., & Weinberg, A. (1984). *The grammatical basis of linguistic performance.* Cambridge, MA: MIT Press.

Bresnan, J. (Ed.). (1982). *The mental representation of grammatical relations.* Cambridge, MA: MIT Press.

Brunswik, E. (1956). *Perception and the representative design of psychology experiments.* Berkeley: University of California Press.

Bybee, J. (1985). *Morphology: A study of the relation between meaning and form.* Amsterdam: John Benjamins.

Foley, W., & Van Valin, R. (1984). *Functional syntax and universal grammar.* New York: Cambridge University Press.

Friederici, A., & Kilborn, K. (1989). Temporal constraints on language processing in Broca's aphasia. *Journal of Cognitive Neuroscience, 1,* 262–272.

Friederici, A., Weissenborn, J., & Kail, M. (in press). Pronoun comprehension in aphasia: A comparison of three languages [Special issue on crosslinguistic aphasia]. *Brain and Language.*

Gallagher, T., & Prutting, C. (Eds.). (1983). *Pragmatic assessment and intervention issues in language.* San Diego, CA: College-Hill Press.

Gibson, E. J. (1969). *Principles of perceptual learning and development.* East Norwalk, CT: Appleton-Century-Crofts.

Gibson, J. J. (1966). *The senses considered as perceptual systems.* Boston, MA: Houghton Mifflin.

Givón, T. (1979). *On understanding grammar*. New York: Academic Press.

Halliday, M. (1966). Notes on transitivity and theme in English: Part 1. *Journal of Linguistics, 2*, 37–71.

Harrington, M. (1987). Processing transfer: Language-specific strategies as a source of interlanguage variation. *Applied Psycholinguistics, 8*, 351–378.

Hawking, S. W. (1988). *A brief history of time: From the big bang to black holes*. New York: Bantam Books.

Heilman, K. M., & Scholes, R. J. (1976). The nature of comprehension errors in Broca's, conduction and Wernicke's aphasics. *Cortex, 12*, 258–265.

Hodson, B., & Padden, E. (1991). *Targeting intelligible speech* (2nd ed.). Austin TX: Pro-Ed.

Kail, M. (1989). Cue validity, cue cost and processing types in sentence comprehension in French and Spanish. In B. MacWhinney & E. Bates (Eds.), *The crosslinguistic study of sentence processing* (pp. 77–117). New York: Cambridge University Press.

Karmiloff–Smith, A. (1979). *A functional approach to child language*. New York: Cambridge University Press.

Kilborn, K. (1987). *Sentence processing in a second language: Seeking a performance definition of fluency*. Ph.D. thesis, University of California, San Diego.

Kilborn, K. (in press). Selective impairment of grammatical morphology due to induced stress in normal listeners: Implications for aphasia [Special issue on crosslinguistic aphasia]. *Brain and Language*.

Kilborn, K., & Ito, T. (1989). Sentence processing strategies in adult bilinguals. In B. MacWhinney & E. Bates (Eds.), *The crosslinguistic study of sentence processing*. New York: Cambridge University Press.

Kuno, S. (1986). *Functional syntax*. Chicago: University of Chicago Press.

Lakoff, G. (1987). *Women, fire and dangerous things*. Chicago: University of Chicago Press.

Langacker, R. (1987). *Foundations of cognitive grammar*. Palo Alto, CA: Stanford University Press.

Leonard, L. B. (1989). Language learnability and specific language impairment in children. *Applied Psycholinguistics, 10*, 179–202.

Leonard, L. B., Bortolini, U., Caselli, M. C., McGregor, K. K., & Sabbadini, L. (1991). Two accounts of morphological deficits in children with specific language impairment. Unpublished manuscript, Purdue University, West Lafayette, IN.

Leonard, L. B., Sabbadini, L., Leonard, J., & Volterra, V. (1987). Specific language impairment in children: A crosslinguistic study. *Brain and Language 32*, 233–252.

Leonard, L. B., Sabbadini, L., Volterra, V., & Leonard, J. (1988). Some influences on the grammar of English- and Italian-speaking children with specific language impairment. *Applied Psycholinguistics, 9*, 39–57.

Loeb, D., & Leonard, L. B. (1988). Specific language impairment and parameter theory. *Clinical Linguistics and Phonetics, 2*, 317–327.

Loeb, D., & Leonard L. B. (in press). Subject case marking and verb morphology in normally developing and specifically language-impaired children. *Journal of Speech and Hearing Research*.

Lund, N. J., & Duchan, J. F. (1988). *Assessing children's language in naturalistic contexts* (2nd ed.). Englewood Cliffs, NJ: Prentice-Hall.

MacWhinney, B. (1978). The acquisition of morphophonology. *Monographs of the Society for Research in Child Development, 43*, 1.

MacWhinney, B. (1987). The competition model. In B. MacWhinney (Ed.), *Mechanisms of language acquisition*. Hillsdale, NJ: Lawrence Erlbaum.

MacWhinney, B., & Bates, E. (Eds.). (1989). *The crosslinguistic study of sentence process-*

ing. New York: Cambridge University Press.

MacWhinney, B., Osmán–Sági, J., & Slobin, D. (in press). Sentence comprehension in aphasia in two clear case-marking languages [Special issue on crosslinguistic aphasia]. *Brain and Language.*

MacWhinney, B., Pléh, C., & Bates, E. (1985). The development of sentence interpretation in Hungarian. *Cognitive Psychology, 17,* 178–209.

Maratsos, M. (1982). The child's construction of linguistic categories. In E. Wanner & L. Gleitman (Eds.), *Language acquisition: The state of the art.* New York: Cambridge University Press.

McDonald, J. (1986). The development of sentence comprehension strategies in English and Dutch. *Journal of Experimental Child Psychology, 41,* 317–335.

McDonald, J. (1989). The acquisition of cue-category mappings. In B. MacWhinney & E. Bates (Eds.), *The crosslinguistic study of sentence processing.* New York: Cambridge University Press.

McDonald, J., & MacWhinney, B. (1989). Maximum likelihood models for sentence processing. In B. MacWhinney & E. Bates (Eds.), *The crosslinguistic study of sentence processing.* New York: Cambridge University Press.

Menn, L., & Obler, L. K. (1990). *Agrammatic aphasia: Cross-language narrative sourcebook.* Amsterdam/Philadelphia: John Benjamins.

Norris, J., & Hoffman, D. (1990). Language intervention within naturalistic environments. *Language, Speech, and Hearing Services in Schools, 21,* 72–84.

Peirce, C. S. (1932). *Language and context: Collected papers.* Cambridge, MA: Harvard University Press.

Pick, A. (1973). *Aphasia.* (J. N. Brown, Ed. & Trans.). Springfield, IL: Charles C. Thomas. (Original work published 1913)

Pinker, S. (1984). *Language learnability and language development.* Cambridge, MA: Harvard University Press.

Prizant, B. (1983). Language acquisition and communicative behavior in autism: Toward an understanding of the "whole" of it. *Journal of Speech and Hearing Disorders, 48,* 296–307.

Prizant, B., & Duchan, J. (1981). The functions of immediate echolalia in autistic children. *Journal of Speech and Hearing Disorders, 46,* 241–249.

Prizant, B., & Wetherby, A. (1988). Providing services to children with autism (ages 0 to 2 years) and their families. *Topics in Language Disorders, 9,* 1–23.

Prutting, C. (1982). *Observational protocol for pragmatic behaviors* [Clinical manual]. Developed for the University of California Speech and Hearing Clinic, Santa Barbara.

Prutting, C., & Kirchner, D. (1987). A clinical appraisal of the pragmatic aspects of language. *Journal of Speech and Hearing Disorders, 52,* 105–119.

Roth, F., & Spekman, N. (1984). Assessing the pragmatic abilities of children: Part I. Organizational framework and assessment parameters. *Journal of Speech and Hearing Disorders, 49,* 2–11.

Rumelhart, D., McClelland, J., & the PDP Research Group. (1986). *Parallel distributed processing: Explorations in the microstructure of cognition.* Cambridge, MA: MIT/ Bradford Books.

Schwartz, M. F., & Dell, G. S. (1990, October). *Comparing speech error patterns in normals and jargon aphasics: Methodological issues and theoretical implications.* Paper presented at the 28th Annual Meeting of the Academy of Aphasia, Baltimore, MD.

Shewan, C. (Ed.). (1990, December). The "future of science and services" seminar. *ASHA Reports 20* (ISSN 0569-8553). Rockville, MD: American Speech-Language-Hearing Association.

Silverstein, M. (1976). Hierarchy of features and ergativity. In R. Dixon (Ed.), *Grammatical categories in Australian languages.* Canberra: Australian Institute of Aboriginal Studies.

Slobin, D. I. (1982). Universal and particular in the acquisition of language. In E. Wanner & L. Gleitman (Eds.), *Language acquisition: The state of the art*. New York: Cambridge University Press.

Sokolov, J. (1989). Cue validity and the acquisition of Hebrew. In B. MacWhinney & E. Bates (Eds.), *The crosslinguistic study of sentence processing*. New York: Cambridge University Press.

Tallal, P. (1988). Developmental language disorders: Part I. Definition. *Human Communication Canada, 12*(2), 7–22.

Taraban, R., McDonald, J., & MacWhinney, B. (in press). Category learning in a connectionist model: Learning to decline the German definite article. *Journal of Memory & Language*.

Vaid, J., & Pandit, R. (in press). Sentence interpretation in normal and aphasic Hindi speakers [Special issue on crosslinguistic aphasia]. *Brain and Language*.

Wetherby, A. (1984). Possible neurolinguistic breakdown in autistic children. *Topics in Language Disorders, 4*, 19–33.

Wetherby, A. (1986). Ontogeny of communicative functions in autism. *Journal of Autism and Developmental Disorders, 16*, 295–315.

Wetherby, A., & Prutting, C. (1984). Profiles of communicative and cognitive-social abilities in autistic children. *Journal of Speech and Hearing Research, 27*, 364–377.

Withee, J., & Tallal, P. (1989). Modality-specific selective attention deficit in developmental dysphasics. [Abs.] *Journal of Clinical and Experimental Neuropsychology, 11*(1), 26.

Wulfeck, B., Bates, E., & Capasso, R. (in press). A crosslinguistic study of grammaticality judgments in Broca's aphasia [Special issue on crosslinguistic aphasia]. *Brain and Language*.

Wulfeck, B., Bates, E., Juarez, L., Opie, M., Friederici, A., MacWhinney, B., & Zurif, E. (1989). Pragmatics in aphasia: Crosslinguistic evidence. *Language and Speech, 32*, 315–336.

Zurif, E., & Caramazza, A. (1976). Psycholinguistic structures in aphasia: Studies in syntax and semantics. In H. Whitaker & H. A. Whitaker (Eds.), *Studies in neurolinguistics* (Vol. I). New York: Academic Press.

CHAPTER 6

Pragmatic Characteristics of the Child with Specific Language Impairment: An Interactionist Perspective

HOLLY K. CRAIG

Pragmatic approaches have dominated research efforts in child language disorder for approximately 10 years. These approaches are concerned with language use in context and focus on both linguistic and conversational rules. This chapter offers a synthesis of accumulating pragmatic information as it relates to children with Specific Language Impairment (SLI) and proposes a theoretical model that depicts the various levels of language production that accordingly seem intact or potentially problematic for these children.

Pragmatics can be defined as the study of the set of rules underlying discourse use of the language code for communication purposes. Determination of the relationship between linguistic and pragmatic rules is critical to the study of pragmatics and to discussions of pragmatic characterizations of the SLI child. Conceptualization of this relationship has important theoretical implications for the formulation of pragmatic models and theories and for the articulation of language acquisition processes. The proposed nature of this pragmatic-linguistic relationship will have a profound impact on definitions of language impairments and organization of clinical management efforts for language-disordered children.

Although pragmatic theorists (Austin, 1962; Hymes, 1971; Searle, 1969, 1974, 1975) proposed a complex interactive relationship between conversational and linguistic systems, early clinical interpretations were less clear. Now, a decade later, some pragmatic researchers are concerned that clinical pragmatics has not fully realized its potential and, indeed, may not do so if it is interpreted and applied as though it were a simple substitute for generative grammar, rather than a paradigmatically different approach (Brinton, Craig, & Skarakis–Doyle, 1990; Gallagher, 1990).

In 1983, Craig observed that clinically the relationship between linguistic and pragmatic rules could be conceptualized in two ways: as a narrow interpretation, or as a broad interpretation. A narrow interpretation views pragmatics as a separate set of discourse rules that are distinct from syntactic, semantic, and morphological rules, and which are linked loosely to these structural behaviors in a simple additive manner (Miller, 1978; Prutting, 1979; Prutting & Kirchner, 1983). By implication, within intervention these rule systems could be taught independently from each other. For example, therapy goals might focus on the acquisition of a particular grammatical form without concomitant consideration of its conversational applications, or a particular discourse function might be targeted without attention to its associated linguistic constraints. A narrow interpretation then highlights the *independence* of these systems and implies few changes in clinical practice. Definitions of language behaviors appropriate for clinical consideration would only have to expand to include functions. In this sense, the term "pragmatic" can be applied appropriately as a contrast to the term "linguistic," for example, linguistic or grammatical rules versus pragmatic functions. Prutting & Kirchner (1987) characterized this approach to pragmatics as a "pragmatics-as-separate'" interpretation in which pragmatics constitutes another language level, analogous to content or form. Johnston (1989) suggested that this view predominates clinically.

In contrast, pragmatics also can be interpreted more broadly from an interactionist perspective so that language is viewed as an integration of rule systems in which communication functions are the underlying force determining the selection of linguistic structures (Bates, 1976b; Bates & MacWhinney, 1979; Halliday, 1975; MacNamara, 1972). From this interactionist perspective, linguistic and conversational rules are distinguishable but functionally inseparable, and an *interdependence* between systems is highlighted. Accordingly, semantic-syntactic rules can be fully understood only relative to their communication purposes. By implication, interactive purposes provide the impetus for language acquisition and linguistic rules are acquired to communicate these purposes in a manner consistent with the child's language community. The child's pragmatic knowledge, therefore, must include linguistic rules, discourse functions, and an understanding of how to integrate the two.

Integration between these systems will reflect the differentiation of linguistic forms by discourse function. Accordingly, some linguistic forms will suit some discourse functions and others will not. For example, the sentences "it's funny" and "well it's funny" are distinguished by the use of the adverb "well." This lexical item is appropriately encoded when the utterance serves a response function and omitted when it serves a comment function. The linguistic choices, including lexical item and syntactic placement, are determined in part by the conversational function of the utterance. In other words, properties of the discourse regulate selection of the unique combinations of linguistic behaviors involved in message formulation. Prutting and Kirchner's (1987) "pragmatics-as-cause-effect" perspective is consistent with this interdependent view. They argued that the communicative outcome is the most useful clinical application of pragmatics and they focused on the appropriateness of linguistic behaviors. These interactionist perspectives, then, use the term "pragmatic" in a different sense. Rather than standing in opposition to the term "linguistic," pragmatic is an overarching description that refers to the integration of "linguistic" rules and "conversational" rules. The terms "conversational" or "discourse-based" may better express these context-dependent relationships.

Pervasive clinical implications derive from the interactionist approach to pragmatics. Language assessment and the resultant determination of goals for intervention would require consideration of linguistic behaviors nested within conversational units. The set of linguistic behaviors associated with the discourse functions of a child with a language disorder which yield unsuccessful communication outcomes would have to be identified and conversational-linguistic goals that have the potential to result in more successful interactive outcomes would have to be specified. Assessment protocols would be more comprehensive and include nonverbal communicative behaviors (Penn, 1988; Prutting & Kirchner, 1983, 1987). Intervention goal statements would be more inclusive so that discourse functions and structural realizations would be formulated in combination for each goal. Clinical activities would highlight social purposes and create intervention contexts that preserve naturalness (Craig, 1983; Halle, 1984).

Clinically, this broader interactionist view would predict that improving the child's linguistic forms in the absence of instruction about the discourse properties governing their expression or their relative effectiveness in communicating specific conversational functions would yield a communicatively ineffective language user. Despite an increasing repertoire of linguistic forms and longer sentence lengths, many utterances would be inappropriate, inadequate, or semantically unrelated to the conversational task.

Over the past few years, a consensus has been emerging that favors the interactionist viewpoint clinically as well as theoretically (Fey, 1986; Lund & Duchan, 1988; Roth & Spekman, 1984). The interactionist model proposed by Bloom and Lahey (1978) has been particularly influential. Their model proposes that language is the interaction of content rules, form rules, and use rules, and they depict this interaction as the partial overlap of three circles. Their model addresses language production and attempts to account for both normal and disordered child language. The problems of the child with SLI are conceptualized as a separation of form from content and use, a deficiency in syntactic rules with essentially intact semantic and pragmatic rules (Bloom & Lahey, 1978; Lahey, 1988). By implication, difficulties experienced semantically and pragmatically would be secondary to the child's primary problems with form.

Considerable information has been accumulating regarding the pragmatic skills of children with SLI. The following discussion will attempt to summarize this information and to address the following questions. How can children with SLI be characterized pragmatically? What future research directions are implied by this characterization? Is this characterization consistent with interactionist theory? What clinical implications pertain?

PRAGMATIC CHARACTERISTICS OF THE CHILD WITH SLI

Children with Specific Language Impairment demonstrate poor expressive or poor receptive and expressive language skills in the absence of clinically significant neurological impairment, hearing loss, emotional problems, or sensory-motor defect, and their general intelligence appears to be within the normal range. The SLI diagnostic label is applied on the basis of well-accepted exclusion criteria (Stark & Tallal, 1981) and may encompass linguistically heterogeneous subgroups (Craig & Evans, 1989; Fey & Leonard, 1983; Stark & Tallal, 1981; Wolfus, Moscovitch, & Kinsbourne, 1980). The terms "language-disorder," "language-impairment," and "language-delay" pre-date widespread acceptance of the term "SLI" but nevertheless refer to the same subgroup of children with primary rather than secondary language problems.

Leonard (1987) proposed that Specific Language Impairment is a misnomer. He argued that there is little "specific" nor "impaired" about the SLI population, and characterized the child with SLI as at the low skill end of the normal continuum for language and for other related skills as well. This controversial proposal implies that pursuing the causal factors underlying SLI is not productive and should cease, and that specific clinical interventions are unwarranted. Again by implication, only generalized language stimulation approaches designed to improve a "subpar" skill would be recommended to address society's intolerance of "below average" language performances. As yet, follow-up empirical data have not been provided to either support or refute Leonard's claims. However, his arguments either ignore or devalue the decades of research that has demonstrated the significant communication deficits definitional to SLI, and the consequent educational, behavioral, and social maladjustments experienced by these children. Therefore, the term SLI will be retained for the purpose of the present discussion because it does denote the widely recognized group of children with developmental language problems that are primary in nature and in that sense provides a common reference point for discussion.

The pragmatic skills of children with SLI have been examined primarily within dialogue and within narrative discourse. Within dialogue, requesting and commenting, presuppositional referencing, verbal and nonverbal turn-taking, and responding have been investigated. The ability of children with SLI to modify their messages based on context has been explored also. Each of these major lines of research will be summarized below.

REQUESTING AND COMMENTING

Performatives refer to the child's communicative intentions (Bates, 1976). Two major categories of intention, *imperative performatives*, which attempt to get the listener to perform an act, and *declarative performatives*, which attempt to inform the listener or focus the listener's attention on an object, have been investigated with SLI children.

Snyder (1978) observed that language-impaired children generated both imperative and declarative performatives but that these children were more likely to rely on nonlinguistic means when formulating their performatives than were normally developing children at the same language level. Rowan, Leonard, Chapman, and Weiss (1983) also found that language-impaired children produced imperative and declarative performatives. In contrast to Snyder, however, the latter investigation did not report a disproportionate use of nonlinguistic means to express the performatives. Language-disordered subjects in the Rowan and colleagues' study performed like their normal-language controls. The authors suggested that the discrepant findings between the two studies were due to subject differences, in particular Snyder's subjects demonstrated a specific representational deficit whereas the Rowan and colleagues' subjects did not. Further, Rowan and colleagues' subjects had expressive command of the lexicon required within the experimental task and this level of control was not apparent for the subjects of Snyder's earlier study.

All of the children in both studies were at the single word stage. Beyond the one-word stage, utterances that serve requesting and commenting functions have been examined for children with SLI. Prinz (1982) examined the requests of more advanced 5- to 7-year-old children who had SLI and also found that the imperative intention was apparent in their conversations. Compared to the discourse of younger children with normally developing language, requests were high in frequency for the children with SLI and were similar in type to those produced by the normal-language children. The normally developing children, however, formulated more grammatically complete requests. In addition, Prinz and Ferrier (1983) also observed requesting by 30 language-impaired children between 3½ and 9 years old.

Children with SLI appear to produce comments in order to try verbally to initiate new games, and to make statements about their own beliefs, actions, or about the situation. Gallagher and Craig (1984) examined the conversations of a 4-year-old SLI boy they called "Clark." Clark attempted verbal initiations of interactive play with age- and language-matched children with normal language skills by repeatedly producing the comment "it's gone." Clark used "it's gone" as an interactive access strategy, repeatedly attempting to engage his child partner in a nonexistence/disappearance game similar to those characteristic of early mother-child interactions. The "it's gone" initiation strategy was comprised of three rules which were sequential, ordered, and had recursive and terminal components. The interactive purpose of "it's gone" was not discerned by three of Clark's four child partners and was generally unsuccessful in engaging the children in play.

Blank, Gessner, and Esposito (1979) studied the conversations of a young language-impaired boy whom they called "John." They observed that John assumed the speaker-initiator role in dialogue with his parents. Initiator utterances included both *comments*, utterances that explicitly did not require a response, and *obliges*, utterances that did. Most of John's talk involved the production of language-based routines and expressed ideas associated with verbal games that he had a history of engaging in with his parents. Like Clark, John's verbal initiations appeared to have emerged from highly routinized play activities that had repetitive and predictable linguistic components. Over time these comments became disassociated from their origins and were used more broadly by the child to serve discourse initiation functions.

Overall these findings indicate that requesting and commenting, major communicative intentions, are apparent in the discourse of children with SLI from single words at approximately 3 years to 9 years of age. These discourse functions are present, although beyond the single word stage their linguistic realizations may differ from those of children with normal language development. The requests of children with SLI were grammatically incomplete compared to those of normal language children, and their comments involved the production of unusual and sometimes ineffective forms. The case reports for Clark and for John are interesting in that the children's talk overall reflected a semantic-syntactic repertoire apparently sufficient to fulfill the structural requirements represented by initiating. The children failed to use their structural resources, however, in ways appropriate to clearly communicate the initiation function of their comments.

REFERENCING PRESUPPOSITIONS

Speakers make assumptions about what their listeners know and do not know about the people, objects, and activities under discussion. *Presuppositions* refer to the speaker's backgrounding and foregrounding of information for the listener.

Snyder (1978) examined the presuppositional behaviors of children with language disorders and children with normal language development at the one-word stage. She found that both groups of children encoded new or changing aspects of the situation rather than old or unchanging aspects. In contrast to children with normal language, however, the children with language disorders used more nonlinguistic means when expressing these relationships.

Rowan and her colleagues (1983) also examined presuppositional abilities of language-disordered children and children with normal language development at the one-word stage. As described previously relative to their investigation of the same children's performative structures, their subjects and Snyder's differed in representational skill. In addition, the design of the Rowan and colleagues' study controlled for the children's previous production of the lexical items required for the experimental tasks. The latter investigation found that language-disordered children performed like children with normal language skills in that they encoded changing rather than unchanging aspects of the situation. Unlike Snyder's previous observations, these children usually expressed their presuppositions with words.

Skarakis and Greenfield (1982) examined the presuppositions of children with language disorders who were beyond the one-word stage. They found that both language-disordered children and normal language-matched controls encoded the new or changing elements in the situation rather than the unchanging elements, and that for both groups this encoding was primarily verbal. Further, they observed a developmental progression in the linguistic strategies used by children with normal language for backgrounding the old information. At an MLU of 3, the children tended to omit old information whereas at an MLU of 5 they pronominalized it. However, more than half of the language-disordered children pronominalized old information regardless of their MLU level, indicating that, for these children, increasing structural resources did not correspond to changes in their conversational uses of the forms.

These studies reveal that children with SLI demonstrate basic presuppositional knowledge. They foreground new information and background old information in a manner that allows them to construct informative messages. However, in contrast to children with normal language, beyond the one-word stage some language-disordered children express these presuppositions in a manner that is not typical of their language structural level. Regardless of the level of their linguistic skill, pronominalization was used by some children with SLI to perform this discourse function.

VERBAL AND NONVERBAL TURN-TAKING

Turn exchanges are a major type of discourse regulation. Both verbal and nonverbal devices for managing the smooth coordination of speakers have been examined in the spontaneous conversations of children with SLI. Van-Kleeck and Frankel (1981) conducted a preliminary investigation of the verbal devices used by language-disordered children to link their utterances to the preceding speaker's utterance. Verbal links between utterances provide cohesion in text and contribute to the maintenance of a topic across a conversation. VanKleeck and Frankel's subjects were found to relate their own utterances to those of the previous speaker using verbal cohesive devices that had been observed earlier for young children with normal language development by Keenan (1974). However, the profile of behaviors used by the language-disordered children differed from that reported previously for the normally developing children. Even at the earliest language level, the children with language disorders used substitution devices, whereas substitutions were not observed for normally developing children until they were linguistically more advanced in other research by Gallagher (1977). Unfortunately, the VanKleeck and Frankel study had no normal-language control groups so the data are difficult to interpret.

In general, it appears that, even at early stages of language development, language-disordered children demonstrate the ability to relate verbally to previous discourse. The linguistic profiles they present, however, incorporate behaviors different from those used by children with normally developing language at comparable stages. Similar to the previously described finding of Skarakis and Greenfield (1982) in which language-disordered children tended to use the same linguistic strategies regardless of changes in their linguistic repertoires when encoding presuppositions, the Van-Kleeck and Frankel (1981) data also indicate that children with SLI may fail to adapt their linguistic structures to particular conversational purposes.

The turn regulation function is managed nonverbally as well as verbally. Craig and Evans (1989) investigated the verbal and nonverbal characteristics of successful and unsuccessful turns produced by boys with SLI and boys with normal language matched for age and language. They found that turn exchange structures for boys with SLI and normal-language controls were similar in essential ways. Like the age-matched and the younger normals with language structural skills more similar to those of the children with SLI, most utterances in the conversations of the children with SLI were nonsimultaneously produced, indicating that the turn exchanged smoothly most of the time. These instances of successful turn negotiation involved primarily an other-directed rather than self-directed utterance focus and response rather than no-response turns. They were single utterance turns, were temporally adjacent (occurred within 2 seconds of the partner's utterance) rather than nonadjacent, and appeared semantically related to prior discourse. Both children with SLI and children with normal language, therefore, engaged in conversations that could be characterized nonverbally by considerable interactive attention and verbally by short conversational turns that were exchanged rapidly and smoothly.

The turns of the children with SLI differed from those of the children with normal language in important ways, however. The children with SLI produced significantly less other-directed speech, fewer multiutterance turns, and less tightly timed turns than their age-mates. The children with SLI produced significantly more responses and more adjacent speech than the younger normal children who had similar structural skills. The profile of behaviors obtained for the children with SLI, therefore, did not match that of either group of children with normal language.

The turn exchange behaviors of the children with SLI differed from both groups of normal-language controls in terms of turns that served an interrupting function. *Interruptions* occur as temporally premature responses, typically relate to the preceding nonoverlapped portion of the partner's utterance, and are effective in securing the turn-at-speaking. Craig and Evans (1989) found that four of their five subjects with SLI never produced interruptions although all of the children with normal language did so. Interestingly, these four children demonstrated both receptive and expressive language deficits, whereas the fifth child exhibited problems only with language expression. The latter child with intact receptive skills appeared to be more like the children with normal language in many aspects of turn management and also produced turn interruptions within conversation. He appeared very different from the other children with SLI who more frequently were slow to respond to prior adult utterances, resulting in turn errors involving overlap of both speakers.

Fujiki, Brinton, and Sonnenberg (1990) examined the ability of a child with SLI to repair interruptions and again observed considerable conversational variability within their sample of 10 subjects who demonstrated both receptive and expressive problems. Subjects with SLI produced a significantly greater number of unrepaired interruptions than normal-language age-mates or language-similar controls; however, these data were attributable primarily to only three of the SLI subjects. The bases for the pragmatic differences within this sample of children with SLI are unclear. It seems important to understand better the pragmatic differences presented by subgroups of children with SLI who demonstrate expressive or both receptive and expressive deficits.

In summary, the child with SLI appears to know the essential structure of the conversational turn exchange. In general, the turns exchange smoothly, rapidly, and are linked semantically to the immediately prior turn. Children with both receptive and expressive language deficits appear less responsive, less adjacent, and less semantically related than normally developing children and indeed perhaps other children with SLI who are receptively intact. These findings indicate that although their changes in structural skill may not result in distinctive profiles of turn linking behaviors, and the turns of children with SLI may be shorter and more self-directed, most behaviors serving a turn regulation function are essentially intact. Some differences may result from slow processing, consistent with the children's receptive language deficits.

RESPONDING

Considerable research effort has been directed toward understanding this function within the conversations of children with SLI. Gallagher and Darnton (1978) examined responses of language-disordered children to the neutral "what?" contingent query form of requests for clarification. They found a very low no-response rate (approximately 8%) for all children with language disorders across Brown's (1973) language structural stages I, II, and III. Their children also produced exact repetitions infrequently (approximately 17%), revealing an understanding of the conversational function of the contingent query. The children seemed to recognize that they needed to do something to their utterance to clarify the message for their partner when requested to do so.

Gallagher and Darnton's subjects revised the linguistic form of their messages but their attempts at revision were linguistically undifferentiated. In a previous study of normal-language children at the same language developmental stages, Gallagher (1977) found that children with normal language revised the linguistic form of their messages in response to the neutral contingent query, but unlike language-disordered children, their recodings were distinctive by stage. The type of revision used by the children with normal language was related to their language stage. In contrast, the revisions of the children with language disorders were structurally the same within and across stages, whereas this uniform profile of revisions did not characterize the normal-language children at any stage. These findings indicate that although the children with SLI demonstrated the full repertoire of revision behaviors observed for the children with normal language, they did not use revision behaviors in linguistically specific ways. Consistent with studies of their encoding of presuppositions and of verbal turn-taking, the repsonses of children with SLI to clarification requests again reflect difficulties in tailoring linguistic forms to achieve specific conversational purposes.

Brinton, Fujiki, Winkler, and Loeb (1986) also examined the responses of children with SLI to requests for clarification, in this instance their responses to "stacked" or consecutively repeated requests for clarification. Like Gallagher and Darnton (1978), Brinton and colleagues found that their subjects with SLI recognized the obligatory nature of the request for clarification, and again no-response rates were low for both subjects with language disorders and age-matched controls with normal language. The translation of the response into an appropriate linguistic form distinguished the SLI and normal-language subject groups, however. Although all of the children most frequently responded to the neutral query, the children with language disorders produced more inappropriate responses than the children with normal language, were not as able to add information to their recodings, and did not attempt verbally to probe the nature of the problem experienced by the listener, as did the normal-language controls. Some of the appropriate response options required syntactic elaborations or complex sentence forms. Therefore, the response differences observed may reflect ways in which the limited linguistic resources of the subjects with SLI constrained their responding. When repetitions failed to clarify the utterance for their partner, the alternative strategies produced by the children with normal language probably required a level of syntactic skill not available to the subjects with SLI.

Responses to other types of requests also have been investigated. Brinton and Fujiki (1982) examined the responses of language-disordered children to three request types. These included their responses to *choice* questions, those involving alternatives, particularly "either-or" and "yes-no" forms; *product* questions those requiring the listener to replace the wh- word in the initial question with a specific item in the response; and *requests for clarification* of various types. They found that the children with language disorders were responsive to the three types of requests but that their response utterances were more likely to be inappropriate or unrelated than those of children with normal language who were functioning at the same grade level.

Leonard, Camarata, Rowan, and Chapman (1982) found that compared to language-matched normals, children with SLI at the one-word stage produced more utterances serving an "answering" function. The children were similar in their production of 14 different classes of communication function but differed in terms of the amount of naming and answering within their samples. The children with normal language produced a significantly higher percentage of utterances serving a naming function, whereas the children with SLI produced significantly more utterances functioning as answers. The investigators reported that the children with SLI were less spontaneous namers overall so the adult examiner probed with "what's that?" questions to which the children with SLI responded.

In contrast to the high discourse obligation request and response pair, comments and their subsequent acknowledgments represent low levels of conversational obligation and, therefore, offer a particularly revealing context for examining the response function. Craig and Gallagher (1986) observed "Clark's" acknowledgment to comments with two age-matched and two language-matched boys with normal language development, and compared his response patterns to those of the boys with normal language when paired with each other. Craig and Gallagher found that Clark was responsive, but that his level of linguistically related responding appeared unsystematic compared to that of children with normal language. His apparent variability was associated with the ratio of other-directed partner turns in play, the frequency of a particular discourse pattern preceding Clark's opportunity for a related response, and the frequency of shared reference across this discourse pattern. Although Clark's acknowledgments to comments were associated with these variables, the responses of the children with normal language to comments were not. Structurally and functionally Clark demonstrated that he was capable of formulating related responses, but properties of the discourse governed his responding in ways not characteristic of the children with normal language.

Blank and colleagues (1979) also found that "John's" response rates were high. His responses were considered functionally inadequate, however, as they were frequently irrelevant to the content of the preceding utterance. Leonard (1986) observed that children with SLI at the one-word stage were more likely to reply to preceding adult utterances than were language-matched normals. The children with SLI produced a greater variety of conversational replies than language-matched normals and used these types of responses relatively more often.

It seems clear, overall, that children with SLI are conversationally responsive, although, at least beyond the one-word stage, they seem to have difficulty tailoring the linguistic structure of their responses to the conversational demand. It is difficult to interpret the behavior of children with SLI at the one-word stage beyond that of being responsive co-conversationalists. Their greater variety and more frequent use of all types of conversational replies may be another instance of relatively uniform, structurally undifferentiated patterns of responding that do not characterize older children with normal language.

Although children with SLI appear conversationally responsive, at least some of their responsiveness may be created by direct probing from the partner when other types of speech acts are not forthcoming more spontaneously. They may recognize the pragmatic obligation to respond to requests and comments, but the linguistic formulation of their responses differs from both age- and language-matched normally developing children. Beyond single words, children with SLI can be characterized by variable levels of linguistically unrelated and inappropriate responding. Response difficulties reflect both their inadequate linguistic resources and their inability to use the linguistic resources they do have to meet their pragmatic obligations in linguistically specific ways. In addition, interactional variables such as high levels of partner attention, prior discourse support, and clear referent identification may influence the ability of the child with SLI to respond in a linguistically related manner.

NARRATIVES

Not all pragmatic investigations of language disorder have focused on spontaneous dialogue. A considerable amount of information is available concerning the knowledge of children with SLI of another type of discourse, the spoken narrative. Like dialogues, narratives have identifiable discourse functions, and differences in their linguistic formulation result in more and less effective communications.

Narration reflects a special set of discourse constraints. More complex syntax and more organizational complexity may need to be managed for narrative compared to dialogue production. MacLachlan and Chapman (1988) investigated the narratives of fifth graders who were language-learning disabled (and appear to meet the SLI exclusion criteria) and found that they demonstrated a significantly greater rate of communication breakdowns for narration than for dialogue. This finding indicates that narrative discourse may be more difficult than dialogue for children with language impairment.

The narratives of children with SLI have been investigated using original story generation, the retelling of stories viewed from movies and videotapes, and the recollection of favorite movies or television shows (Liles, 1985a, 1985b, 1987; MacLachlan & Chapman, 1988; Merritt & Liles, 1987; Sleight & Prinz, 1985). Children with SLI demonstrate fundamental knowledge of *episodes,* an organizational sequence involving initiating events, subsequent actions, and consequences (Liles, 1987); *abstracts,* a summary of the story highlights, orientations, interpretive background information, and *codas,* story completions (Sleight & Prinz, 1985); as well as the need for coherence when producing the narrative (Liles, 1985a, 1985b, 1987).

However, the narratives produced by children with SLI differ from those of children with normally developing language in linguistically important ways. Their narratives seem less complete than those produced by children with normal language development (Liles, 1987; Merritt & Liles, 1987), contain fewer utterances (Liles, 1985a), and exhibit more communication breakdowns (MacLachlan & Chapman, 1988). In addition, children with SLI show more incomplete and erroneous cohesive ties (Liles, 1985a) with fewer accurate conjunctive ties in particular (Liles, 1987) when formulating successive utterances within their narratives. The types of cohesive ties used also differ. Liles (1985b) found that language-disordered children produced more demonstrative and lexically based ties compared to age-matched children with normal language who used more personal pronoun forms.

Overall, children with SLI produce narrative discourse and demonstrate knowledge of the basic discourse features of narratives. They differ from children with normal language in the comprehensiveness of their stories and in the manner in which they formulate specific sentence relationships. Narrative discourse with its particularly demanding grammar and organizational complexity seems to be especially difficult for children with language impairments. Interestingly, the difficulties children with SLI experience during narrative production closely parallel those within the stacked requests for clarification probed by Brinton, Fujiki, and their colleagues (1986). The children with SLI clearly understood their discourse obligations in both situations, but used inappropriate and incomplete linguistic forms across the discourse sequences.

THE INFLUENCE OF SPEAKER CHARACTERISTICS AND LISTENER CONTEXT

Different conversational contexts place different demands on speakers during message formulation. Gallagher (1983) has highlighted the importance of determining which contextual variables are important and which are not. She observed that the notion of contextual influence is infinitely extendible. Not only are the number of potentially important contextual influences conceivably quite large, but characteristics of the speaker also interact with aspects of the context to further increase the set of variables affecting the communication process.

Children with SLI alter their messages based on characteristics of the listener. Fey, Leonard, and Wilcox (1981) observed that children with SLI adjust the linguistic structure of their messages when talking to younger partners with normal language. Fey and Leonard (1984) examined the speech of children with SLI to partners of different ages and compared the patterns obtained to age- and language-matched controls. They also found that the children with SLI modified their speech to partners of different ages. However, the profile of speech modifications for the children with SLI differed from that of the children with normal language. Both subjects with language impairment and age-matched controls with normal language were more active and dominant conversationalists with younger partners. Despite this functional similarity to their chronological peers, the children with SLI were dissimilar to this group also. Although the children with SLI modified their speech when talking to different age partners and were similar to their age-mates in many ways, they differed from them in the frequency of internal state questions, utterance length, and utterance complexity. Although children with SLI clearly code-switched based on partner age, their linguistic choices for speech style modifications were not the same as either age-matched or younger children with normal language. The authors suggested that the expressive syntax problems of the children with SLI probably contributed to their inability to make all of the same partner age-based adjustments in their speech as the children with normal language.

In addition to age of partner, children with SLI seem sensitive to other listener characteristics that require adjustments in the speaker's message. Olswang and Carpenter (1978) compared the expression of language-impaired children during conversation with their mothers and with an unfamiliar clinician. No differences were observed for a variety of lexical, syntactic, and semantic language production characteristics between the mother and the unfamiliar clinician contexts. The children produced more utterances during the mother-child context, however, indicating that they were sensitive to differences in partner familiarity.

In addition, Blank and colleagues' (1979) subject "John" reportedly talked only to his parents, and Gallagher and Craig (1984) observed that "Clark" behaved differently verbally with his mother compared to an unfamiliar speech-language pathologist or to children with normal language. Clark produced his interactive bid "It's gone" in conversation with child partners and the clinician, but never with his mother. These studies indicate that children with SLI are sensitive to the familiarity of their partner and talk differently to different kinds of partners. Amount of speech may be a particularly revealing index of partner familiarity.

Children with SLI also adjust their messages based on whether their partner is aware or unaware of aspects of the topical setting. Liles (1985b) found that children with SLI altered their narratives about a movie they had watched depending on whether their listener had viewed the movie with them or not. She found that both children with SLI and age-mates with normal language adjusted their speech for the uninformed listener and in the same way. The children produced significantly more sentences for the uninformed listener and produced more personal reference and conjunctive ties when linking consecutive sentences in this context. The children also produced more complete ties for the uninformed listener and reduced their production of incomplete or erroneous types of cohesion.

The above line of research as a whole indicates that children with SLI are aware of the need to alter message production based on critical listener variables. They seem to recognize how static characteristics of the listener such as age or familiarity are influential to the production of message formulation. Further, they seem aware that more relative context-dependent characteristics of their listeners, such as level of shared information about a setting or event, may necessitate changes in their messages.

SUMMARY PROFILE

A profile of pragmatic characteristics is emerging for children with SLI. Table 6–1 summarizes this information.

This summary profile indicates that children with SLI do not appear to tailor their linguistic structures to meet conversational demands in the same way as children with normal language. Although a number of dis-

Table 6-1. A profile of pragmatic characteristics of the child with Specific Language Impairment

Conversational Functions	*Linguistic Forms*	*Investigations*
Requesting	Fewer requests are grammatically complete compared to normal-language children	Prinz (1982)
Commenting	Comments may be stereotypic in nature	Gallagher and Craig (1984) Blank, Gessner and Esposito (1979)
Referencing Presuppositions	Their presuppositions depend more on pronominals than do those of normals	Skarakis and Greenfield (1982)
Turn-taking	They relate to preceding discourse using more substitution devices and more inadequate forms	VanKleeck and Frankel (1981) Liles (1985a, 1985b, 1987)
	Turns involve less other-directed speech and are shorter in length	Craig and Evans (1989)
	Their utterances are less "adjacent" than age-mates so that the SLI child takes longer to follow a previous speaker with a turn of his/her own	Craig and Evans (1989)
	They do not use interruptions to gain the turn-at-speaking	Craig and Evans (1989)
Responding	Responses to requests for clarification are structurally diffuse	Gallagher and Darnton (1978) Brinton, Fujiki, Winkler, and Loeb (1986)
	Responses to other types of speech acts are likely to be unrelated, inappropriate, and variable	Blank et al. (1979) Brinton and Fujiki (1982) Craig and Gallagher (1986) Leonard (1986) Leonard, Camarata, Rowan, and Chapman (1982)

Conversational Functions	Linguistic Forms	Investigations
Narratives	Their narratives are less complete, and include different distributions of cohesive ties	Liles (1985a, 1985b, 1987) Merritt and Liles (1987)
Speech Adjustments	Their speech style modifications reflect fewer internal state questions and less adjustment of utterance length and complexity	Fey, Leonard, and Wilcox (1981) Fey and Leonard (1984)

course functions may be apparent within their conversations, children with SLI appear to integrate their forms and functions differently. It is the integration between the two systems that is problematic, not just the operations internal to each system. Unfortunately, little research has focused directly on the ability of the child with SLI to integrate form and function. The current synthesis of pragmatic research would suggest that it will be productive to pursue this type of research, for at least a subset of children with SLI do not use their linguistic forms like children with normal language. For these children, the interactionist perspective is advantageous because it allows conceptualization of these connections between conversational and linguistic structures. Failure to account for the interconnections between systems and an over-reliance on frequency counts of linguistic forms and discourse functions relative to some normal-language standard would result in a view of SLI as only quantitatively different. The next pragmatic step must be taken and the child's ability to integrate the systems must be examined also. The current research synthesis indicates that the quantitative "subpar" view of SLI proposed by Leonard (1987), for example, is only possible if forms and functions are considered separately without then conceptualizing the ability of the child with SLI to integrate the two.

The problem of the child with SLI in differentiating semantic-syntactic uses would only be apparent when the linguistic system has evolved somewhat and offers the child a set of linguistic options. Rules for integrating linguistic behaviors and discourse functions may not be apparent until the child's linguistic system is somewhat advanced. The pragmatic task at the one-word stage in particular may be too generalized and the functions too global to be revealing.

From this perspective, research methodologies must ensure that subjects have the structural repertoires necessary to meet the discourse function involved. Further, it is not clear whether this integration problem is apparent only for children with SLI who have both receptive and expressive problems. It seems important to ensure that future research designs focus on these issues.

METHODOLOGICAL IMPLICATIONS
FOR FUTURE RESEARCH

Some methodological changes might facilitate future pragmatic research with children with SLI. These changes relate to subject issues and are outlined below.

1. *Research designs should factor out the effects of expressive syntax deficits from the use of conversational rules.* In order to determine whether the difficulties of children with SLI include various conversational functions, it seems important to ensure that the subjects have the prerequisite structural skills necessary to perform the task. Considerable effort has been directed toward identifying the SLI child's knowledge of basic discourse functions, but the determination of rules for integrating their emerging linguistic behaviors into these various functions will require additional levels of experimental control. The failure of children with SLI to use language like children with normal language will only be understood when it is clear that the necessary structural repertoire was available but was not applied appropriately to the conversational task. To date, only a small number of studies have exerted this level of control. The linguistically undifferentiated ways in which children with SLI at different structural levels use pronominalization to reference presuppositions (Skarakis & Greenfield, 1982), substitution devices to relate to prior utterances (VanKleeck & Frankel, 1981), the same revision behaviors to clarify their messages (Gallagher & Darnton, 1978), and routinized phrases to comment and to access play (Blank et al, 1979; Gallagher & Craig, 1984) reveal a lack of integration between structure and function that differs from the interdependence between these systems exhibited by normal-language children.

2. *The receptive and expressive bases of the SLI designation need to be identified in subject descriptions.* The SLI designation is applicable to a heterogeneous group of children with language impairments who have primary rather than secondary language problems. Children identified by this label demonstrate receptive and/or expressive language deficits (Ingram, 1972; Johnston, 1982; Stark & Tallal, 1981; Weiner, 1980; Wolfus et al., 1980). Fey and Leonard (1983) have proposed that these subgroups also may vary conversationally, and Craig and Evans (1989) have offered preliminary support for this proposal.

Unfortunately, little of the published research discussed herein clearly identifies the expressive and receptive skills of the children with language impairments who were examined. Future research needs to describe subject subgroups more specifically in order to pursue a valid characterization of children with SLI. If subgroups of children with SLI vary systematically in terms of the linguistic and pragmatic profiles they present, then failure to control for this source of variation will result in inconsistent research findings and will confuse interpretation.

3. *In order to fully interpret the communication behaviors of children with SLI, both chronological normal-language controls and younger normal-language children with language structural skills more similar to children with SLI should comprise control groups.* Some designs have employed no normal language control subjects (Blank et al., 1979; Fey et al., 1981; Prinz & Ferrier, 1983; Van-Kleeck & Frankel, 1981), only age-mates (Bondurant, Romeo, & Kretschmer, 1983; Brinton & Fujiki, 1982; Brinton et al., 1986; Liles, 1985a, 1985b, 1987; Liles, Shulman, & Bartlett, 1977; Merritt & Liles, 1987; Sleight & Prinz, 1985) or only language-matched normal-language controls (Conti–Ramsden & Friel–Patti, 1983; Gallagher & Darnton, 1978; Kamhi & Koenig, 1985; Leonard, 1986; Leonard et al., 1982; Rowan et al., 1983; Skarakis & Greenfield, 1982; Snyder, 1978). A small number of studies have employed both age- and language-matched normal-language control groups (Craig & Evans, 1989; Fey & Leonard, 1984, Gallagher & Craig, 1984; MacLachlan & Chapman, 1988; Meline & Brackin, 1987) and have been important in demonstrating that children with SLI are not easily characterized pragmatically as functioning like either chronological-age or language-similar peers. Studies that involve both age- and language-matched control groups will be particularly helpful in interpreting whether problems with the integration of structure and function are a predictable consequence of the cognitive and social maturity of children with SLI.

4. *The best partner for the child with SLI when collecting spontaneous language samples needs to be explored and determined.* If the goal is to characterize the conversational-linguistic knowledge of the child with SLI, and the child characteristically tries to modify his or her output based on partner attributes, then the partner within the dyadic interaction is an important consideration. Who is the best partner?

It may be simplistic to assume that peer contexts present the same experience to the child with SLI as they do for normal-language controls in a research investigation. Child partners may treat the child with SLI differently than they do other children. The child with SLI experiences more interruptions with peer partners (Wellen & Broen, 1982) and less related talk (Craig & Gallagher, 1986). Adults seem to treat children with SLI like younger children with normal language, simplifying the linguistic form of the messages they address to these children (Bondurant et al., 1983; Conti–Ramsden & Friel–Patti, 1983, 1984; Cramblit & Siegel, 1977; Lasky & Klopp,

1982). These types of contextual variations may be detrimental to valid characterizations of the pragmatic-linguistic knowledge of the child with SLI.

Although there is no easy solution to this set of problems, it seems important to be sensitive to the issue of the partner when comparing the behavior of control subjects and children with SLI. At this stage in our understanding of SLI, when possible adults may provide the best partner contexts because the type of adjustments they make are predictable and are comparable to those they produce with one of the groups of controls. If younger normal-language controls are included in research investigations, then differences in the adult's behavior across groups of children should be observable and interpretatively helpful.

A REVISED INTERACTIONIST MODEL FOR SLI

The system for integrating structure and function appears different for at least some children with SLI and conceptualizing this difference may be central to improving our understanding of their deficits. Overall, children with SLI exhibit many conversational functions within their discourse but some children with SLI seem to approach the expression of these functions with relatively undifferentiated linguistic profiles. Language production models will be helpful only to the extent that they aid conceptualization of this breakdown. Further, some children with SLI require different discourse conditions to exist for particular conversational-linguistic links to occur and these involve discourse constraints that are not operating for children with normal language.

Descriptions of children with SLI as linguistically impaired are long-standing. Children with SLI are deficient in the production of specific syntactic structures compared to children with normal language (Cromer, 1978; Ingram, 1972; Morehead & Ingram, 1973; Steckol & Leonard, 1979) in a manner best characterized as a frequency of use difference (Leonard, 1972). Semantically, frequency of use of specific sentence meanings also distinguishes children with SLI from normal language children (Freedman & Carpenter, 1976; Leonard, Bolders, & Miller, 1976). Recent pragmatic research indicates that these semantic-syntactic differences, typically reported as frequency of use differences, may result at least in part from the child's undifferentiated application of structural behaviors to specific discourse functions (Gallagher & Darnton, 1978; Skarakis & Greenfield, 1982; Van-Kleeck & Frankel, 1981) and may reflect conversational-linguistic rules that involve different discourse constraints (Gallagher & Craig, 1984). To what extent is the emerging pragmatic profile of children with SLI consistent with and aided in interpretation by the interactionist model of language production?

The Bloom and Lahey interactionist model predicts that for children with SLI form problems are primary and content and use problems are artifacts of the basic syntactic deficit. Studies of children with SLI that explore conversational functions in the absence of concomitant structural demands indeed discover few "pragmatic" problems. However, studies that have examined conversational-linguistic rules within research designs that concurrently demonstrate structural skills sufficient for the conversational demand provide less support for an interactionist model that accords form a primary role. Findings that children with SLI have the forms present in their discourse but do not use them relative to specific discourse functions in a manner parallel to children with normal language indicate that conversational-linguistic rule problems may be fundamental. Observations that linguistic structures remain undifferentiated for some conversational purposes across structural stages, and that linguistic expressions are routinized or have different discourse constraints operating for children with SLI compared to children with normal language, all indicate that use rules as well as form rules are impaired for this clinical population. Only an interactionist model that depicts structure, function, and the linkages between the two systems will be revealing for these children. From an interactionist perspective, children with SLI appear pragmatically disordered.

Figure 6–1 presents a preliminary model for conceptualizing both the form and use problems experienced by some children with SLI. The figure is an attempt at refining the interactionist model for SLI proposed by Bloom and Lahey (1978) and Lahey (1988). Unlike the Bloom and Lahey model, the form problems experienced by children with SLI are not depicted as a relatively isolated area of deficit. In this revised interactionist model, the difficulties are conceptualized within the linkages between linguistic behaviors and conversational functions. The model addresses message production of SLI children rather than that of children with normal language. Some other system may be more efficient for normal language users.

It is a model in the sense that it is a tentative description of a system that accounts for the relations among the important conversational-linguistic operating variables derived from the extant empirical data. It is a theoretical model in the sense that it is predictive, identifying communication levels at which other variables should be found to be intact or impaired in future research. Empty boxes are included at each level to represent additional variables yet to be examined for SLI. The model is not explanatory, however, and consequently falls short of theory. In particular, the model does not explain the nature of the language production breakdowns in terms of underlying etiology. Any theory of disorder ultimately must do so. For example, a number of lines of research have revealed that children with SLI have poor symbolic representational and perceptual skills (Johnston & Weismer, 1983; Kamhi, 1981; Kamhi, Catts, Koenig, & Lewis, 1984; Roth & Clark, 1987; Savich, 1984; Tallal, 1976; Tallal & Piercy, 1973, 1975; Tallal & Stark,

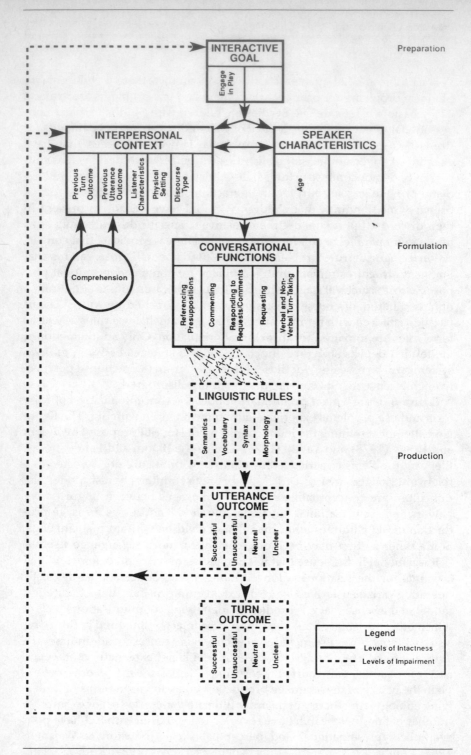

Figure 6-1. A revised interactionist model for SLI.

1981; Tallal, Stark, Kallman, & Mellits, 1980a, 1980b; Terrell, Schwartz, Prelock, & Messick, 1984). To the extent that tasks of these types index neurophysiological integrity, they indicate that the cognitive deficits of children with SLI may be broad based and as such may constitute the etiological foundation for the communication problems experienced by these children. Etiological explanations await future research and hence theory specification does also.

The model retains important features of the models proposed by Bloom and Lahey (1978), Lahey (1988), and Roth and Spekman (1984). All are interactionist in nature, focus on language production, and present form rules as disordered. Unlike the other models, however, Figure 6-1 shows breakdowns in language production at the level where conversational functions are translated into linguistic forms. In this model, the communication deficits of the child with SLI begin at the level of integration between conversational functions and linguistic structures and continue beyond to the levels of communication outcomes. Figure 6–1 portrays language production in terms of a series of choices made by the speaker with SLI in formulating a message. The levels evolve in three phases: preparation, formulation, and production. The model involves a hierarchical process so that each later level depends on selections made at earlier levels in the communication process. Its hierarchical organization implies that a breakdown at one level will result in difficulties at all subsequent levels. An advantage represented by a hierarchical organization is clinical in nature. This arrangement could be applied to the organization of language sampling for assessment purposes and to intervention goal planning.

INTERACTIVE GOALS

Communication purposes are the principal motivation for language growth and provide the basic framework for conversation (Corsaro 1981; Halliday, 1975; MacNamara, 1972). Consistent with this perspective, therefore, the first level in the model involves the determination of an interactive goal. The domain of verbal behaviors related to an interactive goal can be as brief as a single utterance or as extensive as a whole conversation. Lund and Duchan (1988) have described similar units as *agendas*. Conceptualization of this communication level seems necessary to describe the production of discourse units of varying sizes and, therefore, is presented as part of this preliminary proposal.

Various systems for characterizing interactive goals, as expressed in single utterances, are available in the literature (Dore, 1974, 1979; Halliday, 1975; McShane, 1980), but attempts to describe the purposes of larger discourse units are more limited (Garvey, 1975; Lund & Duchan, 1988). Little research has explored the conversations of children with SLI for longer message planning units, particularly all of the utterances pursuant to a single interactive goal. "Clark" tried spontaneously and repeatedly to engage his child partners in a game and the "Its gone" unit with its sequential, recursive, and terminal components seems an example of a larger discourse unit observable for a child with SLI (Gallagher & Craig 1984). Accordingly, Engage-in-Play is represented in the model at this level. Stacked requests for clarification (Brinton et al., 1986) may be another example of the production of a language discourse unit by a child with SLI in which successive attempts are made to clarify information for the conversational partner. It is not included in the model, however, because it is not clear whether successive responses of this type have integrity as a discourse unit or are discrete responses to the experimenter's repeated probes. Narratives also involve larger units, but most studies again prompt directly for this discourse type. It is not clear, at a preparation level, whether children with SLI self-initiate these interactive goals. Therefore, narratives are represented at the next level in the model as a discourse type.

It would be interesting to know whether children with SLI have a large or a limited set of interactive goals compared to children with normal language. The model predicts that this level of message formulation would be intact for children with SLI if research designs were used that permitted their observation despite known structural limitations. The empty cell included at this level might ultimately involve other interactive goals identified for normal language users, such as: to *solicit action or information*, to *inform or misinform* the listener, to *persuade or argue*, to *pass time*, to *entertain or amuse*, to *compliment or praise*, to *intimidate or ridicule* (Dore, 1974, 1979; Halliday, 1975; McShane 1980).

SPEAKER CHARACTERISTICS AND INTERPERSONAL CONTEXTS

Characteristics of the individual as a speaker or as a listener may be context-independent. For example, the individual's language level, social skill, cognitive status, age, gender, and socioeconomic status would be to some extent definitional in nature and invariant. These personal characteristics define the individual in important ways regardless of whether the individual is functioning as a listener or as a speaker. The influence of these variables on message formulation, however, would be context-dependent. For example, a speaker of a certain age might vary his message relative to the age of the conversational partner. The literature indicates that children with SLI are aware of the relative nature of the personal characteristics of conversational interactants and attempt to alter their messages based on features like listener age (Fey & Leonard, 1984; Fey et al., 1981) and interpersonal familiarity (Olswang & Carpenter, 1978). In addition, in their messages children with SLI distinguish pertinent characteristics of the physical setting from less to more informative aspects (Rowan et al., 1983;

Skarakis & Greenfield, 1982; Snyder, 1978) and alter their messages based on the listener's prior knowledge of the information to be discussed (Liles, 1985b).

It is not clear what constitutes the full range of person and setting variables that are contextually important for communication in general and the child with SLI in particular. The child with SLI does seem knowledgeable about different types of discourse, particularly differences in the organization of narratives and face-to-face dialogues. The model represents knowledge of narrative and dialogue differences as "Discourse Type" and at this level in the evolution of a message because they are definitional of the context and a particular type may be better suited to some interactive goals than others. A speaker's overall goal for the interaction should influence the choice of discourse type rather than the reverse. These two types of discourse are represented as intact because the literature examining narratives produced by children with SLI reveals the presence of structures unique to narrative production (e.g., codas) and the presence of dialogue structures, such as stereotypic acknowledgments.

The SLI child's understanding of the prior discourse is represented at this level in the model as Comprehension input. This relates to comprehension monitoring, information derived from a relatively new line of research that, in contrast to studies of static post-sentence comprehension, evaluates more active on-going processing (Meline & Brackin, 1987; Montgomery, Scudder, & Moore, 1990; Skarakis–Doyle, MacLellan, & Mullin, 1990). The child's decoding of his or her own outcomes should influence the SLI speaker's preparation for the next turn-at-speaking. For example, "Clark's" (Craig & Gallagher, 1986) acknowledgment of comments depended in part on whether his partner's immediately prior utterance had in turn been related to Clark's previous talk. Related responding by the child with SLI occurred when the response turn was preceded by a prior partner turn related to a prior utterance by Clark.

It is not clear how best to characterize the comprehension monitoring skills of children with SLI. Meline and Brackin (1987) found similar difficulties in children with language disorders and younger children with normal language in the self-initiation of requests for clarification during communication breakdowns, and in the determination of their sources. They seem slower and less proficient in general than normal-language controls (Montgomery et al., 1990). Children with SLI do detect ambiguity in the messages of others, however, if nonverbal indicants are considered (Skarakis–Doyle et al., 1990). Children with SLI simply may not be as overt in expressing their monitoring of conversational adequacy. In the absence of clear evidence to the contrary, this aspect has been depicted as intact in the model.

Listener characteristics to be considered within the "Interpersonal Context" side of this relationship include age and familiarity with the speaker.

Characteristics of the *physical setting*, particularly shared knowledge about potential discourse referents, seem pertinent also. It would be interesting to pursue other potentially relevant speaker-listener variables to determine their effects on the messages formulated by children with SLI. For example, gender of speaker and the interaction of gender of speaker and gender of listener may influence message formulation of children with SLI in important ways. Perhaps group size is an Interpersonal Context variable that children with SLI find difficult to manage, particularly dyadic compared to multiparty conversations. A comprehensive characterization of the conversational knowledge of the child with SLI needs to include the full range of contextual variables that have potential to constrain communication. The model predicts that examination of additional person and setting variables (represented by the empty cells at this level) will reveal intact knowledge for the child with SLI.

CONVERSATIONAL FUNCTIONS

The conversations of the child with SLI demonstrate the following discourse functions: *requesting and commenting* (Blank et al., 1979; Gallagher & Craig, 1984; Rowan et al., 1983; Snyder, 1978), *presuppositional referencing* (Rowan et al., 1983; Skarakis & Greenfield, 1982; Snyder, 1978), *verbal and nonverbal turn-taking* (Craig & Evans, 1989; VanKleeck & Frankel, 1981), and *responding* (Blank et al., 1979; Brinton & Fujiki, 1982; Brinton et al., 1986; Craig & Gallagher, 1986; Gallagher & Darnton , 1978; Leonard et al., 1982).

The model includes each of these conversational functions and provides space for others. It would be helpful to know whether other discourse meaning and discourse regulation functions are intact and thereby confirm the present proposal for this level of message formulation, or whether the current view is an overgeneralization. Requesting, commenting, and responding are conversational functions in the speech act sense (Searle, 1969). Presuppositional referencing and verbal and nonverbal turn-taking are represented at this level of the model also because they contribute to the formulation aspect of message development involving rules for use rather than linguistic rules. Refinements of this model based on future empirical data may distinguish presuppositional referencing and turn-taking operations from the planning of intentional acts. Systems like these two that serve more of a discourse regulation function ultimately may be best conceptualized as a distinct set of discourse rules from those involving illocutionary force. At this time, there is no evidence that they need to be conceptualized separately for SLI in terms of our understanding of their degree of intactness or impairment. Further, they share the same research problems as the other functions noted at this level.

The model predicts that other conversational functions would be found intact for children with SLI if they were examined using research designs that did not limit their observation for linguistic repertoire reasons, for example, if nonverbal as well as verbal expressive forms were possible. Research on children with normal language has described a number of conversational functions observable as early as the one-word stage (Bates, 1976a; Dore, 1974; Halliday, 1975; Mitchell–Kernan & Kernan, 1977; Sugarman, 1984). It would be interesting to determine whether children with SLI know a comparable range of discourse functions.

At this level in the model, the speaker's message formulation narrows to that of a specific utterance. In contrast, the previous two levels, the determination of an interactive goal and the consideration of contextual variables, could apply to a single utterance or many utterances organized into a turn or series of turns.

LINGUISTIC RULES

Some children with SLI do not express their discourse functions in a manner similar to children with normal language (Blank et al., 1979; Brinton & Fujiki, 1982; Brinton et al., 1986; Craig & Evans, 1989; Craig & Gallagher, 1986; Gallagher & Craig, 1984; Gallagher & Darnton, 1978; Leonard, 1986; Leonard et al., 1982; Liles, 1985a, 1985b, 1987; Merritt & Liles, 1987; Prinz, 1982; Skarakis & Greenfield, 1982; VanKleeck & Frankel, 1981). The connections between conversational functions and their linguistic formulation are the first level within the outlined communication process that breaks down for this type of child. At an utterance level, the child must decide how to coordinate his or her conversational function with linguistic structures, in particular how to make choices about the semantic, vocabulary, syntactic, and morphological expression of the message. The conversational-linguistic mismatches of the child with SLI need to be described more clearly, and the underlying nature of the breakdowns needs to be pursued aggressively in future research.

The connecting linkages between requesting and between verbal and nonverbal turn-taking and the level of linguistic rules have not been depicted in the model. Current literature reveals that conversations of children with SLI include these functions, and at least some children with SLI express them differently than children with normal language. It is not clear, however, whether these linguistic differences involve a problem with the integration of structure into these specific functions or reflect only a linguistic rule problem. Future research demonstrating that children with SLI have the necessary linguistic structures and are or are not using them appropriately will be needed to address this issue.

UTTERANCE OUTCOME AND TURN OUTCOME

Children with SLI probably experience more unsuccessful outcomes than do children with normal language. Craig and Gallagher (1986) found that

Clark's age-mates reduced their level of relatedness to him by approximately half compared to their interactions with chronologically age-matched or younger children with normal language. Wellen and Broen (1982) observed that children with SLI experience more interruptions by normally developing siblings than do children with normal language close to their chronological age. They also found that the type of interruption involved the partner answering questions for the child with SLI. It would be worthwhile to know what effects these less successful outcomes have on the subsequent communication attempts of children with SLI.

The proposed model identifies successful, unsuccessful, neutral, or unclear potential outcomes at both the level of the utterance and the turn. Prutting and Kirchner (1987) defined positive or "appropriate" outcomes as either facilitative to the communicative interaction or neutral. Behaviors that detract from the communication or penalize the speaker were considered "inappropriate." An interactionist approach to communication necessitates dynamic relationships among various levels in the communication process and the model (see Figure 6–1) tries to depict this with arrows looping back from the two outcome levels to the message preparation phase. These loops would allow the speaker to adjust his or her production of the next utterance or turn based on the response of the partner. Current research provides preliminary evidence that the child with SLI is aware of the need to adjust his or her message based on the partner's response (Brinton et al., 1986; Fujiki et al., 1990; Gallagher & Craig, 1984; Gallagher & Darnton, 1978) but is ineffective compared to normal language peers. The model portrays these relationships as production outcomes influencing the preparation of subsequent turns.

Adjusting the expression of messages will depend on the skill of the child with SLI in accurately decoding and assimilating this information into the ongoing communication process. Children with SLI seem to have difficulty recognizing and correcting syntactic and morphological errors (Kamhi & Koenig, 1985; Liles, Shulman, & Bartlett, 1977). They seem able to recognize and correct lexical-semantic and phonological errors, however. Meline and Brackin (1987) found that children with SLI performed more poorly than age-mates in recognizing when messages are vague and nonspecific. The children with SLI, like younger children with normal language, perceived the problem to be the listener's, whereas the age-mates attributed responsibility for inadequate messages to the speaker. Skarakis–Doyle and colleagues (1990), however, observed that although children with SLI detected ambiguity in the messages of the partner, they did not directly communicate this as did chronological age-mates. Perhaps the children with SLI comprehend message outcomes, but do not demonstrate this monitoring in readily observable ways. Children with SLI may have less difficulty accurately decoding messages than appropriately encoding consequent changes throughout the larger communication process.

Information about the relative success of the messages of the child with SLI should influence their subsequent expression. Information about the success of a specific utterance, for example, might motivate the speaker with SLI to change the type of utterance at the next discourse opportunity but to continue to pursue the same interactive goal. Alternatively, the listener's response to a particular speaker utterance might provide information about the achievement or non-achievement of the interactive goal so that the speaker with SLI would decide to change the goal.

These feedback loops provide ways to conceptualize different sizes of discourse units. For example, if the interactive goal is to inform the partner about some upcoming event, utterances leading to different turn sizes, consecutive turns leading to various topic sizes, all might be incorporated within the same interactive goal. Utterances might be quite varied in form, including comment, request, and response types of speech acts, expressed as declaratives, negatives, questions, and so forth. Turns might take the form of single utterances, multiutterances, partial utterance interruptions, or nonverbal back-channel responses.

CLINICAL IMPLICATIONS FOR PLANNING ASSESSMENTS AND INTERVENTION

The accumulating information regarding the pragmatic characteristics of SLI imply a number of clinical changes, as follows.

1. *Assessments should examine the child's conversational knowledge while controlling the linguistic demands of the task and also examine linguistic knowledge while controlling the conversational demands of the task.* If the objective underlying a particular assessment task is to evaluate the child's conversational knowledge, then to be interpretable the assessment task must not require linguistic performances beyond the child's repertoire. For example, the child with SLI who does not evidence knowledge of the auxiliary inversion transformation may not answer questions appropriately. Accordingly, question answering would not be an appropriate linguistic context for evaluation of the child's knowledge of the conversational obligation to respond. Conversely, if a particular evaluation procedure is designed to assess the child's linguistic knowledge, then conversationally it must be presented in the form of a discourse behavior that is within the child's knowledge base. For example, the child with SLI who does not demonstrate knowledge of the conversational initiation function of comments may not perform well on formal tests that utilize picture descriptions to sample the child's sentence production skills. In this example, the latter conversational context would not be appropriate for determining the child's linguistic knowledge.

2. *Once linguistic and conversational skill levels have been determined, assessments should also examine the child's ability to integrate these skills.* In order to

fully assess the ability of the child with SLI to communicate, the literature implies that the child's use of linguistic rules for conversational purposes also should be examined as this type of pragmatic knowledge may be problematic. For some children with SLI, conversational-linguistic mismatches may be apparent, even though the child demonstrates basic knowledge of the conversational function of interest and the necessary linguistic forms. For example, using the kinds of approaches described in the previous section, a child with SLI might be found to respond to comments but only by using stereotypic forms. Complete simple sentence forms are observed when initiating comments, but the child does not use simple sentences when appropriate as responses. In other words, the child does not seem to use linguistic structural knowledge in conversationally appropriate ways. This profile would be suggestive of a pragmatic deficit, characterized by a lack of integration of structural and functional knowledge.

3. *Clinical assessments should document both receptive and expressive language functioning of the SLI child.* Children with receptive-expressive and expressive SLI may function quite differently conversationally. The literature indicates that the children with both receptive and expressive language deficits may also show significate pragmatic deficits, whereas the child with more circumscribed expressive language problems and relatively intact receptive language skills may function more like the child with normal language across a wide range of discourse functions. Compared to the types of assessments designed for the child with expressive language deficits, assessments of the language of the child with expressive-receptive deficits may require more intensive evaluation of the child's discourse functions and his or her ability to use linguistic skills for conversational purposes. Intervention goals may need to target the teaching of new discourse functions and the range of linguistic behaviors that are and are not appropriate to that function. In contrast, intervention with the child with expressive deficits may effectively exploit the child's discourse knowledge to support the acquisition of new forms. For example, if a child with expressive deficits is found to be highly responsive but expresses nothing more advanced than two- and three-word noun phrases, then verb production might be facilitated in question-answering tasks that require responses to yes-no and wh-question prompts that model target verbs. Although considerable research is needed to clarify and replicate the conversational distinctions apparent in the literature to date, quite different strengths and weaknesses ultimately may be confirmed, with associated differences in appropriate approaches to assessment and intervention.

4. *The revised interactionist model proposed in this chapter offers a template for organizing a systematic approach to assessment of language production skills by children with SLI and a hierarchy of intervention goals for treating the problems observed.* Effective communication reflects multilevel processing. The proposed model presents an ordered sequence of achievements for preparing,

formulating, and reformulating communications. Assessments need to determine the ability of the child with SLI to accomplish each subcomponent and to pinpoint areas of breakdown, as all subsequent subcomponents in this process would be impaired also. Treatment goals should be ordered sequentially, also in a top down fashion, as improvement in outcomes would not be predicted until sequentially earlier levels were accomplished.

In summary, this chapter synthesizes information currently available regarding the pragmatic characteristics of children with SLI. A pragmatic profile is presented and future research and clinical implications discussed. A revised interactionist model for viewing the difficulties experienced by some children with SLI is presented that provides a way to conceptualize their primary conversational as well as linguistic deficits. It is offered as a vehicle for describing information available thus far and for interpreting forthcoming research.

REFERENCES

Austin, J. (1962). *How to do things with words.* Oxford, UK: Oxford University Press.

Bates, E. (1976). *Language and context: The acquisition of pragmatics.* New York: Academic Press.

Bates, E. (1976). Pragmatics and sociolinguistics in child language. In D. Morehead & A. Morehead (Eds.), *Language deficiency in children: Selected readings.* Baltimore, MD: University Park Press.

Bates, E., & MacWhinney, B. (1979). A functionalist approach to the acquisition of grammar. In E. Ochs & B. Schieffelin (Eds.), *Developmental pragmatics.* New York: Academic Press.

Blank, M., Gessner, M., & Esposito, A. (1979). Language without communication: A case study. *Journal of Child Language, 6,* 329–352.

Bloom, L., & Lahey, M. (1978). *Language development and language disorders.* New York: John Wiley and Sons.

Bondurant, J., Romeo, D., & Kretschmer, R. (1983). Language behaviors of mothers of children with normal and delayed language. *Language, Speech, and Hearing Services in Schools, 14,* 233–242.

Brinton, B., Craig, H. K., & Skarakis–Doyle, E. (1990). Peer commentary on "Clinical pragmatics: Expectations and realizations." *Journal of Speech-Language Pathology and Audiology, 14,* 7–12.

Brinton, B., & Fujiki, M. (1982). A comparison of request-response sequences in the discourse of normal and language-disordered children. *Journal of Speech and Hearing Disorders, 47,* 57–62.

Brinton, B., Fujiki, M., Winkler, E., & Loeb, D. (1986). Responses to requests for clarification in linguistically normal and language-impaired children. *Journal of Speech and Hearing Disorders, 51,* 370–378.

Brown, R. (1973). *A first language: The early stages.* Cambridge, MA: Harvard University Press.

Conti–Ramsden, G., & Friel–Patti, S. (1983). Mother's discourse adjustments to language-impaired and non-language-impaired children. *Journal of Speech and Hearing Disorders, 48,* 360–367.

Conti–Ramsden, G., & Friel–Patti, S. (1984). Mother-child dialogues: A comparison of normal and language impaired children. *Journal of Communication Disorders, 17,* 19–35.

Corsaro, W. (1981). The development of social cognition in preschool children: Implications for language learning. *Topics in Language Disorders, 2,* 77–95.

Craig, H. (1983). Applications of pragmatic language models for intervention. In T. Gallagher & C. Prutting (Eds.), *Pragmatic assessment and intervention issues in language* (pp. 101–127). San Diego, CA: College-Hill Press.

Craig, H., & Evans, J. (1989). Turn exchange characteristics of SLI children's simultaneous and nonsimultaneous speech. *Journal of Speech and Hearing Disorders, 54,* 334–347.

Craig, H., & Gallagher, T. (1986). Interactive play: The frequency of related verbal responses. *Journal of Speech and Hearing Research, 29,* 375–383.

Cramblit, N., & Siegel, G. (1977). The verbal environment of a language-impaired child. *Journal of Speech and Hearing Disorders, 62,* 474–482.

Cromer, R. F. (1978). The basis of childhood dysphasia: A linguistic approach. In M. A. Wyke (Ed.), *Developmental dysphasia* (pp. 104–105). New York: Academic Press.

Dore, J. (1974). A description of early language development. *Journal of Psycholinguistic Research, 4,* 423–430.

Dore, J. (1979). Conversational and preschool language development. In P. Fletcher & M. Garman (Eds.), *Language acquisition* (pp. 337–362). Cambridge, UK: Cambridge University Press.

Fey, M. (1986). *Language intervention with young children.* San Diego, CA: College-Hill Press.

Fey, M., & Leonard, L. (1983). Pragmatic skills of children with specific language impairment. In T. Gallagher & C. Prutting (Eds.), *Pragmatic assessment and intervention issues in language* (pp. 65–82). San Diego, CA: College-Hill Press.

Fey, M., & Leonard, L. (1984). Partner age as a variable in the conversational performance of specifically language-impaired and normal-language children. *Journal of Speech and Hearing Research, 27,* 413–423.

Fey, M., Leonard, L., & Wilcox, K. (1981). Speech style modifications of language-impaired children. *Journal of Speech and Hearing Disorders, 46,* 91–96.

Freedman, P., & Carpenter, R. (1976). Semantic relations used by normal and language impaired children at stage I. *Journal of Speech and Hearing Disorders, 19,* 784–795.

Fujiki, M., Brinton, B., & Sonnenberg, E. (1990). Repair of overlapping speech in the conversations of specifically language-impaired and normally developing children. *Applied Psycholinguistics, 11,* 201–215.

Gallagher, T. (1977). Revision behaviors in the speech of normal children developing language. *Journal of Speech and Hearing Research, 20,* 303–318.

Gallagher, T. (1983). Pre-assessment: A procedure for accommodating language variability. In T. M. Gallagher & C. A. Prutting (Eds.), *Pragmatic assessment and intervention issues in language* (pp. 1–28). San Diego, CA: College-Hill Press.

Gallagher, T. (1990). Clinical pragmatics: Expectations and realizations. *Journal of Speech-Language Pathology and Audiology, 14,* 3–6.

Gallagher, T., & Craig, H. (1984). Pragmatic assessment: Analysis of a highly frequent repeated utterance. *Journal of Speech and Hearing Disorders, 49,* 368–377.

Gallagher, T., & Darnton, B. (1978). Conversational aspects of the speech of language-disordered children: Revision behaviors. *Journal of Speech and Hearing Research, 21,* 118–135.

Garvey, C. (1975). Requests and responses in children's speech. *Journal of Child Language, 2,* 41–63.

Halle, J. (1984). Arranging the natural environment to occasion language: Giving severely language-delayed children reason to communicate. *Seminars in Speech and Language, 5,* 185–195.

Halliday, M. A. K. (1975). *Learning how to mean: Explorations in the development of language.* London: Edward Arnold.

Hymes, D. (1971). Competence and performance in linguistic theory. In R. Huxley & D. Ingram (Eds.), *Language acquisition: Models and methods.* London: Academic Press.

Ingram, T. (1972). The classification of speech and language disorders in young children. In M. Rutter & J. Martin (Eds.), *The child with delayed speech (Clinics in Developmental Medicine,* Vol. 43). Philadelphia: J. B. Lippincott.

Johnston, J. (1982). The language disordered child. In N. Lass, L. McReynolds, J. Northern, & D. Yoder (Eds.), *Speech, language, and hearing* (Vol. 2). Philadelphia: W. B. Saunders.

Johnston, J. (1989). Specific language disorders in the child. In N. Lass, L. McReynolds, J. Northern, & D. Yoder (Eds.), *Handbook of speech pathology and audiology.* Philadelphia: B. C. Decker.

Johnston, J., & Weismer, S. E. (1983). Mental rotation abilities in language disordered children. *Journal of Speech and Hearing Research, 26,* 397–403.

Kamhi, A. G. (1981) Nonlinguistic symbolic and conceptual abilities of language impaired and normally developing children. *Journal of Speech and Hearing Research, 24,* 446–453.

Kamhi, A., Catts, H., Koenig, L., & Lewis, B. (1984). Hypothesis-testing and nonlinguistic symbolic abilities in language-impaired children. *Journal of Speech and Hearing Disorders, 49,* 169–177.

Kamhi, A., & Koenig, L. (1985). Metalinguistic awareness in normal and language-disordered children. *Language, Speech, and Hearing Services in Schools, 16,* 199–210.

Keenan, E. (1974). Conversational competence in children. *Journal of Child Language, 1,* 163–183.

Lahey, M. (1988). *Language disorders and language development.* New York: Macmillan.

Lasky, E., & Klopp, K. (1982). Parent-child interactions in normal and language-disordered children. *Journal of Speech and Hearing Disorders, 47,* 7–18.

Leonard, L. (1972). What is deviant language? *Journal of Speech and Hearing Disorders, 37,* 427–446.

Leonard, L. (1986). Conversational replies of children with specific language impairment. *Journal of Speech and Hearing Research, 29,* 114–119.

Leonard, L. (1987). Is specific language impairment a useful construct? In S. Rosenberg (Ed.), *Advances in applied psycholinguistics: Vol. I. Disorders of first language development* (pp. 1 39). New York: Cambridge University Press.

Leonard, L., Bolders, J. C., & Miller, J. A. (1976). An examination of the semantic relations reflected in the language usage of normal and language-disabled children. *Journal of Speech and Hearing Research, 19,* 371–392.

Leonard, L., Camarata, S., Rowan, L., & Chapman, K. (1982). The communicative functions of lexical usage by language impaired children. *Applied Psycholinguistics, 3,* 109–125.

Liles, B. (1985a). Cohesion in the narratives of normal and language disordered children. *Journal of Speech and Hearing Research, 28,* 123–133.

Liles, B. (1985b). Production and comprehension of narrative discourse in normal and language disordered children. *Journal of Communication Disorders, 18,* 409–427.

Liles, B. (1987). Episode organization and cohesive conjunctives in narratives of children with and without language disorder. *Journal of Speech and Hearing Research, 30,* 185–196.

Liles, B., Shulman, M., & Bartlett, S. (1977). Judgments of grammaticality by normal and language-disordered children. *Journal of Speech and Hearing Disorders, 62,* 199–209.

Lund, N., & Duchan, J. (1988). *Assessing Children's Language in Naturalistic Contexts.* Englewood Cliffs, NJ: Prentice-Hall.

MacLachlan, B., & Chapman, R. (1988). Communication breakdowns in normal and language learning-disabled children's conversation and narration. *Journal of Speech and Hearing Disorders, 53,* 2–7.

MacNamara, J. (1972). Cognitive basis of language learning in infants. *Psychological Review, 79,* 1–13.

McShane, J. (1980). *Learning to talk.* Cambridge, UK: Cambridge University Press.

Meline, T., & Brackin, S. (1987). Language-impaired children's awareness of inadequate messages. *Journal of Speech and Hearing Disorders, 52,* 263–270.

Merritt, D., & Liles, B. (1987). Story grammar ability in children with and without language disorder: Story generation, story retelling, and story comprehension. *Journal of Speech and Hearing Research, 30,* 539–552.

Miller, J. (1978). Assessing children's language behavior: A developmental process approach. In R. Schiefelbusch (Ed.), *Bases of language intervention* (pp. 269–318). Baltimore, MD: University Park Press.

Mitchell–Kernan, C., & Kernan, K. (1977). Pragmatics of directive choice among children. In S. Ervin–Tripp & C. Mitchell–Kernan (Eds.), *Child discourse.* New York: Academic Press.

Montgomery, J. W., Scudder, R. R., & Moore, C. A. (1990). Language-impaired children's real-time comprehension of spoken language. *Applied Psycholinguistics, 11,* 273–290.

Morehead, D., & Ingram, D. (1973). The development of base syntax in normal and linguistically deviant children. *Journal of Speech and Hearing Disorders, 16,* 330–352.

Olswang, L., & Carpenter, R. (1978). Elicitor effects on the language obtained from young language-impaired children. *Journal of Speech and Hearing Disorders, 42,* 76–88.

Penn, C. (1988). The profiling of syntax and pragmatics in aphasia. *Clinical Linguistics & Phonetics, 2,* 179–207.

Prinz, P. (1982). An investigation of the comprehension and production of requests in normal and language-disordered children. *Journal of Communication Disorders, 15,* 75–93.

Prinz, P., & Ferrier, L. (1983). "Can you give me that one?": The comprehension, production and judgment of directives in language-impaired children. *Journal of Speech and Hearing Disorders, 48,* 44–54.

Prutting, C. (1979). Process\pra/, ses\n: The action of moving forward progressively from one point to another on the way to completion. *Journal of Speech and Hearing Disorders, 44,* 3–30.

Prutting, C., & Kirchner, D. (1983). Applied pragmatics. In T. Gallagher & C. Prutting (Eds.), *Pragmatic assessment and intervention issues in language.* San Diego, CA: College-Hill Press.

Prutting, C., & Kirchner, D. (1987). A clinical appraisal of the pragmatic aspects of language. *Journal of Speech and Hearing Disorders, 52,* 105–119.

Roth F., & Clark, D. (1987). Symbolic play and social participation abilities of language-impaired and normally developing children. *Journal of Speech and Hearing Disorders, 52,* 17–29.

Roth, F., & Spekman, N. (1984). Assessing the pragmatic abilities of children: Part 1. Organizational framework and assessment parameters. *Journal of Speech and Hearing Disorders, 49,* 2–11.

Rowan, L., Leonard, L., Chapman, K., & Weiss, A. (1983). Performative and presuppositional skills in language-disordered and normal children. *Journal of Speech and Hearing Research, 26,* 97–106.

Savich, P. (1984). Anticipatory imagery ability in normal and language-disabled children. *Journal of Speech and Hearing Research, 4,* 494–501.

Searle, J. (1969). *Speech acts.* Cambridge, UK: Cambridge University Press.

Searle, J. R. (1974). Chomsky's revolution in linguistics. In G. Harman (Ed.), *On Noam Chomsky: Critical essays* (pp. 2–33). New York: Anchor Books.

Searle, J. R. (1975). Indirect speech acts. In P. Cole & J. L. Morgan (Eds.), *Syntax and semantics 3: Speech acts.* New York: Academic Press.

Skarakis, E., & Greenfield, P. (1982). The role of new and old information in the verbal expression of language-disordered children. *Journal of Speech and Hearing Research, 25,* 462–467.

Skarakis–Doyle, E., MacLellan, N., & Mullin, K. (1990). Nonverbal indicants of comprehension monitoring in language-disordered children. *Journal of Speech and Hearing Disorders, 55,* 461–467.

Sleight, C., & Prinz, P. (1985). Use of abstracts, orientations, and codas in narration by language-disordered and nondisordered children. *Journal of Speech and Hearing Disorders, 50,* 361–371.

Snyder, L. (1978). Communicative and cognitive abilities and disabilities in the sensori-motor period. *Merrill-Palmer Quarterly, 24,* 161–180.

Stark, R., & Tallal, P. (1981). Selection of children with specific language deficits. *Journal of Speech and Hearing Disorders, 46,* 114–122.

Steckol, K., & Leonard, L. (1979). The use of grammatical morphemes by normal and language-impaired children. *Journal of Communication Disorders, 12,* 291–301.

Sugarman, S. (1984). The development of preverbal communication. In R. Schiefelbusch & J. Pikar (Eds.), *The acquisition of communicative competence.* Baltimore, MD: University Park Press

Tallal, P. (1976). Rapid auditory processing in normal and language-disordered language development. *Journal of Speech and Hearing Research, 19,* 561–571.

Tallal, P., & Piercy, M. (1973). Developmental aphasia: Impaired rate of non-verbal processing as a function of sensory modality. *Neuropsychologia, 11,* 389–398.

Tallal, P., & Piercy, M. (1975). Developmental aphasia: The perception of brief vowels and extended stop consonants. *Neuropsychologia, 13,* 69–74.

Tallal, P., & Stark, R. E. (1981). Speech acoustic-cue discrimination abilities of normally developing and language impaired children. *Journal of the Acoustical Society of America, 69,* 568–574.

Tallal, P., Stark, R. E., Kallman, C., & Mellits, E. D. (1980a). Developmental dysphasia: Relation between acoustic processing deficits and verbal processing. *Neuropsychologia, 18,* 273–284.

Tallal, P., Stark, R. E., Kallman, C., & Mellits, E. D. (1980b). Perceptual constancy for phonemic categories: A developmental study with normal and language impaired children. *Applied Psycholinguistics, 1,* 49–64.

Terrell, B., Schwartz, R., Prelock, P., & Messick, C. (1984). Symbolic play in normal and language-impaired children. *Journal of Speech and Hearing Research, 27,* 424–430.

VanKleeck, A., & Frankel, T. (1981). Discourse devices used by language disordered children: A preliminary investigation. *Journal of Speech and Hearing Disorders, 46,* 250–257.

Weiner, P. (1980). Developmental language disorders. In H. Rie & E. Rie (Eds.), *Handbook of minimal brain dysfunction.* New York: John Wiley and Sons.

Wellen, C., & Broen, P. (1982). The interruption of young children's responses by
    older siblings. *Journal of Speech and Hearing Disorders, 47,* 204–210.
Wolfus, B., Moscovitch, M., & Kinsbourne, M. (1980). Subgroups of developmental
    language impairment. *Brain and Language, 10,* 152–171.

CHAPTER 7

Discourse: A Means for Understanding Normal and Disordered Language

MICHELLE MENTIS AND SANDRA A. THOMPSON

Work in discourse linguistics in the last decade has made it abundantly clear that linguistic knowledge extends beyond sentence level syntax and semantics to include the principles that constrain the structure and ordering of sentences in discourse and the application of social and cognitive knowledge to the generation of coherent, cohesive discourse. Children and adults with language problems may evidence well developed linguistic knowledge at the sentence level, yet experience difficulty in creating a cohesive, coherent text. On the other hand, because well developed discourse is dependent on syntactic and semantic development, linguistic problems at the sentence level may result in problems at the discourse level. Although the clinical application of various discourse analyses is still relatively new, it is already clear that children and adults with language impairments may have significant problems with discourse (e.g., Brinton, Fujiki, & Sonnenberg, 1988; Craig & Evans, 1989; Fey, 1986; Liles, 1985a, 1985b; Mentis & Prutting, 1987; Prigatano, Rouche, & Fordyce, 1985; Prutting & Kirchner, 1987; Tager–Flusberg, 1988). The following sections of this chapter will examine how the study of discourse can provide a means for understanding both normal and disordered language. To provide a framework for this discussion, the intellectual origins of discourse analysis will be traced to demonstrate how the unique origins of this field have shaped its definitions, approaches, and goals.

Discourse analysis only recently has emerged as an established field of enquiry and a distinct branch of linguistics. Until the late 1960s very little attention was paid to discourse. The work of Harris (1952) and Mitchell (1957) in linguistics represents two relatively isolated attempts to study the structure of language above the level of the sentence (Coulthard, 1985, p. 3).

Since the 1970s, however, the field of discourse analysis has become vast and diverse. Its growth and diversity is consistent with its intellectual origins which can be traced back to the contributions of researchers from a wide range of disciplines. Discourse analysis began in linguistics with the work of Harris (1951, 1952), a structural linguist working within the Bloomfieldian tradition (Coulthard, 1985; Schiffrin, 1987). Harris applied distributional methods of analysis to discover structures above the level of the sentence and attempted to identify recurrent morpheme patterns that would differentiate a text from a random string of sentences. In anthropology, the roots of discourse analysis can be seen in the work of Malinowski (1930), who distinguished the referential and social functions of language. Roots can also be seen in the work of the anthropologists Gumperz (1964) and Hymes (1974), who were interested in cultural aspects of naturally occurring discourse. In sociology, Goffman (1959, 1971, 1974) focused attention on the use of language in social interaction, and within this discipline, ethnomethodology has had a considerable influence on the study of conversation. Although ethnomethodology was first articulated by Garfinkel (1967), its application was extended to the analysis of conversation by Sacks and Schegloff in the 1960s (cf. Sacks, Schegloff, & Jefferson, 1974). In philosophy, Austin (1962) and Searle's (1969) discussion of speech acts and Grice's (1975) identification of conversational maxims focused attention on the importance of language use.

Because of its diverse origins, discourse analysis is a field marked by differences in definitions, approaches, and goals. Relatively recently, Stubbs (1983) wrote, "no one is in a position to write a comprehensive account of discourse analysis. The subject is at once too vast, and too lacking in consensus and focus" (p. 12). Even the terms *discourse* and *discourse analysis* are used differently by different scholars. Brown and Yule (1983) noted that discourse analysis "has come to be used with a wide range of meanings which cover a wide range of activities" (p. viii).

There are, however, certain basic concerns that underlie these differences. Common to all forms of discourse analysis is the study of language beyond the level of the isolated sentence (Chafe, in press). One of its central goals is providing an account of the differences between a string of isolated sentences and sentences that form a unified whole (Chafe, in press;

Schiffrin, 1985a). According to Levinson (1983), discourse analysis is concerned with "giving an account of how coherence and sequential organization in discourse is produced and understood" (p. 226).

Another central concern is attempting to understand the nature of the interaction between naturally occurring language, its use in social and cultural contexts, and the acquisition, storage, and use of knowledge by the human mind (Chafe, in press).

UNDERSTANDING NORMAL LANGUAGE FROM A DISCOURSE PERSPECTIVE

Several major lines of research can be identified in the field of discourse analysis. Although these approaches differ in their focus and goals, each makes a unique contribution to the understanding of language from a discourse perspective. The first major line of research looks at discourse as a means for understanding grammar. The second views discourse as a means for understanding conversational structure in the context of social interaction, and the third looks at discourse as a means for understanding cognitive structures and processes. The fourth line of research may be seen as an attempt to provide an integrated approach to discourse by incorporating central aspects from all of the above areas.

DISCOURSE AS A MEANS FOR UNDERSTANDING GRAMMAR

One major line of research in the field of discourse analysis is the study of grammar from a discourse perspective. Although this line of research encompasses a number of approaches, they are related by the centrality of their interest in grammar, that is, morphology and syntax. Studies in the area of discourse and grammar are concerned with how grammar emerges from and can be accounted for by discourse. These approaches are in sharp contrast to sentence-based theories of syntax such as Government and Binding (Chomsky, 1981) and Generalized Phrase Structure Grammar (Gazdar, Klein, Pullum, & Sag, 1985). Some of the more notable grammarians who are interested in discourse and grammar are Chafe (1980, 1987), Givón (1979, 1983, 1984), and Halliday (1985). Chafe's research seeks to understand the relationship between language and cognitive processes involving memory, production, and comprehension. Halliday (1985) has defined syntactic structures in functional terms and argued that differences in syntactic forms are derived from their functions in discourse. Givón's (1979) discourse-oriented approach to grammar is also an attempt to explain syntactic phenomena in terms of the pragmatics of discourse.

In addition to the researchers just cited, examples of the type of research conducted within this framework can be found in a number of articles and books published in the last decade. Hopper (1979) is justifiably celebrated as writing one of the earliest articles to call attention to the role of discourse in explaining grammar. Hopper showed that narrative discourse can be divided into foregrounded and backgrounded portions, where the foregrounded portions provide the essential story line. Hopper also noted that various grammatical devices serve to signal foregrounded events. Du Bois (1980) provided a detailed account of the use of definiteness in English discourse, showing how definitiveness depends on the cognitive assessment that a speaker makes about the hearer's ability to identify referents. Fox (1987) proposed that the choice between a pronoun and a noun in English depends crucially on structural factors in the discourse, and that these structural factors are closely related to the type of discourse being considered (conversation, narrative, or expository). Hopper (1987) and Du Bois (1987) contributed seminal articles that showed how grammatical patterns can be understood as largely determined by regular patterns observable in discourse.

Another approach to the study of grammar from a discourse perspective is the investigation of discourse cohesion, the linguistic means by which sentences are tied together to form a unified text. The most comprehensive treatment of cohesion in English was provided by Halliday and Hasan (1976), who viewed cohesion as the linguistic means through which a set of sentences function as a meaningful unit. Cohesion is established through a set of semantic relations in which one element can be understood only by reference to another. These semantic relations are expressed partly through the grammar and partly through the vocabulary. For example, pronouns may establish referential chains across sentences through the fact that their interpretation is dependent on their being tied to the original referent elsewhere in the text. The study of cohesion is concerned with the nature of cohesive ties, their surface syntactic or semantic form, the direction in which they refer (anaphoric or cataphoric), and the number of intervening sentences between the referring item and the referent. Other work closely related to cohesion concerns the treatment of structures such as articles, demonstratives, and pronomial forms, all of which require reference to prior and following sentences of the discourse (van Dijk, 1981).

DISCOURSE AS A MEANS FOR UNDERSTANDING CONVERSATIONAL STRUCTURE IN THE CONTEXT OF SOCIAL INTERACTION

The second major line of research in the field of discourse analysis is the study of discourse in the context of social interaction. This branch of discourse study is characterized by a number of approaches, and a wide range of topics have been investigated.

One approach is conversational analysis. Much of the work on conversational analysis grew out of the ethnomethodological approach to the analysis of conversational discourse that was pioneered by Sacks, Schegloff, and Jefferson (1974). Levinson (1983) contrasted this approach to other approaches of discourse analysis on the basis of both theory and methodology. He referred to the ethnomethodological approach as conversational analysis and termed the other approaches discourse analysis. He categorized such widely divergent approaches as text grammar (van Dijk, 1972) and work based on speech acts and related notions (Labov & Fanshel, 1977; Longacre, 1976; Sinclair & Coulthard, 1975) as discourse analysis on the basis of their similarities to traditional linguistics. He argued that in discourse analysis the methodology, theoretical principles, and concepts of linguistics are extended beyond the level of the sentence. In contrast, conversational analysis is an empirical approach in which premature construction of theory is avoided. The method is primarily inductive and involves a search for recurring patterns and systematic properties of the sequential organization of talk across a number of texts. A key component is its focus on the local organization of talk as it is accomplished by interactants (Sacks et al., 1974).

Work stemming from the ethnomethodological approach specifically and conversational analysis generally has resulted in detailed structural descriptions of various aspects of conversations. These descriptions are based on the position that the organization of conversations is the result of the application of a set of local interactively managed rules. The procedures that conversationalists use to organize talk are the goals of description for conversation analysts. Their work thus focuses on such problems as how turns at talk are allocated (e.g., De Long, 1974; Goodwin, 1981; Kendon, 1967; Sacks et al., 1974) and how conversations are opened and closed (e.g., Collett, 1983; Corsaro, 1979; Hall & Spencer-Hall, 1983; Schegloff, 1968, 1980; Schiffrin, 1974). Organizational structures that have received particular attention include the adjacency pair, preference organization, and presequences (Atkinson & Drew, 1979; Jefferson, 1972; Levinson, 1983; Pomerantz, 1978, 1984; Schegloff, 1972). Schiffrin (1985b) has analyzed the discourse properties of argument through such aspects of discourse structure as differential distribution of discourse markers, conjunctions, repetition, and different turn-taking strategies and has shown the differences in organizational structure and discourse properties between rhetorical and oppositional argument.

Another aspect of conversational structure that has been the focus of attention is discourse topic. Models of discourse topic have been proposed by Gardner (1987), Keenan and Schieffelin (1976), and Stech (1982). Age-related changes in topic maintenance have been studied by Stover and Haynes (1989). Various aspects of topic shifts and changes in conversation have been investigated by, among others, Crow (1983), Forsyth (1974),

Goodenough and Weiner (1978), Maynard (1980), Okolo (1987), and Planalp and Tracy (1980).

A contrast to the ethnomethodological approach to the analysis of conversational discourse is the study of speech acts. This major line of discourse analysis research investigates discourse in the context of social interaction. The general theoretical framework for the study of speech acts was developed by Austin (1962), Searle (1969, 1975), and Vendler (1972). The early work was done by imagining discourse contexts. Types of speech acts were proposed and justified, for example, threats, warnings, and various types of indirect speech acts. From this general framework and the speech act category systems developed by these scholars, different lines of research have emerged.

Austin identified five categories in his classic categorization of performative verbs: expositives, exercitives, verdictives, commissives, and behabitives. When his system was applied to the analysis of natural discourse, however, several problems emerged. One problem was the overlap between categories, which complicated decisions regarding assignments to speech act categories. Another problem was that his system failed to consider the fact that in natural discourse speech acts are related to other speech acts (D'Andrade & Wish, 1985).

Vendler's (1972) classification of performatives consisted of seven speech act categories, each of which had specific syntactic criteria. There is a certain amount of overlap between his categories and those proposed by Austin (1962). Vendler's whose categories included expositives, verdictives, commissives, exercitives, operatives, behabitives, and interrogatives. Searle (1975) presented a taxonomy of illocutionary acts. He described 12 dimensions along which speech acts could differ, and the criteria on which his categories were based were both clear and explicit. The six major speech act categories he identified included representatives, directives, commissives, expressives, declarations, and representative declarations. Within each of these major categories Searle also included several subcategories of speech acts.

A system of speech acts was developed by Dore (1977) to code the naturally occurring discourse of preschool children. His system was based on those proposed by Austin, Searle, and Vendler with modifications designed to account for the specific characteristics of naturally occurring discourse, such as the relative frequency of use of the various speech acts. Major categories included assertives, requestives, responsives, regulatives, performatives, expressives, and nonverbal responses, with various subcategories within the major categories. Dore's system (or modified versions of it) has been used to describe language development and mother-child interactions in a number of empirical studies (e.g., Folger & Chapman, 1978; Pellegrini, 1982).

Another system of speech acts intended to describe naturally occurring therapeutic discourse was developed by Labov and Fanshel (1977). Their system was hierarchically organized. Any single utterance could be coded at a number of levels depending on the number of different acts the utterance performed. Metalinguistic, representations, requests, and challenges were the four major categories in their system, each with several subcategories. An additional difference from the other systems was that Labov and Fanshel's system incorporated responses and responses to responses. This dimension is important because it begins to address the issue of the sequencing of speech acts in discourse.

Edmondson (1981), however, has criticized Labov and Fanshel on the grounds that they did not explicitly specify a set of sequencing possibilities and that their categories appeared to be ad hoc. Edmonson attempted to address these issues in the development of his own model of speech acts, which emphasized the importance of characterizing conversational discourse in terms of speech act sequences. His model was a multidimensional one that incorporated both interactional and illocutionary acts. According to Edmonson (1987), interactional acts combine to form interactional moves and interactional moves are sequenced to produce various types of exchanges. The combining of various exchanges forms the phases of a conversation, and an ordered sequence of phases describes the structure of an encounter. The nature of the exchange is determined by the illocutionary acts of which the exchange is composed, and the implementation of conversational strategies accounts for the sequencing of communicative acts in any particular conversational encounter.

Van Dijk (1981) argued that a theory of discourse should include both text grammar and a theory of speech acts. The theory of speech acts should delineate the constraints that sequences of speech acts should satisfy. However, in addition to accounting for speech act sequences, speech act theory should also account for their links to textual structures. According to van Dijk, speech act sequences need to be systematically related to simple, compound, and complex sentences and to the sequences of sentences in discourse. In an attempt to solve this problem, van Dijk put forward the notions of macro- and microstructures. Macrostructures correspond to global speech acts that provide an organizing framework for sequences of individual speech acts at the micro level. Van Dijk viewed macrostructures as playing a unifying role in terms of information reduction and organization at several levels of language: at the semantic level where they serve to organize complex sequences of meanings, at the pragmatic level where they serve to organize speech act structures, and at the cognitive level where they facilitate the general handling of complex information.

Another approach to the analysis of discourse based on speech acts and related notions is the approach put forward by Sinclair and Coulthard

(1975). They proposed a framework for describing classroom interaction. Teacher-student transactions were described as having a structure that was expressed in terms of exchanges. Four types of exchanges were identified: boundary exchanges (transactions often begin and end with a boundary exchange), informing, directing, and eliciting exchanges. The structure of exchanges was expressed in terms of three moves: initiation, response, and follow-up. The moves were viewed as consisting of one or more functional interactive acts (as distinguished from Austin's illocutionary acts and Searle's speech acts). Seventeen acts were identified and grouped into three major categories: meta-interactive (marker, metastatement, loop); interactive (initiation—informative, directive, elicitation; response—acknowledge, react, reply); and follow-up (accept, evaluate, comment). A fourth category, acts concerned specifically with turn-taking (cue, bid, nomination), termed an "aside," did not fall into these three categories. It was proposed to deal with utterances that were not directly part of the interaction. Within this model Sinclair and Coulthard also attempted to relate grammatical units (sentence, clause, group, word, morpheme) and external nonlinguistic events (course, period, topic) to the different levels of discourse analysis.

In addition to the ethnomethodological approach and the study of speech acts, another area of discourse analysis that has focused on the study of discourse in the context of social interaction is the study of the effects of social context on discourse. Here the focus is the investigation of features of the social context that impose constraints on discourse. Effects of the social context on such aspects of discourse as the style and thematic structure of gender, status, power, ethnicity, roles, and setting have been studied. For example, Sykes (1985) provided an analysis of discrimination in discourse. She showed how the information content of a message may favor a person or group, while lexical choice or syntax may indicate the reverse. Studies of the discourse in various institutional settings (courtrooms, medical consultations, classrooms, news interviews) have delineated differences between the various types of institutional talk and natural conversation. This is evident from studies of the discourse of immigrant workers (Dittmar & von Stutterheim, 1985), doctor-patient discourse (Cicourel, 1985), discourse in the courtroom (Maynard, 1985; Wodak, 1985), and news interviews (Heritage, 1985).

DISCOURSE AS A MEANS FOR UNDERSTANDING COGNITIVE STRUCTURES AND PROCESSES

The third major line of research in discourse analysis relates to the interaction between discourse and various cognitive structures and processes. This is evident in the study of the cognitive structures used in the production and comprehension of discourse—how the content and structures of world knowledge are used in discourse processing. A wide range of cognitive structures have been proposed, including scripts, schemata, frames, and episodes (Abelson, 1976; Fillmore, 1977; Minsky, 1975; Neisser, 1967; Rumelhart, 1976; Schank & Abelson, 1977). Other research, including the work of van Dijk (1977, 1981) and Mann and Thompson (1988), has focused on how discourse organization can be understood in terms of speaker/writer goals.

Significant work on how knowledge representation influences discourse comprehension has been done by van Dijk and Kintsch (1977, 1983). They have argued that new information is interpreted and recalled according to socially and cognitively established schemata. As mentioned earlier, van Dijk (1977, 1980) proposed the concept of macrostructures which represent the overall global semantic organization of a discourse. Within macrostructures, semantic mappings, or macrorules, are the means by which individual propositions in a given discourse are linked, and any given discourse is organized hierarchically at several different levels of macrostructures. Van Dijk argued that his theory of macrostructures had a linguistic (grammatical) component, which accounted for notions such as topic and semantic relations in discourse, and a general cognitive basis, which accounted for macroprocessing in language production and comprehension. In addition, his theory of discourse incorporated other components such as superstructures, which specified the overall characteristic organization of a particular type of discourse. Related work on the organization of discourse can be found in the research on the Rhetorical Structure Theory of Mann and Thompson (1988), who proposed a framework for describing the organization of texts in terms of the speaker's or writer's goals.

Much of the work done on the relationship between knowledge structures and discourse processing has focused on attempting to characterize the structure of stories. This work has provided some insight into the cognitive processes involved in the comprehension, representation, and production of stories. At least six different story grammars have been postulated (Labov, 1972; Mandler & Johnson, 1977; Rumelhart, 1975; Stein & Glenn, 1979; Thorndyke, 1977; van Dijk, 1980). The results of these studies suggest that stories have a suprasegmental structure and that knowledge of this structure is used in encoding and comprehending stories and in storing and retrieving specific information. Story grammars represent the internal structure of stories and the underlying cognitive organization is reflected in the story schema.

Although story grammars and the characterization of the underlying story schemas differ, the specification of temporal and causal relationships between people and events is central to all story grammars. Mandler and Johnson (1977) described the underlying structure of simple stories in terms of a set of basic nodes in a tree structure. The nodes were connected either causally or temporally and a set of rules governing their sequencing and connection was specified. The story grammar proposed by Stein and Glenn (1979) consisted of six sequentially organized components: settings, initiating events, internal responses, attempts, direct consequences, and reactions.

Although story grammars provide some insight into the cognitive organization underlying the production and comprehension of stories, the literature does not provide an adequate basis for choosing among story grammars. Another problem regarding story grammars, which is now being addressed by researchers, is the nature and significance of the relationship between story grammars and other world knowledge (Black & Wilensky, 1979; Mandler & Johnson, 1980; van Dijk & Kintsch, 1983). This research may lead to a further understanding of the relationship between general cognitive knowledge, knowledge structures, and discourse processing.

The relationship between discourse and cognitive structures has also been studied in terms of the organization of conversational discourse on the basis of script knowledge. Scripts are the conceptual representations of appropriate sequences of events in a particular context (Schank & Abelson, 1977). Nelson and Gruendel (1979) investigated the relationship between script knowledge and conversational structure and argued that scripts may be used as a basis of shared knowledge and a framework for constructing dialogues. They demonstrated how young children use script knowledge to sustain conversations and how the structure of scripts provides a framework for learning general concepts. They suggested that script learning provides an essential foundation for children's social, cognitive, and linguistic development.

The role of discourse in cognitive structures and processes has also been investigated in studies of information flow. Influential work in this area has been done by Chafe (1987, 1988, in press) who investigated changes in the status of knowledge as language is produced and comprehended through time. Chafe (1987) looked at the relationship between mental processing and such linguistic phenomena as given and new information, topics and comments, subjects and predicates, intonation units, and clauses. Chafe argued that spoken language is segmented into intonation units and that each intonation unit is a linguistic expression of the specific information that a speaker is focusing on at that particular moment. Intonation units provide insights into the flow of thought by indicating what kinds of information are being focused on and how movement takes place from one focused piece of information to the next while thought is being verbalized. Although the majority of intonation units are clauses, many are not. As intonation units represent the flow of ideas in the form of successive activations of small amounts of information, intonation units or ideas may be expressed as parts of clauses or combinations of clauses. Chafe's work has focused on the relationship between the flow of ideas as manifested in intonation units and the ways in which these ideas are verbalized in clauses.

TOWARD AN INTEGRATED APPROACH: GRAMMAR, CONVERSATION, AND COGNITIVE STRUCTURES AND PROCESSES

As previously discussed, one of the major goals of discourse analysis is to provide an account of the coherence and sequential organization of discourse. As yet, however, there is no consensus on precisely how coherence in discourse should be defined, or what constitutes a principled account of coherent discourse. Many researchers in this area have, however, agreed that coherence in discourse is the result of the integration of a number of features. For example, Gumperz (1982, 1983) proposed that coherence depends on a speaker's successful integration of different verbal and nonverbal aspects of communication to situate a message in an interpretive frame. Stubbs (1983) suggested a need for multiple theories of discourse coherence, which would include an account of surface lexical and syntactic cohesion, logical propositional development, and the underlying structures relating sequences of speech acts. Ellis (1983) argued that coherence operates at a number of levels in discourse and that an understanding of the contribution of each level is needed before a proper interpretation of coherence is possible. The discourse levels that Ellis identified include speech acts, a system of structural relations that characterize the semantic properties of discourse, discourse topics, and cohesive relations.

Two more fully elaborated, although different, models of coherence in discourse were developed by van Dijk (1977, 1981) and Schiffrin (1987). According to van Dijk's model, coherence is achieved at both micro (local) and macro (global) levels and incorporates linguistic, pragmatic, and cognitive knowledge. Schiffrin's model was based on the integration of different layers of meaning and structure in discourse. In this model, coherence in discourse is seen as the interaction of various components of discourse, which include exchange, action, and ideational structures; a participation framework; and ideational states. Exchange structures refer to the outcome procedures speakers use to alternate speaker turns and to produce and respond to conditionally relevant adjacency pairs. Action structures refer to the organizing principles underlying sequences of speech acts. The units of the ideational structure are semantic and refer to the propositions or ideas conveyed in the discourse. Schiffrin identified three types of ideational structure relations in discourse: cohesive relations, topic relations, and functional relations (how ideas are related to one another in discourse). Schiffrin's participation framework refers to different types of speaker-hearer relationships (teacher-student, doctor-patient, etc.) and to the ways in which speakers and hearers can be related to their utterances (evaluate, present neutrally, or express commitment to propositions; perform actions directly or indirectly). The final component of Schiffrin's model is the information state, which refers to the speaker/hearer's organization and management of knowledge and metaknowledge (what they know about their own knowledge base and what parts of the knowledge base they assume the other to know).

At present researchers have only a preliminary understanding of discourse coherence and what would constitute an adequate account of discourse coherence. There is, however, agreement that an adequate understanding of discourse requires an integration of a number of discourse features at multiple levels. Such an integrated approach to discourse would incorporate central concepts and findings from the three major lines of research previously discussed: grammar, conversational structure in the context of social interaction, and underlying cognitive structures and processes. Understanding of the structure and function of language in normal discourse contexts already has been broadened by the results of research in these areas.

UNDERSTANDING LANGUAGE DISORDERS FROM A DISCOURSE PERSPECTIVE

One of the primary goals of any discipline is to provide systematic, accurate, and explicit descriptions of the phenomena studied and, ultimately, to account for those phenomena through the development of explanatory theories. In the field of speech-language pathology this means that an account of communication disorders needs to include a characterization of the structural and functional features of the aspects of discourse that may be disrupted. The importance of this is highlighted by findings of significant discourse problems in children and adults who are communicatively impaired (e.g., Brinton, Fujiki, & Sonnenberg, 1988; Craig & Evans, 1989; Fey, 1986; Liles, 1985a, 1985b, 1987; Mentis & Prutting, 1987; Prigatano, Roueche, & Fordyce, 1985; Prutting & Kirchner, 1987; Tager–Flusberg, 1988). Just as discourse analysis has led to a broader understanding of normal language, so can it broaden the understanding of language disorders.

The growing body of literature on discourse linguistics suggests that discourse has its roots in linguistic, social, and cognitive domains. This suggests that a systematic and comprehensive account of language disorders requires the delineation of disruptions in discourse in relation to these three domains. The application of discourse linguistics to the study of language disorders goes beyond the description of language disorders in these terms; it necessitates the inclusion of assessment and treatment procedures that focus on the interactions among discourse and the linguistic, social, and cognitive domains. The application of discourse linguistics to the description, assessment, and treatment of language disorders is potentially rich and diverse. Valuable insights may be gained from the study of disorders not only in terms of the three major lines of discourse research, but also in terms of the interaction between the different levels of organization in language.

DISCOURSE AND GRAMMAR: TOWARD AN UNDERSTANDING OF LANGUAGE DISORDERS

The question of how discourse relates to grammatical phenomena in language disorders raises important issues concerning the extent to which the grammatical systems of individuals with language disorders are the result of discourse factors. As important is the corollary to this question: the extent to which disordered grammatical systems result in disrupted discourse. The study of the interaction between disruptions in discourse and grammar can provide valuable insights into the nature of language disorders.

One reason why the relationship between discourse and grammar takes on a unique importance in the study of language disorders is because different language disorders are characterized by disruptions at different levels of functioning. Autistic children may produce complex syntactic structures, yet evidence difficulty in following the principles governing the organization and use of those structures in discourse (Tager–Flusberg, 1987). Selectively intact grammatical development and poor conversational development have also been reported in a retarded child (Curtiss & Yamada, 1981). Similarly, adults who have sustained a traumatic head injury may evidence relatively intact syntactic skills, yet have difficulty consistently formulating coherent, cohesive discourse (Mentis & Prutting, 1987; Prigatano et al., 1985). On the other hand, there are children with language impairment who evidence conversational and narrative skills beyond the level of their syntactic and semantic development (Lahey, 1988). A similar linguistic profile has also been reported in a case of Turner's syndrome (Yamada & Curtiss, 1981). These dissociations suggest that the different levels of organization in language may be differentially affected in language disorders.

Although such dissociations between discourse and grammatical skills are evident in language disorders, the relationships among these different levels of organization are complex. There are at least four possible relationships: problems may occur in isolation at any one level; problems at different levels may be independent from each other; problems at different levels may be independent from each other but result from some common underlying factor; and disruptions at one level may cause disruptions at another. From a clinical perspective, a clear understanding of the effects of disruptions at one level of organization on the others is essential. This is evident in the following examples in which disruptions at one level result in problems at another. A breakdown in the pronominal system of syntax may result in cohesion problems in discourse. The use of pronouns without the appropriate specification of the referent will result in incomplete cohesive ties. Another example is the use of specific syntactic structures to perform such discourse functions as topic initiation and requests for revision. Difficulty in the formulation of questions may limit the devices available to perform these discourse functions.

Research in the area of conversation analysis may be particularly relevant to the investigation of these relationships between discourse and grammar in language disorders. A premise that underlies conversation analysis and has direct and specific clinical implications is the search for how a particular function is fulfilled by a range of forms. For example, there are a number of different ways in which particular conversational tasks, such as turn transitions (Sacks et al., 1974) or disagreements (Pomerantz, 1984), are accomplished in different discursive interactions. Research on such questions may serve as the basis for addressing a number of clinically pertinent issues, such as the extent to which individuals with language impairments use the range and diversity of forms used by normal speakers to accomplish these tasks, and the extent to which restricted linguistic abilities limit the success of a speaker who is language impaired in accomplishing these conversation tasks.

It is clear that the relationship between disorders in grammar and discourse is complex; it differs both across and within disordered groups. As further insights into the nature of this relationship are gained, understanding of the nature of language disorders, as well as of the relationships among the different levels of functioning in language, will be broadened.

The investigation of language disorders from the perspective of the interaction between discourse and grammar also has significant explanatory potential. This is evident from the insights that were obtained from the investigation of a language disordered child's grammatical system from a functional discourse perspective (see Chapter 10). The child's pattern of complex sentence development was explained in terms of his use of a discourse-based strategy. In order to meet the functional demand of introducing new information, complex sentences were scaffolded onto his partner's utterances. The search for additional connections between discourse and specific grammatical patterns may increase speech-language pathologists' understanding of the nature of disordered language as well as their understanding of the relationship between language structure and function.

One grammatically based discourse analysis that has been fruitfully applied to the description of language disorders is cohesion. The framework that has been used most often is that provided by Halliday and Hasan (1976). Different cohesion patterns and the increased use of incomplete and ambiguous cohesive ties have been reported in the discourse of children with language impairments (Liles, 1985a, 1985b), adults with closed head injuries (Liles, Coelho, Duffy, & Zalagens, 1989; Mentis & Prutting, 1987), aphasic adults (Piehler & Holland, 1984; Ulatowska, Doyel, Stern, Haynes, & North, 1983; Ulatowska, North, & Macaluso–Haynes, 1981), and patients with Alzheimer's disease (Ripich & Terrell, 1988). These studies have shown that cohesion may be reduced and disrupted in the discourse of children and adults with language disorders.

Such descriptions of disrupted discourse cohesion in individuals with language disorders suggest that relevant cohesion analyses should be included in assessment and treatment procedures. If cohesion problems are evident, cohesion analyses should be incorporated into the diagnostic evaluation and the information gained should be used for the development of treatment goals directed at each specific level of impairment. Treatment goals based on such evaluations would vary depending on the nature of the cohesion problem. For example, the production of relatively high percentages of incomplete and ambiguous ties leads to semantic confusion and ambiguity in the discourse. Incomplete and ambiguous ties result from a failure to specify appropriate referents. A relevant treatment goal would be to reduce the ambiguity through the appropriate specification of referents and production of complete cohesive ties. In other circumstances, relevant goals might include the reduction of redundancy through the increased use of elliptical and referential ties, or increasing textual cohesion through the use of conjunctive ties to specify the precise relationship between the text preceding the tie and the text that follows. The extent to which ties are connected to the text of the communication partner may provide insight into the extent to which individuals with language disorders use the text of their partners as a scaffold from which to formulate their own text. Such a compensatory strategy may also be used in treatment as a means for facilitating the development and use of different cohesive ties.

The study of the relationship between disorders in discourse and grammar has important implications for understanding the nature of language disorders and for the development of sensitive assessment and treatment procedures. The investigation of the interactions between discourse and grammar in language disorders already has provided some insight into the nature of the differences in discourse-linguistic profiles both within and between language-disordered groups. In addition, the potentially fruitful use of grammatically based discourse analyses for clinical purposes has been demonstrated.

CONVERSATIONAL STRUCTURE IN THE CONTEXT OF SOCIAL INTERACTION: A MEANS FOR UNDERSTANDING LANGUAGE DISORDERS

The study of normal conversational structure in the context of social interaction also has implications for the description, assessment, and treatment of language disorders. Research in this area has provided the basis for preliminary descriptions of the sequential patterns of interactional discourse in language disorders (e.g., Brinton & Fujiki, 1989; Brinton et al., 1988; Conti–Ramsden & Friel–Patti, 1983; Craig & Evans, 1989; Fey, 1986; Linebaugh, Margulies, & Mackisack, 1985). These descriptions suggest that the organization and structure of conversational discourse in individuals who are language impaired may be vulnerable to disruption. They have illustrated how apparently subtle differences in conversational structure can have significant consequences for an individual's overall communicative competence.

The study of conversational structure in the context of social interaction in children with language disorders has been particularly fruitful. Children with language disorders have been reported to have problems in the use of contingent queries and requests for revision (Brinton et al., 1988; Brinton, Fujiki, Winkler, & Loeb, 1986; Fujiki, Brinton, & Sonnenberg, 1990), turn exchanges (Conti–Ramsden & Friel–Patti, 1983; Craig & Evans, 1989), and topic introduction and maintenance (Brinton & Fujiki, 1989; Fey, 1986; Fey, Leonard, & Wilcox, 1981). An important issue, however, is raised by the fact that not all studies have reported differences between children with normal language development and children with language impairments. For example, Prather, Cromwell, and Kennedy (1989) found no differences in the repair strategies used by children with language impairment and normal controls aged 4 years to 5 years, 6 months old. This suggests that there may be subgroups of children with language impairments that present different discourse profiles. This possibility is further suggested by the fact that the diagnosis of a language disorder is normally made on the basis of the results of standardized tests which do not provide an evaluation of discourse skills. Thus children with problems specifically in this area may not be identified. In fact, different discourse profiles within a single disordered group have been described. Fey (1986) described four distinct discourse profiles on the basis of conversational responsiveness and assertiveness in children with language disorders. Prutting and Kirchner (1987) found that subgroups of subjects within different diagnostic groups were characterized by different pragmatic profiles. The possibility of subgroups of children with language impairments presenting different discourse profiles requires systematic investigation and clarification. Descriptions of disruptions in the conversational structure of individuals with language disorders illustrate the importance of incorporating a systematic examination of conversational discourse in the context of social interaction into diagnostic evaluations.

Although the importance of examining conversational discourse in the context of social interaction is clear, the specific type of analyses that should be used is less clear. As yet, reliable, comprehensive, and inclusive analyses of conversational discourse have not been fully developed and a number of issues remain unresolved. For example, there is disagreement regarding what the basic unit of analysis should be. Units such as the sentence, intonation unit, turn at talk, utterance, and move have been suggested (Schiffrin, 1988). Although issues such as these will be addressed by researchers over the next decade, valuable advances have already been made. Speech-language pathologists have been provided with a set of structures and categories that extend across different levels of discourse and range from the sequencing of single turns at talk, to adjacency pairs, to topic structures. These analyses provide a valuable framework for the evaluation of conversational discourse in language disorders. The detail and specificity of such analyses can provide explicit descriptions of disordered conversational structures. Such descriptions can lead to the development of intervention programs directed at each specific level of impairment.

Take, for example, turn-taking. Sacks, Schegloff, and Jefferson (1974) have proposed a model of how turn exchanges are locally achieved on a turn by turn basis with minimal gaps or overlaps. They described the conversational turn-taking system in terms of two components, turn construction and allocation, and a set of rules. The basic unit of a speaker turn is a "unit type," which may be a sentence, clause, phrase, or lexical item. The structure of the unit type allows the speaker to project when the unit type will be completed and this point marks the "transition relevance place," where speaker transfer can take place. The rules that govern turn construction and allocation consist of a set of ordered options which apply at the first transition relevance place. Turns may be allocated either through the current speaker selecting the next speaker or through self-selection. The first option is for the speaker to select the next speaker, the second, for self selection, and the third, for possible continuation of the current speaker.

Although Sacks and colleagues' (1974) account does not provide for the role of information content in turn transition, or for differential interpretation of overlaps in discourse (Schiffrin, 1988), it does specify how the conversational turn exchange is locally achieved. Other relevant factors can then be factored into this account. For instance, Duncan and Fiske (1985) have discussed a wide variety of ways in which the end of a speaker turn may be signalled. Research in this area provides a fertile framework for the generation of assessment procedures relevant to language disorders. Using this framework, an evaluation can be made of the rules that govern turn construction and allocation, the appropriate use of turn initiation or allocation cues (such as pause time, linguistic cues, intonation, and nonverbal cues), and the frequency and diversity of turn initiation and allocation by both the client and partner.

Another example is discourse topic. Although there are no formal methods for the analysis of discourse topic, the insights and informal methods developed by discourse analysis researchers have been employed in the study of both language acquisition and disorders (Brinton & Fujiki, 1984; Fey, 1986; Schober–Peterson & Johnson, 1989; Stover & Haynes, 1989). These studies have provided important information and insights into topic management by both speakers with normal language and language disorders. However, the use of discourse-topic analyses for the description and clinical evaluation of language disorders is hindered by problems related to the definition of topic and the dearth of detailed analyses of multiple topic parameters within a single coherent framework.

In an attempt to address these issues, Mentis and Prutting (in press) have developed and empirically tested a multidimentional analysis of topical coherence based on the work of researchers in the area of conversation and discourse analysis (Atkinson & Heritage, 1984; Brinton & Fujiki, 1984; Crow, 1983; Gardner, 1987; Goodenough & Weiner, 1978; Hurtig, 1977; Keenan & Shieffelin, 1976; Maynard, 1980; Planalp & Tracy, 1980; Reichman, 1978; Schegloff & Sacks, 1973; Stech, 1982; van Dijk, 1981). Their analysis is based on the view that topical coherence requires the successful management of topic introduction and maintenance and the successful embedding of subtopics within topic sequences. Topic and subtopic introduction are analyzed in terms of type and manner. Topic and subtopic maintenance are analyzed in terms of four major categories: the addition of new information or no new information, side sequences, and problematic units. The basic unit of analysis is the intonation unit proposed by Chafe (1987). Each topic and subtopic maintenance category is then further analyzed in terms of several subcategories. Mentis and Prutting's (in press) results suggest that the analysis has the potential to be a reliable means for evaluating topic management and identifying differences between populations. Care should, however, be taken with interpretation, because definitive normative information is not available and research to date suggests that topic management varies according to such factors as individual styles, goals, and differing social and physical contexts (Brinton & Fujiki, 1984; Crow, 1983; Maynard, 1980).

The topic coherence analysis yields clinicial information that pertains to a number of parameters of topic management. Useful clinical data may be obtained through the evaluation of three parameters of topic introduction: the percentage of topics and subtopics introduced by the client, the manner in which topics and subtopics are introduced, and the type of topics and subtopics introduced. In terms of the manner of topic and subtopic introduction, the extent to which topics are introduced by shifts, as compared to changes, and the percentage of noncoherent changes provide an indication of the extent to which a client is capable of appropriately introducing topics into a conversation and the extent to which prior topical talk is used as a source for the introduction of new topics. In terms of the type of topics and subtopics introduced, the percentage of new, related, and reintroduced topics and subtopics can provide information regarding the extent to which a client recycles topics within a conversation.

The following are some of the parameters of topic maintenance that can yield useful clinical information. The length of topic and subtopic sequences and the extent to which the client's contributions to topic development add new information, as compared to no new information, provide indications of the extent to which the client contributes to the ideational development of the interchange. A comparison of the type of new-information and no-new-information units provides an indication of the extent to which the client's contributions are directly elicited by questions as compared to those that are unsolicited. Some insight into the extent to which the client relies on the structure provided by the communication partner and the extent to which the client is an active, contributing partner can be obtained. Such an analysis may also provide an indication of the extent to which repetition is used as a topic-maintaining strategy. The analysis of problematic units in terms of the percentage of unrelated, ambiguous, or incomplete contributions provides an indication of the extent of the client's thematic relevance and information salience.

Analyses such as these, which are based on the study of normal conversational structure in the context of social interaction, provide a comprehensive evaluation of a number of parameters of conversational structure. The resulting information provides detailed descriptions of the nature of the breakdown at each level of organization. This then leads directly to the development of treatment programs directed at each specific level of impairment

Discourse plays a role in many areas of social life and the study of the effects of social context on discourse has important implications for the treatment of language disorders. Children and adults with language disorders need to master not only simple conversational interactions but also the various complex discourse genres encountered in daily life. Ultimately, descriptions of language disorders can only be accurate, and treatment programs maximally meaningful, if the effects of different social features on discourse are taken into account and differences across discourse genres are made explicit. Here, the wealth of information being collected in the field of discourse analysis is of great value. Van Dijk (1990) has suggested that what is needed is "an explicit theoretical framework that relates societal structures with discourse structures, for instance, through a microsociological theory of discursive interaction and a cognitive theory linking interaction and discourse" (p. 150). He thus suggests that a serious account of the interaction between discourse and societal issues requires specification of the nature of the relationship in terms of broader cognitive and microsociological theories. Research with such a focus would have exciting implications in the field of language disorders. It is clear that the study of conversational structure in the context of social interaction in language disorders has implications for the description of the nature of disorders as well as for assessment and intervention.

COGNITIVE STRUCTURES AND PROCESSES: A MEANS FOR UNDERSTANDING LANGUAGE DISORDERS

There is great potential for the clinical application of the finding that discourses have underlying schemata or superstructures that serve an organizational function. The evaluation of narrative production and comprehension in terms of story grammars already has become a standard means of assessing discourse in different language-disordered groups, and has led to a better understanding of the discourse abilities of children (Liles, 1987; Merritt & Liles, 1987; Roth & Spekman, 1985) and adults (Liles et al., 1989) with language disorders. For instance, the results of this type of analysis have led to the postulation that a cognitively based organizational deficit may underlie the linguistic difficulties of some children with language impairments (Merritt & Liles, 1987). Information such as this is essential if a comprehensive picture of the nature of language impairment in different language-disordered populations is to be obtained. Such information may also be useful in the development of treatment programs, where, for instance, the narrative categories of setting, initiating events, internal response, and so forth, which serve to organize the content of narratives, can be explicitly used as the basic framework for structuring narrative production.

Research investigating the relationship among underlying cognitive structures and discourse processes may also be used in treatment as an organizational framework for the development of coherent cohesive discourse. Scripts of social routines or sequences of goal-directed actions may be used to structure conversational interactions. Nelson (1985) has suggested that children use their knowledge of scripts to initiate and maintain topic sequences. Children's knowledge of the sequence of events in such daily routines as bath time and dinner time provide a framework around which discourse may be structured. As certain actions occur in certain sequences, the child is able to recognize and predict action sequences and use this information as a basis for the initiation and maintenance of topics. Foster (1986) has also suggested that children are able to introduce and develop topics more coherently in the context of familiar social routines than outside of these routine situations. Just as children use their knowledge of social routines and scripts to provide a framework for the initiation and maintenance of topics in discourse, so this knowledge can be used by clinicians to structure clients' conversational discourse. Social routines can provide clients with the information necessary for developing a framework around which conversation can be structured.

The interaction between underlying cognitive structures and the development of discourse topics highlights the importance of the interactions among different levels of processing. At present, it is not clear to what extent scripts, schemata, and other forms of cognitive representation underlie discourse coherence or to what extent they are responsible for the global and local organization of discourse. In addition, the precise relationship between discourse structure and such knowledge representations as scripts has not been specified, and the question regarding what strategies relate these two levels of knowledge remains open. Investigation of these issues as they pertain to language disorders is potentially powerful in terms of the descriptive and clinical insights they could provide.

AN INTEGRATED APPROACH TO LANGUAGE DISORDERS: THE INTEGRATION OF A NUMBER OF DISCOURSE FEATURES AT MULTIPLE LEVELS OF LANGUAGE

Discourse linguistics potentially has rich and fruitful implications for the study and remediation of language disorders. These implications extend from the description and explanation of language disorders to principles governing assessment and remediation. Language is not spoken or written in isolated sentences; it is produced in the form of extended discourse. Any account of language impairment, therefore, needs to take into account the principles governing the structure and organization of discourse and the circumstances and manner under which discourse coherence is disrupted.

An integrated approach to discourse in the study of language disorders requires specification of the nature of the interactions among different levels of organization in language. As discourse has its roots in cognitive, linguistic, and social domains, explicit links between the different levels of language within these domains need to be established and the impact of language impairment on these links needs to be understood. The manner in which language impairment affects the interactions among linguistic knowledge, underlying cognitive structures, communicative intentions, and social interaction factors requires elucidation.

This approach to language disorders requires attention to the interactions among the different dimensions of discourse and the integration of what are at present isolated approaches. What is needed is not just an extension of our knowledge base within each *domain* and approach, but specification of the nature of the *interaction* between the different domains and delineation of how breakdowns at one level impact on the others. The ultimate goal should be the generation of a theory of discourse coherence that specifies the relationship among different discourse features at multiple levels of functioning and the nature of the interaction between problems at the different levels.

The proposal of an integrated theory with specific links between the different levels is a task that confronts all who work in the field of discourse analysis. Much is still to be learned about the details of how to link, for example, structural grammatical descriptions with those of conversational analysis. In fact, van Dijk (1990, p. 147) has described this as a "core job of discourse analysis" that will occupy researchers in this area for years to come. The study of language disorders from this perspective is potentially fruitful both from the point of view of broadening understanding of the nature of language impairment and providing information on the nature of these links. The study of language disorders from a discourse perspective, therefore, has implications for language disorders not only in terms of comprehensive and explicit descriptions and an increased understanding of the nature of language disorders, but also for a more general integrated theory of discourse.

The study of language disorders from a discourse linguistics perspective has already broadened and enriched speech-language pathologists' understanding of the nature of language disorders. Descriptions of the discourse abilities of individuals with language disorders suggests that they may experience a range of discourse problems which may or may not be related to their sentence-level linguistic skills. Problems have been reported in the area of discourse and grammar in terms of reduced and disrupted cohesion abilities (Liles, 1985a, 1985b; Mentis & Prutting, 1987; Ripich & Terrell, 1988). Problems also have been reported in the organization and structure of conversational discourse. For example, problems in turn-taking and topic management have been reported in children with language disorders (Brinton & Fujiki, 1984, 1989; Craig & Evans, 1989; Fey, 1986), adults with closed head injuries (Mentis & Prutting, 1987; Prigatano et al., 1985), and patients with Alzheimer's disease (Bayles, 1984; Fromm & Holland, 1989) and right hemisphere impairment (Myers, 1979, 1984; Wapner, Hamby, & Gardner, 1981). Insights into disruptions in the discourse of individuals with language disorders also have been obtained through the investigation of underlying cognitive structures and processes. The results of this research suggest that underlying schemata may serve an organizing function in both narrative and conversational discourse and that a cognitively based organizational deficit may underlie the discourse difficulties of some individuals with language disorders (Foster, 1986; Merritt & Liles, 1987; Nelson, 1985; Roth & Spekman, 1986). Problems thus have been identified across multiple levels of discourse processing: discourse and grammar, conversational structure in the context of social interaction, and underlying cognitive structures and processes. What is needed now is an investigation of how disruptions across these levels are interrelated.

Description of disrupted discourse coherence in language impairment has important clinical implications because an integrated discourse approach to language disorders necessitates the inclusion of discourse-level analyses in the assessment of clients with language disorders. Analyses drawn from the field of discourse linguistics allow speech-language pathologists to go beyond global, anecdotal descriptions of conversational interactions to provide explicit and systematic descriptions of specific aspects of conversational structure and function. This is particularly relevant for those aspects of conversation that previously defied detailed analysis due to their subtle and seemingly elusive nature. These descriptions would then lead to the generation of characteristic discourse profiles across groups with different disorders. Such descriptions are essential if inclusive and comprehensive accounts of language impairment ultimately are to be proposed.

Analyses for individual clients would include the evaluation of a broad range of discourse features at multiple levels of language. If problems at any level are found, more comprehensive analyses based on those generated in the field of discourse analysis could then be used to obtain a more comprehensive picture of the nature of the breakdown. By identifying the nature and level of the breakdown, treatment goals directed at each specific level of impairment could then be developed. Treatment would also focus on the interaction between the different levels of organization in language. Because an integrated discourse approach would focus on the interactions among different discourse features at multiple levels of functioning, treatment would stress the interactions among problems at the different levels. This means that in treatment the various components of language would not be presented to the client in isolation. For instance, the production of various grammatical forms would be taught in relation to their functions in discourse. The focus would be on how syntactic structures can be used to achieve different functions in the production of coherent, cohesive discourse. Thus a client who has mastered the production of the question form should be able to use that form in the service of such discourse functions as initiating a topic and producing a contingent query.

A further potential benefit of the analysis of language disorders from an integrated discourse perspective is that it may also have explanatory potential. Descriptions of the interactions of problems across the domains of discourse and grammar, conversational structure in the context of social interaction, and underlying cognitive structures and processes may lead to accounts of why disordered systems look the way they do.

Discourse linguistics is now an established field of enquiry and has demonstrated its potential to broaden and enrich the understanding of normal and disordered language. Speech-language pathologists can look forward to an exciting era in the investigation and remediation of language disorders from a discourse linguistics perspective.

REFERENCES

Abelson, R. P. (1976). Script processing in attitude formation and decision-making. In J. S. Carroll & J. W. Payne (Eds.), *Cognition and social behavior* (pp. 33–46). Hillsdale, NJ: Lawrence Erlbaum.

Atkinson, J. M., & Drew, P. (1979). *Order in court.* New York: Macmillan.

Atkinson, J. M., & Heritage, J. (1984). Topic organization. In J. M. Atkinson & J. Heritage (Eds.), *Structures of social action: Studies in conversational analysis* (pp. 165–166). Cambridge, UK: Cambridge University Press.

Austin, J. L. (1962). *How to do things with words.* Cambridge, MA: Harvard University Press.

Bayles, K. (1984). Language and dementia. In A. L. Holland (Ed.), *Language disorders in adults* (pp. 209–244). San Diego, CA: College-Hill Press.

Black, J. B., & Wilensky, R. (1979). An evaluation of story grammars. *Cognitive Sci-*

ence, 3, 213–230.

Brinton, B., & Fujiki, M. (1984). Development of topic manipulation skills in discourse. *Journal of Speech and Hearing Research, 27,* 350–358.

Brinton, B., & Fujiki, M. (1989). *Conversational management with language-impaired children.* Rockville, MD: Aspen Publishers.

Brinton, B., Fujiki, M., & Sonnenberg, E. (1988). Responses to requests for clarification by linguistically normal and language-impaired children in conversation. *Journal of Speech and Hearing Disorders, 53,* 383–391.

Brinton, B., Fujiki, M., Winkler, E., & Loeb, D. (1986). Responses to requests for clarification in linguistically normal and language-impaired children. *Journal of Speech and Hearing Disorders, 51,* 370–378.

Brown, G., & Yule, G. (1983). *Discourse analysis.* Cambridge, UK: Cambridge University Press.

Chafe, W. (1980). *The pear stories.* Norwood, NJ: Ablex Publishers.

Chafe, W. (1987). Cognitive constraints on information flow. In R. S. Tomlin (Ed.), *Typological studies in language. XI. Coherence and grounding in discourse* (pp. 21–51). Philadelphia, PA: John Benjamins.

Chafe, W. (1988). Linking intonation units in spoken English. In J. Haiman & S. A. Thompson (Eds.), *Clause combining in grammar and discourse.* Philadelphia, PA: John Benjamins.

Chafe, W. (in press). Discourse. In W. Bright (Ed.), *Oxford international encyclopedia of linguistics.*Oxford, UK: Oxford University Press.

Chomsky, N. (1981). *Lectures on government and binding.* Dordrecht, Holland: Foris Publications.

Cicourel, A. (1985). Doctor-patient discourse. In T. A. van Dijk (Ed.), *Handbook of discourse analysis: Discourse analysis in society* (Vol. 4). London: Academic Press.

Collett, P. (1983). Mossi salutations. *Semiotica, 45,* 191–248.

Conti–Ramsden, G., & Friel–Patti, S. (1983). Mothers' discourse adjustment to language-impaired and non-language-impaired children. *Journal of Speech and Hearing Disorders, 48,* 360–367.

Corsaro, W. A. (1979). "We're friends, right?": Children's use of access rituals in a nursery school. *Language in Society, 8,* 315–336.

Coulthard, M. (1985). *An introduction to discourse analysis.* London: Longman.

Craig, H. K., & Evans, J. L. (1989). Turn exchange characteristics of SLI children's simultaneous and nonsimultaneous speech. *Journal of Speech and Hearing Disorders, 54,* 334–347.

Crow, B. K. (1983). Topic shifts in couples' conversations. In R. T. Craig & K. Tracy (Eds.), *Conversational coherence: Form, structure, and strategy* (pp. 136–156). Beverly Hills, CA: Sage Publications.

Curtiss, S., & Yamada, J. (1981). Selectively intact grammatical development in a retarded child. *UCLA Working Papers in Cognitive Linguistics, 3,* 61–91.

D'Andrade, R. G., & Wish, M. (1985). Speech act theory in quantitative research on interpersonal behavior. *Discourse Processes, 8,* 229–259.

De Long, A. (1974). Kinesic signals at utterance boundaries in preschool children. *Semiotica, 11,* 43–74.

Dittmar, N., & von Stutterheim, C. (1985). On the discourse of immigrant workers. In T. A. van Dijk (Ed.), *Handbook of discourse analysis: Discourse analysis in society* (Vol. 4). London: Academic Press.

Dore, J. (1977). Children's illocutionary acts. In R. O. Freedle (Ed.), *Discourse processes: Advances in research and theory: Discourse production and comprehension* (Vol. 1, pp. 227–244). Norwood, NJ: Ablex Publishing.

Du Bois, J. W. (1980). Beyond definiteness: The trace of identity in discourse. In W. Chafe (Ed.), *The pear stories* (pp. 203–274). Norwood, NJ: Ablex Publishing.

Du Bois, J. H. (1987). The discourse basis of ergativity. *Language, 63,* 805–855.

Duncan, S. D., & Fiske, D. W. (1985). *Interaction structure and strategy.* Cambridge, UK: Cambridge University Press.

Edmondson, W. (1981). *Spoken discourse: A model for analysis.* London: Longman.

Ellis, D. G. (1983). Language, coherence, and textuality. In R. T. Craig & K. Tracy (Eds.), *Conversational coherence: Form, structure, and strategy* (pp. 222–240). Beverly Hills, CA: Sage Publications.

Fey, M. E. (1986). *Language intervention with young children.* San Diego, CA: College-Hill Press.

Fey, M. E., Leonard, L., & Wilcox, K. (1981). Speech style modifications of language-impaired children. *Journal of Speech and Hearing Disorders, 46,* 91–96.

Fillmore, C. J. (1977). Topics in lexical semantics [Lectures 1, 2]. In R. Cole (Ed.), *Current issues in linguistics* (pp. 76–109). Bloomington: Indiana University Press.

Folger, J. P., & Chapman, R. S. (1978). A pragmatic analysis of spontaneous imitations. *Journal of Child Language, 5,* 25–38.

Forsyth, I. J. (1974). Patterns in the discourse of teachers and pupils. In G. Perren (Ed.), *The space between: English and foreign languages at school.* London: Center for Information on Language Teaching.

Foster, S. (1986). Learning discourse topic management in the preschool years. *Journal of Child Language, 13,* 231–250.

Fox, B. (1987). *Discourse structure and anaphora.* Cambridge, UK: Cambridge University Press.

Fromm, D., & Holland, A. L. (1989). Functional communication in Alzheimer's disease. *Journal of Speech and Hearing Disorders, 54,* 535–540.

Fujiki, M., Brinton, B., & Sonnenberg, E. A. (1990). Repair of overlapping speech in the conversations of specifically language-impaired and normally developing children. *Applied Psycholinguistics, 11,* 201–215.

Gardner, R. (1987). The identification and role of topic in spoken interaction. *Semiotica, 65,* 129–141.

Garfinkel, H. (1967). *Studies in ethnomethodology.* Englewood Cliffs, NJ: Prentice-Hall.

Gazdar, G., Klein, E., Pullum, G., & Sag, I. (1985). *Generalized phrase structure grammar.* Oxford, UK: Basil Blackwell.

Givón, T. (1979). *On understanding grammar.* New York: Academic Press.

Givón, T. (Ed.). (1983). *Topic continuity in discourse.* Amsterdam: John Benjamins.

Givón, T. (1984). *Syntax: A functional-typological introduction* (Vol. 1). Amsterdam: John Benjamins.

Goffman, E. (1959). *The presentation of self in everyday life.* New York: Anchor Books.

Goffman, E. (1971). *Relations in public.* New York: Harper & Row.

Goffman, E. (1974). *Frame analysis.* New York: Harper & Row.

Goodenough, D. R., & Weiner, S. L. (1978). The role of conversational passing moves in the management of topical transitions. *Discourse Processes, 1,* 395–404.

Goodwin, C. (1981). *Conversation organization: Interaction between speakers and hearers.* New York: Academic Press.

Grice, H. P. (1975). Logic and conversation. In P. Cole & J. L. Morgan (Eds.), *Syntax and semantics: III. Speech acts* (pp. 41–58). New York: Academic Press.

Gumperz, J. J. (1964). Linguistic and social interaction in two communities. *American Anthropologist, 6,* 137–153.

Gumperz, J. J. (1982). *Discourse strategies.* Cambridge, UK: Cambridge University Press.

Gumperz, J. J. (1983). *Discourse processes.* Cambridge, UK: Cambridge University Press.

Hall, P. H., & Spencer-Hall, D. A. (1983). The handshake as interaction. *Semiotica, 45,* 249–264.

Halliday, M. A. K. (1985). *An introduction to functional grammar.* London: Edward Arnold.

Halliday, M. A. K., & Hasan, R. (1976). *Cohesion in English.* London: Longman.

Harris, Z. (1951). *Methods in structural linguistics.* Chicago: University of Chicago Press.

Harris, Z. (1952). Discourse analysis. *Language, 28,* 1–30.

Heritage, J. (1985). Analyzing new interviews: Aspects of the production of talk for an overhearing audience. In T. A. van Dijk (Ed.), *Handbook of discourse analysis: Discourse and dialogue* (Vol. 3, pp. 95–119). London: Academic Press.

Hopper, P. J. (1979). Aspect and foregrounding in discourse. In T. Givón (Ed.), *Discourse and syntax* (pp. 213–241). New York: Academic Press.

Hopper, P. J. (1987). Emergent grammar. In J. Aske, N. Beery, L. Michaelis, & H. Filip (Eds.), *Proceedings of the thirteenth annual meeting of the Berkeley Linguistics Society* (pp. 139–157). Berkeley: University of California Press.

Hurtig, R. (1977). Toward a functional theory of discourse. In R. O. Freedle (Ed.), *Discourse processes: Advances in research and theory. I. Discourse production and comprehension* (pp. 9–106). Norwood, NJ: Ablex Publishing.

Hymes, D. (1974). *Foundations in sociolinguistics: An ethnographic approach.* Philadelphia: University of Pennsylvania Press.

Jefferson, G. (1972). Side sequences. In D. Sudnow (Ed.), *Studies in social interaction* (pp. 294–338). New York: Free Press.

Keenan, E. O., & Schieffelin, B. B. (1976). Topic as a discourse notion: A study of topic in the conversation of children and adults. In C. N. Li (Ed.), *Subject and topic* (pp. 337–383). New York: Academic Press.

Kendon, A. (1967). Some functions of gaze-direction in social interaction. *Acta Psychologia, 26,* 22–47.

Labov, W. (1972). The transformation of experience in narrative syntax. In *Language in the inner city* (pp. 354–396). Philadelphia: University of Pennsylvania Press.

Labov, W., & Fanshel, D. (1977). *Therapeutic discourse: Psychotherapy and conversation.* New York: Academic Press.

Lahey, M. (1988). *Language disorders and language development.* New York: Macmillan.

Levinson, S. C. (1983). *Pragmatics.* Cambridge, UK: Cambridge University Press.

Liles, B. Z. (1985a). Cohesion in the narratives of normal and language-disordered children. *Journal of Speech and Hearing Research, 28,* 123–133.

Liles, B. Z. (1985b). Production and comprehension of narrative discourse in normal and language disordered children. *Journal of Communication Disorders, 18,* 409–427.

Liles, B. Z. (1987). Episode organization and cohesive conjunctives in narratives of children with and without language disorder. *Journal of Speech and Hearing Research, 30,* 185–196.

Liles, B. Z., Coelho, C. A., Duffy, R. J., & Zalagens, M. R. (1989). Effects of elicitation procedures on the narratives of normal and closed head-injured adults. *Journal of Speech and Hearing Disorders, 54,* 356–366.

Linebaugh, C. W., Margulies, C. P., & Mackisack, E. L. (1985). Contingent queries and revisions used by aphasic individuals and their most frequent communication partners. In R. Brookshire (Ed.), *Clinical aphasiology conference proceedings* (pp. 229–236). Minneapolis, MN: BRK Publishers.

Longacre, R. (1976). *An anatomy of speech notions.* Lisse, The Netherlands: de Ridder.

Malinowski, B. (1930). The problem of meaning in primitive languages. In C. Ogden & I. A. Richards (Eds.), *The meaning of meaning* (2nd ed.). London: Routledge & Kegan Paul.

Mandler, J. M., & Johnson, N. S. (1977). Remembrance of things parsed: Story structure and recall. *Cognitive Psychology, 9,* 111–151.

Mandler, J. M., & Johnson, N. S. (1980). On throwing the baby out with the bath-water: A reply to Black and Wilensky's evaluation of story grammar. *Cognitive Science, 4,* 305–312.

Mann, W. C., & Thompson, S. A. (1988). Rhetorical structure theory: Toward a functional theory of text organization. *Text, 8,* 243–281.

Maynard, D. W. (1980). Placement of topic changes in conversation. *Semiotica, 30,* 263–290.

Mentis, M., & Prutting, C. A. (1987). Cohesion in the discourse of normal and head injured adults. *Journal of Speech and Hearing Research, 30,* 88–98.

Mentis, M., & Prutting, C. A. (in press). Analysis of topic as illustrated in a head injured and normal adult. *Journal of Speeech and Hearing Research.*

Merritt, D. D., & Liles, B. Z. (1987). Story grammar ability in children with and without language disorder: Story generation, story retelling, and story comprehension. *Journal of Speech and Hearing Research, 30,* 539–552.

Minsky M. (1975). A framework for representing knowledge. In P. H. Winston (Ed.), *The psychology of computer vision* (pp. 211–277). New York: McGraw-Hill.

Myers, P. S. (1979). Profiles of communication deficits in patients with right cerebral hemisphere damage. In R. H. Brookshire (Ed.), *Clinical aphasiology conference proceedings*. Minneapolis, MN: BRK Publishers.

Myers, P. S. (1984). Right hemisphere impairment. In A. L. Holland (Ed.), *Language disorders in adults: Recent advances* (pp. 209–244). San Diego, CA: College-Hill Press.

Neisser, U. (1967). *Cognitive psychology.* New York: Appleton-Century-Crofts.

Nelson, K. (1985). *Making sense: The acquisition of shared meaning.* New York: Academic Press.

Nelson, K., & Gruendel, J. (1979). At morning it's lunchtime: A scriptal view of children's dialogues. *Discourse Processes, 2,* 73–94.

Okolo, B. A. (1987). Topic shading in an unplanned Igbo discourse. *Studies in African Linguistics, 18,* 211–237.

Pellegrini, A. D. (1982). A speech analysis of preschoolers dyadic interaction. *Child Study Journal, 12,* 205–217.

Piehler, M. F., & Holland, A. L. (1984). Cohesion in aphasic language. In R. H. Brookshire (Ed.), *Clinical aphasiology conference proceedings* (pp. 208–214). Minneapolis, MN: BRK Publishers.

Planalp, S., & Tracy, K. (1980). Not to change the topic but . . . : A cognitive approach to the management of conversation. In D. Nimmo (Ed.), *Communication yearbook* (Vol. 4, pp. 237–258). New Brunswick, NJ: Transaction Books.

Pomerantz, A. (1978). Compliment responses: Notes on the co-operation of multiple constraints. In J. Schenkein (Ed.), *Studies in the organization of conversational interaction* (pp. 79–112). New York: Academic Press.

Pomerantz, A. (1984). Agreeing and disagreeing with assessments: Some features of preferred/dispreferred turn shapes. In J. Atkinson & J. Heritage (Eds.), *Structures of social action* (pp. 57–101). Cambridge, UK: Cambridge University Press.

Prather, E., Cromwell, K., & Kenney, K. (1989). Types of repairs used by normally developing and language-impaired preschool children in response to clarification requests. *Journal of Communication Disorders, 22,* 49–64.

Prigatano, G. P., Roueche, J. R., & Fordyce, D. J. (1985). Nonphasic language disturbances after closed head injury. *Language Sciences, 1,* 217–229.

Prutting, C. A., & Kirchner, D. M. (1987). A clinical appraisal of the pragmatic aspects of language. *Journal of Speech and Hearing Disorders, 52,* 105–119.

Reichman, R. (1978). Conversational coherency. *Cognitive Science, 2,* 283–327.

Ripich, D. N., & Terrell, B. Y. (1988). Patterns of discourse cohesion and coherence in Alzheimer's disease. *Journal of Speech and Hearing Disorders, 53,* 8–15.

Roth, F., & Spekman, N. (1986). Narrative discourse: Spontaneously generated stories of learning-disabled and normally achieving students. *Journal of Speech and Hearing Disorders, 51,* 8–23.

Rumelhart, D. E. (1975). Notes on a schema for stories. In D. G. Bobrow & A. Collins (Eds.), *Representation and understanding* (pp. 211–236). New York: Academic Press.

Rumelhart, D. E. (1976). Understanding and summarizing brief stories. In D. LaBerge & S. J. Samuels (Eds.), *Basic processes in reading: Perception and comprehension.* Hillsdale, NJ: Lawrence Erlbaum.

Sacks, H., Schegloff, E., & Jefferson, G. (1974). A simplest systematics for the organization of turn-taking in conversation. *Language, 50,* 696–735.

Schank, R. C., & Abelson, R. (1977). *Scripts, plans, goals and understanding: An inquiry into human knowledge structures.* Hillsdale, NJ: Lawrence Erlbaum.

Schegloff, E. A. (1968). Sequencing in conversational openings. *American Anthropologist, 70,* 1075–1095.

Schegloff, E. A. (1972). Notes on a conversational practice: Formulating place. In D. N. Sudnow (Ed.), *Studies in social interaction* (pp. 75–119). New York: Free Press.

Schegloff, E. A. (1980). Preliminaries to preliminaries: "Can I ask you a question?" *Sociological Inquiry, 50,* 104–152.

Schegloff, E. A., & Sacks, H. (1973). Opening up closings. *Semiotica, 7,* 289–327.

Schiffrin, D. (1974). Handwork as ceremony: The case of the handshake. *Semiotica, 12–13,* 189–202.

Schiffrin, D. (1985a). Multiple constraints on discourse options: A quantitative analysis of causal sequences. *Discourse Processes, 8,* 281–303.

Schiffrin, D. (1985b). Everyday argument: The organization of diversity in talk. In T. van Dijk (Ed.), *Handbook of discourse analysis: Discourse and dialogue* (Vol. 3, pp. 35–46). London: Academic Press.

Schiffrin, D. (1987). *Discourse markers.* Cambridge, UK: Cambridge University Press.

Schiffrin, D. (1988). Conversation analysis. In F. J. Newmeyer (Ed.), *Linguistics: The Cambridge survey. IV. Language: The socio-cultural context* (pp. 251–276). Cambridge, UK: Cambridge University Press.

Schober–Peterson, D., & Johnson, C. (1989). Conversational topics of 4-year-olds. *Journal of Speech and Hearing Research, 32,* 857–870.

Searle, J. R. (1969). *Speech acts: An essay in the philosophy of language.* Cambridge, UK: Cambridge University Press.

Searle, J. R. (1975). Indirect speech acts. In P. Cole & J. L. Morgan (Eds.), *Syntax and semantics. III. Speech acts* (pp. 59–82). New York: Academic Press.

Sinclair, J. McH., & Coulthard, R. M. (1975). *Towards an analysis of discourse.* Oxford, UK: Oxford University Press.

Stech, E. L. (1982). The analysis of conversational topic sequence structures. *Semiotica, 39,* 75–91.

Stein, N., & Glenn, C. (1979). An analysis of story comprehension in elementary school children. In R. Freedle (Ed.), *New directions in discourse processing* (Vol. 2, pp. 53–120). Hillsdale, NJ: Ablex Publishing.

Stover, S. E., & Haynes, W. O. (1989). Topic manipulation and cohesive adequacy in conversations of normal adults between the ages of 30 and 90. *Clinical Linguistics and Phonetics, 3,* 137–149.

Stubbs, M. (1983). *Discourse analysis: The sociolinguistic analysis of natural language.* Chicago: University of Chicago Press.

Sykes, M. (1985). Discrimination in discourse. In T. A. van Dijk (Ed.), *Handbook of discourse analysis: Discourse analysis in society* (Vol. 4). London: Academic Press.

Tager–Flusberg, H. (1988). On the nature of language acquisition disorder: The example of autism. In F. Kessel (Ed.), *The development of language and language researchers: Essays in honour of Roger Brown* (pp. 249–267). Hillsdale, NJ: Lawrence Erlbaum.

Thorndyke, P. W. (1977). Cognitive structures in comprehension and memory of narrative discourse. *Cognitive Psychology, 9,* 77–110.

Ulatowska, H. K., Doyel, A. W., Stern, R. F., Haynes, S. M., & North, A. J. (1983). Production of procedural discourse in aphasia. *Brain and Language, 18,* 315–341.

Ulatowska, H. K., North, A. J., & Macaluso–Haynes, S. (1981). Production of narrative and procedural discourse in aphasia. *Brain and Language, 13,* 345–371.

van Dijk, T. (1977). *Text and context: Explorations in the semantics and pragmatics of discourse.* London: Longman.

van Dijk, T. (1980). *Macrostructures.* Hillsdale, NJ: Lawrence Erlbaum.

van Dijk, T. (1981). *Studies in the pragmatics of discourse.* The Hague, The Netherlands: Mouton.

van Dijk, T. (1990). The future of the field: Discourse analysis in the 1990s. *Text, 10,* 133–156.

van Dijk, T. A., & Kintsch, W. (1977). Cognitive psychology and discourse. Recalling and summarizing stories. In W. D. Dressler (Ed.), *Trends in textlinguistics.* New York: Walter De Gruyer.

van Dijk, T., & Kintsch, W. (1983). *Strategies of discourse comprehension.* New York: Academic Press.

Vendler, Z. (1972). *Res cogitans: An essay in rational psychology.* Ithaca, NY: Cornell University Press.

Wapner, W., Hamby, S., & Gardner, H. (1981). The role of the right hemisphere in the apprehension of complex materials. *Brain and Language, 14,* 15–33.

Wodak, R. (1985). The interaction between judge and defendant. In T. A. van Dijk (Ed.), *Handbook of discourse analysis: Discourse analysis in society* (Vol. 4). London: Academic Press.

Yamada, J., & Curtiss, S. (1981). The relationship between language and cognition in a case of Turner's syndrome. *UCLA Working Papers in Cognitive Linguistics, 3,* 93–115.

CHAPTER 8

Experiential Realism: Clinical Implications

JOHN R. MUMA

The purpose of this chapter is to derive some clinical implications from a philosophical perspective known as experiential realism. There are three motivations for doing so. First, experiential realism is a relatively new philosophical view of language and cognition which has considerable implications for the clinical fields. Second, it offers a convincing logical challenge to objectivism which has been the prevailing doctrine underlying traditional clinical views and practices.

Third, there is a compelling need for theoretical continuity from which a well grounded rationale for clinical assessment and intervention may be derived. It is theory that provides appropriate justification. Theory-based clinical assessment and intervention has construct validity.

Carol Prutting and her colleagues (Prutting, 1982, 1983; Prutting, Epstein, Beckman, Dias, & Gao, in press; Prutting, Mentis, & Myles–Zitzer, in press) championed this message in the field of speech-language pathology. She was keenly interested in the philosophy of science precisely because it provides the substantive wherewithal that vindicates a view, a position, a rationale, a practice. The philosophy of science defines a substantive perspective for a field. Issues are derived from a philosophical base and rendered in a theoretical perspective to provide a rationale for doing things particular ways. Continuity counts. Otherwise, clinical endeavors would reduce to nothing more than authoritarianism, intuition, dogma, hype, and eclecticism. Ventry and Schiavetti (1986) expressed a similar concern, "sound clinical practice should be based, in large part, on the relevant basic and applied research rather than pronouncements by authorities, intuition, or dogma" (p. 3). Such research should be governed by an explicit philosophical view.

Prutting (1983) was right. It is philosophy and theory that sanction professional endeavors. It is theory that defines appropriate interpretations of the data. It is theory that provides justifiable rationale for appropriate clinical assessment and intervention. Thus, it is theory that makes things practical.

There are deep and pervasive conflicts between philosophical views and between theoretical perspectives. These conflicts result in a variety of clinical notions concerning the definitions of language impairments and of learning disabilities, a substantive perspective for clinical assessment, criteria for attribution, language intervention, and efficacy. The focus of this chapter is the conflict between the philosophical views of objectivism with the attendant commitment to such notions as normative tests and a priori intervention and the views of experiential realism with the attendant clinical commitment to such notions as descriptive evidence and a posteriori intervention.

In phonology, the shift from normative tests to descriptive evidence has taken place. Rather than relying on the traditional phoneme-oriented tests of articulation, speech-language pathologists have turned to the scholarly literature (Ingram, 1989; Vihman & Greenlee, 1987) for ways of doing a descriptive phonological assessment in regard to phonological processes, phonetic inventory, homonymy, and phonological avoidance. With developments such as these, a larger more pervasive challenge came to the fore. It was the challenge of experiential realism.

EXPERIENTIAL REALISM

Experiential realism is a relatively new view of cognition and language. The main topic in experiential realism is the ontogenesis of meaning in concept formation and in language. This is discussed later. However, this topic is cast within a new philosophical view that has far reaching implications for an appropriate rationale for clinical assessment and intervention. It is the philosophical view that is of primary interest here because it poses a direct challenge to such traditional clinical notions as normative tests and a priori intervention.

The philosophical view of experiential realism is that one's knowledge of the world, or what has come to be known as "possible worlds" (Bruner, 1981; Stalnaker, 1972) and "theory of the world" (Palermo, 1982), issues from active experiences in the world. This means that truth is not external to the human mind. Rather, truth is the product of the human mind. What we know is the product of our experiences in the world.

Such experiences are external as well as internal. External experiences are those derived from actual engagement with objects, events, and relations in the course of living in the world. We bring to these experiences representations of past experiences which in turn govern, to a great extent, what is perceived (Garner, 1966). Representations of past experiences comprise the internal context from which internal experience such as thinking can take place.

The irrefutable nucleus of active experience, whether internal or external, is volition or intent. Intent has emerged as a central issue in cognition and communication. For example, communicative intent is a central issue for pragmatic theory in general (Cazden, 1977; Halliday, 1975; Ninio & Snow, 1988) and speech act theory in particular (Austin, 1962; Grice, 1967; Searle, 1969; Sperber & Wilson, 1986). Needless to say, intent is the nucleus of social commerce (Muma, 1986).

Prutting (1982) recognized the importance of intent in social context for clinical assessment and intervention. This recognition undoubtedly led to the identification of language impairments in terms of cognitive, linguistic, and pragmatic issues (Prutting & Kirchner, 1983, 1987). Indeed, these issues were inherent in speech act theory with its four primary components of utterance, content, intent, and effects on the listener.

In addition to intent, the notion of "institutional facts" has been offered as a more viable account of concepts underlying cognition and language. *Institutional facts* are those rather loosely defined concepts that are mutually manifest in thought or communication in day-to-day social commerce. For example, the concept of "apple" need not be defined precisely between two individuals who wish to talk about apples. Rather, there is a mutual consensus about its essential meaning unless otherwise indicated.

Experiential realism posits that most of social commerce operates on institutional facts. Much of traditional cognition pertains to "brute facts." *Brute facts* are objectively defined in terms of the necessary and sufficient parameters of a category. Moreover, brute facts are context free. That is the kind of meaning that is found in dictionaries. For example, a dictionary provides the necessary and sufficient meanings of words. However, most word meanings are not learned by reading the dictionary but by experience in the world. Such experience yields a variety of meanings, some of which are idiosyncratic. The essential intended meaning of a word in social commerce is largely a matter of the context of use. This means that institutional facts, rather than brute facts, play a major role in day-to-day social commerce.

Institutional facts, then, open the study of cognition and language to active social commerce (Sperber & Wilson, 1986). This in turn raises the role of contexts as a significant influence on what might be thought and said. The role of contexts is the heart of communication in social commerce. As

Bruner (1981, p. 172) said, "Context is all." Once again, Prutting (1982) was an advocate of studying contexts of social commerce or pragmatic theory.

It may be helpful to consider three kinds of communicative contexts (Muma, 1978, 1983, 1986). These are intentional, linguistic, and referential contexts. Intentional contexts, as opposed to elicited contexts, are endemic to natural social commerce. Spontaneous communicative behavior is more representative (assuming a sufficiently large and varied sample) of what a child can do than an elicited language sample.

A linguistic context refers to the verbal relations within a message. For example, a child may know "apple" as an indicative whereby he could point to an apple and say "apple." However, there is more to it. Can he express a variety of relational meanings by placing the word "apple" in various relationships to other words, for example, "my apple," "red apple," "those apples," "some big apples?"

Referential context pertains to message reference. Theories of reference have been the center of the philosophy of language for over a century (Donnellan, 1966; Frege, 1892/1952; Kripke, 1972; Russell, 1905; Strawson, 1950). Drawing on Kripke's (1972) cluster reduction theory of designated reference, a referent may be indexed by selecting the most useful label in a given communicative context. Needless to say, this is precisely what Brown (1958b) posited when he indicated that the words used are those that have the greatest utility in a given communicative context.

Utility in context is the criterion of word selection. Olson (1970) substantiated this proposition by having subjects talk about certain referents, then he changed the referents and noted that the comments changed accordingly. For example, a child may be asked to talk about two identical glasses one of which is half full of water. Then, the referents could be changed by removing or adding water or by changing one glass to a different glass. When a child is asked to talk about the new set of referents, what is said is different from what was said initially. This clearly shows that referential context has a significant influence on what may, or may not, be said.

A superficial view would be that referential context determines what may be said. However, it is necessary to extend the notion of referential context to internal context, what is known of the world and what one wants to say. This means that presupposition, implicature, and intent play significant roles in what can and may be said as well as external objects, events, and relations.

As for external reference, the cognitive distancing hypothesis provides further insights (Sigel & Cocking, 1977). Briefly, an object is more easily processed than a pictorial, a pictorial is more easily processed than a word. Muma and Zwycewicz–Emory (1979) showed that aphasics with word finding difficulties, aphasics with grammatical difficulties, and a matched group of elderly individuals had significantly more difficulty sorting pictures of objects than sorting the actual objects.

In summary, experiential realism posits that experience is the source of knowledge of the world and that such knowledge is volitional or intentional. Knowledge is both internal and external with awareness of external reference and events governed greatly by internal awareness. Social commerce operates primarily on institutional facts whereby reference is mutually manifest unless otherwise indicated. Context plays a major role in what can be thought or said. The three main kinds of contexts are intentional, linguistic, and referential.

EXPERIENTIAL REALISM: COGNITION

The philosophical view that has governed classical thinking about cognition has been objectivism. Classical categorization is a product of this view. It holds that, "All the entities that have a given property or collection of properties in common form a category. Such properties are necessary and sufficient to define the category. All categories are of this kind" (Lakoff, 1987, p. 161).

The criteria of necessary and sufficient were held to be objective. It was the goal of classical cognition to discover the necessary and sufficient parameters of a concept. Indeed, this view worked well within the realm of brute facts. Consequently, much that has been achieved in the study of categorization has been about brute facts. Issues about cognition that have remained unresolved include problem solving, inference, speculation, logic, contemplation of past and future events and relations, and humor.

With so much unaccounted for, it became clear that something was inherently restrictive about the objectivist view. Experiential realism overcomes the restrictions of objectivism in the study of cognition and provides a perspective for the study of heretofore incompletely understood cognitive capacities, including language.

Except for a rudimentary base shared by both experiential realism and objectivism, major new perspectives are offered. Putnam (1980) delineated the common ground between experiential realism and objectivism. He called this common ground "basic realism." Basic realism has the following tenets:

1. Both external reality and internal reality exist. Other scholars have regarded internal reality as "possible worlds" (Bruner, 1981; Stalnaker, 1972) and "theory of the world" (Palermo, 1982).
2. External reality and internal reality are linked.
3. Truth is not merely based on internal coherence. This means that truth may not be whimsical.
4. External reality is based on stable knowledge. This means that, unlike the psychological domains, the nature of the external world is more amenable to study from the perspective of brute facts and that proba-

bility theory offers a reasonable inferential account of external
reality.

5. Postulations about any conceptual system are not equally good. Thus,
in the last analysis, one view will be found to be better than another in
accounting for cognition.

Beyond this common ground, experiential realism provides an explanation of the source of meaningfulness. Briefly, initial meaningfulness comes
from preconceptual gestalt awareness. Subsequent conceptual knowledge
is derived from "metaphorical projection from the domain of the physical
to abstract domains . . . by the projection from basic-level categories to su-
perordinate and subordinate categories" (Lakoff, 1987, p. 268). Early gestalt
awareness comes from early bodily experiences, that is, one comes to know
the world by virtue of experiences in it. Such experiences provide the preconceptual base from which true concepts arise. The sources of basic-level
structure are gestalt perception, bodily movement, and imagery. The sources
of kinesthetic image-schematic structure are everyday bodily experiences
(containers, paths, links, forces, balance) and various orientations and relations (up-down, front-back, part-whole, center-periphery). "These structures are directly meaningful" (Lakoff, 1987, p. 268). They are directly
meaningful because they are embodied by virtue of active experience.

This experiential account of initial meaningfulness and the role of initial
meaningfulness in predicating cognition defines meaningfulness as an inherently human endeavor. Yet, such meaningfulness is only subjective to
the extent of initial embodiment because metaphorical projection and su-
perordinate and subordinate projections are constrained and directed by
the nature of the world in which initial meaningfulness arose and, of
course, by the nature of the human mind. Such constraints make possible
mutual manifestness (Sperber & Wilson, 1986). *Mutual manifestness* is the
mental state in which participants share essentially similar meanings either
conceptually or communicatively.

Basic-level structure has an inherently holistic logic. Thus, a young child
is prone to consider entities holistically. The correlate in early language acquisition is that initial labels are mostly of entities. This logic initially affords
a young child a highly myopic view of the world in which considerations of
myriad other possibilities are simply, and thankfully, not even raised. The
early learner is simply too biased toward considerations of whole entities to
entertain other possibilities. If this is so, the Wittgenstein (1953) dilemma
would be resolved. This dilemma raises the time-honored problem as to
how a child may come to realize entities when he could just as easily attend
to components.

Lakoff identified several kinds of early experiences that are embodied
and thereby provide a meaningful preconceptual base.

A. Container Schema
   Bodily experience: "We experience our bodies as containers and as things in containers constantly" (Lakoff, 1987, p. 272). Embodied experiences with containers may result in the rather direct mental desire to categorize the world.
B. Part-Whole Schema
   Bodily experience: "Awareness of both our wholeness and our parts. We experience our bodies as whole with parts" (Lakoff, 1987, p. 273). Such schemas are asymmetrical. For example, one's hand may be thought of as separate from the body as in the following question-answer sequence: Question: "Were you burned?" Answer: "No, just my hand."
C. Link Schema
   Bodily experience: To secure the location of two things relative to one another, we use such things as string, rope, or other means of connection. In elaborate social structure, other means are used such as uniforms, vows, and articles of faith.
D. Central-Periphery Schema
   Bodily experience: Bodies have centers (identities) and periphery (manipulable). For example, one thinks of the self within the body and the arms and legs as appendages.
E. Source-Path-Goal Schema
   Bodily experience: One moves from place to place with direction and a goal. For example, a child sees a cookie and proceeds to go toward it for the purpose of getting it.
F. Front-Back Schema
   Bodily experience: One is aware of front (forward) as contrasted to back (backward). For most purposes one is oriented forward.
G. Up-Down Schema
   Bodily experience: One is aware of up and down.
H. Linear Order Schema
   Bodily experience: One is aware of serial events and sequences. Such awareness provides a means of dealing with before and after and with sequences.

As a child has such bodily experiences, his preconceptual awareness elaborates until it evolves into true concepts. Once true concepts become available the child is no longer merely responding to direct stimulation. He has obtained a means of representing experience which will govern subsequent learning.

Theories about cognitive representation have continuity with experiential realism. Perhaps the most promising of these theories have been the Piagetian theory and, more recently, the work on categorization generally known as prototype theory (Rosch, 1973; Rosch, Mervis, Gray, Johnson, and Boyes-Braem, 1976).

EXPERIENTIAL REALISM VERSUS OBJECTIVISM

"What have been taken as self-evident truths are really questionable opinions . . . all of the objectivist doctrines concerning human thought and language are problematic if not downright wrong" (Lakoff, 1987, p. 158). This, of course, is a strong claim. If it is correct, it has considerable clinical implications.

Lakoff (1987) and Putnam (1980) contend that objectivism is wrong for the study of cognition and language. They advocate experiential realism because it more adequately accounts for the needed views of day-to-day thought and communication. The needed views are those institutional facts that have the most utility in communicative context.

The crux of the difference between objectivism and experiential realism is that the former claims to be objective, independent of human input—the so-called "God's eye view" of reality, and the latter is subjective, derived from human input. An objectivist account posits, "If human beings are to have real knowledge, then the idiosyncracies of the human organism had better not get in the way" (Lakoff, 1987, p. 174). An experiential realist account posits that knowledge and communication are inherently human endeavors derived from experience.

On the face of it, the objectivist view seems to be right. Objectivity has come to be institutionalized as a desirable criterion for ascertaining truth. It is the view that we are accustomed to believing. However, there is a subtle yet devastating flaw in the criterion for objectivity. The flaw is that there is simply no access to a "God's eye view." Therefore, objectivity is nonaccessible. Whatever is known or said in the name of objectivity derives from our minds by virtue of previous experience and thought. In short, objectivity is actually subjective.

Classical views of cognition in general and categorization in particular are simply not objective. The delimitation of necessary and sufficient parameters of categories are not defined objectively. The entire process is one of human delimitation. Who is to say that one is right or that one is wrong? Certainly, the theory of science has something to say about what is admissible evidence. Yet, here also humanity, not God, is at work. Thus, there is an inherent contradiction within objectivism. Objectivism is based on the premise that it is objective—free from human input—yet all that is known and done by humans comes from human minds.

The fact that the study of language has been committed to objectivism may have limited our understanding of it. For example, empiricism was the objectivist solution to objectivity. That is, it was claimed that a psychometric norm would obscure individual differences, thereby yielding objective evidence of a sort. Indeed, the empirical movement dominated American psychology in general and linguistics in particular from the early 1900s to the 1960s. Chomsky (1957) pointed to the failings of empiricism and redirected the study of language to mental processes and capacities. In a contemporary movement, Brown (1958a) was instrumental in launching the field of psycholinguistics which has provided fruitful studies of individual verbal skills. This work has given credence to descriptive evidence concerning various verbal contexts and appropriate criteria of attribution. Similarly, Grice's (1967) study of speech acts within the field of pragmatics also threatened objectivism.

Even within psycholinguistics, views of generative grammars were influenced by some objectivist notions. For example, language was defined as a hypothetical set of acceptable sentences, and a grammar was a set of rules about such sentences. Lakoff (1987) indicated that some generative linguists have established two major defenses that presumably offer protection against attacks on the basis of objectivism. They are the competence-performance distinction and the notion that grammar is a unique cognitive capacity. Lakoff (1987) suggested that the competence-performance distinction "is sufficiently manipulable so that almost any experimental result from psychology can, at least initially, be claimed to be in the realm of mere performance and thus can be ignored" (p. 181).

The view that grammar is a unique or autonomous mental faculty is an attempt to isolate language from other mental faculties. Thus, if the principles and doctrines that have governed the study of other mental faculties are found wanting, the study of language would be spared. And there is the benefit that those aspects of cognition that hold up could be selectively regarded as robust across all mental faculties.

Lakoff (1987) indicated that these two defenses were unconvincing:

> It seems extremely unlikely that human beings do not make use of general cognitive capacities in language. It is bizarre to assume that language ignores general cognitive apparatus, especially when it comes to something as basic as categorization. Considering that categorization enters fundamentally into every aspect of language, it would be very strange to assume that the mind in general used one kind of categorization and that language used an entirely different one. But strange as such an assumption is, it is a standard assumption behind mainstream contemporary linguistics . . . the classical theory of categorization is as wrong for language as it is for the rest of the mind. (p. 182)

CLINICAL IMPLICATIONS

There are several interesting clinical implications of experiential realism that directly conflict with many traditional clinical beliefs and practices. Put another way, objectivism underlies many traditional clinical beliefs and practices. Experiential realism provides some viable alternatives relating to the following issues: the definitions of language impairment and learning disabilities, language assessment, criteria for attribution, a substantive base for language intervention, and efficacy. Each of these will be briefly addressed.

Definitions of Language Impairment and Learning Disabilities

Traditionally, language impairments were described as a delay or deviance. Both notions were found not to be very useful. Research by Brown (1973), Greenfield and Smith (1976), and others showed that normal variations are considerable, on the order of plus or minus six months. The result was that it was not very useful to reference language learning by rate of learning indices such as age, grade, or MLU because they are not very precise.

The problem with the notion of deviance is that there are two kinds of deviance. One form, which might be called normal deviance, is that which deviates from adult language but is nonetheless normal in acquisition. For example, a young child is likely to say something like the following in the course of language acquisition: "Me here." "Mommy goed home." Such utterances are deviant from adult language but are typical of normal language acquisition. Such normal deviations are commonly found in children with language impairments; these children have been delayed in overcoming such deviations (Leonard, 1987). In this sense, the notion of language "delay" is useful but precision of measurement of a delay remains a problem.

The second kind of deviation might be called true deviation. This pertains to deviations not only from adult language but also from normal acquisition. Such deviations are exceedingly rare, and interestingly enough, they are rather localized to specific aspects of language. Should individuals be found with pervasive true deviations, there are many psycholinguists who would like to study them. The point is that when true deviations occur they are usually a small aspect of language with much more of the person's verbal skills intact or evidencing normal deviance.

The limitations of the use of delay and deviance in defining language impairments resulted in the use of the notion of "specific language impairment." This is a promising perspective because it is possible to "specify" aspects of language—cognitive, linguistic, and communicative repertoires of skill.

Unfortunately, Leonard (1987) contended that language impairments are neither specific nor impaired. There seem to be two problems with his conclusion. First, his notion of "specific" appears to be drawn from an objectivist view. That is, he cast the notion of "specific" in a normative view whereby he attempted to show that children with language impairments have a particular difficulty with language. Elsewhere, Leonard (1989) attempted to specify the particular language difficulty relating to "low phonetic substance" items. However, heterogeneity undermined his efforts resulting in the unfortunate conclusion that specific language impairment was not a useful notion because a specific difficulty could not be ascribed to individuals with language impairments.

Taking an experiential realism view whereby descriptions of individual repertoires of skills are espoused, both the heterogeneity issue and the notion of specific language impairment can be successfully addressed. Descriptions of individual repertoires of skill provide a means of delineating the nature of heterogeneity and they give evidence that it is possible to specify the nature of an individual's verbal skills and difficulties. In this sense, specific language impairment means to specify. Indeed, specification of this sort has been achieved (Fey & Leonard, 1983; Prutting & Kirchner, 1983, 1987).

In short, following an objectivist view with its attendant reliance on normative substantiation, Leonard's conclusion was that specific language impairment was not useful. However, following the experiential realism view with its attendant reliance on descriptive evidence to delineate repertoires of skills, the conclusion would be that it is possible to specify language difficulties and that such specification provides a means of delineating heterogeneity. Inasmuch as such specification has shown that most of the difficulties of children with language impairments are normal deviations, the notion of impairment should recognize that there are true deviations and normal deviations, with the latter being most prominent. Thus, the notion of specific language impairment is viable from an experiential realism perspective.

Three more issues should be made about the definition of a language impairment and the definition of learning disabilities: (a) the issue of a definition by exclusion, (b) atheoretical definitions, and (c) modality orientations. Notions of language impairments and learning disabilities have been based on definitions of exclusion. For example, both the federal (Public Law 94-142) and national (National Joint Committee, 1991) definitions of learning disabilities have been definitions of exclusion. And Leonard (1987) has acknowledged that language impairment has been based on a definition of exclusion. Definitions of exclusion say what something is not but not what it is. For example, the definition of learning disabilities indicates that they are not difficulties with hearing and with mental retardation; but it does not say what the disabilities with learning are.

Cruickshank (1972) not only pointed out this problem but also pointed to the rather strange problem for the field of learning disabilities whereby it is atheoretical. The atheoretical nature of the field points in turn to a reliance on empiricism which is the operational base of objectivism. That is to say, the field of learning disabilities has relied on normative based clinical endeavors at the cost of being atheoretical. This is a fundamental error in assessment because a theoretical base establishes construct validity (Messick, 1980). Everything must be derived from this theoretical base.

A similar story holds for the modality views of language, that is, expressive/receptive modalities, oral/written modalities, visual/auditory modalities. Such views deal with rather superficial notions of language which have obtained status by virtue of normative measures. However, the more substantial cognitive, linguistic, and communicative systems and processes address the core issues of language (Muma, 1978, 1986).

Indeed, the research pertaining to auditory processing has been particularly revealing in this regard because it raises serious questions as to whether auditory processing is a bona fide issue in accounting for language impairments (Leonard, 1987; Rees, 1981; Tallal, 1990). This literature has shown that the mental processing underlying language is nonmodality specific, which is contrary to what advocates of auditory processing claim. Advocates merely claim that if a child looks at something he is processing visually and if he hears something he is using auditory processing. These are superficial views because the literature has established the fact that only very brief initial processing (on the order of .40 seconds) is modality specific but most of the mental processing underlying language is nonmodality specific. Clark and Clark (1977) have shown that initial modality specific information is purged very early in mental processing with most of the mental effort committed to problem solving aimed at constructing an appropriate proposition of a message. Awareness of both grammatical and pragmatic mechanisms provide assistance in deriving an appropriate proposition in the realization of communicative intent.

In summary, there have been some problems with the traditional definitions of language impairments and learning disabilities. Notions of "delay" and "deviant" proved inadequate. The notion of "specific language impairment" was not very useful from an objectivist view in which it may be empirically defined from a normative perspective; however, specific language impairment is useful from the view of experiential realism in which it means to specify a child's cognitive-linguistic-pragmatic skills for communication. The use of a definition by exclusion does not say what something is. Such definitions rely on the normative solution of objectivism. Atheoretical definitions and a modalities view of language also rely on the normative solution.

Clinical Assessment: Appropriate Substantive Base

The traditional substantive base for clinical assessment has been normative tests. This base reflects the empirical solution of objectivism. Briefly, the necessary and sufficient criteria have been invested in norms.

In contrast, experiential realism derives its substance from actual experience and in the realization of communicative intent. Experience and intent are issues that are more adequately accounted for by descriptions of repertoires of skills with attendant criteria of attribution. Consequently, descriptions of an individual's repertoire of skills in communicative context, rather than reference to psychometric norms, should comprise the substantive base for clinical assessment.

The movement in child psychology for ecologically based evidence (Bronfenbrenner, 1979; Donaldson, 1978) also has continuity with experiential realism. It brings with it the need for adequate representative samples (Gallagher, 1983) and appropriate criteria of attribution (Nelson, 1981; Prutting, 1979). Both of these issues have not been adequately broached in the clinical fields. Muma and colleagues (1990) have shown that the prevailing clinical and research practices in speech-language pathology are the use of 50- or 100-utterance language samples and that such samples have very large error rates (on the order of 52% to 47%, respectively) which can lead to inappropriate intervention goals and false claims of efficacy.

A consideration of the seven basic clinical assessment issues reveals that a descriptive model addresses these issues more adequately than a psychometric normative model (Muma, 1983, 1986). The seven issues are: clinical complaint, problem/no problem, nature of a problem, individual differences, intervention implications, prognosis, and accountability. For instance, a descriptive model is better than a normative test in addressing the issue of individual differences. A descriptive account would strive to delineate a child's repertoire of skills within the province of probability theory. On the other hand, normative tests or developmental profiles merely compare a child's performance to a norm. Such assessments are not truly individualized assessments because an individual's actual skills have yet to be identified and described.

In summary, the objectivist view relies on psychometric normative tests to realize claims of objectivity. The experiential realism view relies on descriptions of actual cognitive or communicative skills as estimates of an individual's repertoire of skills in realizing communicative intent.

Criteria of Attribution

With objectivity relying on norms, there was no further need to address the issues of appropriate criteria for attribution. However, with descriptive assessment emerging as a viable account of what a child can do with language, the notion of criteria of attribution has emerged as well. The Piagetian criteria of preparation, attainment, and consolidation may be useful (Muma, 1986; Nelson, 1981; Prutting, 1979). *Preparation* can be attributed when a behavior occurs infrequently, when it is context bound, and when it is difficult to elicit. *Attainment* can be attributed when a behavior occurs relatively frequently, in different referential contexts, and is easily elicited. *Consolidation* can be attributed when a behavior occurs in varied contexts, especially varied linguistic contexts.

Intervention: Substantive Base

The clinical implications of objectivism and experiential realism for intervention are different. As indicated above, the objectivist solution to objectivity is empiricism, the use of norms. The intervention extension of this view is a priori or prepackaged intervention. Moreover, the instructional model is a legitimate extension as well because instructors or teachers assume that the learning process is external.

Behaviorism is a case in point. In behavior modification, the teachers or instructors believe that they are in control of content, sequence, rate, and reinforcement in learning (Muma, 1978, 1983, 1986). And, they are troubled about generalization (Kamhi, 1988).

In contrast to objectivism, experiential realism supports descriptive evidence of individual repertoires of skill with the attendant criteria of attribution. The intervention implication is to facilitate active learning (Bloom & Lahey, 1978; Lahey, 1988; Muma, 1978, 1983, 1986). Facilitation takes place in an ecologically valid context (Bronfenbrenner, 1979), usually play for young children. Often it includes available peer models and parent participation (Muma, 1983, 1986). The goals are to expand and replace verbal behaviors (Bates, 1979) in accordance with the available literature concerning acquisition sequences and alternative strategies of acquisition. An abiding concern throughout is the realization of actual communicative intent (Muma, 1981, 1986).

Facilitation has been advocated by Bloom and Lahey (1978) and Muma (1978). Experiential realism not only gives increased credence to the earlier views of facilitation but it takes on new meaning because of the importance of communicative intent, context, and criteria of attribution. Perhaps it would be helpful to illustrate facilitation. Drawing on several sources, Muma (1986) showed that it is possible to identify active loci of learning from a spontaneous language sample. "Build-ups" coupled with evidence of a child's repertoire of skill can reveal active loci of learning. For example, a child said, "I like soup. I like big soup." Compared to his language sample, this build-up showed that he was attempting a new aspect of object noun phrases, adjectivals for inanimate nouns. Another example given by Muma (1986) pertains to "buttressing." A child had been using object forms of pronouns in subject positions. He would say, "Me here." "Him go." "Them mine." However, he began buttressing whereby he would produce subject forms of the pronouns that were buttressed by some old forms. He said, "Daddy, he go." "Mommy, she here." These were then replaced by subject forms of pronouns, that is, I, he, she, we, they, and so forth. Once a locus of learning has been identified, facilitation can be used.

Facilitation was used with both of these children. In regard to the latter example, the clinician provided appropriate models for the child's intended utterances in communicative contexts. Then, the child began to buttress and subsequently he stopped buttressing and continued with subject pronouns. Thus, facilitation is directed at a child's utterances in actual social commerce. A model is provided for intended utterances. Early on, most children do not alter their utterances. However, after several sessions of facilitation, most children begin altering their utterances in the direction of the available models. There is usually no problem with so-called "carry-over" or generalization simply because the children are not instructed to alter their utterances. Rather, they alter them themselves to realize their communicative intents.

Efficacy

Accountability or efficacy in ASHA (Olswang, Thompson, Warren, & Mingetti, 1991) has also been strongly invested in an objectivist view. Advocates of objectivity have once again picked up the empiricist banner. Indeed, there has been a rather concerted effort to address efficacy as a data-driven issue, usually with within-subject designs (McReynolds & Kearns, 1983).

A more viable approach to the efficacy issue is a rational approach. It is more appropriate to establish the philosophical-theoretical base on which language assessment and intervention are derived and to establish continuity throughout than to generate data. Indeed, data are easily generated; the crucial issue is to obtain data that have continuity with the underlying philosophical-theoretical base with its attendant literature and data that are relevant to an individual's repertoire of skills. Again, experiential realism offers a more viable solution than empricism. A rationale that is consistent with the underlying philosophical-theoretical base has much to offer.

Although it is true that many current tests have established norms, this is not the same as construct validity (Messick, 1980). Construct validity must be established first to ensure that a given test has continuity with its underlying theory. Then, norms may be warranted.

In intervention, it would be inappropriate to turn to a psycholinguistic theory, such as markedness which accounts for a shift from unmarked to marked terms in word acquisition, and then use a behavior modification program in intervention. These are incongruous. The result is likely to be one in which the child will perform well during the instruction but not use the desired behaviors as rule-based behaviors in everyday speech. On the other hand, the use of modeling of marked forms when a child wants (intention) to mark contrastiveness in actual social commerce not only results in an appropriate change in the time but also achieves sustained effects whereby the child uses the new skills anywhere.

Another example is in the pragmatic arena whereby a child wishes to communicate but he lacks what is known as "role taking," wherein the speaker takes the perspective of the listener in constructing a message. Again, a behavior modification approach would result in superficial performance. In contrast, the psycholinguistic activity known as the "over-the-shoulder-game" (Muma, 1978) affords a child an opportunity to monitor the effects of intended messages and revise his utterances accordingly. In this game, a child is behind the listener and looks over the listener's shoulder; thus both speaker and listener have essentially the same perspectives on the available referents. Then, the child issues a message intended for action on the referents and observes how effective that message is as the listener strives to comply with it or asks for clarifying information. Such experiences provide a mechanism for learning that is consistent with the realization of communicative intent.

Two final examples pertain to sheer talking time and communicative payoff. The instructional model strives to control the learning process by using various mechanisms to restrict talking, for example, "Are our hands and voices quiet? Are we ready to learn, children?" (Notice the empirical "We.") Such restraints are usually followed by an activity where the children are told to wait their turns and then called on to participate. This converts what could be actual communication in the realization of intentions to instruction and directives dealing with elicited speech. In the realization of communicative intent, sheer talking time has much more theoretical support in the contemporary literature. It is virtually a given that if talking time is dominated by the teacher or clinician the activity is about elicited rather than intended speech. On the other hand, if the children are dominating the talking, the prospects are good that their communicative intentions are being realized. This brings up the notion of "communicative payoff" (Muma, 1981).

Communicative payoff is a response to a child initiated utterance whereby communicative intent is realized. For example, a child who points to a cookie, says "Cookie," and receives the cookie gets paid off for his intended message. Behaviorists would be quick to say that he was reinforced. However, reinforcement does not offer a viable account of this event simply because children usually do not do what reinforcement theory predicts. The theory predicts that a behavior that has been positively reinforced increases its frequency. However, children in this context rarely continue saying "cookie." What they usually do is maintain their topic and say something like "Um good," then they eat it. What is significant about communicative intent is that children do two important things, neither of which are accountable by reinforcement theory: They talk more because they realize that communicative intent works, and they try to do new things. As Bruner (1981) indicated, the realization of communicative intent has replaced reinforcement theory as a viable account of language acquisition.

Needless to say, the traditional definitions, assessment views and practices, intervention views and practices, and claims of efficacy are receiving increased scrutiny. The crucial issue is to what extent these issues have continuity with the contemporary philosophical-theoretical literature on language and cognition. In this regard, the views of objectivism have been found wanting, whereas the views of experiential realism have been shown to be promising. Indeed, major scholars have received experiential realism positively. For example, Pinker (1989) commented in reference to experiential realism, "I count myself among the impressed" (p. 371).

Before her death I had only a very brief talk with Carol Prutting about the promising philosophical view of experiential realism. She in her characteristic way was interested. I will not claim that she would embrace its vision, although I think she would. I will not claim that she would pit objectivism against experiential realism because she would be more inclined to present experiential realism on its own merits and let the more perceptive among us see its challenge to objectivism and to empiricism ourselves. I will simply say that she wanted to know. That alone is a considerable accolade because Carol was a scholar-clinician.

REFERENCES

Austin, J. (1962). *How to do things with words.* New York: Oxford University Press.

Bates, E. (1979). *The emergence of symbols.* New York: Academic Press.

Bloom, L., & Lahey, M. (1978). *Language development and language disorders.* New York: John Wiley and Sons.

Bronfenbrenner, U. (1979). *The ecology of human development.* Cambridge, MA: Harvard University Press.

Brown, R. (1958a). *Words and things.* New York: Free Press.

Brown,R. (1958b). How shall a thing be named? *Psychological Review, 65,* 18–21.

Brown, R. (1972). *A first language: The early stages.* Cambridge, MA: Harvard University Press.

Bruner, J. (1981). The social context of language acquisition. *Language & Communication, 1,* 155–178.

Cazden, C. (1977). The quest of intent. In M. Lewis & L. Rosenblum (Eds.), *Interaction, conversation, and the development of language.* New York: John Wiley and Sons.

Chomsky, N. (1957). *Syntactic structures.* The Hague, The Netherlands: Mouton.

Clark, H., & Clark, E. (1977). *Psychology and language.* New York: Harcourt, Brace, Jovanovich.

Cruickshank, W. (1972). Some issues facing the field of learning disabilities. *Journal of Learning Disabilities, 5,* 380–387.

Donaldson, M. (1976). *Children's minds.* New York: W. W. Norton.

Donnellan, K. (1966). Reference and definite descriptions. *Philosophical Review, 75,* 281–304.

Fey, M., & Leonard, L. (1983). Pragmatic skills of children with specific language impairment. In T. Gallagher & C. Prutting (Eds.), *Pragmatic assessment and intervention issues in language.* San Diego, CA: College-Hill Press.

Frege, G. (1952). On sense and reference. In P. Geach & M. Block (Eds.), *Translations from the philosophical writings of Gottlob Frege.* Oxford, UK: Blackwell. (Original work published in 1892/1952)

Gallagher, T. (1983). Pre-assessment: A procedure for accommodating language use variability. In T. Gallagher & C. Prutting (Eds.), *Pragmatic assessment and intervention issues in language.* San Diego, CA: College-Hill Press.

Garner, W. (1966). To perceive is to know. *American Psychologist, 21,* 11–19.

Greenfield, P., & Smith, J. (1976). *Communication and the beginnings of language: The development of semantic structure in one-word speech and beyond.* New York: Academic Press.

Grice, H. (1967). 1957 William James Lectures, Harvard University. (Published in part as "Logic and conversation.") In P. Cole & J. Morgan (Eds.), *Syntax and semantics: 3. Speech acts.* New York: Seminar Press.

Halliday, M. (1975). Learning how to mean. In E. Lenneberg & E. Lenneberg (Eds.), *Foundations of language development: A multidisciplinary approach.* New York: Academic Press.

Ingram, D. (1989). *Phonological disability in children* (2nd ed.). New York: Elsevier.

Kamhi, A. (1988). A reconceptualization of generalization and generalization problems. *Language, Speech, and Hearing Services in Schools, 19,* 304–313.

Kripke, S. (1972). Naming and necessity. In D. Davidson & G. Harman (Eds.), *Semantics of natural language* (2nd ed.). Boston: Reidel.

Lahey, M. (1988). *Language disorders and language development.* New York: Macmillan.

Lakoff, G. (1987). *Women, fire, and dangerous things: What categories reveal about the mind.* Chicago: University of Chicago Press.

Leonard, L. (1987). Is specific language impairment a useful construct? In S. Rosenberg (Ed.), *Advances in applied psycholinguistics. I. Disorders of first language development.* New York: Cambridge University Press.

Leonard, L. (1989). Language learnability and specific language impairment in children. *Applied Psycholinguistics, 10,* 179–202.

McReynolds, L., & Kearns, K. (1983). *Single-subjects experimental designs in communicative disorders.* Austin, TX: Pro-Ed.

Messick, S. (1980). Test validity and the ethics of assessment. *American Psychologist, 35,* 1012–1027.

Muma, J. (1978). *Language handbook: Concepts, assessment, and intervention.* Englewood Cliffs, NJ: Prentice-Hall.

Muma, J. (1981). *Language primer for the clinical fields.* Austin, TX: Pro-Ed.

Muma, J. (1983). Speech-language pathology: Emerging clinical expertise in language. In T. Gallagher & C. Prutting (Eds.), *Pragmatic assessment and intervention issues in language.* San Diego, CA: College-Hill Press.

Muma, J. (1986). *Language acquisition: A functionalist perspective.* Austin, TX: Pro-Ed.

Muma, J., Morales, A., Day, K., Tackett, A., Smith, S., Daniel, B., Logue, B., & Morriss, D. (1990). Representative language samples: Grammatical repertoires. Unpublished manuscript.

Muma, J., & Zwycewicz–Emory, C. (1979). Contextual priority: Verbal shift at seven? *Journal of Child Language, 6,* 301–311.

National Joint Committee on Learning Disabilities. (1991). Learning disabilities: Issues on definition. *Asha, 33* (Suppl. 5), 18–20.

Nelson, K. (1981). Toward a rare-event cognitive comparison theory of syntax acquisition. In P. Dale & D. Ingram (Eds.), *Child language.* Austin, TX: Pro-Ed.

Ninio, A., & Snow, C. (1988). Language acquisition through language use: The functional sources of children's early utterances. In Y. Levy, I. Schlesinger, & M. Braine (Eds.), *Categories and processes in language acquisition.* Hillsdale, NJ: Lawrence Erlbaum.

Olson, D. (1970). Language and thought: Aspects of a cognitive theory of semantics. *Psychological Review, 77,* 257–273.

Olswang, L., Thompson, C., Warren, S., & Mingetti, N. (Eds.). (1991). *Treatment efficacy research in communication disorders.* Rockville, MD: American Speech Language Foundation.

Pinker, S. (1989). *Learnability and cognition.* Cambridge, MA: MIT Press.

Palermo, D. (1982). Theoretical issues in semantic development. In S. Kuczaj (Ed.), *Language development* (Vol. 1). Hillsdale, NJ: Lawrence Erlbaum.

Prutting, C. (1979). Process. *Journal of Speech and Hearing Disorders, 44,* 3–30.

Prutting, C. (1982). Pragmatics as social competence. *Journal of Speech and Hearing Disorders, 47,* 123–133.

Prutting, C. (1983). Scientific inquiry and communicative disorders: An emerging paradigm across six decades. In T. Gallagher & C. Prutting (Eds.), *Pragmatic assessment and intervention issues in language.* San Diego, CA: College-Hill Press.

Prutting, C., & Kirchner, D. (1983). Applied pragmatics. In T. Gallagher & C. Prutting (Eds.), *Pragmatic assessment and intervention issues in language.* San Diego, CA: College-Hill Press.

Prutting, C., & Kirchner, D. (1987). A clinical appraisal of the pragmatic aspects of language. *Journal of Speech and Hearing Disorders, 52,* 105–119.

Prutting, C., Epstein, L., Beckman,S., Dias, I., & Gao, X. (in press). Inquiry into and tampering with nature: A clinical perspective. *Journal of Speech and Hearing Disorders.*

Prutting, C., Mentis, M., & Myles-Zitzer, C. (in press). Philosophy of science: A template for understanding our science. *Asha.*

Putnam, H. (1980). Models and reality. *Journal of Symbolic Logic, 45,* 464–482.

Rees, N. (1981). Saying more than we know: Is auditory processing disorder a meaningful concept? In R. Keith (Ed.), *Central auditory and language disorders in children.* San Diego, CA: College-Hill Press.

Rosch, E. (1973). Natural categories. *Cognitive Psychology, 4,* 328–350.

Rosch, E., Mervis, C., Gray, W., Johnson, D., & Boyes–Braem, P. (1976). Basic objects in natural categories. *Cognitive Psychology, 8,* 382–439.

Russell, B. (1905). On denoting. *Mind, 14,* 479–493.

Searle, J. (1969). *Speech acts: An essay in the philosophy of language.* Cambridge, UK: Cambridge University Press.

Sigel, I., & Cocking, R. (1977). Cognition and communication: A dialectic paradigm for development. In M. Lewis & L. Rosenblum (Eds.), *Interaction, conversation, and the development of language.* New York: John Wiley and Sons.

Sperber, D., & Wilson, D. (1986). *Relevance: Communication and cognition.* Cambridge, MA: Harvard University Press.

Stalnaker, R. (1972). Pragmatics. In D. Davidson & G. Harman (Eds.), *Semantics of natural language* (2nd ed.). Boston, MA: Reidel.

Strawson, P. (1950). On referring. *Mind, 59,* 320–344.

Tallal, P. (1990). Fine-grained discrimination deficits in language-learning impaired children are specific neither to the auditory modality nor to speech perception. *Journal of Speech and Hearing Research, 33,* 616–617.

Ventry, I., & Schiavetti, N. (1986). *Evaluating research in speech pathology and audiology* (2nd ed.). New York: Macmillan.

Vihman, M., & Greenlee, M. (1987). Individual differences in phonological development: Ages one and three years. *Journal of Speech and Hearing Research, 30,* 503–521.

Wittgenstein, E. (1953). *Philosophical investigations.* New York: Macmillan.

CHAPTER 9

Profiling Pragmatic Abilities in the Emerging Language of Young Children

AMY M. WETHERBY

Two things that distinguish human development from that of other primates are the extended length of human childhood and the relative immaturity of human infants at birth. Gould (1985) has explained humans' lengthened childhood by the process of evolutionary slowdown in maturation called *neoteny*, which literally means "holding on to youth." Relative to the extension of human childhood, Gould estimated that human infants should have a gestation period of about 18 months. However, because of the evolutionary growth of the human infant's brain, the female pelvic bone could not accommodate the size of the infant skull after an 18-month gestation period. Therefore, one of two processes had to occur: either the female's pelvic bone had to increase dramatically in size or human infants had to be born earlier when their craniums were still small enough to fit through the pelvic bone. Women can be grateful to know that the evolutionary outcome was not a pelvis large enough to accommodate a baby the size of a 9-month-old infant in present chronology. Instead, the outcome was a shortening of the gestation period, or what Gould referred to as an "accelerated birth." Gould (1977, 1985) suggested that human babies "are born as embryos" and cited evidence that the rate of maturation during the first nine months of postnatal life is very rapid and matches prenatal fetal development.

Thus, extended childhood and accelerated birth in humans are evolutionary processes that have operated on the timing of development. The outcome of these processes on human development has contributed to humans' greater capacity for flexible behavior, problem solving, learning, symbol use, and social dependency (Gould, 1985). A decade-long childhood provides an extended amount of time for exploring, playing, developing social ties, and learning before human behavior becomes rigid and inflexible, which is typical of mammalian development after puberty. Premature birth allows for the early nurturing environment to have a greater impact on brain development at a time when the brain is maturing at its fastest rate.

The relative immaturity of the human infant at birth is one factor that accounts for humans' propensity, compared to nonhuman primates, for learning language. The word infant is derived from the Latin word *infans* which literally means "one unable to speak" (Prutting, 1982a). Although it is accurate to say the infant cannot yet speak, the infant does have an impressive repertoire of communicative abilities and plays an active role in language learning. Communicative abilities that develop during infancy form the foundation for emerging language. The child language literature has emphasized the importance of prelinguistic communicative development for the acquisition of language (Bates, 1979; Bruner, 1981; Dore, 1986; McLean & Snyder–McLean, 1978). Research has indicated that human communication development involves continuity from preverbal communication through referential language (Bates, 1979; Harding & Golinkoff, 1979).

From birth the infant's behavior systematically affects the caregiver, and thus serves a communicative function, although the infant is not yet aware of the outcome. The caregiver's interpretation of and contingent responsiveness to the infant's preintentional communicative signals play an important role in the development of intentional communication (Dore, 1986; Dunst, Lowe, & Bartholomew, 1990). At about nine months of age, the child begins to use gestures and/or sounds to communicate intentionally; that is, the child deliberately uses particular signals to communicate for preplanned effects on others (Bates, 1979). It is interesting that this is the age when Gould suggested human infants would have been born had birth not been accelerated.

Thus, the development of preverbal intentional communication is rooted in social interaction and may be considered a necessary precursor to the development of the intentional use of language to communicate. The shift in focus to pragmatics in the child language literature in the 1970s has led to more emphasis on the communicative and social/affective aspects of language. Pragmatics was introduced into the child language literature by Bates (1976). She defined *pragmatics* as the "rules governing the use of language in context" and delineated three categories of pragmatic rules: (a) performatives or communicative intentions expressed by the speaker; (b) presupposition or the use of given versus new information; and (c) conversational postulates or rules governing discourse. Prutting (1982b) suggested a broader view of "pragmatics as social competence" and emphasized that the social interactional context provides the foundation for language acquisition. The acquistion of pragmatics involves a complex interplay of emerging abilities in social/affective, communicative, cognitive, and linguistic domains (Bates, 1979; Prizant & Wetherby, 1990).

It is important for the language clinician to have a strong understanding of early social and communicative development in order to address pragmatic abilities of young children with communication and language impairments. This chapter will focus on the emergence of language in the first two years of life. The cognitive, social, and communicative bases of symbolic development will be examined in more detail. Literature on children developing language normally and children with communicative impairments at emerging language stages will be briefly reviewed. Clinical vignettes of children with and without social impairments will be presented to demonstrate the importance of profiling a child's pragmatic abilities. Clinical implications for designing the content and context of intervention will be offered.

COGNITIVE BASES OF SYMBOL USE

The cognitive bases of language acquisition have received continuing attention in the literature. Piaget (1952) suggested that the child's sensorimotor cognitive knowledge provides the basis for the emergence of symbol use. Language is but one manifestation of the symbolic function shared by other symbolic processes (i.e., deferred imitation, play, drawing, and visual imagery). Piagetian theory has influenced current views that language is derived from a broad cognitive knowledge base and has stimulated the search for cognitive prerequisites to language acquisition. There is some evidence to suggest that cognitive development sets the pace for language acquisition (Sinclair, 1975; Slobin, 1973) and that impairments in the acquisition of language may stem from deficits in specific cognitive attainments (Leonard, 1978). However, several hypotheses about the relationship between language and cognition that differ from Piaget's have been proposed (see Rice, 1983, for a review). The two major questions addressed in the various theories are: (a) to what extent is language influenced by cognition and (b) can cognition be influenced by language?

Cromer (1976) offered a "weak cognition hypothesis" which stated that certain cognitive achievements are necessary, but not sufficient, to explain normal language acquisition. More recently, Cromer (1981) renewed interest in the nativist position and emphasized the interaction of environmental factors with an innate potential that is specific to language. Curtiss and colleagues (Curtiss, 1981; Curtiss, Yamada, & Fromkin, 1979) have argued more strongly than Cromer that grammatical aspects of language have unique organizing principles that are independent of general cognition. Their conclusions are based on case studies of children with mental retardation who showed dissociations between cognition and language.

Although there is continued debate over the role of cognition in the acquisition of grammatical aspects of language, there is accumulating evidence of parallels between cognition and the emergence of preverbal communication, first words, and first-word combinations (see Bates & Snyder, 1987; Rice, 1983). In a review of research on the relationship between language and cognition, Bates and Snyder (1987) concluded that there are meaningful associations between specific achievements in communication/language and cognition, but that these relationships change from the prelinguistic stage to the acquisition of syntax.

In an attempt to account for the parallels between language and cognition, Bates (1979) formulated an explanatory theory of the origins of the human symbolic capacity. Based on a cross-sectional study of 25 normally developing children, Bates isolated three cognitive-social components that contribute to the symbolic capacity: imitation, tool use, and communicative intent. The symbol-using capacity is manifested in the development of both language and play. This relationship is illustrated in Figure 9–1.

Bates (1979) explained the developmental dependence among linguistic, cognitive, and social domains with the "homology through shared origins" model. In biology, the term *homology* refers to different structures that are related because they are derived from a common origin or source. In this homology model, the cognitive-social components are related structures that emerge from a separate source, referred to as an underlying "software" or cognitive substrate. The model predicts that two homologous structures related through a shared underlying software should emerge in no particular sequence, because no causal relationship exists between the two structures. For example, the homologous structures of communicative intent and tool use are related through a shared cognitive substrate. Communicative intent may emerge earlier or later than tool use, perhaps due to environmental influences, but when either capacity is present, it can be inferred that the cognitive substrate is present. Further, the homology model predicts that transfer from one component skill to another should be bidirectional. For example, training or experience in communicative intent may enhance the underlying cognitive substrate and spill over into tool use ability and vice versa.

Bates (1979) hypothesized that the symbolic capacity evolved in phylogeny (i.e., the evolutionary development of a species) as a "new product" built from the interaction of available "old parts." The human symbolic

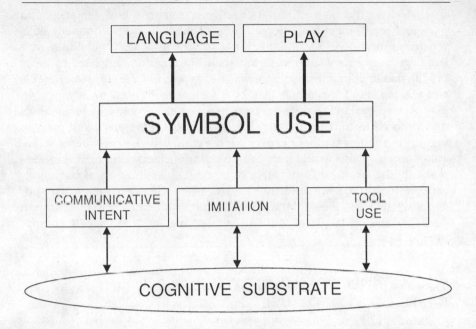

Figure 9-1. Illustration of the homology through shared origins model described by Bates (1979).

capacity was generated through the process of "heterochrony," which refers to changes in the developmental timing and rate of maturation of preexisting capacities. Through the operation of heterochrony, specific, dissociable cognitive and social components evolved in the service of nonlinguistic functions. In other words, specific cognitive and social components evolved for purposes unrelated to language functions. When the relative proportions of available cognitive-social components reached a certain threshold level, new interactions among the components resulted, creating new capacity for symbols. Thus, the "new product," symbolic capacity, was constructed in phylogeny from the interactions of at least three "old parts"—imitation, tool use, and communicative intent. Quantitative variations in timing have led to a qualitatively new capacity. Bates suggested that the heterochronous process that occurred in phylogeny is replicated in ontogeny (i.e., the biological development of the individual).

CLINICAL IMPLICATIONS

The homology model presented above has clinical implications. Some children with language impairments may have an underlying deficit in symbol use, which would be manifested in an impairment in both language and play, and may reflect limitations in one or more of the component skills (i.e., communicative intent, imitation, and tool use). Other children with language impairments may have a specific blockage, as suggested by Bates (1979), that impairs the development of language, but the component skills and the capacity for symbols may be intact, as evidenced by advances in play. As depicted in Figure 9–1, assessment of a child's capacity for symbols may proceed from the top-down (i.e., evaluation of language and play) to identify the child's symbolic capacity. If the child shows impairments in language and play, this would imply a symbolic deficiency, and further assessment should proceed from the bottom-up (i.e., evaluation of communicative intent, imitation, and tool use) to isolate impairments in component skills. These assessment findings would lead naturally to intervention goals addressing language, general symbol use, and/or specific component skills.

SOCIAL AND COMMUNICATIVE BASES OF SYMBOL USE

One limitation of Bates' homology model is that it does not directly address the role of the caregiving environment in language acquisition. Although the model does include component skills of the child that fall in the social domain (i.e., communicative intent and imitation) and a nurturing language-learning enviroment is presumed necessary, it does not account for the role of social interaction as a contributing factor that influences the child's socioemotional communication and language development. This has been addressed in other theories that emphasize the social bases of language acquisition.

In the last two decades, pragmatic and social interactive theories have placed a great emphasis on the role of social interaction in language development (Bloom & Lahey, 1978; McLean & Snyder–McLean, 1978). Pragmatic theory has emphasized that successful communication involves reciprocity and mutual negotiation. Preverbal turn-taking provides the foundation for learning to exchange roles in conversation (Bruner, 1978). Joint action between the child and caregiver forms the social context in which children learn to use more sophisticated and conventional means to communicate. Children are viewed as active participants who learn to affect the behaviors, thoughts, and ideas of others through active signalling (Prizant & Wetherby, 1989). From early in life, infants make deliberate attempts to share experiences with caregivers by sharing attention and affective states (Stern, 1985). Early displays of affect and directed eye gaze serve as signals to regulate interaction and help the caregiver read the infant's emotional state (Dunst et al., 1990; Tronick, 1989). Thus, it is the combination of the readability of the child's signals and the caregivers' contingent social responsiveness that influences the successful acquisition of communication and language.

The transactional model proposed by Sameroff (Sameroff, 1987; Sameroff & Chandler, 1975) emphasized the developmental interplay between a child and his or her social environment. This model states that the child's behavior influences the caregiver's responsiveness which influences the child's development. The child's developmental outcome is determined by the mutual interaction or transaction of the child and the environment. Research findings on mother-child interactions exemplify this transactional process. Compared to mothers of children who develop normally, mothers of children who are communicatively impaired have been found to use a lower proportion of utterances that are semantically related to the child's previous verbal or nonverbal behavior and to use a higher proportion of topic initiations and directives. (See Cross [1984] and Tiegerman and Siperstein [1984] for review of this literature.) Thus, mothers of children with communicative impairments provide a more controlling and less responsive language learning environment than mothers of children with normal communicative development. Although a directive interactional style may be the result of the child's communicative impairment, it may also contribute to the difficulties that the child has in developing communication and language (Newhoff & Browning, 1983).

Consistent with the transactional model of Sameroff, Dunst and colleagues (1990) recently formulated a model for conceptualizing the role of the social context in the development of communicative competence. They proposed that the degree of readability of the child's behavior influences the caregiver's ability to respond contingently to the child. They also stressed the impact that the caregiver's social system has on the child. Included in the caregiver's social system were the immediate family, informal supports (i.e., friends, neighbors, co-workers, church members), and formal supports (i.e., professionals providing services to the child). They argued that the caregiver's well-being is influenced by the support system available to the caregiver and thereby influences the caregiver's social responsiveness to the child. Thus, biological and environmental factors that affect the caregiver as well as those that affect the child mutually influence the child's development over time through a transactional process.

CLINICAL IMPLICATIONS

The theoretical shift to pragmatic social interactive theories of language development has had a major impact on clinical practice (see Craig, 1983). This shift has identified the need for assessment and intervention efforts to focus on the level of the dyad, rather than the individual child (MacDonald, 1985; Prizant & Wetherby, 1988). In considering the role of the social context on the child's developing language, it is critical for the language clinician to examine the affect each communicative partner has on the other in language assessment, to address the social support system available to the caregiver, and to foster a facilitative language learning environment in intervention (MacDonald, 1985; Newhoff & Browning, 1983).

IMPORTANCE OF PROFILING COMMUNICATION AND SYMBOLIC ABILITIES

The current theories on child language acquistion reviewed above indicate that a child's profile of social/affective, communicative, cognitive, and linguistic abilities are essential components of the assessment of a developmentally young child's communicative competence. Furthermore, the child's communicative abilities should be considered in relation to the social context of language learning. However, the formal assessment instruments that are most frequently used to assess communication and language for young children focus on the form of communication and rely on elicited responses (Wetherby & Prizant, in press).

   Assessment instruments need to go beyond measures of language form or placement of a child in a respondent role. The child's communicative abilities need to be examined in natural communicative exchanges, with the child's symbolic abilities serving as a developmental frame of reference (Prizant & Wetherby, 1988). In the assessment of pragmatics, the child's deficits in specific aspects of development need to be considered in relation to his or her communicative competence (Prutting & Kirchner, 1987). Patterns of communication and symbolic development identified in the literature on children with normal language development and children with communicative impairments will be reviewed briefly below to indicate areas that need to be addressed in the assessment and remediation of a child's communicative competence.

COMMUNICATION DEVELOPMENT OF NORMALLY DEVELOPING CHILDREN

Prior to the emergence of words, children who are developing normally use prelinguistic gestures and vocalizations beginning as early as eight to nine months of age to communicate for a variety of purposes (Bates, 1979; Coggins & Carpenter, 1981; Harding & Golinkoff, 1979; Wetherby, Cain, Yonclas, & Walker, 1988). Bruner (1981) suggested that three "innate communicative intentions" emerge during the first year of life: (a) *behavior regulation* (i.e., acts used to regulate another's behavior for purposes of obtaining or restricting environmental goals); (b) *social interaction* (i.e., acts used to direct another's attention to oneself for affiliative purposes); and (c) *joint attention* (i.e., acts used to direct another's attention for purposes of sharing the focus on an entity or event). During the prelinguistic stage, children who are developing normally use intentional communicative signals for these three major functions (Wetherby et al., 1988). Thus, before the emergence of words, children are able to use signals intentionally to communicate for a broad range of purposes.

Developmental progressions have been identified in the acquisition of communicative means, for example, in the forms used to express communicative intentions. At about nine months of age children first use "contact" gestures in which their hands come in contact with an object or person (e.g., giving an object, showing an object, and pushing an adult's hand). By about 11 months children use distal gestures in which their hands do not touch a person or object (e.g., open-hand reaching, distant pointing, and waving) (Bates, O'Connell, & Shore, 1987). At about 13 months children begin using a small number of words that are symbolic or referential. That is, they use names to refer to objects, events, or classes of objects or events. Between 12 and 18 months new word acquisition is slow but children show an increase in their rate of communicating, use of sounds in coordination with gestures, and use of consonants in multisyllabic utterances (Carpenter, Mastergeorge, & Coggins, 1983; Kent & Bauer, 1985; Wetherby et al., 1988). These language achievements increase the readability of young children's communicative signals.

At about 18 months there is a sudden surge in vocabulary growth from a rate of learning about one new word a week to learning several new words a day (Ingram, 1978). Children begin to produce word combinations and to predicate, that is, to describe states and qualities about agents, actions, and objects (Bates et al., 1987; Prutting, 1979). Children grow in conversational skills as they begin to request information, talk about events that are remote in place and time, and maintain topics across several turns (Goldin–Meadow, Seligman, & Gelman, 1976; Ingram, 1978; Prutting, 1979). Thus, from 9 to 24 months, children show rapid advances in the means they use to express intentions and in their ability to engage in conversation.

COMMUNICATION DEVELOPMENT IN CHILDREN WITH COMMUNICATIVE IMPAIRMENTS

Communication skills have been studied in school-age and older preschool children with identified communicative impairments. Several differences from children with normally developing communicative skills have been noted. The range of communicative functions expressed by children with specific language-impairment has been found to be restricted compared to that of children with normal language development of similar chronologic age but similar to that of children with normal language development of similar language age (Fey, Leonard, Fey, & O'Connor, 1978; Leonard, Camarata, Rowan, & Chapman, 1982; Rom & Bliss, 1981). In the prelinguistic and early stages of language development, children with autism use a predominance of communicative acts to regulate other's behavior and few or no acts to engage in social interaction and to reference joint attention, compared to normally developing children at the same language stage (Wetherby, 1986; Wetherby & Prutting, 1984; Wetherby, Yonclas, & Bryan, 1989). A similar pattern was noted in institutionalized adolescents who were profoundly mentally retarded and nonverbal (Cirrin & Rowland, 1985). These findings indicate the importance of examining the communicative functions expressed by children at prelinguistic or early language stages.

By definition, children with communicative impairments show delays or differences in their acquisition of communicative means. Children with specific language impairments and autism have been found to use fewer vocalizations and more gestures to express intentions during the prelinguistic and early one-word stage, compared to language-age matched normally developing children (Rowan, Leonard, Chapman, & Weiss, 1983; Snyder, 1978; Wetherby & Prutting, 1984; Wetherby, Prizant, & Kublin, 1989). There have been few investigations of the quality of prelinguistic communicative vocalizations used by children with communicative impairments. Wetherby and associates (1989) found that the vocalizations of children with specific language impairments and autism contained few consonants. Thus, reliance on gestures and a limited consonantal repertoire appear to be typical patterns of children with communicative impairments, and should be apparent during early communication development.

SYMBOLIC DEVELOPMENT IN NORMALLY DEVELOPING CHILDREN

In normal development, preverbal intentional communication contributes to the emergence of symbols, which can be seen in a child's use of language and play (Bates, 1979). Much attention has been given to the relationship between language and play. Fewell and Kaminski (1988) defined *play* as "a spontaneous activity that involves interaction with objects in a pleasurable manner" (p. 147). The literature on early childhood development has described growth in play skills along cognitive and social dimensions (Mindes, 1982; Ruben, 1977; Ruben, Watson, & Jambor, 1978, Smilansky, 1978). This characterization of the cognitive and social aspects of play underscores the interdependence of language and play. Level of play reflects advances in cognition that may also enhance language acquisition, and participation in play activities provides a social context for cognitive and language development.

A cognitive perspective on play considers the developmental progression in level of play from exploratory actions on objects to representational thought. Piaget (1962) distinguished between symbolic and constructive play, based on the classification of Buhler (1935). *Symbolic play* is make-believe play in which the child uses one object to stand for or represent an absent object. Pretend objects may range in size from macrospheric (i.e., realistic size that the child shares with others, such as large dolls and grooming utensils, plastic food, housekeeping equipment, costumes and dress-up clothes) to microspheric (i.e., miniature relative to the child, such as small people figures, zoo and farm animals, small playhouses and furniture, small vehicles) (Erikson, 1963). Development in symbolic play progresses along three dimensions:

1. *decontextualization,* which is the ability to produce an action scheme using objects that are not realistic or in a different context than the action usually occurs;
2. *decentration,* which is the ability to use others as agents and recipients of actions;
3. *sequential organization,* which is the ability to organize action schemes in sequence (Fewell & Kaminski, 1988; Westby, 1988).

The development of symbolic play in the preschool years culminates in the ability to participate in sociodramatic play in which the child takes on the role of someone else and elaborates on a theme in cooperation with at least one other player (Smilansky, 1968). Smilansky pointed out that sociodramatic play is reliant on language in that verbalizations are used to take on make-believe roles, to change the identity of objects, to substitute for actions, to describe pretend situations, and to cooperate with other players.

Constructive play is the systematic manipulation of materials to create a product. Materials used in constructive play may range from *fluid* (e.g., water, finger paint, dry sand, easel paint, clay, markers, crayon) to *structured* (e.g., unit blocks, interlocking blocks, paste and paper, string and beads, form boards, puzzles) (Levy, Schaefer, & Phelps, 1986; Wolfgang, Mackender, & Wolfgang, 1981). Buhler (1935) described constructive play as children's "work" that is not complete until the product is finished and suggested that the "work attitude" that children learn in their play is important for achievement in school. Piaget (1962) pointed out that there is not a clear boundary between symbolic and constructive play; for example, a child can build an elaborate house out of blocks, which involves constructive play, and then act out a scenario about a family living in the house, which involves symbolic play. During the sensorimotor period in the first two years, children develop the ability to use objects in a functional manner, in combination with other objects, and in planned sequences. These achievements lead to representational levels of symbolic and constructive play during the preoperational period.

The relationship between cognitive advances in play and language has been studied in both symbolic and constructive play. In normal development, achievements in language have been found to parallel those in symbolic play (McCune–Nicolich & Carroll, 1981; Shore, O'Connell, & Bates,

1984; Wolf & Gardner, 1981). For example, as children begin to produce single words they use single action schemes in play. As they move to the use of word combinations, they display multiple action schemes in play. However, by 28 months of age, language has been found to surpass play in combinatorial capacity (Shore et al., 1984). Similar developmental relationships have been explored in studies of constructive play and language. Parallels between linguistic rules and strategies used in constructive play have been identified with materials including seriated nesting cups (Greenfield, Nelson, & Saltzman, 1972; Goodson & Greenfield, 1975), block building (Case & Khanna, 1981; Greenfield, 1978; Shore, 1986; Wolf & Gardner, 1981), and drawing (Greenfield, 1978; Wolf & Gardner, 1981). These findings in symbolic and constructive play have been interpreted as reflecting structural parallels in a combinatorial capacity across linguistic and nonlinguistic domains (Greenfield, 1978; Shore, 1986; Shore et al., 1984).

Play development has also been characterized by the degree of social participation among children. Parten (1932) described the following six sequential stages of social participation: unoccupied behavior, onlooker behavior, solitary play, parallel play, associative play, and cooperative play, which are widely used as a measure of social maturity of play. Rubin and colleagues have developed a nested play scale that rates cognitive level of play (i.e., exploratory, constructive, symbolic) for each of Parten's categories of social participation (Rubin, 1976; Rubin, Maioni, & Hornung, 1976; Rubin et al., 1978). In studying the play behavior of normally developing children from 3 to 5 years of age, Rubin and colleagues found that the amount of time spent in associative and cooperative play increased whereas time spent in parallel play decreased with advancing age. However, the amount of solitary play that was constructive or symbolic increased with age while solitary exploratory play decreased. They concluded that large amounts of time spent in parallel play indicated social immaturity but that the amount of time spent in Parten's first three categories of play (i.e., unoccupied behavior, onlooker behavior, and solitary play) did not correspond with sophistication of play behavior. The difference is that in parallel play the child wants to play with other children but may lack the social skills to engage in play with others; whereas in unoccupied behavior, onlooker behavior, and solitary play a child may be choosing to play alone and may be productive during that time with constructive or symbolic play activities. Additionally, they indicated that the use of a nested play scale helped to distinguish between the quality of individual and group play in preschool- and kindergarten-age children.

DIFFERENCES IN SYMBOLIC DEVELOPMENT IN CHILDREN WITH COMMUNICATIVE IMPAIRMENTS

Children who have communicative impairments may also have impairments in other aspects of symbolic development. Children with developmental delays have been found to display less sociodramatic play than peers of the same age who are not handicapped (Guralnick & Groom, 1988; Mindes, 1982). Performance in symbolic play of young children with specific language impairments has been found to be deficient compared to normally developing children matched for chronologic age but commensurate with or higher than normally developing children matched for language age (Terrell, Schwartz, Prelock, & Messick, 1984; Terrell & Schwartz, 1988). A large number of research studies have demonstrated that children with autism show significant deficits in symbolic play (Dawson & Adams, 1984; Sigman & Ungerer, 1984; Wetherby & Prutting, 1984; Wing, Gould, Yeates, & Brierly, 1977). Compared to normally developing children matched for language age, children with autism have been found to perform at lower levels on symbolic play but at higher levels on combinatorial play (i.e., combining objects in ordinal relations, which is an aspect of constructive play) (Wetherby, Prizant, & Kublin, 1989; Wetherby & Prutting, 1984). This is presumably because of the greater social demands of symbolic play compared to combinatorial play.

Curtiss, Yamada, and Fromkin (1979) demonstrated the dissociation of grammar and cognition in children with mental retardation by providing evidence that some of these children had a grammar that was more advanced than their level of nonverbal combinatorial play abilities and vice versa. These findings indicate that symbolic play, constructive play, and language may not develop in synchrony in children with developmental disorders and highlight the importance of examining a child's symbolic abilities across domains. Wetherby and Prizant (in press) have suggested that comparing a child's ability to use symbols in language with his or her level of symbolic versus constructive play provides important information that contributes to the early identification of a communication impairment along a continuum of more specific language delays to more pervasive social-communicative impairments.

Studies of the quality of social participation displayed by preschool children with handicaps have found less group play (i.e., associative and cooperative play combined) than is displayed by children of the same age who are developing normally (Guralnick & Groom, 1988; Mindes, 1982). The limited amount of group play may be related to the lower level of symbolic play displayed by these subjects. This is supported by the findings of Kohl, Beckman, and Swenson–Pierce (1984) who found that social interaction with peers increased as cognitive level of play increased. In comparing play behavior in integrated versus segregated preschool settings, Guralnick and colleagues (Guralnick, 1981; Guralnick & Groom, 1988) demonstrated that children with both mild and severe delays in overall development display a higher rate of social interaction and a higher level of play in integrated settings. Rate of social interaction during play in integrated preschool settings also has been found to be related to the types of materials available (Stoneman, Cantrell, & Hoover–Dempsey, 1983). Play materials that necessitated cooperation among children (e.g., house play, vehicle play) were found to promote social interaction. Thus, in evaluating the play of children with communicative impairments, it is important for the language clinician to consider a variety of factors that may influence the social and cognitive level of play of children with handicaps, including the availability of nonhandicapped peers and interactive play materials.

PROPOSED MODEL OF ASSESSMENT

Over the past 10 years, Barry Prizant and I have been developing a framework for assessing the communicative, social-affective, and symbolic abilities of developmentally young children. This work culminated in the *Communication and Symbolic Behavior Scales* (CSBS) (Wetherby & Prizant, 1990). The CSBS is an assessment instrument designed to examine the communicative, social/affective, and symbolic abilities of children whose functional communication abilities range from prelinguistic intentional communication to early stages of language acquisition (i.e., between 8 months and 2 years in communication and language). The two major purposes of this assessment instrument are (a) the early identification of children with communication impairments and (b) the establishment of a communicative and symbolic profile to provide directions for further assessment, to plan intervention goals, and to chart changes in these abilities over time.

The procedures used in the CSBS originally were conceived as informal procedures to sample communication abilities of autistic children at preverbal and early verbal stages (Wetherby & Prutting, 1984). The need for communication sampling procedures arose from the limited utility of the formal language and communication measures that were available. What was needed was a means to gather information about children's abilities in spontaneous communicative interactions that was more efficient than naturalistic observations. Of particular concern was providing ample opportunity for the child to initiate communication without relying on the child's comprehension of or compliance with verbal instructions. The CSBS sampling procedures are, in part, an expansion and refinement of the procedures described by Wetherby and Prutting (1984) and Wetherby and colleagues (1988).

The CSBS uses a standard but flexible format for gathering data through a variety of procedures. The sampling procedures enable the examiner to engage the parent as an interactant for the direct assessment with the child and as an informant for the caregiver questionnaire. The sampling procedures allow for direct assessment of children using a continuum from structured to unstructured contexts. Rather than setting up discrete trials with expected responses, the sampling procedures resemble natural ongoing adult-child interactions and provide opportunities for use of a variety of communicative behaviors. The communication sample begins with the presentation of a series of communicative temptations, which are structured situations that entice child-initiated communicative behavior and are set up nonverbally. Opportunities to use repair strategies are provided systematically. The communication sample is completed in a less structured book sharing context. The communication sample is followed by probes of symbolic play, language comprehension, and combinatorial play. The caregiver and examiner are instructed to use a facilitative interaction style by following the child's lead and to avoid asking the child questions or telling the child what to do.

Behaviors collected in the sample are rated along a number of parameters and are converted to scores on 20 five-point rating scales of communicative and symbolic behaviors. Seven cluster scores are derived from the 20 scales:

1. Communicative functions
2. Communicative means—gestural
3. Communicative means—vocal
4. Reciprocity
5. Social/affective signalling
6. Verbal symbolic behavior
7. Nonverbal symbolic behavior

Definitions of each of the 20 scales are provided in Table 9–1.

The growing body of literature on developmental pragmatics provided the theoretical constructs from which the scales were derived. Determination of the 20 scales was based on pilot studies of the CSBS with normally developing and communicatively impaired children (Wetherby, Prizant, & Kublin, 1989). The scales included on the CSBS were selected because they were able to differentiate children developing normally, children with specific language impairments, and children with more pervasive social communicative impairments. It is expected that the scales will continue to be refined after national field-testing and further research investigations.

The scales were designed so that children who are developing normally would achieve a score close to the highest point (5) on the communication scales (i.e., scales 1–16) by 18 months, and close to the highest point (5) on the symbolic scales (i.e., scales 17–20) by 24 months.

CASE PRESENTATIONS

In order to demonstrate how the CSBS can be used to generate profiles in young children, three clinical vignettes of children with communicative impairments will be presented. These include one child with a specific lan-

Table 9–1. Definitions of the communication and symbolic parameters measured on the *Communication and Symbolic Behavior Scales.* Adapted from Wetherby and Prizant (1990)

Communicative Functions

1. *Range of Function:* The variety of specific purposes for which a child communicates (e.g., request object, protest, call, show off, comment).
2. *Behavioral Regulation:* Communicative acts used to regulate the behavior of another person to obtain or restrict an environmental goal.
3. *Joint Attention:* Communicative acts used to direct another's attention to an object, event, or a topic of a communicative act.

Communicative Means-Gestural

4. *Conventional Gestures:* Gestural communicative acts whose meaning is shared by a general community, including giving, showing, pushing away, open-hand reaching, pointing, waving, nodding head, and shaking head.
5. *Distal Gestures:* Gestural communicative acts in which the child's hand does not touch a person or object (e.g., open-hand reaching, pointing at a distance, waving).
6. *Coordination of Gesture and Vocal Acts:* Communicative acts that are composed of a gesture and a vocalization produced simultaneously or overlapping in time.

Communicative Means—Vocal

7. *Isolated Vocal Acts:* Transcribable vowels or vowel plus consonant combinations that are used as a communicative act and are not accompanied by a gesture.
8. *Inventory of Consonants:* The total number of different consonants produced as part of communicative acts.
9. *Syllable Shape:* Vocal communicative acts that are transcribable vowel plus consonant combinations (i.e., syllables must contain at least one consonant).
10. *Multisyllables:* Vocal communicative acts that contain two or more syllables; syllables may be a vowel only or a vowel plus consonant combination.

Reciprocity

11. *Discourse Structure—Respondent Acts:* Communicative acts that are in response to the adult's conventional gesture or speech.
12. *Rate:* The frequency of communicative acts displayed per minute.
13. *Repair Strategies:* Persistence in communication measured by repetition and/or modification of a previous communicative act when a goal is not achieved.

Social/Affective Signalling

14. *Gaze Shifts:* Alternating eye gaze between a person and an object and back; it may be either a person-object-person or an object-person-object gaze shift.
15. *Positive Affect with Eye Gaze:* Clear facial expressions of pleasure or excitement, which may or may not be accompanied by a vocalization, that are directed toward the adult with eye gaze.

Social/Affective Signalling *(continued)*

16. *Episodes of Negative Affect:* Clear vocal expressions of distress or frustration that commence when the vocalization begins and continue until the child has recovered and has displayed a neutral or positive affect.

Verbal Symbolic Behavior

17. *Expressive Language:* A measure of the number of different words used (i.e., spoken or signed) and the number of multiword combinations produced; a word or word approximation must be used to refer to a specific object, action or attribute and only that word class.
18. *Language Comprehension:* A measure of comprehension of contextual cues, single words, and multiword utterances.

Nonverbal Symbolic Behavior

19. *Symbolic Play:* A measure of the child's use of agents and actions with objects in pretend play.
20. *Combinatorial Play:* A measure of the child's ability to use one object in combination with another object or group of objects to construct a product (e.g., a tower).

---

guage impairment, one child with more general developmental delays, and one child with autism (APA, 1987). These three children were selected to illustrate the communicative and symbolic profiles of children with and without social impairments. The names used are fictitious. The results of the CSBS for these three children were compared to those of children developing normally at the same language stage, which are available from preliminary field testing (Wetherby & Prizant, 1990). The profiles of these three children are illustrated in Figure 9–2. A filled circle indicates that they achieved a score at least 1 point above normally developing children at the same language stage, a half-filled circle indicates a score within 1 point of normally developing children, and an unfilled circle indicates a score at least 1 point below normally developing children.

CASE 1

The first case portrays the profile of a child who shows a specific impairment in language, with other aspects of cognitive and social development relatively spared. Alex, a 2-year-5-month-old white male, was an only child and lived with both parents. He was referred for a speech/language evaluation by his pediatrician because of concerns about his expressive language

Communication and Symbolic Behavior Scales

1990, Amy M. Wetherby and Barry M. Prizant

	Alex	Alan	Jamie
Communicative Functions			
1. Range of Functions	◖	◖	○
2. Behavioral Regulation	◖	◖	◖
3. Joint Attention	◖	◖	○
Communicative Means: Gestural			
4. Conventional Gestures	●	◖	○
5. Distal Gestures	●	●	○
6. Coordination of Gesture and Vocal Act	◖	◖	◖
Communicative Means: Vocal			
7. Isolated Vocal Acts	○	●	○
8. Inventory of Consonants	○	◖	◖
9. Syllable Shape	○	◖	◖
10. Multisyllables	◖	◖	◖
Reciprocity			
11. Discourse Structure	●	◖	◖
12. Rate	●	●	○
13. Repair Strategies	●	◖	◖
Social/Affective Signalling			
14. Gaze Shifts	◖	◖	○
15. Positive Affect	◖	○	○
16. Negative Affect	◖	◖	○
Verbal Symbolic Behavior			
17. Expressive Language	◖	◖	◖
18. Language Comprehension	●	◖	○
Nonverbal Symbolic Behavior			
19. Symbolic Play	●	○	○
20. Combinatorial Play	◖	○	●

Key

● *above normally developing children at same language stage*
◖ *commensurate with normally developing children at same language stage*
○ *below normally developing children at same language stage*

Figure 9–2. Results of the CSBS for three children with communicative impairments. A filled circle indicates that they achieved a score at least 1 point above normally developing children at the same language stage, a half-filled circle indicates a score within 1 point of normally developing children, and an unfilled circle indicates a score at least 1 point below normally developing children.

development. Both parents were present during the evaluation. His parents reported no unusual events in his medical and developmental history. According to his mother, development in all other areas except speech and language was progressing normally. Alex began using single words at 12 months of age but by 18 months of age his vocabulary was limited to three words. Alex stayed at home with his mother during the day and had minimal opportunity to interact with other children.

Alex's results on the CSBS are displayed in the first column of Figure 9–2 in comparison to normally developing children who were 13 to 18 months of age and functioning in the one-word stage. Alex communicated for a full range of communicative functions, including requesting objects/actions, protesting, requesting a social routine, and commenting on objects/actions. The communicative means used by Alex included giving, showing, pointing, reaching, manipulating adult's hand, throwing, shaking his head, covering his face with his hands, using depictive gestures, and vocalizing. He used a variety of conventional gestures and many of his gestures were distal. He was able to coordinate gestures with vocalizations, but showed a striking lack of isolated vocal acts (i.e., vocal communicative acts that are not accompanied by gestures), which indicates that he relied on gestures to communicate. Many of his gestures were compound (e.g., pulling at the clinician's hand and then pointing to a jar he wanted open). His vocalizations consisted of isolated vowels, consonant-vowel combinations, and some extended jargon. He had a limited inventory of consonants but did not show any signs of a motor speech disorder (i.e., apraxia or dysarthria).

Alex was reciprocal in his communicative interactions. He responded to the adults' verbal and gestural communicative acts. His rate of communicating was 3.7 communicative acts per minute, which is typical of children in the multiword stage. He was able to persist when a goal was not obtained and to repair by repeating a previous act or by changing the act to clarify his message. His social/affective signalling was appropriate. He demonstrated good use of directed eye gaze, frequent gaze shifts, and appropriate positive affect. He showed minimal frustration or distress and no episodes of negative affect during the evaluation, although he did express displeasure by protesting.

Alex used approximations for the following words during the communication sample: mamma, daddy, gone, boom, uh-oh, balloon, bye bye, and no. His parents reported that he did not use any additional words at home. The limited size of his lexicon and his lack of intelligible word combinations indicate that he is functioning expressively in the one-word stage. He demonstrated comprehension of possessor-possessive utterances (e.g., point to mama's mouth, Alex's hair, baby's eyes), indicating comprehension of at least two-word combinations, which is beyond his expressive language level. With the symbolic play materials Alex demonstrated multiple related action schemes involving himself and a doll using grooming and feeding toy sets. For example, with the feeding set he pretended to prepare and to eat food by moving the pan as if to flip the pretend "food," pouring the "food" into a bowl, scooping the "food" with a spoon, and eating some "food." His level of symbolic play is typical of children in the preoperational period and exceeds his expressive language. With the combinatorial play materials he stacked 6 blocks and put on 5 rings without regard to order. The symbolic scales indicate that he is at a combinatorial level in language comprehension and symbolic play and shows a particular weakness in expressive language.

Alex's profile of communicative and symbolic abilities are characteristic of a child with a specific language and speech impairment. He shows deficits in phonetic inventory, syllable structure, lexicon, and sentence construction for his age. However, gestural communicative means, reciprocity, language comprehension, and play are advanced for his expressive language stage.

CASE 2

The second case depicts the profile of a child with general developmental delays. Alan was a 3-year-5-month-old white male who was living with his parents, grandparents, and 6-year-old sister. He was referred by his parents because of concerns about his language development. His mother was present during the evaluation. She reported that Alan had had trouble breathing for a brief period of time at birth but no other unusual events had occurred in his medical history. She indicated that he was delayed in motor development. He sat alone at about 7 months, stood up alone at about 32 months, and began walking at about 33 months. He had frequent middle ear infections and had pressure equalizing tubes inserted in his ears at 16 months. He began using single words at about 28 months. His mother indicated that his words had been primarily monosyllabic but that he began putting together strings of syllables which were not clear words about 2 weeks prior to the evaluation. The *Denver Developmental Screening Test* (Frankenburg & Dodds, 1969) was administered on the day of the evaluation and Alan failed at least two items in all four sectors tested: personal-social, fine motor-adaptive, language, and gross motor.

Alan had been attending full-time preschool since about 6 months of age. Prior to the evaluation he was observed at this preschool, which was using a developmental whole language and play curriulum and was an integrated program with less than 15% of the children having disabilities. During the observation he was generally passive and nonverbal. He wandered aimlessly, did not initiate interactions with peers, and did not engage in focused play. His preschool teacher indicated that his behavior during the observation was typical and requested recommendations on how to develop language and social interaction.

The results of the CSBS for Alan are presented in the second column of Figure 9–2 in comparison to normally developing children who were 19 to 24 months of age and functioning in the multiword stage. Alan communicated for a full range of communicative functions, including requesting objects/actions, protesting, requesting a social routine, showing off, and commenting on objects/actions. The communicative means used by Alan included giving, showing, pointing, reaching, and vocalizing. He displayed many distal gestures. He was able to coordinate gestures and vocalizations but also produced many isolated vocal communicative acts. His vocalizations consisted of monosyllabic and multisyllabic utterances with a large variety of consonants.

Alan displayed strengths in reciprocity. He responded to the speech and gestures of the adults during the communication sample giving the interaction a smooth flow of turn-taking. He displayed a very high rate of communicating, 5.0 communicative acts per minute, which is typical of children in the multiword stage. He was able to repair by repeating or changing a previous act to clarify the message. He demonstrated appropriate facial expression, eye gaze, and affect during the sample. Although he showed frequent positive affect, he showed a low frequency of positive affect directed toward the adults, measured in scale 15.

Alan's lexicon was greater than 15 words during the sample and he produced a few two-word utterances, suggesting that he is in the early multiword stage. He displayed frequent vocal imitation, some of which was used communicatively, which is typical of this language stage. He demonstrated comprehension of two-word possessor-possessive combinations. In contrast to his strengths in communication and language, he displayed limited play skills. When given the feeding toy set and a stuffed Kermit, he initially did not pretend with the materials but rather organized and stacked them. When told that Kermit was hungry and that he should feed Kermit, he displayed single action schemes (e.g., feeding Kermit with a spoon and a bottle). However, he did not display any sequences of pretend action schemes, which would be expected for his age and language level. With the combinatorial play materials he stacked 8 blocks but did not combine objects in order (i.e., stacking rings, nesting cups). His motor delays may have contributed to his relative weakness in play but cannot fully account for it because he displayed adequate manual dexterity to stack 8 blocks and to carry out pretend actions with the materials, as well as to form a variety of gestures.

Alan displayed communicative and language strengths during the CSBS evaluation that were not evident at his preschool. One possible explanation for this discrepancy is the difference between the social context at school and during the CSBS sample. He responded well to structured interactions with adults. However, at preschool, most of his opportunities to interact with peers were during unstructured play activities. In light of Alan's weakness in play, the cognitive demands of play may have limited his social participation in play with peers.

CASE 3

The third case exemplifies how the limited social abilities of this child affect his communication, social/affective, and symbolic profile, which is typical of children with autism. Jamie, a 4-year-5-month-old white male, was an only child and lived with both parents. According to his mother, who was present during the evaluation, he had a normal birth and developmental history and had no unusual accidents or illnesses. He had been diagnosed autistic by a psychologist and meets the criterion of DSM III-R (APA, 1987), which includes impairments in social interaction, impairments in verbal and nonverbal communication, and a restricted repertoire of activities and interests. He was echolalic and had a spontaneous vocabulary of over 50 words according to his mother. However, she expressed concern because, although he had a large vocabulary, she indicated that he did not "use words in sentences for conversation."

Jamie had been attending a self-contained preschool classroom for children with emotional handicaps for the past 3 months. He was referred for evaluation by his classroom teacher who was concerned about his communication abilities. Prior to the evaluation he was observed at his preschool. He did not initiate or respond to interactions with peers. He was able to respond to routine questions about the date and weather when asked by his teacher during circle time. During unstructured center time Jamie played with blocks and looked at books.

The results of the CSBS for Jamie are presented in the third column of Figure 9–2 in comparison to normally developing children who were 19 to 24 months of age and functioning in the multiword stage. Jamie used gestures and vocalizations to communicate but initated a very limited range of communicative functions. During the communication sample he communicated only behavioral regulation functions (i.e., to request objects/actions and protest) and did not use more social functions of communication. He was limited in his use of conventional and distal gestures. The gestures that he used included giving, reaching, manipulating an adult's hand, banging on objects, and aggression (e.g., squeezing his mother's arm). Although he had a limited repertoire of gestures, his reliance on gestures was apparent in his minimal use of isolated vocal acts. His vocalizations consisted of multisyllabic utterances and many words and phrases. He used a large number of different consonants and produced clearly articulated words and sentences. His verbalizations were primarily echolalic, both immediate and delayed. An example of his immediate echolalia was using the word "sit" to request more Cheerios after his mother had told him to "sit down." An example of his delayed echolalia was the phrase "let me taste your wares" which he repeated from a nursery rhyme. He produced this phrase with negative intonational affect to request objects or assistance when he was frustrated.

Jamie had good turn-taking skills during the communication sample, as seen in his frequency of respondent acts. He displayed a rate of 1.8 communicative acts per minute, which is relatively low for his language stage. Jamie demonstrated the ability to use repair strategies when his goal was not met by repeating or modifying a particular communicative act. However, at times of more extreme frustration, his repairs became more diffuse rather than specific. For example, when a request for assistance was not responded to, Jamie began crying, whining, and/or banging the object that he needed assistance with. On one occasion his frustration grew to the point that he squeezed his mother's arm to urge her to open a jar. Jamie displayed minimal positive affect during the sample and a few episodes of negative affect when he was frustrated about not achieving his goal. He showed minimal directed eye gaze and no gaze shifts during the communication sample. On two occasions during the evaluation it appeared that he hurt himself but he did not display negative affect and did not seek comfort. One time he tripped and fell on the rug, and the other time he bit his tongue while chewing a snack.

Jamie's level of symbolic development was examined in language and play. In addition to his echolalia, Jamie used a few words spontaneously (e.g., "microphone" to request this object). He also used some word combinations imitatively and spontaneously (e.g., hold it, you hold it, hold this, open bubbles, open it, open it mommy). Even though Jamie used some phrases of 3 to 6 words in length, most of these were "chunks" learned as a whole through imitation. Jamie did not appear to know the individual meanings of the words in these longer phrases (e.g., "let me taste your wares"), and the whole phrase appeared to be equivalent to one word or morpheme for Jamie. Thus, it appears that Jamie was functioning at an early multiword stage of expressive language development. Jamie demonstrated comprehension of single words (i.e., some agents and body parts) but did not respond to instructions containing two-word combinations.

Jamie showed a striking discrepancy between his levels of symbolic and combinatorial play. He demonstrated mostly exploratory actions toward objects during the symbolic play sample. He did imitate feeding a stuffed animal with a spoon following the clinician's model of this action scheme but did not display any action schemes spontaneously. This indicated a deficit in symbolic play compared to his language level. In contrast, he was able to combine up to 5 objects in order during the combinatorial play probe; he stacked 5 rings in order and nested 6 seriated cups with 4 in order.

The communicative, social/affective, and symbolic profile displayed by Jamie is characteristic of a child with a pervasive social impairment with nonsocial cognitive skills relatively spared. The effects of his social impairment were seen in his failure to use communication to engage in social interaction and reference joint attention, his minimal use of conventional and distal gestures, his minimal use of social/affective signalling, and his limited symbolic play skills. His nonsocial cognitive strengths were seen in his use of communication to regulate behavior, his ability to persist and repair, and his combinatorial play skills. In spite of his social impairment, he showed relative strengths in structural aspects of language, including vocal production, vocabulary, and sentence construction.

EXPLANATORY HYPOTHESES FOR THE PRAGMATIC PROFILES

The interaction vis-a-vis social knowledge, cognition, and language in normal development has been highlighted in this chapter. The interdependence of cognitive and social knowledge is reflected in the recent development of the field of social cognition, which refers to the way individuals perceive, interact with, and organize knowledge about people (Sherrod & Lamb, 1981). Although social, cognitive, and linguistic domains normally develop in synchrony, the clinical vignettes of the three communicatively impaired children that were presented provide evidence of a dissociation between social cognition and language in these children. Alex (Case 1) showed impaired expressive language with social and other aspects of symbolic development relatively spared. Alan (Case 2) showed impaired play skills with more advanced abilities in language and communication, at least during interactions with adults. Jamie (Case 3) showed impaired social skills that affected communicative functions, social-affective signalling, use of conventional gestures and meanings for words, and symbolic play. These skills rely on social cognition and are learned in a social context. Jamie's ability to use communication for behavior regulation, to acquire structural aspects of language, and to develop combinatorial play skills was relatively spared. The dissociation of social cognition and language is evidenced by the relative strengths and weaknesses displayed by Case 1 and Case 3.

Individual variation in normal language acquisition may help to explain the dissociation of social cognition and language abilities seen in these children with communicative impairments. The study of normal language acquisition in children has demonstrated individual variation in language learning styles or strategies (Bates, Bretherton, & Snyder, 1988; Nelson, 1981). In characterizing the nature of this variation, a number of dichotomies in language learning strategies have been identified, such as referential/expressive children (Nelson, 1973), intonation/word babies (Dore, 1974), nominal/pronominal children (Bloom, Hood, & Lightbown, 1974), and analytic/gestalt learners (Peters, 1983). Bates (1979) proposed that variations in the relative timing of the emergence of cognitive-social component skills may lead to differences in language-learning strategies. In a recent review of the literature on individual differences, Bates and colleagues (1988) concluded that from first words to grammar, the development of semantics, morphology, syntax, and phonology are all paced by the same underlying mechanism that leads to one style over the other. Differences in language-learning strategies have been explained by internal and external factors. Internal factors that have been identified include gender, age at first words, temperament, cognitive style, and cerebral hemispheric organization; external factors include birth order, maternal style and input, and socioeconomic level (Bates et al., 1988; Furrow & Nelson, 1984; McCabe, 1989; Nelson, 1985). Thus, the child's individual makeup, the language learning environment's influence on the child, or the interaction of these potential sources may contribute to individual variation. The result is heterogeneity in the strategies used by normally developing children to acquire language.

The process of heterochrony (i.e., variation in time of emergence and rate of development) may account for the individual variation in children with normal language development as well as deviation from normal development. Although this concept has been used to account for changes in phylogeny, it may also be applied to ontogenetic changes (Bates, 1979; Wetherby & Prutting, 1984). The profiles of the three children with communicative impairments presented in this chapter suggest heterochrony in development between linguistic and social cognitive domains. Variations in timing at early stages in ontogeny may have developmental consequences that are cumulative and potentially deleterious. The relative proportions of component skills available at varying times in development may influence the child's communicative and symbolic profile. Slight variations in the developmental timing of individual components may result in pervasive differences in later stages, based on the interaction of the components available at particular times in development. The particular combination of skills available to a child may lead to a distinct interaction with the caregiving environment and contribute to the specific profile of abilities and limitations of the individual child. Heterochrony may be the mechanism that operates to produce discrepancies in a child's profile and may be caused by normal variation in or disruption of the precise orchestration of events that unfold during neural maturation (Wetherby, 1985).

The particular combination of skills and experiences available to a child with communicative impairments is not seen at any point in normal development and leads to distinct patterns and strategies for communicating because of the interplay among the available components and interaction with the caregiving environment. However, the child's skills within specific domains may follow normal developmental progressions. The combination of skills available to the child may be better understood if considered from a developmental perspective (Prizant & Wetherby, 1989). Simply identifying a child's deficiencies is insufficient in clinical practice. A developmental pragmatics perspective underscores the importance of profiling the child's abilities and limitations across social, cognitive, and linguistic domains.

Rees (1982) suggested two possible interpretations of the role of pragmatics in language development. First, the development of pragmatics may be viewed as a mastery of skills related to conversational competence. Second, in a broader interpretation, pragmatics may be viewed as a more dynamic influence on language acquisition, "not only as a set of skills to be acquired but as motivating and explanatory factors for the acquisition of the language itself" (p. 8). A child's developing pragmatic abilities influence and are influenced by other areas of social, cognitive, and language development. The profiles of the three clinical cases presented do not support the view of pragmatics as merely an inventory of communication skills. Rather, they support Rees' broader interpretation of pragmatics as an influence on language acquisition, which is consistent with Prutting's (1982b) view of pragmatics as social competence. From a clinical perspective of developmental pragmatics, it is necessary to consider a child's abilities and limitations in the social domain as well as the child's proficiency in learning in a social context.

IMPLICATIONS FOR INTERVENTION

Professionals have come a long way from the traditional practice of waiting to evaluate a child for a language impairment until that child is talking. Current theories on child language acquisition, reviewed earlier in this chapter, indicate that a great deal of diagnostic information can be obtained from a child at preverbal or emerging language stages. Procedures for sampling communication and symbolic abilities in children who are not yet talking or are at early language stages have been described in this chapter. These sampling procedures resemble natural adult-child interactions and provide an opportunity for the caregiver and clinician to observe the child's behaviors together. The sample provides the basis for generating a profile of the child's strengths and weaknesses and integrating information about social, communicative, and symbolic development.

Profiling a child's pragmatic abilities entails examining the effect of a child's social skills on communicative competence and the child's ability to learn and use language in a social context. Three case examples of children with communicative impairments, one without social impairments and two with varying degrees of social impairments, were presented to illustrate the influence of social impairments on a child's pragmatic profile. A child's profile of communication, social/affective, and symbolic abilities can contribute to the early identification of a language impairment as well as profile guidelines for the design of an early intervention program (Wetherby & Prizant, in press).

The CSBS provides a profile of the child's strengths and weaknesses in communicative and symbolic abilities that can be used for making decisions regarding the *content* of intervention. The child's particular strengths and weaknesses on the communication and symbolic parameters should be used to prioritize intervention goals. For example, a high priority goal for Jamie (Case 3) would be to develop social interaction and joint attention functions of communication. For children showing discrepancies in verbal and nonverbal symbolic levels, symbolic strengths may be used to enhance weaknesses. For Alex (Case 1) his strengths in play skills can be utilized to develop language by providing developmentally appropriate verbal models of language in reference to the action schemes he uses in symbolic play. For Alan (Case 2) his strength in language can be used to develop symbolic play by providing simple verbal scripts of appropriate developmental levels of play to focus and guide his actions.

The child's communicative behavior displayed during the different contexts utilized in the CSBS in comparison with less structured observations with significant others provides important information for designing the *context* of intervention. Intervention should provide contexts with an optimal degree of structure in the language-learning environment and adult "scaffolding" needed to foster successful interactions. For example, Alan (Case 2) showed a discrepancy between how communicative he was during structured interactions with adults and during unstructured activities with peers. Structured situations, such as communicative temptations, could be set up to foster communication with peers. Teaching symbolic play scripts to Alan and normally developing peers, as described by Goldstein and Strain (1988), may be used to foster social interactions during play. Intervention agents should plan activities with greater communicative demands in contexts of relative strengths. For example, Jamie (Case 3) showed strengths in structured turn-taking activities during the communicative temptations and combinatorial play activities. For Jamie, activities like these can be used as the context to develop social interaction with peers. Peers with normal skills can be taught to use strategies that will facilitate interaction with children who are communicatively impaired (Goldstein & Wickstrom, 1986; Kohler & Fowler, 1985).

Although the CSBS sampling procedures resemble natural adult-child interactions, the focus of this instrument is on profiling the child's strengths and weaknesses. Assessment of children at the younger stages of development should also include a measure of the quality of caregiver-child interactions. Dunst, Lowe, and Bartholomew (1990) have suggested that "caregiver social responsiveness to infant behavior is a major determinant of a child's acquisition of communicative competence" (p. 39). Having the caregiver present and participating in the CSBS assessment process may help the caregiver understand the child's developmental level and identify the child's communicative attempts. Additionally, this may be a first step toward improving the caregiver's responsiveness to the child's communicative initiations.

CONCLUDING COMMENTS

The process of heterochrony operated in phylogeny to produce the human capacity to use symbols and to form complex social relationships. In this chapter it has been suggested that heterochrony can also operate in ontogeny to produce individual variation in language-learning strategies as well as deviations from normal development. The issue of timing is critical in understanding children with communicative impairments because of the developmental interplay among component skills within and across social, cognitive, and linguistic domains. Minor variations in developmental timing in early stages of maturation may have major clinical manifestations. Profiling pragmatic abilities in a child with a communicative impairment provides information about how the child's deficits in specific aspects of development affect the child's communicative competence. The theoretical perspective espoused in this chapter supports the view of pragmatics as a factor contributing to the child's developing competence as a communicator.

ACKNOWLEDGMENTS

This chapter is an extension of theories developed in my dissertation, which was directed by Carol Prutting. Therefore, I would like to acknowledge the influence that she had on my knowledge of child language and on developing these ideas. I would also like to acknowledge Barry Prizant who has co-authored many papers on this topic with me and therefore has influenced the formulation of theories presented in this chapter.

REFERENCES

American Psychiatric Association. (1987). *Diagnostic and statistical manual of mental disorders* (3rd ed. Rev.). Washington, DC: American Psychiatric Association.

Bates, E. (1976). *Language and context: The acquisition of pragmatics.* New York: Academic Press.

Bates, E. (1979). *The emergence of symbols: Cognition and communication in infancy.* New York: Academic Press.

Bates, E., Bretherton, I., & Snyder, L. (1988). *From first words to grammar: Individual differences and dissociable mechanisms.* Cambridge, UK: Cambridge University Press.

Bates, E., O'Connell, B., & Shore, C. (1987). Language and communication in infancy. In J. Osofsky (Ed.), *Handbook of infant development* (pp. 149–203). New York: John Wiley and Sons.

Bates, E., & Snyder, L. (1987). The cognitive hypothesis in language development. In I. Uzgiris & J. Hunt (Eds.), *Infant performance and experience* (pp. 168–204). Chicago: University of Illinois Press.

Bloom, L., Hood, L., & Lightbown, P. (1974). Imitation in language development: If, when, and why. *Cognitive Psychology, 6,* 380–420.

Bloom, L., & Lahey, M. (1978). *Language development and language disorders*. New York: John Wiley and Sons.

Bruner, J. (1978). From communication to language: A psychological perspective. In I. Markova (Ed.), *The social context of language*. Chichester, UK: John Wiley and Sons.

Bruner, J. (1981). The social context of language acquisition. *Language and Communication, 1,* 155–178.

Buhler, C. (1935). *From birth to maturity: An outline of the psychological development of the child*. London: Lund Humphries.

Carpenter, R., Mastergeorge, A., & Coggins, T. (1983). The acquisition of communicative intentions in infants eight to fifteen months of age. *Language and Speech, 26,* 101–116.

Case, R., & Khanna, F. (1981). The missing links: Stages in children's progression from sensorimotor to logical thought. *New Directions for Child Development, 12,* 21–32.

Cirrin, F., & Rowland, C. (1985). Communicative assessment of nonverbal youths with severe/profound mental retardation. *Mental Retardation, 23,* 52–62.

Coggins, T., & Carpenter, R. (1981). The communicative intention inventory: A system for observing and coding children's early intentional communication. *Applied Psycholinguistics, 2,* 235–251.

Craig, H. (1983). Applications of pragmatic models for intervention. In T. Gallagher & C. Prutting (Eds.), *Pragmatic assessment and intervention issues in language* (pp. 101–128). San Diego, CA: College-Hill Press.

Cromer, R. (1976). The cognitive hypothesis of language acquisition and its implications for child language deficiency. In D. Morehead & A. Morehead (Eds.), *Normal and deficient child language*. Baltimore, MD: University Park Press.

Cromer, R. (1981). Reconceptualizing language acquisition and cognitive development. In R. Schiefelbusch & D. Bricker (Eds.), *Early language: Acquisition and intervention* (pp. 51–137). Baltimore, MD: University Park Press.

Cross, T. (1984). Habilitating the language-impaired child: Ideas from studies of parent-child interaction. *Topics in Language Disorders, 4*(4), 1–14.

Curtiss, S. (1981). Dissociations between language and cognition: Cases and implications. *Journal of Autism and Developmental Disorders, 11,* 15–30.

Curtiss, S., Yamada, J., & Fromkin, V. (1979). How independent is language? On the question of formal parallels between grammar and action. *UCLA Working Papers in Cognitive Linguistics, 1,* 131–157.

Dawson, G., & Adams, A. (1984). Imitation and social responsiveness in autistic children. *Journal of Abnormal Child Psychology, 12,* 209–226.

Dore, J. (1974). A pragmatic description of early language development. *Journal of Psycholinguistic Research, 3,* 343–350.

Dore, J. (1986). The development of conversational competence. In R. Scheifelbusch (Ed.), *Language competence: Assessment and intervention* (pp. 3–60). San Diego, CA: College-Hill Press.

Dunst, C., Lowe, L. W., & Bartholomew, P. C. (1990). Contingent social repsonsiveness, family ecology, and infant communicative competence. *National Student Speech Language Hearing Association Journal, 17,* 39–49.

Erikson, E. (1963). *Childhood and society* (2nd ed.). New York: W. W. Norton.

Fewell, R., & Kaminski, R. (1988). Play skills development and instruction for young children with handicaps. In S. Odom & M. Karnes (Eds.), *Early intervention for infants and children with handicaps* (pp. 145–158). Baltimore, MD: Paul H. Brookes.

Fey, M., Leonard, L., Fey, S., & O'Connor, K. (1978). *The intent to communicate in language-impaired children*. Paper presented at the Third Annual Boston University Conference on Language Development, Boston, MA.

Frankenburg, W., & Dodds, J. (1969). *Denver developmental screening test.* Denver: University of Colorado Medical Center.

Furrow, D., & Nelson, K. (1984). Environmental correlates of individual differences in language acquisition. *Journal of Child Language, 11,* 523–534.

Goldin–Meadow, S., Seligman, M., & Gelman, R. (1976). Language in the two-year-old. *Cognition, 4,* 189–202.

Goldstein, H., & Strain, P. S. (1989). Peers as communication intervention agents: Some new strategies and research findings. *Topics in Language Disorders, 9*(1) 44–57.

Goldstein, H., & Wickstrom, S. (1986). Peer intervention effects on communicative interaction among handicapped and nonhandicapped preschoolers. *Journal of Applied Behavior Analysis, 19,* 209–214.

Goodson, B. D., & Greenfield, P. M. (1975). The search for structural principles in children's manipulative play: A parallel with linguistic development. *Child Development, 46,* 734–746.

Gould, S. J. (1977). *Ever since Darwin: Reflections in natural history.* New York: W. W. Norton.

Gould, S. J. (1985, December). The most compelling pelvis since Elvis. *Discover Magazine,* pp. 54–58.

Greenfield, P. (1978). Structural parallels between language and action in development. In A. Lock (Ed.), *Action, gesture, and symbol* (pp. 415–445). London: Academic Press.

Greenfield, P. M., Nelson, K., & Saltzman, E. (1972). The development of rulebound strategies for manipulating seriated cups: A parallel between action and grammar. *Cognitive Psychology, 3,* 291–310.

Guralnick, M. J. (1981). The social behavior of preschool children at different developmental levels: Effects of group composition. *Journal of Experimental Child Psychology, 31,* 115–130.

Guralnick, M. J., & Groom, J. M. (1988). Peer interactions in mainstreamed and specialized classrooms: A comparative analysis. *Exceptional Children, 54,* 415–425.

Harding, C., & Golinkoff, R. (1979). The origins of intentional vocalizations in prelinguistic infants. *Child Development, 50,* 33–40.

Ingram, D. (1978). Sensori-motor intelligence and language development. In A. Lock (Ed.), *Action, gesture, and symbol* (pp. 261–290). London: Academic Press.

Kent, R., & Bauer, H. (1985). Vocalizations of one-year-olds. *Journal of Child Language, 12,* 491–526.

Kohl, F. L., Beckman, P. J., & Swenson–Pierce, A. (1984). The effects of directed play on functional toy use and interaction of handicapped preschoolers. *Journal of the Division of Early Childhood, 8,* 114–118.

Kohler, F. W., & Fowler, S. A. (1985). Training prosocial behaviors to young children: An analysis of reciprocity with untrained peers. *Journal of Applied Behavior Analysis, 18,* 187–200.

Leonard, L. (1978). Cognitive factors in early linguistic development. In R. Schiefelbusch (Ed.), *Bases of language intervention.* Baltimore, MD: University Park Press.

Leonard, L., Camarata, S., Rowan, L., & Chapman, K. (1982). The communicative functions of lexical usage by language impaired children. *Applied Psycholinguistics, 3,* 109–127.

Levy, A., Schaefer, L., & Phelps, P. (1986). Enhancing the language abilities of 3- and 4-year-old children through planned sociodramatic play. *Early Childhood Research Quarterly, 1,* 133–140.

MacDonald, J. D. (1985). Language through conversation: A model for intervention with language-delayed persons. In S. Warren & A. Rogers–Warren (Eds.), *Teach-*

ing functional language: Generalization and maintenance of language skills (pp. 89–122). Baltimore, MD: University Park Press.

McCabe, A. (1989). Differential language learning styles in young children: The importance of context. *Developmental Review, 9,* 1–20.

McCune–Nicolich, L., & Carroll, S. (1981). Development of symbolic play: Implications for the language specialist. *Topics in Language Disorders, 2*(1), 1–15.

McLean, J., & Snyder–McLean, L. (1978). *A transactional approach to early language training.* Columbus, OH: Charles E. Merrill.

Mindes, G. (1982). Social and cognitive aspects of play in young handicapped children. *Topics of Early Childhood Special Education, 2*(3), 39–52.

Nelson, K. (1973). Structure and strategy in learning to talk. *Monographs of the Society for Research and Child Development, 38* (Serial No. 149).

Nelson, K. (1981). Individual differences in language development: Implications for development and language. *Developmental Psychology, 17,* 170–187.

Nelson, K. (1985). *Making sense: The acquisition of share meaning.* Orlando, FL: Academic Press.

Newhoff, M., & Browning, J. (1983). Interactional variation: A view from the language-disordered child's world. *Topics in Language Disorders, 4*(1), 49–60.

Parten, M. B. (1932). Social participation among preschool children. *Journal of Abnormal and Social Psychology, 27,* 243–269.

Peters, A. (1983). *The units of language acquisition.* Cambridge, UK: Cambridge University Press.

Piaget, J. (1952). *The origins of intelligence in children.* New York: Basic Books.

Piaget, J. (1962). *Play, dreams and imitation in childhood.* New York: W. W. Norton.

Prizant, B., & Wetherby, A. (1988). Providing services to children with autism (0–2) and their families. *Topics in Language Disorders, 9*(1), 1–23.

Prizant, B., & Wetherby, A. (1989). Enhancing language and communication in autism: From theory to practice. In G. Dawson (Ed.), *Autism: Nature, diagnosis, and treatment* (pp. 282–309). New York: Guilford Press.

Prizant, B., & Wetherby, A. (1990). Toward an integrated view of early language, communication and socioemotional development. *Topics in Language Disorders, 10,* 1–16.

Prutting, C. (1979). Process: The action of moving forward progressively from one point to another on the way to completion. *Journal of Speech and Hearing Disorders, 47,* 123–134.

Prutting, C. (1982a). Infans—"(one) unable to speak." In J. Irwin (Ed.), *Pragmatics: The role in language development* (pp. 15–27). LaVerne, CA: Fox Point Publishing.

Prutting, C. (1982b). Pragmatics as social competence. *Journal of Speech and Hearing Disorders, 47,* 123–134.

Prutting, C., & Kirchner, D. (1987). A clinical appraisal of the pragmatic aspects of language. *Journal of Speech and Hearing Disorders, 52,* 105–119.

Rees, N. (1982). An overview of pragmatics or what is in the box? In J. Irwin (Ed.), *Pragmatics: The role in language development* (pp. 1–13). LaVerne, CA: Fox Point Publishing.

Rice, M. (1983). Contemporary accounts of the cognition/language relationship: Implications for speech-language clinicians. *Journal of Speech and Hearing Disorders, 48,* 347–359.

Rom, A., & Bliss, L. (1981). A comparison of verbal communicative skills of language impaired and normal speaking children. *Journal of Communication Disorders, 14,* 133–140.

Rowan, L., Leonard, L., Chapman, K., & Weiss, A. (1983). Performative and presuppositional skills in language-disordered and normal children. *Journal of Speech and Hearing Research, 26,* 97–106.

Rubin, K. H. (1976). Relation between social participation and role-taking skill in preschool children. *Psychological Reports, 39,* 823–826.

Rubin, K. H. (1977). Play behaviors of young children. *Young Children, 32,* 16–24.

Rubin, K. H., Maioni, T. L., & Hornung, M. (1976). Free play behaviors in middle- and lower-class preschoolers: Parten and Piaget revisited. *Child Development, 47,* 414–419.

Rubin, K. H., Watson, K. S., & Jambor, T. W. (1978). Free play behaviors in preschool and kindergarten children. *Child Development, 49,* 534–536.

Sameroff, A. (1987). The social context of development. In N. Eisenburg (Ed.), *Contemporary topics in development* (pp. 273–291). New York: John Wiley and Sons.

Sameroff, A., & Chandler, M. (1975). Reproductive risk and the continuum of caretaking causality. In F. Horowitz (Ed.), *Review of child development research* (Vol. 4, pp. 187–244). Chicago, IL: University of Chicago Press.

Sherrod, L., & Lamb, M. (1981). Infant social cognition: An introduction. In M. Lamb & L. Sherrod (Eds.), *Infant social cognition: Empirical and theoretical considerations* (pp. 1–10). Hillsdale, NJ: Lawrence Erlbaum.

Shore, C. (1986). Combinatorial play, conceptual development, and early multiword speech. *Developmental Psychology, 22,* 184–190.

Shore, C., O'Connell, B., & Bates, E. (1984). First sentences in language and symbolic play. *Developmental Psychology, 20,* 872–880.

Sigman, M., & Ungerer, J. (1984). Cognitive and language skills in autistic, mentally retarded and normal children. *Developmental Psychology, 20,* 293–302.

Sinclair, H. (1975). The role of cognitive structures in language acquisition. In E. H. Lenneberg & E. Lenneberg (Eds.), *Foundations of language development* (Vol. 1). New York: Academic Press.

Slobin, D. (1973). Cognitive prerequisites for the development of grammar. In C. Ferguson & D. Slobin (Eds.), *Studies of child language development.* New York: Holt, Rinehart & Winston.

Smilansky, S. (1968). *The effects of sociodramatic play on disadvantaged preschool children.* New York: John Wiley and Sons.

Snyder, L. (1978). Communicative and cognitive abilities and disabilities in the sensorimotor period. *Merrill-Palmer Quarterly, 24,* 161–180.

Stern, D. (1985). *The interpersonal world of the infant.* New York: Basic Books.

Stoneman, Z., Cantrell, M., & Hoover–Dempsey, K. (1983). The association between play materials and social behavior in a mainstreamed preschool: A naturalistic investigation. *Journal of Applied Developmental Psychology, 4,* 163–174.

Terrell, B. Y., & Schwartz, R. G. (1988). Object transformations in the play of language-impaired children. *Journal of Speech and Hearing Disorders, 53,* 459–466.

Terrell, B. Y., Schwartz, R. G., Prelock, P., & Messick, C. K. (1984). Symbolic play in normal and language impaired children. *Journal of Speech and Hearing Research, 27,* 424–429.

Tiegerman, E., & Siperstein, M. (1984). Individual patterns of interaction in the mother-child dyad: Implications for parent intervention. *Topics in Language Disorders, 4*(4), 50–61.

Tronick, E. (1989). Emotions and emotional communication in infants. *American Psychologist, 44,* 112–119.

Westby, C. (1988). Children's play: Reflections of social competence. *Seminars in Speech and Hearing, 9,* 1–14.

Wetherby, A. (1985). Speech and language disorders in children: An overview. In J. Darby (Ed.), *Speech and language evaluation in neurology: Childhood disorders* (pp. 3–32). New York: Grune & Stratton.

Wetherby, A. (1986). Ontogeny of communicative functions in autism. *Journal of Autism and Developmental Disorders, 16,* 295–316.

Wetherby, A., Cain, D., Yonclas, D., & Walker, V. (1988). Analysis of intentional communication of normal children from the prelinguistic to the multi-word stage. *Journal of Speech and Hearing Research, 31,* 240–252.

Wetherby, A., & Prizant, B. (1990). *Communication and symbolic behavior scales—Research edition.* Chicago, IL: Riverside Publishing.

Wetherby, A., & Prizant, B. (in press). Profiling young children's communicative competence. In S. Warren & J. Reichle (Eds.), *Causes and effects in communication and language intervention.* Baltimore, MD: Paul H. Brookes.

Wetherby, A., Prizant, B., & Kublin, K. (1989). *Assessing infants and toddlers with an eye toward intervention.* Short course presented at the Annual Convention of the American Speech-Language-Hearing Association. St. Louis, MO.

Wetherby, A., & Prutting, C. (1984). Profiles of communicative and cognitive-social abilities in autistic children. *Journal of Speech and Hearing Research, 27,* 364–377.

Wetherby, A., Yonclas, D., & Bryan, A. (1989). Communicative profiles of handicapped preschool children: Implications for early identification. *Journal of Speech and Hearing Disorders, 54,* 148–158.

Wing, L., Gould, J., Yeates, S., & Brierly, L. (1977). Symbolic play in severely mentally retarded and in autistic children. *Journal of Child Psychology and Psychiatry, 18,* 167–178.

Wolf, D., & Gardner, H. (1981). On the structure of early symbolization. In R. Schiefelbusch & D. Bricker (Eds.), *Early language: Acquisition and intervention* (pp. 287–327). Baltimore, MD: University Park Press.

Wolfgang, C., Mackender, B., & Wolfgang, M. (1981). *Growing and learning through play.* New York: McGraw-Hill.

CHAPTER 10

A Discourse Approach to
Language Disorders: Investigating
Complex Sentence Production

ELIZABETH SKARAKIS–DOYLE AND MICHELLE MENTIS

Pragmatics has been popularly viewed as the fourth component of language, in addition to syntax, semantics, and phonology. From this perspective, each separate component is viewed as interacting with the others. The Bloom and Lahey (1978) model of language, which integrates the separate components of form, content, and use, exemplifies this approach. However, some language researchers have considered pragmatics to be a basis from which to understand all other linguistic components. This perspective is the main tenet of the functionalist approach to grammar (Leech, 1983).

FUNCTIONALISM

Essentially, proponents of the functionalist approach maintain that grammar (i.e., morphology and syntax) emerges from its functions in discourse. The approach is based on the assumption that grammatical structures can be explained in terms of the principles of discourse organization and communicative interaction. Functionalist theories focus on the interaction between linguistic structures and communicative functions and appeal to communicative or discourse pressures and causes in their explanations of those grammatical forms (Levinson, 1983). Functionalist theories contrast sharply with formalist theories which are based on central concepts such as an autonomous system of rules generating structural descriptions of sentences. Linguists working from a functionalist perspective focus on providing an account of grammatical phenomena in terms of recurrent discourse patterns (DuBois, 1987; Givón, 1979, 1983, 1984; Halliday, 1985).

A central concern of functionalist theories is the role of language in social interaction and the belief that language should be studied in relation to its function as a system of human communication. Foley and van Valin (1985) suggest that functional explanations for morphosyntactic phenomena are related to "pragmatic principles, and discourse and sociolinguistic universals, which themselves must be related to necessary properties of communication systems in general and human perceptual mechanisms and social interactions in particular" (p. 13).

During the past 10 years, Bates and MacWhinney (1979) have developed a similar functionalist approach. They define functionalism as the belief that: "The forms of natural languages are created, governed, constrained, acquired and used in the service of communicative functions" (MacWhinney, Bates, & Kliegl, 1984, p. 128). Their model is one of language performance in which the acquistion of morphosyntactic forms is guided by the pragmatic and semantic structure of communication and their interaction with competing constraints on the speech channel. According to Bates and MacWhinney (1979), the speech channel is constrained in that there are only four kinds of surface form signals that are available for expressing multiple underlying meanings and intentions, these being lexical items, word order, morphological markers, and intonation. With these limited resources semantic information such as reference to particular objects and actions, reference to qualities and aspects of objects and actions, and case role relations must be conveyed. Additionally, the following pragmatic information must be expressed: the speech act, status of the relationship between partners, attitude of the speaker toward the information, relative newness of the information, topicalization of information, and presupposition. All of these functions compete for access to the limited surface forms available in the speech channel. The surface grammatical forms are the result of this competition. That is, "these forms are the emergent solution to the problem of communicating multiple, simultaneous meanings onto a linear speech channel" (Bates & MacWhinney, 1979).

Such a functionalist orientation to language provides a valuable framework for understanding language disorders. From this perspective, it is possible to explain the patterns of surface forms of a child with a language disorder in terms of the functions those forms serve in discourse.

Kirchner and Skarakis–Doyle (1983) proposed a model from which to understand developmental language disorders. In this model, they adopted the position of Bates and MacWhinney that multiple meanings compete for access to the limited surface forms possible in a linear speech channel. They suggested that the child with a language disorder must contend with the same communicative task demands (i.e., competition of multiple meanings for limited surface forms) as children with normal language, but due to incomplete acquisition of surface forms and tenuous control over acquired forms, the communicative system of the child with a language disorder is in a state of disequilibrium. The natural tendency of any organism in such a condition is to adapt. Consequently, the child with a language disorder does so by employing a compensatory strategy or an alternative means of controlling information. The result is a unique pattern of communication, or what Bates and MacWhinney (1979) would consider an "inevitable solution" to the competition of multiple meanings for limited surface forms. This model suggests that unique patterns of communication can be revealed by examining the communicative demands (e.g., the discourse role of a surface form) faced by the child with a language disorder. Although such patterns are encountered daily by clinicians who work with children who have language disorders, they have eluded researchers working from a traditional formalist perspective.

This chapter will illustrate how specific features of the grammatical system of a child with a language disorder are better explained in terms of the interaction between surface syntactic forms and discourse functions than through formal linguistic representations. Specifically, a case is presented that illustrates the influence of discourse demands on the complex sentence production of a preadolescent child with a language disorder. To understand the importance of complex sentence forms to the communicative system of a school-age child, a discussion of their structure and functions, as well as their developmental course follows.

COMPLEX SENTENCE DEVELOPMENT

Complex sentences are the surface forms through which the power and efficiency of the linguistic system is realized. The processes involved in forming complex sentences represent the basic ways in which ideas can be related to one another. In a complex sentence, two or more propositions are combined into relationships that link, qualify, or expand the ideas being expressed. In each case, new information is incorporated into a simple sentence form. Thus, these structures reveal something about the way information is generally organized. Syntactically, these forms are characterized by the presence of at least two main verbs and by either conjoined or embedded structure types. Complex sentences become increasingly important for academic and social success during the school years. The language of instruction, both curriculum materials and classroom discourse, demands increasing proficiency with complex sentences because they are integral to higher level comprehension processes and problem-solving abilities.

In the study of complex sentence acquisition, research efforts have been concentrated primarily on comprehension. However, acquisition studies focused on the production of these forms have steadily accumulated over the past 10 years (Bloom, Lahey, Hood, Lifter, & Fiess, 1980; Paul, 1981; Scott, 1988; Tyack & Gottsleben, 1986). Early investigations of complex sentence acquisition were either part of larger studies of general syntactic development (Limber, 1973; Menyuk, 1969; Trantham & Pederson, 1976) or focused on only one type of complex sentence (e.g., conjunction or relativization) (Clancy, Jacobsen, & Silva, 1976; Ingram, 1975). These early studies revealed that the acquisition of complex sentences begins in the latter half of the third year of life. Development continues for several years and is possibly refined by instruction in written language. Further, of the general types of complex forms, researchers have determined that complements are the earliest to emerge with some disagreement as to whether conjoined forms or relatives follow next in the order of acquisition.

Contemporary investigations have focused solely on complex sentences and have enhanced the database in several ways. Bloom and colleagues (1980) investigated not only the acquisition of the syntactic form, but also the semantic function and use of these sentence types. They found a slightly different order of acquisition when they considered the interaction of all of these parameters of language. Their data suggested that conjunction emerged first, followed by complements, which were in turn followed by relatives. Supportive of earlier research, their longitudinal study also identified a gradual process of acquisition for complex sentences which begins in the latter half of the third year of life.

Paul (1981) and Tyack and Gottsleben (1986) both provided acquisition data for a large number of normal children according to syntactic development stages based on mean length of utterance (MLU). Paul (1981) studied the stages from MLU 3.0 to 5.0 and greater (levels were divided into 0.5 intervals). Tyack and Gottsleben (1986) investigated MLU stages beginning at 2.0 and used a 1.0 interval from level 3.0 upward. Both studies investigated the onset and order of acquisition of specific types of complex sentences within the general types of complements, conjunctions, and relatives. Again, the early onset and gradual process of acquisition was confirmed. Additionally, both investigations found that MLU was a good predictor of the proportion of complex sentences to be found in a spontaneous language sample. For example, at an MLU of 4.0 approximately 20% of the sample was found to consist of complex sentences. The order of acquisition identified in the earliest studies, infinitive complements, conjunctions, and relatives, was confirmed again in both of these investigations.

Complex sentence development has been a prominent feature of investigations of syntactic development during the school years (Scott, 1988). For school children the context of complex sentence use becomes an important issue. Contextual factors such as the discourse genre (e.g., narratives, expository prose) and the channel of expression (i.e., spoken versus written) influence the frequency and types of complex sentences used by a child. For example, complex sentences with subordinated clauses occur more frequently in the spoken language than in the written language of school children up to approximately Grade 8. Conversely, after Grade 8 subordination is more frequent in written language (Hunt, 1965, 1970; Klecan–Acker & Hedrick, 1985; Loban, 1976; O'Donnell, Griffin, & Norris, 1967; Scott, 1984).

Scott (1988) has reviewed developmental changes occurring in the school years for specific types of complex sentences which have subordinated nominal, adverbial, or relative clauses. In the case of these specific forms the impact of contextual factors is also seen. Scott (1988) reported that the production frequency of nominal clauses (e.g., that– and to– complements) is determined primarily by grammatical function. That is, nominal clauses rarely serve in the preverbal position of subject, resulting in a low frequency of occurrence in this sentence position. However, a much greater frequency would be found in postverbal positions due to a tendency for important information to occur at the end of a sentence.

For subordinated adverbial clauses, Scott (1988) further reported that those that denote time (e.g., when, after) and cause (e.g., because) occur with great frequency in the language of school children, whereas the conditional "if" and resultant "so" occur with only moderate frequency. Hunt (1965) found that developmental increases in the use of these high- and mid-frequency adverbial clauses plateau in Grades 4 through 6. Subsequent use of these subordinate adverbial clauses is influenced more by discourse context and topic than by syntactic development alone.

Finally, according to Scott (1988), relative clauses occur the least frequently of all three types of subordinate clauses, yet are significant in school children's syntactic development. A steady increase in the frequency of occurrence of relative clauses was evidenced in Grade 3 through Grade 12 children's written language samples (Hunt, 1965; Loban, 1976; O'Donnell et al., 1967). Romaine (1984) found that the most frequently occurring type of relative clauses were those that postmodify object nouns and in which the relative pronoun serves as the subject for the embedded clause (e.g., She married the boy *who lives next door*). Other frequently occurring relatives postmodify complements or adverbial nouns in postverbal positions. In comparison, center-embedded relative clauses following subjects of the main clause are rare (Scott, 1984).

In summary, the literature on the acquisition of complex sentences suggests that, although the process begins in early childhood, it continues through the school years. In the latter years, communicative contexts such as genre and mode of expression, as well as grammatical function, influence the production frequencies of complex sentence types. In comparison to this burgeoning database for normal children's complex sentence development, relatively little is known about complex sentence development in children with language disorders. Currently, data regarding the acquisition of complex sentences must be extrapolated from the general studies of the syntactic development of children with language disorders, because studies that focus solely on complex sentences are rare (Klecan–Acker, 1985; Skarakis–Doyle, 1985). Given the paucity of specific data on these forms, we are left to conclude little other than that complex sentences, like simple sentences, are acquired later, at a slower rate by children with language disorders than by normal children and may be incompletely developed (Leonard, 1972; Menyuk, 1964; Morehead & Ingram, 1973; Trantham & Pederson, 1976; Wiig & Fleischman, 1980). Thus, complex sentence production was of particular interest in the following case presentation because of the dearth of information available about these forms in children with language disorders. Perhaps even more importantly they were of interest because the child studied was at the age when the powerful and efficient communication afforded by complex sentence use was necessary for his academic and social success.

A STUDY IN THE PRODUCTION OF COMPLEX SENTENCES: A CASE PRESENTATION

The subject of this case study was a male whom we shall call Sandy. He was studied over a two-year period, between 10 years, 6 months and 12 years, 6 months of age. He was the second and most severely impaired of three children with language disorders of a middle class family. He had no history of peripheral hearing loss or other significant medical history or psychopathology. He had a normal performance I.Q. on the *WISC-R* (Wechsler, 1974) and *Leiter* (Arthur, 1980). He had had a special education placement for six years with intensive language intervention provided as a supplemental service. Grammatical and lexical comprehension performance was never better than -1.5 standard deviations below the mean for his age or grade. Criterion-referenced comprehension measures also substantiated Sandy's marginal comprehension abilities. Table 10–1 shows the results of numerous standardized tests assessing comprehension which were administered during the two-year period. Complex sentence comprehension, production, and conversational contingency had never been targeted for treatment.

DATA COLLECTION

During the two-year period, seven informal conversational language samples between Sandy and a familar adult (i.e., his clinician or his mother)

Table 10–1. Summary of language comprehension assessment measures

Test	Score[a]
Token Test for Children (all subtests)	> −3 SD
Clinical Evaluation of Language Functions	
Processing words and sentences	−1.5 SD
Processing linguistic concepts	−1.5 SD
Processing oral directions	−1.5 SD
Peabody Picture Vocabulary Test—Revised	−1.5 SD
Test of Problem Solving	> −2 SD[b]
Test of Syntactic Ability (9 subtest criterion-referenced measure)	52%[c]

a. Standard deviations based on mean for age or grade.
b. Compared to norms for 9-year-old children.
c. Mean percent correct; range = 16% to 85%.

were collected. The samples were collected at school prior to or during his language treatment session or at home after school. Given the informal nature of these conversational samples, the opportunity existed for either partner to initiate topics for discussion. Topics were most often removed in time and space from the immediate physical context, although on several occasions the discussion focused on an ongoing activity (e.g., making a map, a homework assignment, etc.). Topics included discussions of future events (e.g., an upcoming field trip, the fall term, a class performance), past events (e.g., movies or television programs recently seen, vacation experiences, sporting events), and role play activities (e.g., a television broadcast of a football game). The adult partner occasionally had background knowledge of the event Sandy was discussing, but this was not always the case. The samples were audiotape recorded and both participants' utterances were orthographically transcribed for later analysis.

DATA ANALYSES

The data were analyzed in a two-step process. Initially, the seven individual transcripts were combined and in-depth morphosyntactic and speech act/topic analyses were conducted using several programs from the *Computerized Profiling* software analysis program (Long & Fey, 1988). The first step of analysis was conducted to characterize Sandy's repertoire of surface forms in a traditional formalist manner, as well as to describe social communicative style. It was necessary to establish the relative strengths and weaknesses of his linguistic system to provide the context necessary for the interpretation of the second step in the analysis process. This phase of analysis consisted of in-depth investigations of his complex sentence repertoire, including the discourse analysis of these surface forms.

ANALYSES OF MORPHOSYNTACTIC AND PRAGMATIC REPERTOIRES

The morphosyntactic and pragmatic analyses were conducted on the total number of child (and adult) utterances in the seven samples. The *Language Analysis and Remediation Screening Procedure* (LARSP) (Crystal, 1982) which includes both major and minor utterances was employed to describe Sandy's syntactic and morphological repertoire. Minor utterances were defined as those in which the elements do not combine according to grammatical rules to produce an infinite number of sentences (Crystal, 1982). A total of 1,056 child utterances were employed in the first step of data analysis.

The *Conversational Act Profile* (CAP) (Fey, 1986, Chapter 5) analysis was employed to assess Sandy's social conversational style by means of an utterance level speech act analysis and a discourse level topic analysis. Additional information about communicative interaction abilities was obtained from discourse sections of the LARSP.

COMPLEX SENTENCE ANALYSES

The complex sentence analyses were conducted on the total number of major child utterances, resulting in a total sample size of 759 child utterances. Two complex sentence analyses were conducted. The first analysis provided a measure of the proportions of ill-formed simple and complex sentences in the composite sample. Thus, the impact of communicative demands on complex sentence form production could be viewed relative to his entire repertoire of surface forms. The second analysis was performed to provide an in-depth evaluation of complex sentence production. Complex sentences were analyzed as one of the following three types:

1. *True Complete Complex* (TCC). These sentences were characterized by the presence of two main verbs. Both conjoined and embedded forms were included. A connective form was usually present, except in cases of optional coding (e.g., complement that). Forms in which clause reduction occurred were also included (Paul, 1981; Quirk, Greenbaum, Leech, & Svartvik, 1972).

EXAMPLE: "John missed the bus because he put the dog in the gate."

2. *Semigrammatical Complex* (SGC). These sentences were characterized by: (a) the omission of an obligatory clause element, such as subject, verb, or complement, (b) a within grammatical class substitution, (c) constituent disagreement, or (d) word order reversals and as such were considered ill-formed. However, these forms were clearly an attempt to produce the type of utterance described earlier. This category did not include elliptical forms for which such a deletion may be appropriate in conversation.

> EXAMPLE: "I dunno when see Superman III or Star Trek III, The Search for Spock."

3. *Discourse Complex.* These utterances were characterized by the encoding of complex propositions which extended across: (a) utterance boundaries of the same speaker, with or without an intervening utterance by the partner, and (b) consecutive utterances of the adult and the child, when a connective form was used by the child in the second clause (Bloom et al., 1980). These forms are distinguished from the "pragmatic connectors" described by van Dijk (1979) in that the primary link provided by the connector is between the semantic propositions of the utterances rather than the speech acts of each utterance. That is, the primary linking function of the connectors was to challenge or add to the *assertion* made in the initial utterance rather than to question or protest the *appropriateness conditions* of the initial speech act.

> EXAMPLE 1: *Child–Child:* Within speaker (C–C)
>   C: # "I don't know what" #
>   C: # "But he threw whatever its called." #
> EXAMPLE 2: *Child–Adult–Child:* Intervening utterance (C–A–C)
>   C: # "I wish we put tile" #
>   A: # "Where would you put it?" #
>   C: # "In my room but its carpet" #
> EXAMPLE 3: *Adult–Child* (A–C)
>   A: # "Oh, they had sheep there" #
>   C: # "and they ran around" #

CONTROL GROUPS

The frequency of occurrence for the three types of complex sentence forms in Sandy's samples was compared to that for two control groups of children. The first of these groups included three children between the ages of 11 and 13 years (age-matched) and the second consisted of five children with a mean length of utterance (MLU) between 4.5 and 5.5 morphemes, who were between 2 years, 10 months and 4 years, 5 months of age (language matched). Both groups were from middle class homes and had normal intellectual abilities for their ages. Language samples of approximately equal size to Sandy's (759 utterances) were collected from both groups. A total of 712 and 737 utterances were collected from the language-matched control group and the age-matched group, respectively, during interactions with familiar adults. Similar to that of Sandy, opportunities for either partner to initiate topics existed in these interactions. While the age-matched group tended to discuss topics that were removed in time and space from the immediate context, the language-matched group tended to discuss ongoing activities in the "here and now."

RESULTS

MORPHOSYNTACTIC AND PRAGMATIC REPERTOIRES

The results of the LARSP analysis suggest that at the clause, phrase, and word levels of the profile (see Appendix A for a complete profile), Sandy's utterances fell predominantly at Stages III and IV. An MLU of 4.18 morphemes was obtained for the composite sample, with minor utterances included. A somewhat higher range of MLUs (4.5 to 5.5 morphemes) was obtained for the seven samples when minor utterances were excluded.

At the clause level, the majority of Sandy's statements were Stage III structures with the canonical subject-verb-object (SVO) form predominating as can be seen in Table 10–2. However, even at this early stage, lexical restrictions appeared to limit the adequacy of clause structure development. This issue will be discussed in more detail in the forthcoming phrase level section. Although a range of Stage IV clause structures were evidenced in the samples, several factors suggested restricted development at this level. Only 50% of the Stage IV statement structures met productivity criteria (Lahey, 1988), and 40% of the productive forms contained either a clause element deletion or other phrase level errors. Incomplete acquisition of Stage V structures was also demonstrated in that only 50% of structures were productive. Again, of the productive forms demonstrated, 43% contained either clause or phrase level errors. The most common error at any stage (34% of all errors) was the omission of an obligatory clause element. Imperatives were extremely rare and usually without error. Stage II and III question forms were most predominant, but some Stage IV and V forms were demonstrated. However, the latter would not be considered productive because tokens of these types were accounted for by the stereotyped phrases "How 'bout . . ." and "What happens if . . ."

Analyses of phrase and word structures (shown in Table 10–3 and Table 10–4) once again revealed Stages III and IV to be the most completely developed in Sandy's repertoire. However, it is at the phrase and word levels

Table 10–2. Clause level structures in three sentence modes

		Imperative	Question	Statement	
Stage	Connectives				
II		VX5	QX 26	SV 69	AX 25
	–			SO 4	VO 16
	–			SC 4	VC 2
				Neg X 1	Other
III	–	VXY	QXY 22	SVC 81	VCA
	–			SVO 145	VOA 4
	–	Let XY 1	VS (X) 22	SVA 64	VOdOi
		Do XY 1		Neg XY	Other 7
IV	>	+S	QVS 3	SVOA 31	AAXY 12
	–	VXY+2	QXY+7	SVCA 8	Other 10
			VS (X+) 6	SVOdOi 1	
			tag	SVOC	
V	and 60	Coord 1	Coord 2	Coord −1	42−1+
	c 47	Other 1	Other 11	Sub A−1	7−1+
	> s 62			Sub S2	
	Other 93			Sub C6	Sub O 10
				Comparative 21	

that limitations in grammatical category development can be seen. Although pronouns were the predominant structure at both Stages II and III, they were not always used appropriately. In 17% of the instances where personal pronouns were used, a noun phrase (NP) was required in order for the referent to be specified. Of these vague referents, 85% served as the subject of the utterance.

A further limitation was evident in the types of NP expansions produced by Sandy. His repertoire of Adjective + Noun, Determiner + Adjective + Noun, and Adjective + Adjective + Noun expansion structures was limited. Only 19 different adjectives were produced in five hours of conversation. Limited lexical category development and ineffective use of pronouns without the appropriate specification of referents in turn influenced development at the clause level. Sandy had relatively few structures available at the phrase level for use in clause structure expansion. The subject element appeared to be particularly vulnerable to the restricted elaboration of the clause elements as shown in Table 10–5. In addition to the restricted elaboration of the subject, there was a tendency to produce nonspecific personal pronouns in this position, and to delete the subject altogether (45% of all clause element deletions occurred in this position).

Table 10–3. Phrase level structures at four stages

Stage	Noun Phrase	Verb Phrase
II	DN 119 AdjN 65 NN 43 PrN 80	VV 20 VPart 11 IntX 7 Other 64
III	DAdjN 44 AdjAdjN 7 PrDN 32 Pron-P 369 Pron-O 91	Cop 134 Aux-M 38 Aux-O 108 Other 87
IV	NPPrNP 32 PrDAdjN 6 cX 5 XcX 83	NegV 70 NegX 41 2 Aux 4 Other 38
V	Postmod C1 − 1 20 Postmod C1 − 1+ Postmod Phr − 1+1	

Table 10–4. Word level elements

Stage	Word Elements
II	−ing 23 pl 153 −ed 100
III	−en 18 3s 162 gen 9
IV	n't 57 'cop 80 'aux 28
V	−est −er 8 −ly 10

Table 10–5. Transition structures: Phrase elaboration of two and three clause element constructions

Stage	Phrase Elaborations				
II/III	X+S:NP 16	X+V:VP 51	X+C:NP 3	X+O:NP 25	X+A:AP 23
III/IV	XY+S:NP 37	XY+V:VP 92	XY+C:NP 59	XY+O:NP 95	XY+A:AP 59

Verb phrase constructions also appeared well developed at Stages III and IV. Again, this is qualified by the lexical category analyses of these constructions. LARSP verb profile and valency analyses revealed a restricted verb profile. Only 25 different verbs occurred in five hours of conversation. Sandy's modal system consisted of three productive forms, "could," "will," and "can" (can't included).

The auxiliary verb repertoire was particularly illustrative of Sandy's restricted verb system. Only two productive auxiliary verb structures were identified, "Be + Verb" and "Do + Verb" of which 61% was accounted for by the latter. In-depth analysis of the "Do + Verb" form revealed additional restrictions. Specifically, of all the tokens of that structure in the composite sample, 76% were of the form "Do + Negative + Verb." Further, of these forms, 52% were realized as "Don't Know" and an additional 15% as "Don't have/got." Thus, little flexibility existed in the types of auxiliaries mastered and in the lexical realization of those that were productive. In addition, 26% of auxiliary structures exhibited an omission, tense, or agreement error.

Restricted verb development and use was common throughout other forms as well. The copula occurred most frequently in its contracted form (62%). In addition, 86% of the time that the copula was used in any form it occurred with an empty subject (i.e., it, that, there, here). As shown in Table 10–4, Sandy's verb inflection repertoire was also limited. Fifty-two percent of all verbs were unmarked. Further, 7% of verb forms were in error. Complex verb phrases were demonstrated (13 tokens). Half of these examples had errors in the auxiliary used, while the remainder could be accounted for by one of two structures, "Auxiliary + Modal + Main Verb" or "Auxiliary + Negative + Main Verb."

In summary, the LARSP analyses have revealed that Sandy demonstrated his most adequately developed forms at Stages III and IV, although even at these stages restrictions in development were evident. Although he attempted production of complex sentence structures, gaps at earlier stages of development and tenuous control over earlier acquired forms limited the success of those attempts.

PRAGMATIC REPERTOIRE

Sandy's social communicative style is characterized by the data presented in Table 10–6. This represents the results of both the CAP analyses and the LARSP discourse measures. These data suggest that Sandy demonstrated a passive conversational style. This is evident in the comparison of assertive and responsive speech acts produced, and the extent to which Sandy's responses served to maintain the conversational topic without adding to its development. The relatively low proportion of total assertives produced by Sandy suggests that he was not dominant in the conversational interactions. This is substantiated by the predominance of responsive speech acts in the sample of which only 22% were used in extending the topic. Seventy-five percent of the minor utterances (responses to assertives and performatives) and one element elliptical utterances also served to maintain topic without contributing new unsolicited information. These data suggest that Sandy was responsive to his partners by responding to their questions and minimally acknowledging the obligation to take a turn in the conversation. He did not, however, take an active role in contributing unsolicited novel information in order to develop the conversation.

The linguistic profile that emerges from the initial analyses of Sandy's spontaneous language is that of incomplete and tenuous control over the syntactic, morphological, and lexical aspects of the linguistic system and a dependency on the conversational partner for the development of a conversation. It is with this fragile communicative system that Sandy must meet the demands of producing complex sentences.

COMPLEX SENTENCE ANALYSES

Figure 10–1 shows the proportion of ill-formed simple sentences compared to the proportion of ill-formed complex sentences. Ill-formedness (i.e.,

Table 10–6. Characteristics of pragmatic repertoire

Responsiveness to Partner's Initiations	
Questions responded to adequately	99.6%
Ratio of percent maintaining to percent extending utterances	1.65:1
Frequency of RSAS and one element ellipsis	47%
Ratio of adult to child utterances	3:1
Proportions of Assertive and Responsive Speech Acts	
Ratio of percent responsive acts to percent assertive acts	2.7:1
Proportion of responsives that extend topic	22%
Percent of total assertives that were produced by the child	25%

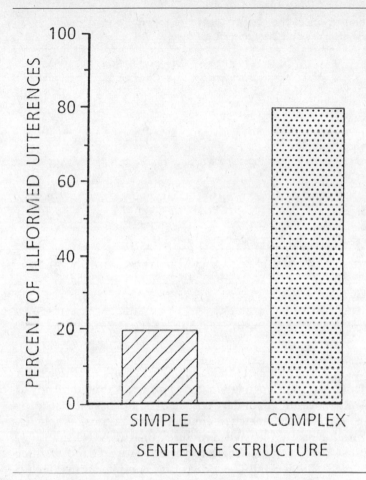

Figure 10–1. A comparison between the proportion of ill-formed simple and complex sentences.

omission of an obligatory clause element, constituent disagreement, grammatical class substitutions) increased fourfold for attempts at complex sentences as compared to attempts at simple sentences. This suggests that the weakness demonstrated when Sandy attempted to produce simple sentence forms was increased four times when he attempted complex sentences.

Table 10–7 shows the comparison of Sandy's complex sentence repertoire to the two control groups. Considering conventional within boundary coding first, Sandy produced proportionately fewer true complete complex sentence forms than either group of normal children, but a substantially greater proportion of semigrammatical forms (ill-formed utterances). When all within utterance boundary attempts at complex sentences are

Table 10–7. Comparison of the complex sentence repertoire of the child with a language disorder and two control groups

	Child with a Language Disorder	Language-Matched Children (N = 5)	Age-Matched Children (N = 3)
Total Utterances	759	712	737
True complete complex (TCC)	6%	9.8%	29%
Semigrammatical complex (SGC)	10%	3.3%	1.4%
Discourse			
Adult–child	5%	.7%	.5%
Child–child	1.8%	3.5%	1.8%
Attempt conventional coding (TCC + SCC)	16%	13.2%	31.3%
Total attempts at complex sentences	23%	17.4%	33.7%

considered, Sandy produced about the same proportion of complex sentences as the children in the language-matched group. Although Sandy attempted conventional within boundary coding of complex sentence forms as frequently as the language-matched children, he was considerably less successful in producing well-formed structures than they were.

When discourse-based complex sentences were compared, other differences also emerged. Child–child (C–C) discourse complex forms (including those with intervening adult utterances) occurred infrequently, 3.5% or less in any of the children's samples; however, Sandy was similar to the age-matched controls in the frequency of production of these forms. The younger normal children produced a slightly greater number than both Sandy and the age-matched controls. When adult–child (A–C) forms were considered, the results indicated that they comprised a similar proportion of the sample for either group of normal children. However, A–C forms comprise about 10 times more of Sandy's sample than that of the age-matched group's sample and about seven times more than that of the language-matched group's sample. Thus, by expanding the unit of analysis beyond the boundary of a single utterance to view discourse units that cross utterance boundaries, a discourse solution to the problem of producing complex sentences emerges.

DISCUSSION

The purpose of this case presentation was to illustrate the utility of the functionalist approach to the study of language disorders. Specifically, our goal was to demonstrate how features of the complex sentence repertoire of a preadolescent child with a language disorder can be explained in terms of the interaction of surface syntactic forms and discourse functions. To this point, we have approached this task by first conducting traditional formalist analysis of both simple and complex sentence forms. These have revealed *what* elements comprise Sandy's system. In addition, the social communicativeness analyses broadly revealed *how* he used his system. Finally, the discourse-based analysis revealed a potential strategy for dealing with the problem of producing complex sentences, which allows us to suggest *why* his pattern of complex sentence production presented as it did.

As the initial morphosyntactic and pragmatic analysis revealed, Sandy's repertoire of the four surface form signals identified by Bates and MacWhinney (1979) (i.e., lexical items, word order, morphological markings, and intonation) was neither fully developed nor well controlled. Yet with this fragile system, Sandy met the demands of complex sentence production. The specific constraints that compete when producing complex sentences include the semantic functions of qualifying, linking, or expanding ideas. In order to accomplish these semantic goals, one must incorporate new information into an existing form which is a pragmatic function. Thus, the production of complex sentences involves mapping the function of introducing new information that either qualifies, links, or expands existing information onto the appropriate syntactic form. In Sandy's case, the form-function mapping was constrained by the limitations imposed by his fragile communicative system. To meet the demands of introducing new information in the production of complex sentences, Sandy relied heavily on the production of discourse complex sentences. He accomplished the function of introducing new information and circumvented the limitations imposed by his restricted linguistic system by producing a discourse-based complex sentence which was scaffolded onto his partner's prior utterance. Thus, he developed a discourse-based solution to the problem of producing complex sentences.

Research in the area of normal language acquisition has identified the strategy of expressing propositions across utterance boundaries as occurring early in the developmental process. Bloom and colleagues (1980) found that complex surface forms initially emerged across utterance boundaries, but that children created them first and most frequently by building on one of their own utterances (C–C) with or without the assistance of an intervening adult utterance (C–A–C). Joining one's proposition to that of a partner (A–C) was a subsequent development. Further, such A–C forms occurred substantially less frequently than C–C codings of complex forms.

Other researchers (Ochs, Schieffelin, & Platt, 1979; Scollon, 1979) have termed these jointly constructed forms "Vertical Constructions" and have identified them as an alternative to conventional grammatical surface forms in normal children at the one- and two-word stage of language development. Thus early in development, discourse provides a framework that enables a child to produce structures that she or he would be incapable of producing alone (Bruner, 1975).

Although the expression of propositions across utterance boundaries is a normal occurrence, the comparison of Sandy's *pattern* of complex sentence production to that of the two control groups clearly illustrates that this discourse-based solution was a unique aspect of his communicative system. Sandy's overall pattern of complex sentence production was quite different than that of either control group. Discourse-based A–C forms made up approximately the same proportion of his total sample as the TCC forms (and in the presence of twice as many semigrammatical forms). In comparison, the normal children's proportion of discourse-based forms decreased with a larger proportion of conventional within boundary codings of complex sentences. The normal children's pattern was consistent with the Ochs, Schieffelin, and Platt (1979) hypothesis which states that the development of communicative competence in young children is a process of moving from the expression of propositions across utterance boundaries to expression within the boundary of a single utterance. Sandy's pattern was not consistent with this position.

The characteristics of Sandy's use of the discourse strategy that distinguished him from normally developing children were the manner and extent to which the strategy was used, factors that identify a compensatory strategy (Kirchner & Skarakis–Doyle, 1983). That is, his solution to the problem of introducing new information in order to produce complex sentences with a fragile linguistic system was to find an alternative means for expression. Sandy compensated by relying heavily on the dialogue of his conversational partner as a scaffold for complex sentence production. Such a strategy could only have been revealed by analyzing surface complex sentence forms from the perspective of their discourse function.

CONTRIBUTIONS TO CLINICAL PRAGMATICS

As this case presentation has demonstrated, the functionalist approach makes a twofold contribution to clinical pragmatics. The first principle to be derived is that function can enlighten the understanding of form. Speech-language pathologists must, of course, understand the forms they seek to develop or change in their clients before they can undertake intervention. In recent discussions concerning the contributions of pragmatic models to the understanding of language disorders, the point has been made that the pragmatic abilities of children with language disorders are deficient only to the degree that the child's form is deficient (Connell, 1987; Leonard 1986). Although there is truth in this position, to stop with this observation alone is to oversimplify the issue. The relationship between form and function is symbiotic (Saddock, 1984). Function not only follows form, form also follows function. One enlightens the other. Traditional analyses of forms have yielded the answer to the question of "what" elements are present, absent, or are in some way inadequate in a language disordered child's system. Additionally, taxonomies of communicative functions have yielded a broad answer to the question of "how" available forms are used for purposes of interpersonal communication. A functionalist discourse approach reveals the answer to "why" patterns of form emerge in the manner they have for any particular child. All three of these questions are of clinical importance. Thus, the clinical assessment of the child with a language disorder should seek not only to answer the "what" and "how" questions, as is the current practice in speech-language pathology, but also the question "why." However, a brief clarification is warranted.

A functionalist approach does not attempt to explain the etiology of a language disorder. It has been argued that an answer to the question of why a language disorder exists (i.e., the identification of its etiology) would reveal little about the goals for treatment of the language disorder anyway (Lahey, 1988). Rather, the functionalist approach explains why a particular pattern emerged by identifying the communicative conditions under which a breakdown in form may occur. In the example provided by Sandy's case, the breakdown in production of complex sentences was identified under the discourse condition of adding new information. It is quite likely that for other children with language disorders different conditions may be critical in the outcome, because the population is heterogeneous in the relative strengths and weaknesses demonstrated. The value of the functionalist approach is its applicability across individuals of varying linguistic ability.

The functionalist framework also permits the identification of a child's own solution to the problem of communicating. That is, self-generated compensatory strategies can be recognized in the child's communicative behavior. Frequently, intervention practices consist of finding alternative means for clients to express themselves. A functionalist approach can reveal alternative means created by clients. Thus, the clinician may be provided with behaviors to build on and, hence, maximize client strengths in the intervention process.

Practical considerations in undertaking the task of uncovering such behaviors include: the sample size necessary to establish behaviors as more than idiosyncratic forms and the time involved in the collection, transcription, and analyses of the samples. Consistent with the view espoused by Miller (1981), the functional, discourse analysis employed in this study

must be viewed as part of an ongoing assessment process. For clinical application, several samples of the size typically obtained for clinical purposes
(i.e., 50 utterances) would be necessary. Additionally, samples should be
obtained at several different occasions (minimum of three) to complete this
procedure. As Brinton (1990) has pointed out, such extensive sampling is
characteristic of the best clinical applications of pragmatic models. However, with some experience in the use of computer software programs, clinicians can reduce the time involved in data analysis, particularly in the
process of searching for recurrent patterns. The time involved in collecting,
transcribing, and analyzing the samples will be justified by the valuable insights obtained for identifying intervention goals and procedures.

The second principle to be derived from a functionalist approach is clearly related to the first and echoes a critical procedure offered by others interested in clinical pragmatics (Craig, 1983; Prutting, 1982). Specifically, a unit
of analysis that extends beyond single utterance boundaries is essential.
Again, using the present case as an example, had we confined our analyses
to traditional within boundary units we would have been left with only the
observation that Sandy's complex sentence attempts usually resulted in
fragments that were replete with grammatical inadequacies. Instead, by extending the unit of analysis beyond utterance boundaries, and in particular
to consider multiutterance units, a very different view of his complex sentence repertoire emerges. By viewing the scaffolded combination of Sandy's
proposition with that of his conversational partner as a unit, an alternative
means of expressing complex sentences was revealed. This alternative allowed him greater ability to produce these forms. Just as changing the mag-
nification of a microscope's lens allows us to see things that otherwise
would not be visible, changing the unit of analysis allows us to observe aspects of our clients' behavior that otherwise would not be visible to us.
Thus, we have employed multiutterance units to reveal an aspect of Sandy's
complex sentence repertoire. Other researchers have used multiutterance
units to reveal the segmentation process that children with language disorders use in learning syntactic forms (Kirchner & Prutting, 1987; Schwartz,
Chapman, Terrel, Prelock, & Rowan, 1985).

Once strategies have been identified, the same units suggest a basis for
intervention. Kirchner (see Chapter 11) has suggested procedures for facilitating complex sentence production using a bootstrapping strategy very
much like that created by Sandy. In addition, she has developed similar
procedures for facilitating simple sentence types in children with pervasive developmental disorders (Kirchner, in press). Futher, Schwartz and
colleagues (1985) have demonstrated that multiword utterances could be
facilitated in children with language disorders using multiutterance units as
the core of their treatment program. Clearly, the use of multiutterance units
is of value in both assessment and intervention and, therefore, appears to
provide an innovative addition to the clinical armamentarium.

Despite the apparent contribution of the functionalist perspective to the understanding of language disorders in children, its potential remains largely unexplored in speech-language pathology. Currently, it appears popular to advocate the abandonment of pragmatic models in clinical research and practice, yet prudence dictates that additional research and clinical application of the functionalist approach and other pragmatic models be pursued. Indeed, the functionalist perspective provides an exciting and viable means for approaching the complex and challenging task of refining and expanding clinical pragmatics in the 1990s.

ACKNOWLEDGMENTS

The effort and cooperation of several individuals were essential to the success of this project. Thus, the first author wishes to thank Linda Fredeen for the countless hours she spent in the computer analyses, Dr. Steven Long for his consultation on the computer analyses, Sonya Gale and Kathleen Mullin for their contributions to the processing of the data, and finally Sandy who was the catalyst for it all.

REFERENCES

Arthur, G. (1980). *The Arthur Adaptation of the Leiter International Performance Scale*. Los Angeles: Western Psychological Services.
Bates, E., & MacWhinney, B. (1979). A functionalist approach to grammar. In E. Ochs & B. Schieffelin (Eds.), *Developmental pragmatics* (pp. 167–211). New York: Academic Press.
Bloom, L., & Lahey, M. (1978). *Language development and language disorders*. New York: John Wiley and Sons.
Bloom, L., Lahey, M., Hood, L., Lifter, K., & Fiess, K. (1980). Complex sentences: Acquisition of syntactic connectives and semantic relations they encode. *Journal of Child Language, 7*, 235–261.
Brinton, B. (1990). Peer commentary on "Clinical pragmatics: Exceptions and realizations" by Tanya Gallagher. *Journal of Speech-Language Pathology and Audiology, 14*, 7–8.
Bruner, J. (1975). The ontogenesis of speech acts. *Journal of Child Language, 2*, 1–19.
Clancy, P. M., Jacobsen, T., & Silva, N. (1976). The acquisition of conjunctions: Cross-linguistic study. *Stanford Papers and Reports on Child Language Development, 12*, 71–80.
Connell, P. J. (1987). Teaching language form, meaning and function to specific language-impaired children. In S. Rosenberg (Ed.), *Advances in applied psycholinguistics: Disorders of first language development* (Vol. 1, pp. 40–75). New York: Cambridge University Press.
Craig, H. (1983). Application of pragmatic language models for intervention. In T. Gallagher & C. Prutting (Eds.), *Pragmatic assessment and intervention issues in language* (pp. 101–127). San Diego, CA: College-Hill Press.
Crystal, D. (1982). *Profiling linguistic disability* (Chap. 2). London: Edward Arnold.
DuBois, J. H. (1987). The discourse basis of ergativity. *Language, 63*, 805–855.

Fey, M. E. (1986). *Language intervention with young children.* Boston: College-Hill Press.

Foley, W., & van Valin, R. D. (1985). *Functional syntax and universal grammar.* Cambridge, UK: Cambridge University Press.

Givón, T. (1979). *On understanding grammar.* New York: Academic Press.

Givón, T. (1983). *Topic continuity and discourse.* Amsterdam: John Benjamin.

Givón, T. (1984). *Syntax: A functional-typological introduction* (Vol. 1). Amsterdam: John Benjamin.

Halliday, M. A. (1985). *An introduction to functional grammar.* London: Edward Arnold.

Hunt, K. W. (1965). *Grammatical structures written at three grade levels* (Research Report No. 3). Champaign, IL: National Council of Teachers of English.

Hunt, K. W. (1970). Syntactic maturity in school children and adults. *Society for Research in Child Development Monographs, 35*(1, Serial No. 134).

Ingram, D. (1975). If and when transformations are acquired by children. In D. Dato (Ed.), *Developmental psycholinguistics: Theory and applications* (pp. 99–127). Washington, DC: Georgetown University Press.

Kirchner, D. (in press). Using verbal scaffolding to facilitate conversational participation and language acquisition in children with pervasive developmental disorders. *Journal of Childhood Language Disorders.*

Kirchner, D., & Prutting, C. A. (1987). Spontaneous verbal repetition: A performance based strategy for language acquisition. *Clinical Linguistics and Phonetics, 1,* 147–169.

Kirchner, D., & Skarakis–Doyle, E. (1983). Developmental language disorders: A theoretical perspective. In T. M. Gallagher & C. A. Prutting (Eds.), *Pragmatic assessment and intervention issues in language* (pp. 215–246). San Diego, CA: College-Hill Press.

Klecan–Acker, J. S. (1985). Syntactic abilities in normal and language deficient middle school children. *Topics in Language Disorders, 5,* 46–54.

Klecan–Acker, J. S., & Hedrick, L. D. (1985). A study of the syntactic language skills of normal school age children. *Language Speech and Hearing Services in Schools, 16,* 53–81.

Lahey, M. (1988). *Language disorders and language development.* New York: Macmillan.

Leech, G. N. (1983). *Principles of pragmatics.* London: Longman.

Leonard, L. B. (1972). What is deviant language? *Journal of Speech and Hearing Disorders, 37,* 427–446.

Leonard, L. B. (1986). Conversational replies of children with specific language impairment. *Journal of Speech and Hearing Research, 29,* 114–119.

Levinson, S. (1983). *Pragmatics.* Cambridge, UK: Cambridge University Press.

Limber, J. (1973). The genesis of complex sentences. In T. E. Moore (Ed.), *Cognitive development and the acquisition of language* (pp. 169–185). New York: Academic Press.

Loban, W. (1976). *Language development: Kindergarten through grade twelve* (Research Report No. 18). Champaign, IL: National Council of Teachers of English.

Long, S., & Fey, M. (1988). *Computerized profiling* [Computer program]. Ithaca, NY: Computerized Profiling.

MacWhinney, B., Bates, E., & Kliegl, R. (1984). Cue validity and sentence interpretation in English, German and Italian. *Journal of Verbal Learning and Verbal Behavior, 23,* 127–150.

Menyuk, P. (1964). Comparison of grammar of children with functionally deviant and normal speech. *Journal of Speech and Hearing Research, 7,* 109–121.

Menyuk, P. (1969). *Sentences children use.* Cambridge, MA: The MIT Press.

Miller, J. F. (1981). *Assessing language production in children: Experimental procedures.* Baltimore, MD: University Park Press.

Morehead, D., & Ingram, D. (1973). The development of base syntax in normal and linguistically deviant children. *Journal of Speech and Hearing Research, 16,* 330–352.

O'Donnell, R. C., Griffin, W. J., & Norris, R. D. (1967). *Syntax of kindergarten and elementary school children: A transformational analysis* (Research Report No. 8). Champaign, IL: National Council of Teachers of English.

Ochs, E., Schieffelin, B., & Platt, M. (1979). Propositions across utterances and speakers. In E. Ochs & B. Schieffelin (Eds.), *Developmental pragmatics* (pp. 251–268). New York: Academic Press.

Paul R. (1981). Analyzing complex sentence development. In J. F. Miller (Ed.), *Assessing language production in children: Experimental procedures* (p. 36). Baltimore, MD: University Park Press.

Prutting, C. (1982). Pragmatics as social competence. *Journal of Speech and Hearing Disorders, 47,* 123–133.

Quirk, R., Greenbaum, S., Leech, G., & Svartvik, J. (1972) *A grammar of contemporary English.* London: Longman.

Romaine, S. (1984). *The language of children and adolescents.* Oxford, UK: Basil Blackwell.

Saddock, J. (1984). Whither radical pragmatics? In D. Schiffren (Ed.), *Meaning, content, and use in context: Linguistic application* (pp. 139–149). Washington, DC: Georgetown University Press.

Schwartz, R., Chapman, K., Terrel, B., Prelock, P., & Rowan, L. (1985). Facilitating word combinations in language-impaired children through discourse structure. *Journal of Speech and Hearing Disorders, 50,* 31–39.

Scollon, R. (1979). A really early stage: An unzippered condensation of a dissertation on child language. In E. Ochs & B. Schieffelin (Eds.), *Developmental pragmatics* (pp. 215–228). New York: Academic Press.

Scott, C. M. (1984). *What happened in that: Structural characteristics of school children's narratives.* Paper presented at the annual meeting of the American Speech-Language-Hearing Association. Cincinnati, OH.

Scott, C. M. (1988). Spoken and written syntax. In M. Nippold (Ed.), *Later language development: Ages nine through nineteen* (pp. 49–95). Boston: Little, Brown.

Skarakis–Doyle, E. (1985). *Complex sentences in a language disordered preadolescent: Language production.* Paper presented at the annual convention of the American Speech-Language-Hearing Association. Washington, DC.

Trantham, C., & Pederson, J. (1976). *Normal language development.* Baltimore, MD: Williams & Wilkins.

Tyack, D., & Gottsleben, R. (1986). Acquisition of complex sentences. *Language Speech and Hearing Services in Schools, 17,* 160–174.

Van Dijk, T. A. (1979). Pragmatic connectives. *Journal of Pragmatics, 3,* 447–456.

Wechsler, D. (1974). *Manual for the Wechsler Intelligence Scale for Children—Revised.* New York: Psychological Corporation.

Wiig, E., & Fleischman, N. (1980). Prepositional phrases, pronominalization, reflexivization and relativization in the language of learning disabled college students. *Journal of Learning Disabilities, 13,* 45–50.

Appendix A

```
NAME: COMPOSITE    AGE: 11/12    DATE: 1983/84    TYPE: CONVERSATION
===============================================================================
A  UNANALYZED:      Unintelligible       Symbolic Noise 1      Deviant
   PROBLEMATIC:     Incomplete 9         Ambiguous             Stereotypes 2
===============================================================================
```

	REPET-	NORMAL RESPONSE					ABNORMAL	PROB-
TOTALS	ITIONS	Elliptical			Red-			Struc-	LEMS
		1	2	3+	uced	Full	Minor	tural Null	
B 319 R-Q		76	11	10	12	77	157		
317 R-O		78	10	10	8	77	121		
C 230 Spon		36	19	8	36	149	19		

```
===============================================================================
  M I N O R       Responses 294      Vocatives 2      Other 21      Problems
-------------------------------------------------------------------------------
```

_	COMM	QUEST	STATEMENT			
	'V'	'Q' 36	'V' 3	'N'1	Other 5	Problems

```
===============================================================================
```

CONN	CLAUSE				PHRASE		WORD
_	VX 5	QX 26	SV 69	AX 25	DN 119	VV 20	
_			SO 4	VO 16	AdjN 65	VPart 11	-ing23
			SC4	VC 2	NN 43	IntX 7	
			Neg X 1	Other	PrN 67	Other 64	pl 153

```
===============================================================================
```

	X+S:NP16	X+V:VP 51	X+C:NP 3	X+O:NP25	X+A:AP 23		-ed100
_	VXY	QXY22	SVC 81 VCA		DAdjN 44 Cop134		-en 18
_			SVO145 VOA 4		AdjAdjN 7 Aux-M 38		
	Let XY1	VS(X)22	SVA 64 VodOi		PrDN 32 Aux-O108		3s162
	Do XY1		NegXY Other 7		Pron-P369 Other 87		gen 9
					Pron-O 91		

```
===============================================================================
```

	XY+S:NP 37	XY+V:VP 92	XY+C:NP 59	XY+O:NP 95	XY+A:AP 59		n't57
>	+S	QVS3	SVOA31 AAXY12		NPPrNP32 NegV70		'cop80
_		QXY+ 7	SVCA 8 Other10		PrDAdjN 6 NegX41		
	VXY+2	VS(X+) 6	SVOdOi 1		cX 5 2 Aux4		'aux28
		tag	SVOC		XcX 83 Other38		

```
===============================================================================                                               -est
```

and 60	Coord 1	Coord 2	Coord-1 36 -1+		Postmod Cl-1 20		
c 47	Other 1	Other11	Sub A-1 7 -1+		Postmod Cl-1+		-er 8
> s 62			Sub S 2		Postmod Phr-1+ 1		
Other93			Sub C 6 Sub O 10				-ly10
			Comparative 21				

```
===============================================================================
   (+) Initiator 7      Complex VP 13        Passive 2          Complement 11
       Coord NP 3                             how                what
-------------------------------------------------------------------------------
   (-) and &    Elem 0 74 Det 2      Prep10   Modal      Oth Aux 13  Irr N 1
>      conn 1   Elem -> 8 D 0 26     Pr 0 14  Aux 0 12   Copula 4    Irr V 27
       subord1  Concord 1 D ->       P ->                            Reg N
                          Pronoun             Ambiguous 4            Reg V 4
       Other 37                      Ambiguous 4
===============================================================================
   it 4    there 16    A Connectivity 5  ·  Comment Clause 7    Emphatic Order 3
===============================================================================
Total P Sentences1056   Mean P Sentences/Turn  1.44     MLR 3.8      MLU 4.18
Spontaneous Utterances   19.5%          Questions Responded to Adequately 98.3%
Total T Sentences1509   Mean T Sentences/Turn  2.24     MLR 7.79
Questions 358   Other 354            P Utterances/T Utterances  0.65
```

CHAPTER 11

Reciprocal Book Reading: A Discourse-Based Intervention Strategy for the Child with Atypical Language Development

DIANE M. KIRCHNER

One of the most important components to developing a good intervention procedure—pragmatic or not—is that the intervention strategy should rest on a sound theoretical framework for taking such remedial action. The problems related to the development of intervention procedures, and their solutions are many and varied. Nevertheless, speech-language pathology is a profession with deep historical roots in clinical endeavors, and the overwhelming majority of speech-language pathologists are service providers rather than researchers. Still, the single greatest need in the profession is for an adequate bank of applied research that documents intervention techniques applied to children with atypical language development. There is an even greater need for innovation in clinical strategies, particularly with respect to the application of a pragmatic or discourse-based framework for intervention.

The practical and theoretical significance of pragmatic research to date is evident throughout the literature of the past 15 years. A body of both theoretically and clinically meaningful research has been produced which delineates the effects of context on communicative competence and the functional bases of structural acquisitions (Bates & MacWhinney, 1979, 1982). In its early years, pragmatics was accepted positively in recognition of its potential contribution to an understanding of language acquisition and disorders. Now, position attitudes are expressed less enthusiastically by some speech-language pathologists, which may reflect the problems they have experienced in attempting to apply such a complex framework to intervention in a manner that facilitates documentation of its value. Some clinicians may see the emphasis on the interpersonal and communicative aspects of language in the past 15 years as a "bandwagon" that has taken the focus off the real "stuff" of language intervention—syntax and semantics. It has even been suggested that the application of the pragmatic framework does little more than create a terminological confusion that makes practioners feel outdated (Wilcox, 1988). Unfortunately, statements of this nature, perhaps innocently but devastatingly, mislead practitioners into thinking that pragmatics is little more than a "renaming" of previously known concepts in contemporary language. It appears that many speech-language pathologists have fallen prey to a host of misunderstandings and misinterpretations about pragmatics, but the theory must not be faulted for its misapplication. Unfortunately, much clinical "mischief" has accompanied the confusion over the meaning of pragmatics and its application in practice.

This chapter is written from the perspective of a practicing clinician and clinical researcher who has interacted with thousands of clinicians, teachers, and parents across the country around this single question: How do you teach pragmatics? This is fundamentally the wrong question. Applying a pragmatic theory does not simply entail learning a special set of new terminology for previously known concepts. Applying a pragmatic theory is not teaching a list of communicative functions such as requesting, greeting, or justifying. Pragmatics is not group therapy. Pragmatics is not attending behavior or eye contact. In fact, it is really not a matter of how to teach "pragmatics" at all. Rather it is embracing and understanding a new and broadened theoretical framework from which to understand syntax and semantics. For clinical purposes, it involves more than an understanding of pragmatic theory, how theory guides practice, and how a pragmatic perspective influences the way in which speech-language pathologists assess language development and create intervention contexts for children with atypical language development.

At all costs, clinicians must not be misled into thinking that they "don't necessarily need to understand . . . theory" (Wilcox, 1988). With respect to pragmatics, nothing could be further from the truth. In fact, this attitude may explain why application of the theoretical constructs that can be considered pragmatic have not been forthcoming to the extent that was once expected. If the theory and the research literature that provides support for a developmental construct or theory are not understood, appropriate clinical application of the principles of that theory or construct cannot be achieved. Whatever the form or focus of intervention, practitioners must be prepared to offer theoretical justification for their approaches. Consider the alternatives—clinical decisions based on intuition or an appeal to authority. There is a point where such decisions must be supported by data rather than intuition. Beyond this, the most robust clinical approaches are conceptually sound and empirically supported.

This chapter attempts to demonstrate how understanding the theoretical bases of cognitive development from an interactive perspective and language acquisition from a discourse perspective can be directly applied in intervention. Such approaches need not separate the teaching of the structure or meaning of the language from interaction or the requirements of learning in the literate classroom. This point raises the issue of what is the "correct" way to apply the pragmatic literature. First of all, categorical distinctions between what is syntactic, semantic, pragmatic, or literate can be avoided by exploring integrated approaches to intervention. That is, the goal is the development of intervention strategies in which the content is linguistic and academically based, while the context for teaching is interaction oriented and driven. Although this concept may seem rather obvious, intervention approaches such as these have scarcely been explored.

LANGUAGE AND COGNITION: AN OUTGROWTH OF INTERACTION

From a psycholinguistic perspective it has long been argued that the skilled use of language is an outgrowth of early interactive routines between adult and child (Snow, 1979, 1981; Bruner, 1975, 1976, 1981, 1983). In the context of predictable routines and carefully constructed dialogues between child and adult the child learns not only what to say, but how and when to say it (Bruner, 1983). The majority of the psycholinguistic literature emphasizing the social-interactive contribution to language acquisition has focused on the preverbal and/or one-word stage. However, this work has produced some important principles that hold true for the continuum of language learning and a range of cognitive activities well beyond this stage. Of special importance among these strategies is the notion of "scaffolding."

"Scaffolding" is a rather well-known term used by Bruner and his colleagues (Ratner & Bruner, 1978; Wood, Bruner, & Ross, 1976) which could be applied more creatively in the intervention context. *Scaffolding* refers to a shared process whereby the adult and child jointly construct supportive, interactive environments for learning. These interactions are "contingent" in that the responses of each partner depend on the prior utterance or action of the other. This scaffolding is evident in the early, predictable and highly structured play formats between child and adult (Ratner & Bruner, 1978). Collectively these authors have suggested that these semantically constrained, predictable, and interactive contexts not only contribute to children's understanding of appropriate dialogue but also assist them in mastering the forms of the language. One important aspect of scaffolding is that the dialogue (both verbal and nonverbal) allows for the expression of meaning across speech acts. Scaffolded utterances, which incorporate content words from the immediately preceding adult utterance through imitation, are less demanding to produce than spontaneous utterances and are frequently used by young talkers and children with language disorders (Kirchner & Prutting, 1987; Snow, Perlman, & Nathan, 1987). Additional research has shown that children continue to link propositions across speech acts in the discourse rather than within sentence units at the multiword stage (Ochs, Schieffelin, & Platt, 1979; Scollon, 1979) and, even later, to link speech acts across utterance boundaries in the use of pragmatic connectives (Gallagher & Craig, 1987; van Dijk, 1979). What this suggests is that throughout development the discourse itself provides a sort of "scaffold" or supportive context for the construction of both meaning and structure.

With respect to cognition Vygotsky's position has been presented in the translations of his own work (1962, 1978, 1986) as well as by numerous other researchers who have applied his original ideas in the contemporary literature (Bruner, 1984; Wertsch, 1985a, 1985b). Vygotsky argued that cognitive growth itself is dependent on language and is developed and maintained through interpersonal experience One of the most important concepts to come out of Vygotsky's work was the "Zone of Proximal Development" (ZPD). Belmont (1989) provided a clear and concise summary of the important constructs proposed by Vygotsky, in which he stated that the ZPD can be thought of as "a domain-specific predictor of benefit from able, domain-specific instruction . . ." (p. 145), which is the difference between how the child performs with and without assistance. According to Belmont, for evaluative purposes, the ZPD might usefully be considered as an alternative to the psychological construct of IQ. However, he cautioned that for instructional or educational purposes the resemblance of ZPD to the term "readiness" is a superficial one at best. Readiness, in Belmont's view, is often used as an excuse not to try to teach something (e.g., the child will learn when he is "ready"). Instead, in the Vygotskian approach, the clinician would provide instruction in supported learning environments. Instruction is not provided at a level where the child is capable of performing independently, but rather at a level of proficiency where the child manages to reach the desired level of performance only in close collaboration with a more capable partner.

Summing up this section, then, Vygotsky stated that learning is interpersonal and collaborative, an outgrowth of the skillful collaboration between the child and a partner who is more skilled, much like the early acquisition of language in the interactions between child and adult. Furthermore, it is the context of this partnership that allows the child to practice, understand, organize, and internalize aspects of that skill until eventually the skill or knowledge becomes his or her own.

With respect to application, two questions must be answered: What principles or notions link the constructs of a social-interactionist theory of language development and Vygotsky's view of cognitive development? And how can these principles be integrated to develop intervention approaches? The following principles are proposed:

1. The child learns language and a range of cognitive constructs as the result of active participation in reciprocal, collaborative, and interpersonal contexts.
2. Initially, the more skilled partner (clinician, teacher, or parent) structures and guides the interaction, enabling the child to perform at a level he or she would otherwise not be capable of.
3. Eventually, although gradually, there is a transfer of control to the child who, having automated and derived meaning from his performance in the collaborative context, is now able to assume a greater level of initiative in the interaction.

The question for language intervention is whether it is possible to make use of or construct supported communicative intervention contexts that can address conversational management and discourse, specific linguistic structures, and early literacy at once. In the pages that follow, one example of the application of these principles is demonstrated in an intervention context utilizing joint book reading routines. The book reading contexts, which are the subject of this chapter, were developed as an adaptation and outgrowth of the literature on these joint routines early in development. Following a summary of this literature, a description of the construction of reciprocal reading contexts and examples that clarify the use of the strategy pragmatically, structurally, and educationally will be presented.

BOOK READING ROUTINES: CHARACTERISTICS OF A DISCOURSE CONTEXT FOR LANGUAGE ACQUISITION

Psycholinguists' general interest in the relationship between interactive routines and language development has led to the examination of joint book reading as a specific instance. Investigations along these lines are an extension of the more general literature that characterizes the relationship between adult input and child language acquisition. The role of book reading routines in the development of labeling and vocabulary acquisition in young children during the one-word stage has been documented (Ninio, 1980, 1983; Ninio & Bruner, 1978). This line of research has provided evidence that labeling, and more generally the concept of reference, may be partially an outgrowth of the reciprocal dialogue structured by the adult in early interactive routines. Elaborating on this research, Wheeler (1983) demonstrated that mothers make linguistically sensitive changes in the structure and organization of the dialogue accompanying the activity according to the child's language level. Therefore, in the earliest stages of development the book reading routine may focus on labeling and lexical acquisition, whereas later dialogues may contain higher proportions of utterances relating more than one aspect of a picture in the same utterance, more requests for information, and eventually more abstract aspects of what the picture implies or how the pictured situation may have come about.

Snow and Goldfield (1983) investigated the incremental growth in language ability of a child between the ages of about 2 years, 5 months and 3 years, 4 months of age. In this study, a book reading routine functioned as a collaborative, predictable, and interactive activity in which the child learned to say "what he had heard others say in precisely the same situation" (p. 566). Snow and Goldfield (1983) proposed that this was evidence of the child's exploitation of the strategy of identifying utterances associated with frequently recurring situations and producing these utterances in predictable contexts. Rather than focus on the issues of simplicity, redundancy, and semantic contingency as critical variables in the supportive environment, Snow and Godlfield (1983) emphasized the role of routinization of interactive activity and predictability in adult-child interactions.

In addition to providing evidence for the role of predictability and situation-specific learning in language development, this study provides additional support for a context in which many young children initially function as effective communicators by acquiring unanalyzed utterance forms for immediate use (Clark, 1974, 1976; Peters, 1977, 1983; Wong–Fillmore, 1979). Children appear to segment and analyze the utterances that they produce rather than carry out analysis on the utterances they hear (Peters, 1977, 1983). However, the "pedagogical challenge," as Peters (1983) has put it, is how to construct learning environments that facilitate segmentation through the active analysis of longer utterance into their constituent parts. According to Peters (1983), the characteristics of a learning context that might facilitate segmentation and linguistic analysis would include a set of "fixed" phrases which, once fairly well learned, could be varied by introducing rephrasings, expansions, reductions, and substitutions. The combination of this systematic, controlled variation along with the frequent and selective exposure to linguistic forms would allow the learner to distinguish patterns in surface forms as well as their functions in the discourse.

It has been suggested that the initial acquisition of unanalyzed forms on which analytic work can be performed is accomplished largely through immediate imitation (Snow, 1981). It has been further hypothesized that the child with limited generative capability and atypical language development may rely to an even greater extent or for longer periods in development on similar strategies due to the discrepancy between communicative need and linguistic capability (Kirchner & Prutting, 1987). With respect to intervention, then, contexts should be constructed to exploit, rather than eliminate, the child's adaptive strategies.

Although the research just discussed focused primarily on language development in the preschool years, from a slightly different point of view, a remarkably similar set of characteristics have been identified for the contexts in which children learn to read. The significance of "predictability" and more specifically the impact of "patterning" in children's literature on the development of early reading skills has been well documented in the educational research literature (Bridge, 1979; Bridge & Burton, 1982; Bridge, Winograd, & Haley, 1983; McCracken & McCracken, 1979, 1986; Rhodes, 1981; Tompkins & Webeler, 1983). The same characteristics of repetition, predictability, and patterning identified in the literature on early language acquisition have been found to lead to the development of reading skills such as the ability to use contextual cues to aid meaning (Bridge et al., 1983), predict and apprehend meaning in reading comprehension (McCracken & McCracken, 1979, 1986), acquire a printed sight vocabulary, acquire knowledge of word families and sound letter correspondence, use sentence or story "frames" to form novel creations, as well as expand knowledge and vocabulary (Bridge et al., 1983). In both language and early literacy the value of repetition, predictability, and the ability to distinguish patterns in language has been demonstrated. Because these same characteristics surface in the interaction between the child and language development as well as in the interaction between child and print, the collective application of these characteristics in intervention could be of enormous potential.

SETTING UP THE RECIPROCAL BOOK READING CONTEXT: SELECTING THE LITERATURE AND SEGMENTING THE TEXT

For the purposes of this chapter, *reciprocal book reading* is the use of patterned children's literature to construct a structured, reciprocal (two-way) discourse activity as a context for language intervention. A book is selected for appropriateness in the areas of content, complexity, and interest level relative to the child's linguistic and congitive profile. Books should also be selected with respect to the particular linguistic structures that have been targeted for a particular child. A number of excellent sources have been compiled that group individual books according to their repetitive patterns and structural characteristics (Bridge et al., 1983; Tompkins & Webeler,

1983). Types of patterns, organized by Tompkins and Webeler (1983), include the following categories.

1. Books with repetitive language patterns in which a certain phrase or sentence is repeated at various points in a story (cf. The kindergarten classic, *Brown Bear Brown Bear, What Do You See?* by Bill Martin [1967]).
2. Books with a repetitive-cumulative pattern in which a word, phrase, or sentence is repeated in each succeeding episode with each episode adding a new word, phrase, or sentence to the sequence (cf. *I Know an Old Lady* by Rose Boone [1961]; *The Very Hungry Caterpillar* by Eric Carle [1969]; and *The Little Red Hen* by Paul Galdone [1969]).
3. Books with rhyming patterns or rhyme combined with repetition and cumulative repetition (cf. *A Rocket in My Pocket* by Carl Withers [1967]).
4. Books with patterns based on familiar cultural sequences such as cardinal and ordinal numbers, alphabet, months of the year, days of the week, seasons, colors (cf. *A Ghost Story* by Bill Martin [1970]).
5. Books with predictable plots in which the events occur in such a way as to enable the reader to predict future events (cf. *Spoiled Tomatoes* by Bill Martin [1967]).

The most predictable books would be those in Category 1 where the children can quickly learn to recite the repetitive pattern. Books in Category 2 and beyond are more complex. They may incorporate a repetitive language pattern, but largely are written using cumulative sequences and elaborated plots. Consequently, more linguistic and cogitive sophistication is needed to discover the pattern.

Once a book is selected, the following steps can be implemented to begin teaching language using reciprocal reading either individually or with choral responses in a small group.

1. Begin reading the book to the child or group over several repetitions using prosodic cues to segment and highlight the patterns in the selection.
2. Depending on the level of the child or group, when they have enough exposure to the text, begin to pause, creating a type of "cloze" condition wherein the child or group in choral fashion produce the next word, phrase, or line of the book. This portion of the invervention is referred to as "segmentation" of the book content. Pauses are inserted in linguistically specific ways to mark and select the portion of text the child will produce. (See McCracken and McCracken [1979, 1986] for additional uses of the "cloze" technique and a description of more general procedures for working with groups of children.)

3. Initially the child will "memorize" the text producing, perhaps, an un-analyzed form. The clinician, however, will continue to segment the text in variable yet explicit ways to facilitate linguistic analysis.
4. Segment the text in ways that allow the child to produce increasingly longer portions of the text until eventually children, if they are capable, "read" the entire book.
5. Once the text is well practiced, reverse roles. The child produces the clinician's utterances and the clinician responds by assuming the child's role.
6. Construct novel contexts using similar linguistic patterns to facilitate creative use of language outside the context in which it was original-ly learned.

It should be emphasized that the use of patterned children's literature and the techniques proposed by the McCrackens (1979, 1986) are not new to many regular education teachers in the primary grades. However, class-room teachers may be applying such techniques for somewhat different reasons and with different goals in mind. In this particular application the emphasis is on the development of oral language in a dialogic context for children with atypical or delayed language development, and this tech-nique can be used to focus specifically on the language aspect of the activ-ity rather than on reading per se. At the same time, however, the clinician is making use of the link between oral language and early literacy.

Theoretically, this is an ecellent example of a pragmatically based meth-odology because the success of this intervention procedure, even though it can be designed to address specific linguistic forms, depends on the colla-borative and interactive context between teacher, parent, or clinician and child for its execution. This is a specific application of what Snow, Perl-mann, and Nathan (1987) have suggested the goal of any intervention in the child's linguistic environment should encompass. That is, the building of discourse frames that provide a context for the child's utterances—"put-ting language before and after the child's expected utterance so that utter-ance is part of a longer coconstructed text" (p. 78). In this case, the more skilled partner presents a predictable text often enough that the child be-gins to understand the structure of the text and the language associated with it. Furthermore, the dialogue and the way the dialogue is structured is the heart of the intervention. When adjustments upward or downward must be made relative to complexity or level of support, the structure of the dialogue, not the words of the book, is modified.

Of greatest importance in constructing the discourse context is the clini-cian's purposeful selection and segmentation of book text for children of varying cognitive abilities, receptive language levels, and expressive skills. This is the kind of controlled and systematic variation that Peters (1983) suggested may be at the heart of "triggering" segmentation as a process linked to linguistic analysis. Importantly, however, it is the way in which the text is segmented, as well as the content and form of particular books, that dictates what the child will learn and at what level the child will be asked to respond. The best way to demonstrate this is through examples of segmentation using the language that comprises the text of a number of familiar children's books. The productions in the left column are those of the facilitator; the productions in the right hand column are the responses expected from the child.

The book most frequently referred to as the "kindergarten classic" is *Brown Bear, Brown Bear, What Do You See?* by Bill Martin (1970). The following examples reflect different ways of segmenting the same text, depending on what the clinician is trying to teach, the child's linguistic ability, and the child's ability to respond.

EXAMPLE 1

Brown Bear, Brown Bear, what
do you

see?

I see a . . . .

red bird

Looking at me.

EXAMPLE 2

Brown Bear, Brown Bear

What do you see?

I see

a yellow duck

Looking at me.

EXAMPLE 3

Brown Bear, Brown Bear

What do you see?

I see

a blue horse, looking at me.

etc.

Here is an example from a book by Eric Carle (1984) entitled *The Very Busy Spider*. The text is somewhat more complicated but lends itself to creating a dialogue in more creative and linguistically sophisticated ways using a sort cloze format with "slots" (Peters, 1979, 1983) where similar but slightly varied responses are required. The patterned "frame" of this text is as follows:

_____ said the _____.

Neigh, Neigh	horse
Moo, Moo	cow
Baa, Baa	sheep
Maa, Maa	goat
Oink, Oink	pig

Want to _____?

    go for a ride
    eat some grass
    run in the meadow
    jump on the rocks
    roll in the mud

The spider didn't answer. She was very busy spinning her web.

It is also possible to construct a reciprocal reading context which addresses more complex syntactic relationships in a similar interactive context. Several additional examples illustrate a more complicated application of a reciprocal reading strategy to teach meaning and production of connectives in a dyadic context.

Bloom, Lahey, Hood, Lifter, and Fiess (1980) have demonstrated that syntactic connectives are often used to connect relations that extend across utterance boundaries, for example, between two consecutive utterances produced by the child (Child–Child) or across two or more different speaker turns (Adult–Child; Child–Adult–Child). Bloom and colleagues suggested that discourse and the structure of utterances "mutually influence one another" with the presence of adult-child cohesion signaling the child's increasing ability to participate in discourse using newly or already learned linguistic forms. Others (Gallagher & Craig, 1987; van Dijk, 1979) have demonstrated that "pragmatic" connectives (to be distinguished from connectives primarily used to link semantic propositions) are used across speaker turns to link speech acts that serve an interactional function critical to the negotiation of interpersonal relationships. Skarakis–Doyle and Mentis (Chapter 10) have shown that some children with language disorders may rely to a greater extent on the "dyadic," or adult-child, construction of complex linguistic forms containing connectives across utterance boundaries. To create a context for teaching these more complex forms, speech-language pathologists need not—and perhaps should not—be restricted to thinking about teaching the meaning and production of connectives at the level of the sentence. To make what may be implicit and easily understood for the normal child explicit and salient for the atypical or delayed language user, interactive book reading can be used to construct contexts where the child and clinician collaborate to built complex forms intersententially as a way of teaching the meaning conveyed by specific connectives. This is in essence a more specific and applied use of vertical construction (Scollon, 1979), which takes into account both the cognitive and production factors that may initially serve as limitations to the construction of complex meanings intrasententially. What remains constant here with respect to intervention, regardless of the form, is the fact that both the meaning and the form are taught and learned in a dialogic context. Furthermore, the child's active participation and collaborative role in the construction of the dialogue is what facilitates learning of both form and meaning.

Three examples of books, although there are many more, that are ideally suited to the intersentential construction of complex utterances are *Dear Zoo* by Rod Campbell, *Where Is It?* by Robert and Marlene McCracken (1989), and *The Runaway Bunny* by Margaret Wise Brown (1972). The latter has a fairly complex textual structure from a semantic and syntactic standpoint.

EXAMPLE 1
Dear Zoo

I wrote to the zoo.

To send me a pet.

They sent me an elephant . . .

BUT he was too big.

So . . .

I sent him back.

etc.

They sent me a giraffe . . .

but he was too tall.

They sent me a camel . . .

but he was so grumpy.

They sent me a lion . . .

but he was too fierce.

etc.

EXAMPLE 2
Where Is It?

I had a blue ball. I bounced it to play. A dog took my blue ball. The dog ran away. I wanted my blue ball. I wanted to play. So . . . . .

I looked for my blue ball

The rest of the day.
I looked in the dog house

I looked in the wheelbarrow . . .

BUT the ball wasn't there.

I looked in the garbage can . . .

BUT the ball wasn't there.

BUT the ball wasn't there.

etc.

EXAMPLE 3
The Runaway Bunny

Once there was a little bunny who wanted to run away. So he said to his mother "I am running away."

"If you run away," said his mother, "I will run after you for you are my little bunny."

If you run after me I will become a fish in a trout stream

and . . . .

I will swim away from you.

If you become _____

        a fish in a trout stream
        rock on the mountain
        a crocus in a hidden garden
        a bird and fly away from me

I will _____

        become a fisherman
        become a mountain climber
        be a gardener
        be a tree that you come home to

and _____

        I will fish for you
        I will climb to where you are
        I will find you

It is possible to exploit predictability in the dialogue of more complex text wherein the clinician reads, pausing for child productions along the way. Take this example from the book *50 Below Zero* by Robert Munsch (1986). The book has a cumulative structure but also contains several sentences that are repeated throughout the story. The predictable and repetitive portions of the text which the child produces are highlighted.

EXAMPLE 4
50 Below Zero

In the middle of the night, Jason was asleep. He woke up! He heard a sound. He said, . . .

WHAT'S THAT? WHAT'S THAT? WHAT'S THAT?

Jason opened the door to the kitchen and there was his father who walked in his sleep. He was sleeping on top of the refrigerator. Jason yelled . . . PAPA, WAKE UP!

His father ran around the kitchen three times and went back to bed. Jason said,

THIS HOUSE IS GOING CRAAAAZY!!!

One final example provides an excellent, albeit more complex, example of a book text that can be used to teach connectives and logical, predictive answers. This is the story entitled *If You Give a Mouse a Cookie* by Laura Joffe Numeroff (1985). This book contains a pattern, but one that does not stem from phrases of exact wording which are repeated throughout the text. Rather, the pattern is cumulative and consequential based on a little boy's encounter with a demanding and energetic mouse.

EXAMPLE 5
If You Give a Mouse a Cookie

IF you give a mouse a cookie . . . .
                    he's going to ask for a glass of milk.
WHEN you give him the milk . . . .
                    he'll probably ask you for a straw.
WHEN he's finished . . . .
                    he'll ask for a napkin.
THEN he'll want to look in a mirror . . . .
                    to make sure he doesn't have a milk mustache.
WHEN he looks into the mirror . . . .
                    he might notice his hair needs a trim.
SO . . . . . .
                    he'll probably ask for a pair of nail scissors.
etc.

Just as early discourse environments are "highly mother managed" (Snow et al., 1987, p. 79), book reading are routines initially highly clinician managed. Therefore, at the outset the participation structure (Shugar &

Kmita, 1990) is adult-guided and provides opportunities for children to contribute in fairly explicit and predetermined ways. Initial learning, then, is embedded in interactional contexts that are specific and fixed (Peters & Boggs, 1986). Once the original text is learned it is important for the clinician to systematically vary roles in the dialogue, structure opportunities for child initiation, vary segmentation of the text, structure opportunities for the child to control and manipulate the language and interactional patterns, and construct dialogues in interactive contexts outside the book reading activity which elicit the language learned based on the pattern in the book. This is easily done using "substitution" and "replacement" strategies which hold the predictable frame and meaning constant, while varying the constituent parts (Crystal, Fletcher, & Garman, 1976; Kirchner & Prutting, 1987; Peters 1983). The previous examples from the books illustrate the utterance "frames," and the possibilities for construction of new utterances through lexical or constituent substitution and replacement are endless.

WHO WILL BENEFIT: FITTING INTERVENTION STRATEGIES TO CHILDREN'S PROFILES

Just as there are individual differences in the language of children who are developing normally (cf. Fillmore, Kempler, & Wang, 1979), one can assume that the range of differences in atypical language learners is equally great. Features of a child's particular profile, can predict the potential effectiveness of one intervention strategy over another. I have been collecting data on the application of the reciprocal book reading for language acquisition in atypical users. In the following pages, an example from a case report that illustrates application of the reciprocal reading strategy will be presented.

A CASE EXAMPLE

This is a child of 4.0 years of age, who carries the diagnosis of Asperger's syndrome. There are some rather specific characteristics associated with this diagnosis which necessitated the development of an intervention approach which was at once interactive and language-based. Asperger's syndrome has been described fairly regularly in the literature (Gillberg, 1985; Schopler, 1985; Szatmari, Tuff, Finlayson, & Bartolucci, 1990; Tantum, 1988; Wing, 1981, 1989; Wing & Gould 1979; Wolff & Barlow, 1979; Wolff & Chick, 1980). It is now thought to be a subclassification of the DSM-III-R (1987) classification of Pervasive Developmental Disorder. Asperger's syndrome presents as a distinct profile from the subclassification of autism, although it shares some of the more general features of the disorder as well as some features of the schizotypical personality. The characteristic profile of a child with Asperger's syndrome is unique and particularly relevant to the issues addressed at the pragmatic or discourse level of communication development. Children with this syndrome often show significant motor delays, and there have been reports that some of these children acquire speech before they learn to walk. Eventually, although often at a slower rate than normal children, a majority of these children appear to demonstrate a relatively full command of grammar except for pronominal errors, but they show a range of deficits which could be classified as pragmatic in nature. For example, despite the appearance of relatively "normal" linguistic structure in many of these children, it has been argued that much of their language is acquired by "rote" and that these children can be observed using rather complex or obscure vocabulary without corresponding knowledge of its meaning (Wing, 1981). As language develops, analysis of the discourse in the children I have evaluated (Kirchner, 1989) reveals the presence of irrelevant or tangential replies to questions, deficits in topic continuation or maintenance, inability to join meanings using connectives in a logical and semantically correct manner, and more global deficits in cohesion and coherence.

Structural deficits aside, the most obvious impairment in these children is the development of a two-way social interaction. Importantly, however, the social interactive deficit in this group of children is not thought to arise from a desire to withdraw from interaction but rather from an inability to understand and use the rules governing social behavior (Wing, 1981). In addition to demonstrating social behavior that is naive and peculiar, they show deficits in nonverbal aspects of communication such as using little facial expression, monotonous vocal intonation, inappropriate use of gesture, and inappropriate use of gaze as a discourse regulator. Although children with Asperger's syndrome are often reported to be of normal or above average intelligence, they are also restricted in imaginative play, engage in repetitive activity, and function with greater confidence in predictable contexts. These are children who, while odd and socially inept, require an age-appropriate academic curriculum, language-based instruction, peers of average or above intelligence, peers who demonstrate age-appropriate language development, and structured opportunities for interaction with socially appropriate children.

Baseline language samples collected daily for a period of 1 week indicated that the child being evaluated produced spontaneous utterances ranging in length from about 1.65 to 5.00 morphemes. Despite the presence of many shorter and grammatically simple utterances, there were numerous examples throughout the samples of longer, more complex utterances that were used frequently and in stereotypic ways. The child was able to produce many longer language segments grammatically and quite fluently, particularly in the form of songs, nursery rhymes, finger plays, and excerpts from dialogues produced as delayed imitations from prior conversations. There were also examples of the sometimes appropriate use of quite

complex utterances which appeared incongruous with the child's usual level of spontaneous production. Of special significance, this child showed
evidence (although not at high rates) of "scaffolded" speech where he produced appropriate responses in conversational contexts by incorporating
content words from the clinician's prior utterance. He was, however, completely unwilling to produce any imitative speech on demand, and a variety
of avoidance behaviors (reduced eye contact, increases in self stimulatory
behaviors such as eye squinting) were noted in all environments where any
demands for verbal language were placed on him.

The most remarkable feature of the child's communicative profile was
the marked discrepancy between what he was capable of producing linguistically and his ability to use language for social interaction—even at linguistically simple levels. The child's social skills were markedly discrepant
from all other areas of functioning. Communicatively, this child would be
described as unassertive, demonstrating characteristics of both passive and
inactive communicators (Fey, 1986). He was usually unresponsive to initiations from adults and always unresponsive to initiations (verbally or in
play) from his peers. He almost never gave verbal or nonverbal replies to
direct requests for information or action. Despite age-level performance on
standardized measures of receptive and expressive vocabulary as well as
cognitive functioning, the child displayed a profound communicative disorder with failures primarily at the level of discourse rather than structure.

Given this profile, the main concern at the outset of intervention was not
the production of verbal language, but rather facilitating a level of engagement and participation in a reciprocal and interactive context. In addition,
an effort was made to identify a context that could be used individually but
later could be used with a peer or in the preschool classroom to provide an
opportunity for the child to participate interactively with a small group.
Having noted the child's interest in book reading as an activity in which he
would engage with his mother and alone, the reciprocal reading strategy
was applied.

The child received 2 hours of individual language intervention per week,
and during one six-week period, several book reading contexts were constructed. Books were segmented incrementally, gradually increasing the
length of the expected child response until the child was able to produce
the text from the books verbatim. A particular book was selected because of
it's linguistic simplicity and it's question-answer format, the latter being
particularly deficient for this child and a way of specifically addressing responsiveness. It is important to note, however, that the segmentation was
not incremental because the child was unable to recall and reproduce longer responses but rather because of the child's reluctance and often clear re-
fusal to participate verbally, be responsive, and be reciprocal. Therefore, in
addition to controlling the language, the level of participation required
was controlled.

The book selected was *Mommy Where Are You?* by Harriet Ziefert and Emilie Boon (1988). The text of the book is very short and in it's final form was segmented as follows:

I'm looking for my mommy.
Mommy is that you?

> Yes, it's me. I'm home.

Mommy, I can't see you.

> Here I am. [picture is
> hanging laundry]

Mommy where are you?

> Here I am. I'm picking
> vegetables.

Mommy, what are you doing?

> I'm cooking supper.

Mommy where are you?

> Here I am. I'm taking a bath.

Little Hippo, where are you?

> Here I am. I'm hiding.

Goodnight Mommy. [Picture is
mommy tucking little Hippo
into bed.]

When training was introduced, the child listened but provided no verbal responses for fully the first four sessions using the books. What is important, however, is that after only one to two readings of the book he began to point to the picture corresponding to the verbal answer required. Verbal or not, this was a level of reciprocity and participation in an interactive context that had not been present previously in any of his interactions with the clinician.

As the child was exposed repeatedly, two to three times per session, to the book reading context he participated verbally and began to extend the language of the text in ways that were not modeled or specifically taught. These linguistic additions are highlighted in the text.

Mommy is that you?

> Yes it's me. I'm home.

Mommy, I can't see you.

> Here I am. I'M DOING
> THE LAUNDRY.

Mommy where are you?

> Here I am. I'm picking
> vegetables. CARROTS, CORN.

Mommy what are you doing?

> I'm cooking supper.
> SPAGHETTI, MACARONI
> AND CHEESE, ROAST BEEF.

Mommy where are you?

> Here I am. I'm taking a
> BUBBLE bath. I'm taking a
> BUBBLE bath.

Little Hippo where are you?

> Here I am. I'm hiding
> UNDER THE BED.

Goodnight mommy.

> THIS IS THE END OF
> MOMMY WHERE ARE YOU.

Transfer of use to play contexts was noted by the end of the six-week period during which data were collected for this particular text. An example of utterances produced using toys that could be physically manipulated in a variety of ways included the following examples. The clinician's input is presented in the column on the left; the child's responses are presented on the right. Specific examples of text or textual "frames" presented in the book reading context, but not observed previously in any spontaneous samples taken, not taught in any other context, but used appropriately in the sample are highlighted in this short segment of dialogue.

Shall we use Ernie and Bert?

> Yes, let's use Ernie and Bert.
> Ernie and Bert. Ernie and Bert.
> Ernie WHERE ARE YOU?
> HERE I AM. There's no bed.

Here's the bed.

> Ernie, WHERE ARE YOU?
> HERE I AM. I'M IN THE
> BED. Bert. There's Bert. He
> has no bed.

Here we go. "B" for Bert.

> "B." Bert's bed. It's Bert's bed.

Bert, WHERE ARE YOU?

> HERE I AM. I'M IN MY BED.

These data are not inclusive, but rather are illustrative of a great number of generalized productions which provided evidence of this child's knowl-

edge of the linguistic data learned in the book reading context and the
child's ability to apply similar language appropriately in contexts outside
that in which it was originally learned. Some children will naturally be
more restricted in their abilities to generalize use of language, regardless of
the strategy used. The extent to which the child possesses the cognitive and
linguistic competencies to elaborate within the original dialogue may be
predictive of the degree to which the child will eventually be less dependent on the supportive aspects of a dialogue.

Using these data and supportive research in the psycholinguistic literature, it is possible to delineate the characteristics of the learner who will
profit most from this kind of language intervention. It is also possible to
speculate as to why the strategy is so powerful—not only in establishing
initial use of the language in the structured book reading context, but also
in the generalized use of similar language patterns beyond the original
teaching context.

The most important characteristic in predicting the child's ability to learn
the language in the context of the routine appears to be that the child is imitative or presents evidence of spontaneous complete or partial repetition in
conversational samples. Snow and colleagues (1987) suggested that imitative children may need to have appropriate responses available for situations
before they can analyse and produce novel behaviors in them. Similarly,
the best candidates for application of this particular strategy are children
who show evidence of the "gestalt" learning (Peters, 1977, 1983). For these
children the initial "units" of language acquisition may be formulaic
phrases and multiword units that only later are analyzed for their structure. These are also the children who make use of repetition in a "scaffolded" manner, borrowing content from the partner's prior utterance as a
way of using the discourse to construct utterances (Clark, 1974, 1977, 1978,
1982; Snow, 1981). As Snow and colleagues (1987) pointed out, children
can respond to routinized speech without understanding or analyzing it
because of the characteristics of the routine itself—familiarity and predictability. The effect, then, is to give even the child with limited generative skill
a way of participating in the interaction by exploiting the child's tendency
to repeat as a way of making up for both his limitations of cognitive capacity and incomplete analysis of the language (Kirchner & Prutting, 1987;
Peters, 1983). Equally important for the child whose data served as an example here is that the reciprocity and interactive nature of the learning context served to facilitate a level of responsiveness and participation in the
dialogue which was not present at the outset of intervention. It was the absence of this responsiveness and reciprocity which characterized the primary communication deficit displayed by the child and which could not be
addressed in a context emphasizing syntactically correct productions to describe pictured actions. For that matter, any other activity of this nature, in
which the interactional component is deemphasized or even eliminated al-

together in service of structural objectives, would have been inappropriate to this child's needs.

The reasons why an intervention strategy embedded in a routine works at this more sophisticated language level are really no different from the reasons why routines and rule-governed play are effective aids to acquisition earlier in development. First, the child is systematically exposed to language in a semantically restricted, well understood context with a clearly delineated structure (Bruner, 1983; Ratner & Bruner, 1978). The child is an active participant in the co-construction of a meaningful dialogue. Teaching language as part of a dialogue is substantially different from teaching identical linguistic forms and meanings in a picture description task. Second, within the context of this dialogue, flexibility can be created by interchanging roles and segmenting the text in varied ways to make specific aspects of the language salient and thus permit structural analysis. Third, there is an aspect of the book reading context which is extremely important with respect to the generalizability of use outside the original teaching context and which is a feature not always shared of mother-child routines early in development. Snow and colleagues (1987) pointed out that early mother-child routines often are somewhat "nonsensical" in a practical way (e.g., "This Little Piggy Went to Market"), making them high in predictability but low in semantic contingency. Therefore, there is little chance that the child will encounter these routines or opportunties to use the language associated with them in other contexts. What is important about the interactive book reading contexts presented here is that they are not nonsensical, which makes them at once both predictable and contingent. The child then can be exposed to opportunities outside the book reading context itself, where the utterances can be used in interactions structured for elicitation or as naturally occurring parts of a dialogue. Finally, this is an active, integrated learning environment where the child learns language as part of a dialogue that incorporates conversational management through turn-taking and reciprocity which are part of the instructional context. In addition, what has been proposed here is an instructional plan that can be organized to place varying levels of demand on the child for responsiveness, contingency, linguistic structure, comprehension, prediction, and the relationship between patterns in language and patterns in print, depending on the child's intervention needs.

CONCLUSION

There is no question that the contribution of the pragmatic literature in the past 10 to 15 years has provided a necessary and expanded view of language acquisition and language disorder. There is also no question that it will require an ambitious effort to delineate the characteristics of successful, integrated intervention approaches. However, the field of speech-language pathology is now under strenuous pressure to begin translating the fundamentals of pragmatic theory into clinical applications. Pragmatic approaches may be, by their very nature, more difficult to validate than approaches that compartmentalize the teaching of syntactic constituents outside the contexts in which they are used (cf. Connell, 1987). However, focusing research on the teaching of small structural segments of the discourse to excess serves only to fragment speech-language pathologists' understanding of the contexts in which language is acquired and used. Language assessment must always include an analysis of structural features because conclusions drawn from this source of evaluative data provide necessary information relative to the formulation of a diagnosis and an intervention plan. However, beyond this, a pragmatic theory stipulates that structure must be evaluated, interpreted, and remediated within the larger framework of discourse. It would seem, then, that any set of criteria applied to the definition of either an assessment profile or an intervention plan would include some explanation of function both structurally and contextually.

There are no precise rules about how to proceed in accumulating the necessary body of applied research that is so desperately needed. As a point of departure for future research, consider the words of Luria, quoted by Oliver Sacks (1985) in *The Man Who Mistook His Wife for a Hat.*

Luria wrote: the power to describe, which was too common to the great nineteenth-century neurologists and psychiatrists, is almost gone now . . . It must be revived. (p. viii)

There is a limit, based on experimental research, to what speech-language clinicians can know about the processes at work when they intervene to teach language to children with atypical profiles. But it is precisely the process of acquisition, not the product, that requires our attention at this moment. A careful description of an approach justified on the basis of theoretical weight will clarify the processes and conditions under which children learn what we attempt to teach them. Perhaps the realization of how little we really know about these processes is a sort of signal—a piece of news that will provide the foundation for a rigorous effort aimed at understanding how best to teach the children we are obligated to treat.

ACKNOWLEDGMENT

This chapter is lovingly dedicated to the memory of Carol A. Prutting. Carol was my advisor, mentor, colleague, and dear friend. Carol inspired me to work, encouraged me to think creatively, and taught me to defend that in which I believed. In her memory and in memory of our partnership I will continue to work. I confess, I am at once overwhelmed by her absence as well as the importance and complexity of the work that lies ahead. I suppose we could all stop now and say this is the best we could do. However, Carol's work served to lay a rich foundation of knowledge from which we have only begun to extract the potential contribution. Not until we had Carol's insight in hand did it become a certainty that pragmatics would occupy a position of true importance in the field of speech-language pathology. We are now obligated to move forward in acknowledgment of this contribution and in a manner befitting of Carol's respect for scholarship.

REFERENCES

Bates, E., & MacWhinney, B. (1979). A functionalist approach to the acquisition of grammar. In E. Ochs & B. Schieffelin (Eds.), *Developmental pragmatics* (pp. 167–211). New York: Academic Press.

Bates, E., & MacWhinney, B. (1982). Functionalist approaches to grammar. In E. Wanner & L. Gleitman (Eds.), *Language acquisition: The state of the art* (pp. 173–218). Cambridge, UK: Cambridge University Press.

Belmont, J. (1989). Cognitive strategies and strategic learning: The socio-instructional approach. *American Psychologist, 44*(2), 142–148.

Bloom, L., Lahey, M., Hood, L., Lifter, K., & Fiess, K. (1980). Complex sentences: Acquisition of syntactic connectives and the semantic relations they encode. *Journal of Child Language, 7*, 235–262.

Bridge, C. (1979). Predictable materials for beginning readers. *Language Arts, 56*, 503–507.

Bridge, C., & Burton, B. (1982). Teaching sight vocabulary through patterned language materials. In J. Niles & L. Harris (Eds.), *New inquiries in reading research and instruction. Thirty-First Yearbook of the National Reading Conference* (pp. 119–123). Washington, DC: National Reading Conference.

Bridge, C. A., Winograd, P. N., & Haley, D. (1983, May). Using predictable materials vs. preprimers to teach beginning sight words. *The Reading Teacher*, pp. 884–891.

Bruner, J. S. (1975). From communication to language—a psychological perspective. *Cognition, 3*, 255–288.

Bruner, J. S. (1976). Early rule structure: The case of peekaboo. In J. S. Bruner, A. Jolly, & K. Sylva (Eds.), *Play: Its role in development and evolution* (pp. 277–285). New York: Basic Books.

Bruner, J. S. (1981). The social context of language acquisition. *Language and Communication, 1*, 155–178.

Bruner, J. S. (1983). *Child's talk*. Oxford, UK: Oxford University Press.

Bruner, J. S. (1984). Vygotsky's zone of proximal development: The hidden agenda. In B. Rogoff & J. V. Wertsch (Eds.), *Children's learning in the zone of proximal development* (pp. 93–97). San Francisco, CA: Jossey-Bass.

Clark, R. (1974). Performing without competence. *Journal of Child Language, 11*, 1–10.

Clark, R. (1977). What's the use of imitation? *Journal of Child Language, 4*, 341–358.

Clark, R. (1978). Some even simpler ways to learn to talk. In N. Waterson & C. Snow (Eds.), *The development of communication* (pp. 391–414). New York: John Wiley and Sons.

Clark, R. (1982). Theory and method in child-language research: Are we assuming too much? In S. Kuczaj (Ed.), *Language development. I. Syntax and semantics* (pp. 1–35). Hillsdale, NJ: Lawrence Erlbaum.

Connell, P. (1987). Teaching language form, meaning, and function to specific language-impaired children. In S. Rosenberg (Ed.), *Advances in applied psycholinguistics* (Vol. 1, pp. 40–76). New York: Cambridge University Press.

Crystal, D., Fletcher, P., & Garman, M. (1976). *The grammatical analysis of language disability.* New York: Elsevier.

Diagnostic and statistical manual of mental disorders. (1987). (3rd ed., Rev. [DSM-III-R]). Washington, DC: American Psychiatric Assn.

Fey, M. E. (1986). *Language intervention with young children.* San Diego, CA: College-Hill Press.

Fillmore, C. J., Kempler, D., & Wang, W. (1979). *Individual differences in language ability and language behavior.* New York: Academic Press.

Gallagher, T. M., & Craig, H. K. (1987). An investigation of pragmatic connectives within preschool peer interactions. *Journal of Pragmatics, 11,* 27–37.

Gillberg, C. (1985). Asperger's syndrome and recurrent psychosis. *Journal of Autism and Development Disorders, 15,* 389–397.

Kirchner, D. M. (1989). Unpublished data.

Kirchner, D. M., & Prutting, C. A. (1987). Spontaneous verbal repetition: A performance based strategy for language acquisition. *Clinical Linguistics and Phonetics, 1*(2), 147–169.

Kirchner, D. M., & Skarakis–Doyle, E. (1983). Developmental language disorders: A theoretical perspective. In T. M. Gallagher & C. A. Prutting (Eds.), *Pragmatic assessment and intervention issues in language* (pp. 215–246). San Diego, CA: College-Hill Press.

McCracken, M. J., & McCracken, R. A. (1979). *Reading, writing, and language.* Winnepeg, Canada: Peguis Publishers.

McCracken, R. A., & McCracken, M. J. (1986). *Stories, songs, and poetry to teach reading and writing: Literacy through language.* Winnepeg, Canada: Peguis Publishers.

Nelson, K., & Gruendel, J. M. (1979). At morning it's lunchtime: A scriptal view of children's dialogues. *Discourse Processes, 2,* 73–94.

Ninio, A. (1980). Picture book reading in mother-infant dyads belonging to two subgroups in Israel. *Child Development, 51,* 587–590.

Ninio, A. (1983). Joint book reading as a multiple vocabulary acquisition device. *Developmental Psychology, 19*(3), 445–451.

Ninio, A., & Bruner, J. S. (1978). The achievements and antecedants of labeling. *Journal of Child Language, 5,* 1–15.

Norris, J. A. (1988, March). Using communication strategies to enhance reading acquisition. *The Reading Teacher,* pp. 668–673.

Ochs, E., Schieffelin, B., & Platt, M. (1979). Propositions across utterances and speakers. In E. Ochs & B. Schieffelin (Eds.), *Developmental pragmatics* (pp. 251–227). New York: Academic Press.

Peters, A. (1977). Language learning strategies: Does the whole equal the sum of the parts? *Language, 53,* 560–573.

Peters, A. (1983). *The units of language acquisition.* Cambridge, UK: Cambridge University Press.

Peters, A., & Boggs, S. T. (1986). Interactional routines as cultural influences upon language acquisition. In B. Schieffelin & E. Ochs (Eds.), *Language socialization across cultures* (pp. 80–96). Cambridge, UK: Cambridge University Press.

Ratner, N., & Bruner, J. S. (1978). Games, social exchange, and the acquisition of language. *Journal of Child Language, 5,* 391–401.

Rhodes, L. K. (1981, February). I can read! Predictable books as resources for reading and writing instruction. *The Reading Teacher,* pp. 511–518.

Sacks, O. (1985). *The man who mistook his wife for a hat.* New York: Harper & Row.

Schopler, E. (1985). Convergence of learning disability, higher level autism, and Asperger's syndrome. *Journal of Autism and Developmental Disorders, 15,* 359.

Scollon, R. (1979). A real early stage: An unzipped condensation of a dissertation of child language. In E. Ochs & B. Schieffelin (Eds.), *Developmental pragmatics* (pp. 215–227). New York: Academic Press.

Shugar, G. W., & Kmita, G. (1990). The pragmatics of collaboration: Participant structure and the structures of participation. In G. Conti–Ramsden & C. Snow (Eds.), *Children's language* (Vol. 7, pp. 273–303). Hillsdale, NJ: Lawrence Erlbaum.

Snow, C. (1979a). Social interaction and language acquisition. In P. Dale & D. Ingram (Eds.), *Child language: An international perspective* (pp. 195–214). Baltimore, MD: University Park Press.

Snow, C. (1979b). The role of social interaction in language acquisition. In A. Collins (Ed.), *Children's language and communication: 12th Minnesota symposium on child psychology* (pp. 157–182). Hillsdale, NJ: Lawrence Erlbaum.

Snow, C. (1981). The uses of imitation. *Journal of Child Language, 3,* 205–212.

Snow, C., & Goldfield, B. A. (1983). Turn the page please: Situation-specific language learning. *Journal of Child Language, 10,* 551–570.

Snow, C., Perlmann, R., & Nathan, D. (1987). Why routines are different: Toward a multiple-factors model of the relation between input and language acquisition. In K. E. Nelson & A. van Kleeck (Eds.), *Children's langauge* (Vol. 6, pp. 65–97). Hillsdale, NJ: Lawrence Erlbaum.

Szatmari, P., Tuff, L., Finlayson, A. J., & Bartolucci, G. (1990). Asperger's syndrome and autism: Neurocognitive aspects. *Journal of the American Academy of Child and Adolescent Psychiatry, 29,* 130 136.

Tompkins, G. E., & Webeler, M. (1983, February). What will happen next? Using predictable books with young children. *The Reading Teacher,* pp. 489–502.

van Dijk, T. A. (1979). Pragmatic connectives. *Journal of Pragmatics, 3,* 447–456.

Vygotsky, L. S. (1962). *Thought and language* (E. Harfmann & G. Vakar, Trans.). Cambridge, MA: MIT Press. (Original work published 1934)

Vygotsky, L. S. (1978). *Mind in society: The development of higher psychological processes* (M. Cole, V. John–Steiner, S. Scribner, & E. Souberman, Eds. & Trans.). Cambridge, MA: Harvard University Press.

Vygotsky, L. S. (1986). Thinking and speech. In R. W. Rieber & A. S. Carton (Eds.), *The collected works of L. S. Vygotsky: I. Problems of general psychology* (pp. 39–285). New York: Plenum Press. (Original work published 1934)

Wertsch, J. W. (1985a). *Vygotsky and the social formation of mind.* Cambridge, MA: Harvard University Press.

Wertsch, J. W. (1985b). *Culture, communication, and cognition: Vygotskian perspectives.* New York: Cambridge University Press.

Wheeler, M. P. (1983). Context-related age changes in mother's speech: Joint bookreading. *Journal of Child Language, 10*(1), 259–263.

Wilcox, J. (1988). *Pragmatics: A retrospective analysis* (Cassette Recording No. H81118-110). Rockville, MD: American Speech-Language-Hearing Assn.

Wing, L. (1981). Asperger's syndrome: A clinical account. *Psychological Medicine, 11,* 115–129.

Wing, L., & Gould, J. (1979). Severe impairments of social interaction and associated abnormalities in children. *Journal of Autism and Developmental Disorders, 9,* 11–29.

Wolff, S., & Barlow, A. (1979). Schizoid personality in childhood: A comparative study of schizoid, autistic, and normal children. *Journal of Child Psychology and Psychiatry, 20,* 29–46.

Wolff, S., & Chick, J. (1980). Schizoid personality in childhood: A controlled follow-up study. *Psychological Medicine, 10,* 85–100.

Wong–Fillmore, L. W. (1979). Individual differences in second language acquisition. In C. J. Fillmore, D. Kempler, & Sy-Y. Wang (Eds.), *Individual differences in language ability and language behavior* (pp. 203–228). New York: Academic Press.

Wood, D. J. (1980). Teaching the young child: Some relationships between social interaction, language, and thought. In D. R. Olson, (Ed.), *The social foundations of language and thought: Essays in honor of Jerome Bruner* (pp. 211–230). New York: W. W. Norton.

Wood, D. J., Bruner, J. S., & Ross, G. (1976). The role of tutoring in problem solving. *Journal of Child Psychology and Psychiatry, 17*(2), 89–100.

PREDICTABLE CHILDREN'S LITERATURE CITED

Brown, Margaret Wise. *The Runaway Bunny,* 1972.

Carle, Eric. *The Very Busy Spider,* 1984.

Carle, Eric. *The Mixed Up Chameleon,* 1984.

Galdone, Paul. *The Little Red Hen,* 1969.

Martin, Bill. *Brown Bear, Brown Bear What Do You See?,* 1970.

Martin, Bill. *A Ghost Story,* 1970.

Martin, Bill. *Spoiled Tomatoes,* 1967.

McCracken, Robert and McCracken, Marlene. *Where is it?,* 1987.

Munsch, Robert. *50 Below Zero,* 1986.

Numeroff, Laura Joffe. *If You Give a Mouse a Cookie,* 1985.

Westcott, Nadine Bernard. *I Know an Old Lady Who Swallowed a Fly,* 1980.

Withers, Carol. *A Rocket in My Pocket,* 1967.

CHAPTER 12

Facilitating Grammatical Development: The Contribution of Pragmatics

LAURENCE B. LEONARD AND MARC E. FEY

In Fey and Leonard (1983), we reviewed the growing literature on the pragmatic abilities of children with specific language impairment. We concluded that, as in other areas, these children do not represent a homogeneous group with respect to their pragmatic skills. Rather, we proposed that there are at least three different groups of children with specific language impairment as determined by their profiles of social-conversational participation.

The first pattern is represented by children who are neither as assertive nor as responsive to their social partners as expected, based on the formal linguistic means at their disposal. These children have general pragmatic deficits that extend well beyond any delays they are experiencing in the acquisition of language forms. Fey (1986) referred to these children as inactive conversationalists. The second group of children are considerably more cooperative in conversational settings. Indeed, many of these children are highly responsive to the requestive and nonrequestive acts of their conversational partners. Importantly, however, they are either unwilling or unable to make frequent substantive contributions to the conversation. They have the linguistic resources to initiate and extend topics and to perform assertive speech acts, such as requests for information and action, but they do so infrequently. Fey (1986) referred to these children as passive conversationalists. The third group of children are less pragmatically impaired than children in the first groups. These children, referred to by Fey (1986) as active conversationalists, are limited by deficits in language form, but they use their limited linguistic resources to participate actively in conversations. They typically produce a wide range of both assertive and responsive conversational acts, and they appear to attend to the informational requirements of their partners.

Fey (1986) added a fourth category of children, verbal noncommunicators, to our original formulation. These children willingly and frequently produce assertive conversational acts. In so doing, however, they seem relatively unconcerned with making semantic ties between their own utterances and those of their partners. Their narratives may also be characterized by incoherence. Their reasonably well-formed sentences simply do not make sense in the context.

Prior to the introduction of pragmatics into speech-language pathology, this type of categorization of children with language impairment would have been difficult to conceive. But the impact of pragmatics on language assessment and intervention extends well beyond simply making it possible to categorize children based on their pragmatic performance. Pragmatics gives speech-language pathologists the theoretical rationale for developing intervention objectives that are not based on language form. Furthermore, it obligates them to search for intervention approaches that are effective in achieving these nonformal goals.

For example, if a child does not perform a variety of illocutionary acts and is not participating actively both as speaker and as listener, it probably is not appropriate to focus the intervention program on the child's grammar (Fey, 1986). This is precisely the case for inactive conversationalists. A new Auxiliary or Article is not likely to have any significant effect on the communicative effectiveness of a child who is unwilling or unable to use existing formal abilities. Instead, intervention may focus on spontaneous talking, the use of topic initiations and extensions, the use of more assertive acts, and greater responsivity (Fey, 1986; Hubbell, 1977, 1981).

A similar case can be made for verbal noncommunicators. Omitted Auxiliaries, Articles, and inflectional morphemes seem rather insignificant obstacles to effective communication for a child who seems to have a basic deficit in the sense-making capacity (Lund & Duchan, 1988). At least initially, intervention must focus instead on helping the child to attend more carefully and respond more consistently to the informational requirements of the conversational partner.

By directing attention toward language as a tool for social action, pragmatics has freed speech-language pathologists from the necessity to focus on grammatical or even lexical form in intervention programs. But there are some children, especially active conversationalists, for whom the primary obstacle to effective communication is their delay in grammatical development. How can pragmatics, with its emphasis on language in context, inform speech-language pathologists in such cases? It is crucial to recognize, in this regard, that the emphasis on communication mandated by a pragmatic perspective in no way minimizes the importance of grammar (Kamhi & Nelson, 1988). In fact, a primary objective of functionalist theorists (e.g., Bates & MacWhinney, 1987) is to demonstrate how grammatical structure derives from semantic and pragmatic sources.

Indeed, one of the basic principles of functional linguistics is that clause-internal morphosyntax can only be understood with reference to the semantic and pragmatic functions of its constituent units, and consequently the major task is to describe the complex interaction of form and function in language. (Foley & Van Valin, 1984, p. 14)

Clearly, then, the application of pragmatic principles to language intervention does not require the abandonment of grammar as a potential treatment objective. To the contrary, grammar must share center stage with semantic and pragmatic functions.

In this chapter, some of the ways in which pragmatics and grammar interact will be illustrated. The emphasis will be on how clinicians can capitalize on knowledge of pragmatics to facilitate the grammatical development of children with language impairment.

SOME LINKS BETWEEN GRAMMAR AND PRAGMATICS

Any attempt to integrate pragmatics and grammar must recognize the reciprocal nature of their relationship. On the one hand, pragmatics is needed to define the conditions under which syntactic and semantic phenomena apply. For example, do is not simply optional in affirmative declarative sentences. It is used for contrast or emphasis. Auxiliaries are not free to appear in either sentence-initial or sentence-medial position. They appear in sentence-initial position when a question or indirect request is intended. Pragmatics is also necessary to explain apparent violations of grammatical rules. For example, in English a Sentence cannot consist entirely of a Prepositional Phrase. Yet, utterances such as *To the farm* are perfectly appropriate in the context of a prior utterance such as *Where is Maggie going?*

On the other hand, certain pragmatic abilities seem to depend on grammar. Because this is not the direction of influence usually considered in discussions of the relationship between pragmatics and grammar, a number of details will be provided here.

SPEECH ACTS

Studies of children's pragmatic abilities often include an examination of the speech acts, or communicative functions served by the children's utterances. Three such speech acts are indirect requests (e.g., *Can you give me the pencil?*), permission requests (e.g., *May I go?*), and rules (e.g., *You should/ hafta spin the dial*). It is doubtful that a child could be given credit for expressing the first two of these unless he or she included the Modal Auxiliary verb. Quite possibly, Auxiliary inversion would be required as well. In the case of rules, it is difficult to see how a child could receive credit for this speech act without producing the Modal or Semi-Auxiliary.

CONVERSATIONAL REPLIES

One of the bulwarks of conversation is ellipsis. Without it, much of a conversationalist's speech would simply be a repetition of material already contained in prior utterances. However, ellipsis, too, requires control of aspects of grammar. Consider the utterance in (1):

(1) Adult: Who eats worms?
     Child: I don't!

In the child's response, *don't* replaces an entire Verb Phrase, *eats worms*. A response to the same question such as *Brenda!* would also require knowledge of the category Verb Phrase, for it is precisely this category that is deleted.

The pragmatic device called the follow-on (McShane, 1980) also appears to depend on knowledge of grammatical categories. The following utterance pair provides an example:

(2) Adult: The truck is pulling a car
     Child: A broken car

The child's elaboration of the point made by the adult requires extraction of a Noun Phrase.

CONVERSATIONAL REPAIR AND REGULATION

When the child receives feedback from a listener that his or her original message requires modification, any repair that the child can muster will be dependent in part on his or her grammatical abilities. For example, the repair below seems to require knowledge of the category Noun Phrase:

(3) Child: It's crying
    Adult: What?
    Child: The baby bird's crying

The child's attempts to obtain clarification from others also seems dependent on this type of knowledge:

(4) Adult: Gonna take that tidbit
    Child: Take what?
    Adult: That little piece

CODE SWITCHING

Adults are not the only ones to simplify their speech when talking to young children. Other children show evidence of this behavior as well. But to engage in this type of modification, children must have implicit knowledge of which categories can be reduced. For example, in (5), the child seems to recognize that a Modal Auxiliary is dispensable and that a full Prepositional Phrase can be replaced by a deictic term:

(5) We should put the toys on the shelf.
    See? We put the toys here.

COHESION

Perhaps the best example of an interaction between grammar and pragmatics can be found in the rules for using pronouns. From the standpoint of pragmatics, one can say that a pronoun is used whenever the referent is obvious from the physical context, or when the referent has already been made explicit in the prior discourse. However, if we limit ourselves to these considerations, we would be unable to explain why, for example, *him* can refer to *Dante* in (6) but not in (7):

(6) Dante thinks that Kevin might hurt him
(7) Dante might hurt him

To explain the difference in these two utterances, we must recognize that him cannot refer to another Noun Phrase that is within the same embedded clause. In (6), *him* can refer to Dante because Dante is outside the embedded clause, *Kevin might hurt him.* In (7), *him* can only refer to some male other than Dante. It is difficult to see how these constraints on pronoun interpretation could be explained by pragmatic principles alone.

IMPLICATIONS FOR INTERVENTION

There are at least three ways in which information about pragmatics can play an important part in grammatical intervention. The first involves the selection of goals. In particular, a pragmatic skill found to be deficient in a child with language impairment may, on close inspection, require some grammatical knowledge and/or ability that the child has not yet attained. Effective intervention might require a focus on the child's acquisition of the prerequisite grammatical forms.

The second contribution made by pragmatics concerns the activities within which intervention takes place. Activities represent the physical and social contexts in which clinical procedures are implemented (Fey, 1986). The pragmatic focus on language as a means for social expression motivates clinicians to carry out intervention in more naturalistic and functional contexts than previously believed necessary. Pragmatic principles provide clinicians with some methods for enhancing the naturalness of even relatively structured intervention activites.

The third area in which pragmatics has influenced approaches to grammatical intervention concerns the specific procedures that are employed within the activities. In particular, knowledge of pragmatics provides clinicians with information about how to alter the specific conversational context to highlight the targeted grammatical form or, in some cases, to exemplify its communicative function. These three contributions will be discussed in turn.

USING PRAGMATIC FUNCTIONS TO DICTATE GRAMMATICAL GOALS

The literature on children who are language impaired reveals a number of specific pragmatic areas that can be deficient in these children (see Chapter 6). In some cases, these deficits clearly are not attributable to limitations in grammar. For example, some limitations might be due primarily to a poor understanding of listener needs or to a low degree of conversational assertiveness (Fey, 1986). As a case in point, Conti–Ramsden and Friel–Patti (1983) found that children with language impairment initiated fewer conversational turns when speaking with their mothers than did a group of younger normally developing children at a comparable stage of language development. This reluctance of many children with specific language impairment to initiate conversational bids cannot be easily attributed to deficient grammatical abilities.

In some cases, however, the pragmatic difficulties of children with language learning problems seem to be dependent on particular grammatical attainments. Accordingly, a reasonable strategy would be to select for treatment those areas of grammar that seem linked to documented pragmatic difficulties. A few examples are provided here.

Craig and Evans (1989) compared the turn exchanges of children with language impairment and younger normally developing children at a similar stage of language development. They found that when the normally developing children began an utterance in the middle of an adult's utterance, it occurred in a "transition-relevant position." That is, although the utterance overlapped with the adult's utterance, it followed the adult's completion of (or elliptical reference to) a simple proposition expressed in structures such as Subject + Verb, or Subject + Verb + Object. The overlaps of the children with language impairments were not so strategically placed. If children with language impairment who show inappropriate turn exchanges were found to have problems with grammatical structures of this type, such structures would be an especially appropriate goal for intervention.

MacLachlan and Chapman (1988) found that communication breakdowns frequently occurred in the narratives of children with language impairment, even when they showed relatively few such breakdowns in conversation. The largest proportion of breakdowns took the form of stalls (filled pauses and repetitions). Because the narratives involved utterances of greater length and complexity than in conversation, MacLachlan and Chapman suggested that the increases in communication breakdowns they observed might have reflected an interaction between the longer narrative utterances and the children's limited linguistic skills. If these children were more facile with grammatical elaborations, such as relative clauses and various forms of sentence coordination and subordination, such breakdowns might have been less frequent. It might be noted in this regard that Tyack (1981) presented evidence that increased use of complex sentences was related to improvements in story recall in a 10-year-old child who was learning disabled.

In a well-known study by Gallagher and Darnton (1978), the conversational repairs of children with language impairment were investigated. Relative to a group of younger normally developing children with similar mean utterance length, the children with language impairment showed less use of a repair involving a constitutent substitution:

(8) Child: He ride bike
    Adult: What?
    Child: He ride it

As noted earlier, these substitutions seem to require greater knowledge of syntactic categories such as Noun Phrase. If evidence of such knowledge were not otherwise available from the child, these categories would constitute an appropriate intervention goal.

Liles (1985) conducted an investigation of use of cohesion in narratives by children with language impairment. Relative to a group of normally developing children, the children with language impairment used fewer personal pronouns as cohesive devices and showed a greater number of incomplete and erroneous cohesive ties. Although several different factors might contribute to problems of this type, before intervention were to proceed with children experiencing such difficulties, it would be important to ensure that they knew which grammatical structures permitted pronouns to refer to preceding Noun Phrases (see [6] and [7] on p. 337).

In summary, although not all pragmatic limitations will have a grammatical basis, an examination of the interactions between pragmatics and grammar can alert clinicians to some of the grammatical underpinnings that might serve as important goals in language intervention. What is important for the present discussion is that without attention to the child's pragmatic abilities, some grammatical deficiencies critical to the child's communication success may go undetected.

CONSIDERATION OF THE INTERVENTION ACTIVITY

Perhaps the greatest disappointment stemming from early efforts to teach grammar to children was the finding that, in many cases, the abilities children displayed in the treatment context were not used outside the clinical setting (Hughes, 1985; Leonard, 1981). The literature on pragmatics made it clear that in at least some cases, this failure was due to the fact that these early efforts focused almost entirely on language form. Children were given direct intervention on what to say but were provided with very little evidence of when to use their new acquisitions or how their new forms could be socially useful (Rees, 1978; Spradlin & Siegel, 1982). Under these circumstances, children may be inclined to learn rules that enable them to play "the therapy game" yet fail to recognize the broader communicative relevance of the target forms (Johnston, 1988).

The solution to this problem that is offered by pragmatics lies in the basic principle that language form cannot be meaningfully dissociated from its social function. This principle has two broad implications for creating intervention activities. First, the principle suggests that activities should provide the clinician with many opportunities to model grammatical targets under semantically and pragmatically appropriate conditions. Under such conditions, the child is likely not only to hear the new grammatical form but to identify its meaning and pragmatic function. Second, the principle suggests that activities should provide numerous opportunities for the child to produce communicative acts in which the target form is useful, if not obligated. If the child uses the target form under these circumstances, the child's act can be consequated naturally by the adult's appropriate conversational and/or nonverbal response.

The activities that result from the application of these basic principles will look different in several respects from the drills commonly used in the 1960s and 1970s. In these drills, children are required to produce lists of sentences containing the target forms in response to unrelated pictures or events acted out by the clinician. The child's utterances serve no communicative function, such as informing, requesting, or clarifying, and are in no way related to the accomplishment of some higher objective, such as telling a story, making sandwiches, or baking cookies.

In pragmatically motivated activities, the child's production of the target form constitutes only a part of a broader goal. It is a means to an end rather than an end in itself. This can be the case whether the activity is loosely or tightly structured.

In loosely structured, highly naturalistic activities, the motivation for producing an utterance that obligates the use of a target form arises from within the child. For example, the incidental teaching approach of Hart and Risley (1975, 1980; see also Warren & Kaiser, 1986) takes place during the child's play periods. Intervention episodes arise only when the child initiates a communicative bid, usually a request or command.

The clinician can increase the number and quality of teaching episodes in natural contexts by altering the play environment in ways that make communication necessary. Suppose, for example, that a particular child enjoyed the art center in the classroom. If all relevant materials were stored where the child could get them without assistance, there would be no need for the child to communicate to complete the art project. The clinician could create a need to communicate, however, by placing necessary materials out of reach. Similarly, the clinician could "sabotage" the art activity by providing, say, crayons of only one color, coloring books that were already completed, or scissors that didn't work properly (see Constable, 1983; Fey, 1986; Lucas, 1980, for additional examples). Note that by modifying the physical setting in this way, the clinician has not done anything that directly facilitates grammatical development. Such changes in grammar must rest with the specific intervention procedures adopted within these activities (see below). However, it seems likely that these procedures can be more effective if the activities in which they take place increase the child's motivation to communicate, and if the child's communicative efforts have a potent effect on the listener's behavior.

In many instances, more tightly structured activities may be necessary. This is especially true in cases of low frequency grammatical forms such as passives. However, such activities are also helpful when the clinician feels the child needs to hear relatively common forms even more frequently and/or have a large number of opportunities to use the target form. For example, during a restaurant activity, the child might be asked to be the server and convey to the cook how many of each item on the menu the customer (alias clinician) orders. The structure of this activity would make it easier for the clinician to model, and the child to practice, a large number of noun plurals in an appropriate communicative context. Fey (1986) gives numerous examples of how structured activities can be made natural.

CHILD-INITIATED AND CLINICIAN-INITIATED PROCEDURES

The potential influence of pragmatics goes beyond the selection of activities. The specific intervention procedures employed within these activities can also be significantly shaped by pragmatic considerations. In this section, the case is made that two quite different classes of intervention procedures can accommodate pragmatic notions, those in which the child initiates the occasion for grammatical instruction and those in which the clinician is the initiator.

In child-initiated procedures the clinician follows the child's lead and responds to the child's communicative attempts in a way that is presumed to facilitate language learning. Such procedures can be a useful means of presenting new grammatical information to the child. For example, if the clinician repeats the child's prior utterance and, in so doing, adds grammatical details, the child might be quite likely to register the changes (Nelson, 1989). Because the child's interest in the topic and knowledge of the basic vocabulary are assured (by virtue of the child's having just said essentially the same thing a moment before), the child's attention can focus more directly on these grammatical additions. This state of affairs seems to correspond to Johnston's (1985) proposal that intervention "fit the child's social purposes, interpretive resources and emergent meanings" while advancing his or her knowledge one step beyond its current level (p. 128).

Several specific procedures can be considered to be child-initiated. One of these is expansion, first employed as an intervention approach by Cazden (1965) and later adopted in a range of studies (e.g., Farrar, 1990; Scherer & Olswang, 1984). In this procedure, the child and clinician engage in an activity that promotes conversation and the clinician responds to the child's utterance with a grammatically expanded version of the utterance:

> (9) Child: Baby go sleep
>   Adult: The baby's going to sleep
>   Child: Now want water
>   Adult: Oh, now she wants some water

Because expansions are intended to capture the child's original meaning, the grammatical details that are added in the clinician's subsequent utterance will vary by necessity, as seen in (9). Thus, expansion might be most accurately characterized as providing more general grammatical stimulation. A clinician who wishes to emphasize certain grammatical forms and not others must be highly selective in the utterances he or she expands.

Alternatively, the clinician might employ a related procedure, such as recasting. This procedure was first used in an intervention study by Nelson, Carskaddon, and Bonvillian (1973), and subsequently by Nelson (1977). In this case, the clinician uses the child's prior utterance as the basis for a modified sentence that contains the grammatical form that the clinician wishes to emphasize. For example, if the clinician's goal were to facilitate the child's use of questions, the following types of recasts might be appropriate:

(10) Child: Car's gonna crash
     Adult: Is the car gonna crash?
     Child: Yeah, and driver's hurt
     Adult: Is the driver hurt? Oh no

For some children, it may not be sufficient to present new grammatical information in this way. These children might detect the new grammatical form in the clinician's speech, but fail to see how it adds to the original message. For these children, it may be necessary to highlight the precise function of the grammatical form.

Procedures in which the clinician initiates the interchange can be called on for this purpose. By manipulating the specific conversational context, the clinician can create instances in which the role of the grammatical form is demonstrated on an intensive basis. This format permits the clinician to conform to another of Johnston's (1985) tenets—that focused input be provided, to "narrow the child's search for order" (p. 130).

A number of examples of how both child- and clinician-initiated procedures can be used to facilitate the development of a range of grammatical structures are presented in the next section. Although the two types of procedures differ in the nature of their contributions, both can be pressed into service of Johnston's (1985) final principle, that intervention provide the child with "functional language tools" (p. 131).

New Syntactic Categories

Syntactic categories include Preposition, Auxiliary, and Noun Phrase, among others. These categories often pose problems for children with language impairment. Consider how a clinician might facililtate a child's acquisition of Prepositions, using expansion. The grammatical requirements for this category (see Valian, 1986) should first be considered. One of these is that a Preposition takes a Noun Phrase as an object but, unlike Verbs, is not inflected for Tense (e.g., one can say *He placed the dish in the refrigerator* but not **He place the dish inned the refrigerator*). Another requirement is that a

Preposition must sometimes precede full Noun Phrases, not just single Nouns. The first of these requirements calls for the clinician to ensure that he or she expands utterances that vary in Tense, so that the child is in a position to note that Tense is marked on the Verb, not the Preposition:

(11) Child: Put cup table
     Adult: Put the cup on the table
     Child: Drop floor
     Adult: Yup, it dropped on the floor.

The second requirement suggests the need to expand utterances in which a full Noun Phrase follows the Preposition, as well as those in which only a Noun follows:

(12) Child: Hat Bob
     Adult: The hat's on Bob
     Child: Now cowboy
     Adult: Now the hat's on this big cowboy

The syntactic category Noun Phrase is also difficult for some children with language impairment. Before a child is credited with this category, considerably more is required than an ability to use Nouns (see Valian, 1986). First, Determiner + Noun combinations must be seen (e.g., *the car, a frog*). There must also be evidence that these combinations can serve as a single unit in the child's speech. This might be seen in the substitution of a single term such as *it* for, say, *the ball*. In addition, these combinations must appear in several different sentence positions with the same Determiner, namely, pre-Verb (e.g., *The frog fell*), post-Verb (e.g., *She hit the ball*), and post-Preposition (e.g., *Put it in the box*).

How might information on pragmatics facilitate teaching new categories such as Noun Phrase? Consider a clinician-initiated procedure that makes use of two interacting pragmatic notions, ellipsis and the given-new distinction. Ellipsis permits the child to begin the task of using Determiner + Noun in two-word utterances without violating conversational conventions. Further, the clinician's questions that permit ellipsis can vary in the type of information given and the type of (new) information that is requested such that the Determiner + Noun responses of the child represent constituents that are pre-Verb, post-Verb, and post-Preposition, as seen in (13), (14), and (15), respectively:

(13) Adult: What's making that noise?
     Child: A bear
(14) Adult: What's Dinah pushing?
     Child: A car

(15) Adult: What's Mom putting the bird in?
       Child: Cage
       Adult: Yeah, a cage. Mom's putting him in a cage

Thus, the linguistic context provided by the clinician makes it appropriate for the child to respond with a Noun Phrase only. Under these conditions, the child may be more likely to utilize his or her developing knowledge of Determiner + Noun. Note, however, that if the child fails to use a well-formed Noun Phrase, as in (15) above, the clinician has an opportunity to expand the child's utterance.

Once the child's use of Determiner + Noun in two-word utterances becomes established, the clinician can make use of the given-new distinction to assist the child in using Determiner + Noun in longer utterances. For example, by using sequence pictures in which only the action and object change, the child's ability to use post-verb Determiner + Noun might be enhanced. By using pictures in which only the agent changes, the use of pre-Verb Determiner + Noun might be facilitated.

The remaining criterion for crediting a child with the category Noun Phrase is that *it* (or *him, her,* etc.) must replace Determiner + Noun on occasion. This, too, can be promoted through the given-new distinction. For example, by keeping the object acted upon constant while varying the agent and action, subsequent reference to the object can be made with a pronoun:

(16) Adult: Tell me a story about these pictures
       Child: A hat
       Adult: Now what (indicating next picture)
       Child: Monkey take it
       Adult: Yes, but now what? (next picture)
       Child: Put hat in tree
       Adult: Yeah, he put it in a tree

Again, if the child fails to use the target form as planned, an expansion or recast can be used to create a learning opportunity.

Another syntactic category that is often problematic for children with language impairment is Auxiliary (e.g., Fletcher & Garman, 1988). In current theories of grammar, Auxiliary is separate from the Verb Phrase, which enables one to explain how Auxiliary verbs can be so easily separated from main verbs (e.g., *John will surely pass the test this time,* but not **John will pass surely the test this time*). Another illustration of the separate status of Auxiliary can be seen in ellipsis, in which the Auxiliary verb can stand alone:

(17) I don't know if she's going to the party, but I am.

It seems that this property of Auxiliary can be utilized in the initial teaching of this category. For example, a question-and-answer activity can be devised such that for all affirmative answers the child must use the form *yes, I* + Auxiliary. Initially, Auxiliary verbs that require no agreement marking for person or number can be used, such as the Modal *can*:

(18) Adult: Can you ride a bike?
      Child: Yes, I can

Subsequently, Auxiliary verbs requiring person and number agreement can be used:

(19) Adult: Is the girl riding a bike?
      Child: Yes, she is

Eventually, the child could be required to change the form of the Auxiliary verb to agree with the Subject:

(20) Adult: Are you sitting on the table?
      Child: Yes, I am

Expansions and recasts of the child's responses in these circumstances might be highly useful to the child:

(21) Adult: Are the girls going to fall?
      Child: Yes, they is
      Adult: They are. They are going to fall

At this point, there seem to be two possible directions to proceed in helping the child acquire Auxiliary. One is to devise activities in which the child asks questions using sentence-initial Auxiliary verbs (e.g., *Can you see my toes? Are you watching cartoons?*). An advantage of this option is that the Auxiliary verb is uncontractible and more salient in this context. However, because the sentence-initial position is not the typical location of Auxiliary verbs, and because the child's only other practice with Auxiliary verbs was in elliptical utterances, there is no assurance that the child will understand the proper placement of Auxiliary in the phrase structure tree (viz., Noun Phrase + Auxiliary + Verb Phrase).

For this reason, it might be advantageous to proceed directly to the use of Auxiliary in full declarative sentences. By making use of the principle of contrast, as in Fey's (1986) "false assertion" technique, this step might be somewhat easier to accomplish. For example, the clinician and child might monitor each other's descriptions of pictures, providing corrections when needed. Some of the clinician's descriptions can be in error, for example, by stating that some action is not being performed when it actually is. Because corrections in these cases could be elliptical (e.g., *Oh yes she is*), each description could contain two or more actions appropriate to the picture. Consider a picture in which some children are sleeping and some are not:

(22) Adult: Let's see who's sleeping in this picture. This baby is not sleeping, she's eating; this boy is not sleeping, and this girl is not sleeping, she's reading a book
     Child: Uh uh, the boy *is* sleeping
     Adult: Oh, now I see. The girl is not sleeping, but the boy *is* sleeping

Note how these manipulations make it possible to place pragmatically appropriate stress on the target form. This, in turn, might make the form more salient to the child.

New Grammatical Functions

If children have good command of the syntactic categories of the language, they possess one necessary ingredient for sentence construction. However, they must also learn the grammatical functions of these categories. Some of these functions are obligatory in all (English) sentences (except, as we know, when certain pragmatic conditions come into play). A prime example is Subject. Others are obligated when certain types of verbs are used. For example, *hit* requires Object, but *sleep* does not. In addition, there are functions, such as Adjunct, that are not obligated at all grammatically, but do serve to elaborate the meaning of the sentence. For example, in the sentence *Hugh ate his lunch on the terrace*, the Adjunct *on the terrace* is not required to make the sentence well-formed.

Although young normally developing children often omit Subjects from their early sentences (e.g., P. Bloom, 1989; Gerken, 1990), it appears that children with language impairment may do so even more frequently (Leonard, 1972). Although there are several factors at work in the use of this grammatical function, children's inclusion of Subjects might be promoted initially through use of the given-new distinction. Again, a clinician-initiated procedure with sequence pictures might be employed:

(23) Adult: Tell me a story about these pictures. It's about our old friends Archie, Betty, and Veronica. I'll start, and you finish. Here, Veronica is kissing Archie. And here?
     Child: Betty kissing him
     Adult: Yes, it's Betty. She's kissing Archie

It can be seen that the final adult turn in (23) contains a recast in which the Subject is pronominalized. This might help the child recognize that Subjects are obligatory in English even when the referent is already established in the discourse.

Adjunct is a grammatical function that can be useful because it provides the child with a means of elaborating sentences at little cost in the form of syntactic complexity. To teach Adjuncts, the principle of contrast might be used:

(24) Adult: Well, Betty's washing her hair in the sink. But what about Archie?
     Child: Washing hair in swimming pool

Syntactic Features

Children with language impairment often have great difficulty with features such as Person, Number, Tense, Definiteness, and Case. For example, language-impaired children seem to omit the Past Tense inflection *-ed* more frequently than younger normally developing children at comparable levels of mean length of utterance (MLU) (Johnston & Schery, 1976). To assist a child in acquiring this inflection, a clinician might use a child-initiated procedure in which he or she selectively expands those utterances of the child that seem to refer to past events:

(25) Child: Daddy watch tv. But mommy, no
     Adult: Daddy watched tv. But mommy didn't?
     Child: No. Work
     Adult: Oh, she worked

Case constitutes another difficult feature. For example, children with language impairment appear to substitute Accusative Case for Nominative Case more often than younger MLU-matched controls (Loeb & Leonard, 1991). Utterances such as *Me do it* and *Them not here* are quite frequent in the speech of these children.

Connell (1986) presented an interesting (clinician-initiated) method of facilitating children's use of Nominative Case. Noting that the use of forms such as *him* and *her* in pre-Verb position might reflect the children's expression of the topic of the sentence, Connell attempted to separate the topic function from the Subject function. Each child was taught to respond in a specific manner in carefully selected sentence pairs. For example, a picture depicting different persons performing diverse actions was presented, and the clinician and child proceeded as follows:

(26) Adult: Which one is walking?
     Child: Him, he is walking
     Adult: What is the man doing?
     Child: He is walking

As can be seen from (26), in the response to the first question there was a greater need for the topic to be highlighted. Yet, the following pronoun *(he)* contrasted with the topic pronoun *(him)* in Case and agreed in Person and Number with the Auxiliary Verb. Hence, it served as a clear indication that the notion of topic is not identical to Subject.

Another feature that might prove troublesome to children with language impairment is Definiteness, as reflected in Articles. Because children with language impairment frequently omit Articles, clinicians often focus principally on teaching the inclusion of these forms. However, inclusion of an Article does not necessarily mean that the child knows the distinction between *the* and *a*.

By highlighting the use of the Definite Article as a cohesive tie, this distinction might become clearer. For example, suppose the activity involves shopping. The clinician is the storekeeper and the child is the shopper. On the table, the clinician has arranged several objects. The child must buy several of them.

(27) Adult: Welcome to our store. We have books, crayons, pens, and balls. What do you want?

Child: Book

Adult: A book. You want a book, ok. But wait, we also have other nice things. Do you still want the book? Or do you want a pen?

Child: A pen

Adult: Good, you'll like it. Here it is. Now, we also have a ball. Or do you want the book?

Child: The book

As can be seen from (27), the clinician introduces each object with the Indefinite Article, but proceeds to the Definite Article when re-introducing the object.

Eventually, the child must be able to make the distinction between *the* and *a* without the support of the clinician's cues. For example, in a later procedural step, the child might be asked to describe his or her shopping experience using multi-utterance turns. In the first utterance of the turn, the child might name the objects purchased. Then, the child would be asked to describe each, focusing on some salient attribute such as size or color:

(28) Adult: So, what did you buy at the new store?

Child: I bought three pens and a book.
The pens blue and the book red

The crucial aspect of this task is that the child learn that the initial reference to an object should be made using an Indefinite Article, and that sub-

sequent reference to it should employ the Definite Article. To foster Indefinite Article use, the objects should probably not be visible to the clinician.
By ensuring that several different objects are depicted at the same time, the
clinician can increase the likelihood that the child will use a Noun and not a
Pronoun in his or her second utterance. The use of plural objects (e.g., three
pens) as well as single objects (one book) might lead the child to produce,
for example, *one book* instead of *a book*. Such use is not a problem, provided
that the child uses *the* only in the second utterance. Subsequently, the clinician can employ only single objects (e.g., one ball, one doll) to reduce the
salience of number.

Alternate Word Orders

Although word order errors in production are not frequently reported for
children with language impairment who are acquiring English, comprehension studies suggest that these children may not understand the variation in
word order that is permitted in the language (van der Lely & Harris, 1990).
One such variation is Dative alternation. It is assumed that children eventually learn that certain verbs (e.g., *give*) permit two different subcategori-
zation frames, one making use of a Prepositional Phrase, as in (29), the
other involving a double-Object construction, as in (30):

(29) Tina gave the microphone to Mick
(30) Tina gave Mick the microphone

It appears that Dative alternation can be made clearer to children with
language impairment through use of procedures that capitalize on the
given-new distinction. A task devised by McKee and Emiliani (in press)
might be adapted for this purpose. For example, assume that while a confederate is blindfolded, the child and clinician manipulate toys or puppets
in a prescribed manner. Upon questioning by the confederate, the child
must then describe what transpired. As can be seen from (31) and (32), the
nature of the confederate's question can highlight different elements in the
activity, prompting either of the word orders:

(31) Adult: Well, I still see Olive Oil and Popeye. But why is he
               hugging her?
       Child: Because she gave him some spinach
(32) Adult: Well, there's Olive Oil. But why doesn't she have
               her spinach?
       Child: Because she gave it to Popeye

Another troublesome construction that implicates word order is the passive. Because attempts at this construction are not especially frequent, a

procedure such as expansion may not be plausible. However, another child-initiated procedure, recasting, might prove quite effective in this case. Here, the clinician restates the child's utterance in such a manner that the original Object serves as Subject:

(33) Child: The guy hit the ball
Adult: Yeah, the ball was really hit by that guy
(34) Child: Mommy bought these presents
Adult: These presents were all bought by Mommy?

Clinician-initiated procedures can be designed to illustrate the important point that passives are employed in English when the Object receives focus. The following example demonstrates this use along with some relevant adult responses to the child's attempts:

(35) Adult: Here is a picture with a boy and a girl. First, tell me about the boy
Child: The dog bited him
Adult: Yeah, he was bitten by that dog. What happened to the girl?
Child: She was bit by a raccoon
Adult: Yeah, she was bitten by the raccoon. The boy was bitten by a dog, and the girl was bitten by a raccoon. They both were bitten by an animal. Ouch!

Conjunction and Relativization

As clinicians employed in school settings can attest, many children who reach school age continue to exhibit problems with spoken language (see reviews in Aram & Hall, 1989; Weiner, 1985). Problems center not only on understanding humor, metaphors, and other aspects of figurative language, but also on aspects of grammar such as the use of complex sentences.

Here, too, pragmatics can be used to full advantage. Consider first simple conjunction. When two independent clauses are joined by *and*, three types of relationships can be expressed: additive (e.g., *Here's the corn and there's the endive*), temporal (e.g., *I got up and brushed my teeth*), and causal (e.g., *He saw the reflection of his face in the water and screamed*) (Bloom, Lahey, Hood, Lifter, & Fiess, 1980). The clinician might make use of any or all of these relationships to produce an expansion of the child's utterance that includes *and*. Consider, for example, the following procedure, adapted from Schwartz, Chapman, Terrell, Prelock, and Rowan (1985):

(36) Child: Baby lie down
Adult: Oh, and now what?
Child: She go night-night
Adult: The baby lies down and goes night-night

Relativization is a complex sentence construction that seems to be acquired after conjunction and complementation (Bloom et al., 1980). Relative clauses are used to modify Noun Phrases. This construction might be taught through use of the classic referential communication task (e.g., Glucksberg, Krauss, & Higgins, 1975). Assume that a child and clinician are seated at opposite sides of a table and that a screen blocks each participant's view of the other. Each person is given a set of drawings depicting, for example, a dog running, a dog sleeping, a cat running, and a cat sleeping. The child's task is to select a picture and instruct the clinician to select the identical one in his or her possession, using a particular sentence frame:

(37) Child: Pick up the cat
     Adult: Which one? Remember our rule.
     Child: Pick up the one that's running
     Adult: Good ... Or do you mean the dog that's running?
     Child: The cat!

The value of this task is that the most communicatively relevant aspect of the child's instruction (the specification of which dog or cat is to be selected) is contained in the relative clause, thus highlighting the function of this construction.

SUMMARY

In this chapter, ways in which grammar and pragmatics interact, and how this interaction has clinical relevance have been discussed. Although some children may have pragmatic limitations that are unrelated to grammar, children with grammatical difficulties—even active conversationalists—appear to be at risk for certain problems in pragmatics. This is because a number of pragmatic abilities seem to rely on knowledge of some grammatical category, function, feature, or construction. Clinicians can take advantage of this dependency by using it as a basis for choosing grammatical targets during intervention: Of those grammatical problems exhibited by the child, choose for intervention one that seems to be hindering the development of some pragmatic skill.

Even when a child's grammatical limitations are a concern in their own right, the effectiveness of intervention might be bolstered through application of pragmatic principles. We have attempted to show that the activities and procedures selected can go a long way toward teaching the child the relevant social contexts in which to use particular grammatical forms, and the specific communicative functions these forms serve.

The intervention examples that were provided are only suggestive; future research must determine their ultimate worth. However, we are more confident in the larger message, that pragmatics and grammar should be considered together when plotting the course of intervention for a child with language impairment.

REFERENCES

Aram, D., & Hall, N. (1989). Longitudinal follow-up of children with preschool communication disorders: Treatment implications. *School Psychology Review, 18,* 487–501.

Bates, E., & MacWhinney, B. (1987). Competition, variation, and language learning. In B. MacWhinney (Ed.), *Mechanisms of language acquisition* (pp. 157–193). Hillsdale, NJ: Lawrence Erlbaum.

Bloom, L., Lahey, M., Hood, L., Lifter, K., & Fiess, K. (1980). Complex sentences: Acquisition of syntactic connectives and the semantic relations they encode. *Journal of Child Language, 7,* 235–262.

Bloom, P. (1989). Why do children omit subjects? *Papers and Reports on Child Language Development, 28,* 57–63.

Cazden, C. (1973). Environmental assistance to the child's acquisition of syntax. Unpublished doctoral dissertation. Harvard University, Cambridge, MA.

Connell, P. (1986). Teaching subjecthood to language-disordered children. *Journal of Speech and Hearing Research, 29,* 481–492.

Constable, C. (1983). Creating communicative context. In H. Winitz (Ed.), *Treating language disorders: For clinicians by clinicians* (pp. 97–120). Baltimore,MD: University Park Press.

Conti–Ramsden, G., & Friel–Patti, S. (1983). Mothers' discourse adjustments to language-impaired and non-language-impaired children. *Journal of Speech and Hearing Disorders, 48,* 360–367.

Craig, H., & Evans, J. (1989). Turn exchange characteristics of SLI children's simultaneous and nonsimultaneous speech. *Journal of Speech and Hearing Disorders, 54,* 334–347.

Farrar, M. (1990). Discourse and the acquisition of grammatical morphemes. *Journal of Child Language, 17,* 607–624.

Fey, M. (1986). *Language intervention with young children.* San Diego,CA: College-Hill Press.

Fey, M., & Leonard, L. (1983). Pragmatic skills of children with specific language impairment. In T. Gallagher & C. Prutting (Eds.), *Pragmatic assessment and intervention issues in language* (pp. 65–82). San Diego, CA: College-Hill Press.

Fletcher, P., & Garman, M. (1988). Normal language development and language impairment: Syntax and beyond. *Clinical Linguistics and Phonetics, 2,* 97–113.

Foley, W., & Van Valin, R. (1984). *Functional syntax and universal grammar.* Cambridge, UK: Cambridge University Press.

Gallagher, T., & Darnton, B. (1978). Conversational aspects of the speech of language-disordered children: Revision behaviors. *Journal of Speech and Hearing Research, 21,* 118–135.

Gerken, L. (1990). Performance constraints in early language: The case of subjectless sentences. *Papers and Reports on Child Language Development, 29,* 54–61.

Glucksberg, S., Krauss, R., & Higgins, E. (1975). The development of referential communication skills. In F. Horowitz (Ed.), *Review of child development research.* (Vol. 4, pp. 305–346). Chicago: University of Chicago Press.

Hart, B., & Risley, T. (1975). Incidental teaching of language in the preschool. *Journal of Applied Behavioral Analysis, 8,* 411–420.

Hart. B., & Risley, T. (1980). In vivo language intervention: Unanticipated general effects. *Journal of Applied Behavioral Analysis, 13,* 407–432.

Hubbell, R. (1977). On facilitating spontaneous talking in young children. *Journal of Speech and Hearing Disorders, 42,* 216–232.

Hubbell, R. (1981). *Children's language disorders: An integrated approach.* Englewood Cliffs, NJ: Prentice-Hall.

Hughes, D. (1985). *Language treatment and generalization: A clinician's handbook.* San Diego, CA: College-Hill Press.

Johnston, J. (1985). Fit, focus and functionality: An essay on early language intervention. *Child Language Teaching and Therapy, 1,* 125–134.

Johnston, J. (1988). Generalization: The nature of change. *Language, Speech, and Hearing Services in Schools, 19,* 314–329.

Johnston, J., & Schery, T. (1976). The use of grammatical morphemes by children with communication disorders. In D. Morehead & A. Morehead (Eds.), *Normal and deficient child language* (pp. 239–258). Baltimore, MD: University Park Press.

Kamhi, A., & Nelson, L. (1988). Early syntactic development: Simple clause types and grammatical morphology. *Topics in Language Disorders, 8,* 26–43.

Leonard, L. (1972). What is deviant language? *Journal of Speech and Hearing Disorders, 37,* 427–446.

Leonard, L. (1981). Facilitating linguistic skills in children with specific language impairment. *Applied Psycholinguistics, 2,* 89–118.

Liles, B. (1985). Cohesion in the narratives of normal and language-disordered children. *Journal of Speech and Hearing Research, 28,* 123–133.

Loeb, D., & Leonard, L. (1991). Subject case marking and verb morphology in normally developing and specifically language-impaired children. *Journal of Speech and Hearing Research, 34,* 340–346.

Lucas, E. (1980). *Semantic and pragmatic language disorders: Assessment and remediation.* Rockville, MD: Aspen Systems.

Lund, N., & Duchan, J. (1988). *Assessing children's language in naturalistic contexts (2nd ed.).* Englewood Cliffs, NJ: Prentice-Hall.

MacLachlan, B., & Chapman, R. (1988). Communication breakdowns in normal and language learning-disabled children's conversation and narration. *Journal of Speech and Hearing Disorders, 53,* 2–7.

McKee, C., & Emiliani, M. (in press). Some Italian two-year-olds' morphosyntactic competence and why it matters. *Natural Language and Linguistic Theory.*

McShane, J. (1980). *Learning to talk.* Cambridge, UK: Cambridge University Press.

Nelson, K. E. (1977). Facilitating children's syntax acquisition. *Developmental Psychology, 13,* 101–107.

Nelson, K. E. (1989). Strategies for first language teaching. In M. Rice & R. Schiefelbusch (Eds.), *The teachability of language* (pp. 263–310). Baltimore, MD: Paul H. Brookes.

Nelson, K. E., Carskaddon, G., & Bonvillian, J. (1973). Syntax acquisition: Impact of experimental variation in adult verbal interaction with the child. *Child Development, 44,* 497–504.

Rees, N. (1978). Pragmatics of language: Applications to normal and disordered language development. In R. Schiefelbusch (Ed.), *Bases of language intervention* (pp. 191–268). Baltimore, MD: University Park Press.

Scherer, N., & Olswang, L. (1984). Role of mothers' expansions in stimulating children's language production. *Journal of Speech and Hearing Research, 27,* 387–396.

Schwartz, R., Chapman, R., Terrell, B., Prelock, P., & Rowan, L. (1985). Facilitating word combination in language-impaired children through discourse structure. *Journal of Speech and Hearing Disorders, 50,* 31–39.

Spradlin, J., & Siegel, G. (1982). Language training in natural and clinical environments. *Journal of Speech and Hearing Disorders, 47,* 2–6.

Tyack, D. (1981). Teaching complex sentences. *Language, Speech, and Hearing Services in Schools, 12,* 49–53.

Valian, V. (1986). Syntactic categories in the speech of young children. *Developmental Psychology, 22,* 562–579.

van der Lely, H., & Harris, M. (1990). Comprehension of reversible sentences in specifically language-impaired children. *Journal of Speech and Hearing Disorders, 55,* 101–117.

Warren, S., & Kaiser, A. (1986). Incidental language teaching: A critical review. *Journal of Speech and Hearing Disorders, 51,* 291–299.

Weiner, P. (1985). The value of follow-up studies. *Topics in Language Disorders, 5,* 78–92.

Index